Escape Artist

WISCONSIN FILM STUDIES

Patrick McGilligan
Series Editor

Escape Artist

The Life and Films of John Sturges

Glenn Lovell

THE UNIVERSITY OF WISCONSIN PRESS

This book was published with the support of
the Anonymous Fund of the College of Letters and Science
at the University of Wisconsin–Madison.

The University of Wisconsin Press
1930 Monroe Street, 3rd Floor
Madison, Wisconsin 53711-2059

www.wisc.edu/wisconsinpress/

3 Henrietta Street
London WC2E 8LU, England

1   3   5   4   2

Printed in the United States of America

Library of Congress Cataloging-in-Publication Data
Lovell, Glenn.
Escape artist: the life and films of John Sturges / Glenn Lovell.
p.   cm. — (Wisconsin film studies)
Includes bibliographical references and index.
ISBN 978-0-299-22830-9 (cloth: alk. paper)
ISBN 978-0-299-22834-7 (pbk: alk. paper)
1. Sturges, John, 1910–1992.
2. Motion picture producers and directors — United States — Biography.
I. Title. II. Series.
PN1998.3.S779L68   2008
791.4302´33092 — dc22   2008011967
[B]

For
DONNA,
Magnificent, too

Contents

Escape Artist

Prologue
The Case for "The Other Sturges"

John Sturges may be the most popular but least discussed director of the postwar era. The man behind such seminal action films as *Bad Day at Black Rock, The Magnificent Seven,* and *The Great Escape* has all but passed beneath the radar of critics and academicians who laud his more morally ambiguous contemporaries, such as Robert Aldrich and Anthony Mann. The stock argument against Sturges, who toiled on the studio assembly line before proclaiming his independence as producer-director, is that he was a technically proficient popcorn merchant, a plier of escapist entertainment who seldom tackled social issues or peered deeply into the conflicted soul. Further, the argument goes, Sturges, like Robert Wise and Mark Robson, his editing buddies at RKO Pictures, eventually let ego get the better of him, and allowed his later films—most notably *Ice Station Zebra* and *Marooned*—to balloon into flashy and impersonal roadshow attractions. In *The American Cinema: Directors and Directions,* under the heading "Strained Seriousness," Andrew Sarris lumped Sturges with Wise, John Frankenheimer, and Stanley Kubrick as a solemn and self-conscious practitioner of the big action movie.

Those who have taken the time to review Sturges's full career—from the tautly drawn *Mystery Street* and *Jeopardy* to the melancholic Wyatt Earp–Doc Holliday reunion *Hour of the Gun*—may want a second opinion. To turn another Sarris section heading, "Less Than Meets the Eye," back on itself, there is more than meets the eye, quite a bit more, to the Sturges oeuvre. A protégé of William Wyler and George Stevens, he was a gifted storyteller and keen judge of emerging talent who worked in just about every genre: besides the signature buddy Westerns, he turned out Gothic romances, period biopics, science-speculation thrillers, and at least one quasi-musical (*The Hallelujah Trail*). And when CinemaScope arrived, Sturges, whose eyes were never very good, saw its potential for power proxemics. To this day, his minimalist *Bad Day at Black Rock* stands with Elia Kazan's *East of Eden* as the finest early example of the widescreen process. Its dynamic groupings have been quoted by half the action directors in Hollywood, including, most notably, Steven Spielberg, John Carpenter, Walter Hill, Lawrence Kasdan, and Michael Bay.

To appreciate Sturges's influence on the revisionist Western, one need but draw a line from the Wyatt and Doc of *Gunfight at the O.K. Corral* to the mercenaries of *The Magnificent Seven* to the mismatched paladins of Kasdan's *Silverado* and Clint Eastwood's *Unforgiven*. And where would Sergio Leone and the spaghetti Western be without Sturges? For good or ill, their hyperbolic theatricality and mordant sight gags owe as much to the acrobatic gunplay at the O.K. Corral as they do to the anarchic spirit of Sam Peckinpah, who in the 1960s almost teamed with Sturges for a *Magnificent Seven* TV series.

Politically, Sturges was a fascinating whirl of contradictions—"a funny kind of liberal conservative," in son Michael's words. He called himself "a professional Democrat—very much on the liberal side." In *Hour of the Gun*, he commented on the dehumanizing effects of extra-legal law enforcement. In *McQ*, starring John Wayne, he appeared to applaud police brutality as dispensed to long-haired "hippie types." He prided himself on being fair and open-minded, almost courtly in de-meanor, but he also could be as cold and intractable as General Patton. He took a stand against Cecil B. DeMille's communist-smear tactics, was active in both the directors and writers guilds, and contributed generously to the ACLU—until it veered from his pro-death penalty stance. In the early 1970s, he, along with John Lennon, was named to Nixon's enemies list, and when a reporter called to ask how he felt about it, he replied, "Honored."

Though he for the most part avoided soapboxes, Sturges did not shy away from thorny issues. In the guise of Saturday-night diversion, he tackled racism (*Black Rock, Last Train from Gun Hill, A Girl Named Tamiko*), alcoholism (*The People against O'Hara*), biological warfare (*The Satan Bug*), the abuse of power (*Hour of the Gun*), and Cold War détente (*Ice Station Zebra*). Like Budd Boetticher and Peckinpah, he spent considerable time south of the border and worked diligently to cast Latinos in strong, non-race-specific roles. Ricardo Montalban, a Massachusetts detective in *Mystery Street* and a New York prizefighter in the casually interracial *Right Cross*, applauded Sturges's "courageous" refusal to buy into studio stereotyping.

The portrayal of Sturges as a "man's man" comfortable only in the presence of macho types always has smacked of pat generalization. On closer inspection we find the prototypical child of divorce who for the first half of his life seeks the approval and counsel of his mother and then, following her death, indulges an, if not stifled, at least suppressed, masculinity. On the set, more than one actress observed he could be stony, distant. *By Love Possessed* and *A Girl Named Tamiko,* his 1960s women's pictures, were, in his own words, "definite miscues." They also can be seen as unintentional parodies of the form, attributable as much to a desperate-to-appease Hollywood as any lack of directorial finesse with the opposite sex. Sturges at this point had already directed Ethel Barrymore, Donna Reed, and Barbara Stanwyck in some of their liveliest performances, and later he would pan from Kirk Douglas and John Wayne to shrewd scene stealing by Jo Van Fleet and Colleen Dewhurst.

This book—culled from family albums, letters, production logs, and interviews with Sturges during the two years prior to his death in 1992—is offered not as a *reappraisal* of the action auteur but rather as a long-overdue appraisal. The scholarship on John Sturges, often confused with Preston Sturges, is as haphazard at it is patronizing. In the words of assistant director Robert E. Relyea, who would serve as production chief for Sturges's Alpha Company, "It's a crime what has happened to John's legacy: He's the most underrated director in the history of Hollywood."

He is also—with DVD re-releases, cable retrospectives, and Hollywood's return to stylized heroics—a filmmaker who speaks to a generation reared on high-concept escapes. Though they seldom impressed the Academy or brought the critical establishment to its feet, Sturges's later films can be seen as the forerunners of such blockbusters as *Raiders of the Lost Ark* and *Armageddon*. Indeed, Spielberg and Jerry Bruckheimer are on record as tracing their passion for the medium to epiphanous afternoons spent with *The Magnificent Seven* and the POWs of Stalag Luft III. Quentin Tarantino, the bad-boy cinéaste, paid impudent homage to Charles Bronson's Tunnel King in *Reservoir Dogs*, his debut feature.

The fact is, John Sturges was doing good work long before Spencer Tracy detrained in the jerkwater town of Black Rock. His early films at Columbia and MGM, as well as his sprawling and soon-to-be-anachronistic Cinerama epics, have never really received their due. This book attempts to rectify that by putting the director's work into social and historical context: his emergence coincided with the dismantling of the studio system and the rise of the independent producer-director who would exercise control over all phases of production. Sturges, like Otto Preminger and Billy Wilder, was emblematic of a shift in how Hollywood did business, and as such, he learned to work both sides of the street, so to speak. The key difference between Sturges and his more proprietary competition: he was far less interested in self-aggrandizement. His name preceded only a handful of titles, including, most famously, "John Sturges' *The Great Escape*." The once de rigueur "A film by . . ." was an affectation that never failed to elicit a wince from him.

There is no attempt to cast Sturges as heir to John Ford, whose cavalry tableaux inspired *Escape from Fort Bravo*, or, as some would have it, the American Kurosawa. He was neither, and to suggest otherwise would do him a disservice and raise false expectations in the reader. Sturges's place is not at the head of the table but rather to the side, seated with such distinguished guests as Mann, Wise, Boetticher, and Henry Hathaway.

The case for the director rests in large part on his gift for showmanship. He was a born yarn spinner, who, when the resources were at hand, could operate on a grand scale—a David Lean by way of Mike Todd. In his twenty-year heyday, as boomers gathered weekly for TV broadcasts of *Bonanza* and *The Wonderful World of Disney*, he offered the big-screen alternative—flamboyant, sometimes allegorical fables that pushed the Hawksian ideal of duty and teamwork to new and more operatic levels. Like others quoted here, I still can recall the Saturday matinees where I discovered *Gunfight at the O.K. Corral* and *The Magnificent Seven*. The giddy pleasures of those afternoons, I would wager, had something to do with my eventually becoming a film critic, and my later desire to track down Sturges and proffer thanks.

This book is meant as a reassuring pat on the back to those who have always loved the escapes but have been bullied into ignoring the escape artist.

1

Sturges with a Blast of Rum

The man on the carport obviously had been a commanding presence. Now the six-foot-two frame was closer to six feet, the white hair short-cropped and sparse, like a victory laurel. The large hands were wedged in his back pockets, the eyes obscured by tinted aviator glasses. He wore a Western shirt, Levis, and moccasins—standard attire.

"You found us, good," he said through a smoker's wheeze (twelve years earlier he had been diagnosed with emphysema). "We just built this place. They finally ran me out of town. Did you know they mugged me? Beat me black-and-blue, hogtied me. So now we're here."

This was my introduction to John Sturges. It had taken three years of calls and false leads to track the director to San Luis Obispo on California's Central Coast. He had always been just out of reach, wintering at a beach house in Baja, deep-sea fishing in Kona, living the Hemingway-esque existence of one of his heroes. But now the rugged outdoor life—and the picture making—was behind him.

During the first of several interviews, Sturges proved the consummate host, forthcoming and friendly. He did not get many visitors, he said as he draped himself over a chair. Reading his mind, wife Kathy arrived with the first of the day's ten rationed cigarettes. He sipped hot tea, spiked with "a blast of rum." Then he sat back, crossed his long legs, and began to recount his remarkable career, from lucky apprenticeship at RKO to angry exit from *The Eagle Has Landed*, his last completed film in 1976. Though he had trouble juggling the remotes, he screened the laserdisc of *Bad Day at Black Rock,* contributing live commentary on the film's genesis. He also set the record straight on a few things, including why he fired and rehired Steve McQueen on *The Great Escape,* why he walked off *Day of the Champion* and *Das Boot,* and why he indulged in an epic folly called *The Hallelujah Trail*—"a clear miss," he admitted.

He was living an almost Spartan existence. There was little about his ranch house (which he designed himself) to suggest it was home to one of the most successful directors in Hollywood history. No awards on the mantle. No plaques on the wall. No signed photos of Spencer Tracy or Ethel Barrymore or Clint Eastwood. Just posters from *The Magnificent Seven* and *The Satan Bug* and an assortment of biographies and bestsellers, including Carl Sagan's *Cosmos,* Stephen Hawking's *A Brief History of Time,* and, a particular favorite, Guy Murchie's *Song of the Sky.* The opposite of a packrat, he was what Kathy called a "throw-awayer."

But he did tell the most wonderful stories. That's what drew Kathy to him. They met in Mulegé, Baja, where they were seasonal neighbors. Though half Sturges's age and just tolerated by the director's daughter, Kathy was good company and shared his love of all things nautical. The newlyweds looked for property and a slip in Santa Barbara—to berth the twenty-six-foot, twin-engine *Cochinito* (Baja slang for dolphin)— but everything was taken.

"We got fed up with the traffic, smog, and crime," he said. "So we came up here and lived temporarily in an old house, and then I built this one. It's a little isolated, but we spend most of our winters in Mexico, two-thirds of the way down the peninsula, on Conception Bay. . . . That's where we keep the boat."

Nine years earlier, Sturges had been living alone in Marina del Rey. He had a one-bedroom condo on the channel. It was there that he had been mugged and robbed. It was 8:30 at night, and people were milling about. He had been reading when he heard the glass door slide open. It was never locked. Two men came in. One pointed a gun at his head and said, "Don't move." The other guy pulled the curtains. They tied his hands and feet and took the television and expensive audio equipment. It was like a scene from one of his movies, only there was no hero played by John Wayne living on a nearby boat and getting the better of the assailants.

What Sturges remembered most about the ordeal was that the thieves, instead of reaching for the leftover nylon rope from his boat, had tied him up with a telephone cord. "Their knots slipped," he laughed. "If they'd known how to tie plastic knots, I guess I'd have been there for a good while."

He was trying to make light of it, but the indignation of being bound and gagged in his own living room was still eating at him. He was used to being in control, and though it had been fifteen years since he oversaw his last film, and he had pretty much lost touch with his friends in the industry, he still carried himself like someone who could marshal the troops.

He had never set out to retire, he said, but the last two projects—a Hollywood version of *Das Boot* and a Vietnam War drama—had fallen through, and all he was offered subsequently were formula pictures, the ones where a stranger faces down a hostile town or soldiers of fortune band together for a suicide mission.

Finally he said, "To hell with it—I'm not going to do a picture just to do a picture. I don't need the money; I don't need to keep stretching my career. I guess I proved I'm a pretty good storyteller."

A little more than a year later, the eighty-two-year-old Sturges would be dead from congestive heart failure. The obituaries, which heralded the passing of one of Hollywood's preeminent action auteurs, didn't appear until several days later.

"Johnny dead? NO! When did he die?" asked RKO colleague and sailing buddy Robert Wise when given the news. Wise, like the rest of the industry, had lost touch with Sturges.

2

Youth

Though he would spend much of his career cultivating the less refined image of rugged, hard-drinking outdoorsman, John Eliot Sturges sprang from Chicago blue blood and, on his mother's side, could trace his lineage to the Mayflower Pilgrims and, beyond that, to ninth-century Norwegian royalty, in particular Turgesius, son of the king of Norway. John's father, Reginald G. R. Carne, was an English-born banker who, after the crash of 1929, turned to real estate. John's mother, Grace Delafield Sturges, was one of five children born to Charles M. Sturges, a British-born, Harvard-educated corporate lawyer and future president of the Illinois Bar Association, and Ella Delafield of Tennessee. Grace and her siblings enjoyed a privileged childhood straight out of Booth Tarkington, except that they were not coddled. Grace, who aspired to belles lettres, graduated with honors from the University of Illinois, and sister Mary became one of the first women physicians in the United States.

Sturges's official studio biography would make selective use of this lineage. The director, it trumpeted, was from "a distinguished early American family whose history goes back to Fairfield, Conn., in 1636." Among his ancestors, the studio release said, were General Israel Putnam and the Puritan doctor Increase Matthews. "Most of the men in the family were Harvard-educated lawyers." But was John Sturges, as some assume, a distant cousin of the comedy director Preston Sturges? Their paths crossed at Paramount. Sandy Sturges, Preston's widow, said, "I remember Preston referring to John Sturges as related, but distantly—only through Preston's adoption. They were not blood relatives."

Reginald and Grace married in 1897 and settled in Oak Park, Illinois, in a large Victorian house with bay windows and front parlor. The census listed two live-in maids from Germany, a butler and chauffeurs, and a summer house by the lake. Sturges Delafield Carne, called "Sturge," was welcomed into the world in 1899, and Alice followed a year later. In the summer of 1909, Grace surprised the family by announcing, at thirty-seven, she was pregnant again. John Eliot was born on January 3, 1910. The family photos of a chubby baby with thick curly hair, smiling back from a shiny black pram and waving from atop a snow fort, suggest a typical, happy infancy.

Life in the Carne household, however, was anything but happy. Reginald, according to family lore, was "a rip-roaring drinking Irishman," and Grace, like her sisters, was a teetotaler who flaunted her sobriety. Reginald was not above dipping into his wife's future inheritance. She was from money and he was not, and this caused him to overcompensate, lavishing the children with expensive toys, including an ornate, pony-drawn cart. As the arguments escalated, the parents sought allies. Grace drew Alice and John to her; Reginald confided in Sturge, his eldest son.

In 1912, Reginald moved the family to Southern California, where he founded the Bank of Ojai and dabbled in real estate. Three years later, amid rumors of alcoholism and abuse, Grace divorced him. This was a bold move because, as Emily Dunning Barringer pointed out in her memoir *Bowery to Bellevue* (adapted in 1952 by Sturges as *The Girl in White*), "divorce in those days was considered a social disgrace." Grace was granted custody of the children; Reginald had visitation rights, until he fell behind on support payments. Grace further shocked family and friends by reclaiming her family name. Sturge, who at age nineteen would ship out to the war in France, remained a Carne; but John and Alice (who had changed her first name to Jean)—in a tacit us-against-the-world declaration—henceforth would be Sturges. Grace announced that she wanted all vestiges of Reginald and his family out of her life. She and the children would go it alone, or with the help of her sisters and brother. "Grandmother was a tough woman with real presence, a grande dame," said Deborah Wyle, the director's daughter. "She wielded a great deal of power in that family."

That same year, Grace moved the family to a small wood-frame house in Santa Monica. Though the family album does not chronicle apparent hardship or privation, Sturges would recall these days as "a long period of starvation" when the family ate bread dipped in bacon grease and walked to a nearby farm to pick lima beans. Still, the child beaming back in family photos appears happy mowing the front lawn in his cowboy boots, feeding an uncle's chickens, playing with his pit bull terrier, Milestone. A letter to Santa from the six-year-old provides detailed directions to a house with "a field on each side, not just one side." It goes on to ask for a tricycle, a stuffed gray elephant, and "a little train and cars, and switches to pull back." He then inquired, "Where do you get the steel to make them with down in the snow?" (A parenthetical to whoever took dictation: "Don't ask him for the tunnel. I know how to make one myself, I did out in our yard.")

Grace seldom saw her older son, who lived with his father, but she doted on John, dressing him like Little Lord Fauntleroy in sailor suits and knickerbockers. More important, she passed on to him her love of the outdoors. Indeed, she saw John as a "raw-boned backwoods boy, who knows every reach of his native waters." That idealized youth figured in Grace's unpublished story, "A Likely Spot," about a family hike up Hogback Mountain, North Carolina, to see the spectacular gorge and falls.

Grace's rhapsodic odes—with their "daring leaps of Whitewater" and "dazzling snowy plunges"—bespoke a genuine passion for nature and exploration. And John, who one day would film the Walking Hills of Death Valley and the jungles of Ceylon, came to share his mother's adventurous spirit. Clearly no "sissy," he made up for his precious attire with a hands-akimbo bravado. Among his interests: cowboys and the Wild West, underworld confidence games, and silent movies. He attended Roosevelt Grammar School in Santa Monica and, in a 1920 class picture, appeared taller and cockier than his classmates. While the other boys wore their hair neatly trimmed or slicked back, John's curly mop was a force unto itself. A typical Sunday outing took Grace and the children to Cawston Ostrich Farm in South Pasadena, where John in hightop shoes and wool cap fearlessly rode an ostrich or sat astride a muzzled alligator. He joined the Boy Scouts and rigged a makeshift wireless receiver. "Always be prepared for the unexpected," he repeated after his mother. (Even as a successful filmmaker, he would carry a canteen,

sleeping bag, and first-aid kit in the trunk of his car.) His prized posses-
sions included a pump-action BB gun and a soapbox racer. Scientific
curiosity, a love of speed, and the rough-and-tumble life—the man that
the boy would become was beginning to emerge.

At age ten, John learned what others already knew: just how control-
ling and vindictive his mother could be. Sturge, twenty-one, stopped by
the house on his way to Ojai to see Reginald. John, of course, was excited by the prospect of seeing his father and jumped into the rumble
seat of his brother's Model T. When Grace heard what had happened,
she called the police. The brothers were intercepted as they started up
the Santa Paula Pass. Sturge was ordered to turn around and take his
brother home, which he did. Consequently, John would never reunite
with his father, who died in 1930. (Sturges's press bio not only ignored
the family melodrama but sanitized it, renaming the director's father
Reginald Sturges.)

"He didn't talk about his father," said Kathy Sturges. "But I remember him telling that story. I don't know that he was upset about it, or re-
gretted it. He just told the story, acted like it was no big deal. He held
things like that in a lot."

In 1923, upon her father's death, Grace inherited a sizable fortune
and moved the family to Berkeley. In 1924, John—now a studious, spec-
tacled fourteen-year-old—entered Berkeley High School. Sturge and
Jean attended the University of California at Berkeley. Sturge pursued
his passion for design at the architectural engineering school; Jean, described as "a socialite" who liked to drive around town in a green road-
ster, majored in sociology.

How rich was Grace Sturges? "Money wasn't really a topic that ever
got discussed, but she was very well off," said Deborah Wyle. "Grandmother was wealthy up until the Depression—a millionaire by some accounts," said Jon Stufflebeem, the son of John's sister, Jean. The inheritance was generous enough for the family to afford a gleaming-white
Mediterranean-style home on Shattuck Avenue and a Model T sedan.
John, already comfortable behind the wheel, taught his mother to drive,
and they began a series of summer trips that eventually would take them
to Alaska. In Lake Tahoe, John was photographed on snow-topped
mountain ridges, showing off his limit in trout, and just mugging for
the camera. "Drinking snowballs on Mount Ellis slope," Grace wrote

on the back of a snapshot. "Note the thermos pitcher, which contained ice cream, which we ate at the top." Three days later, outside Tahoe City, "G-Man" John posed by a police car that had just come from a raid on an illegal still in Truckee.

In the summer of 1925, Grace and John, now fifteen, embarked on their most ambitious outing, a two-month road trip to Banff National Park in the Canadian Rockies. By now John was over six feet tall, slim and athletic. He swam in the frigid mountain lakes and rock-climbed with the agility of a would-be Sir Edmund Hillary. At the coast they set up camp. As soon as the tent was pitched, John disappeared down the beach. Two hours later he returned with a huge smile — and enough crab for a feast.

Sturges would trace his love of fishing and the American West to these trips with his mother. He was never less than exhilarated when about to hit the road, he said, and this sense of excitement infused his early adventure movies, such as *The Walking Hills* (1949) and *Jeopardy* (1953). To quote Barbara Stanwyck in the latter film, "Vacation time in the United States means traveling, and traveling in the United States is wonderful. Fill your gas tank and hit the road. There is a turn-off to everywhere."

It was at Berkeley High that John became involved in theater. As a sophomore, he appeared in school productions as a pilgrim and King Tut's mummy, who, in harem pants and headband, looked more like Valentino in *The Sheik*. Later that same season, he played Richard III.

John's earliest movie memories were of silent Westerns and cliff-hangers. His favorite stars were Tom Mix and Rod La Rocque, the mustachioed hero of Cecil B. DeMille's *The Ten Commandments* (1923) and *The Shadow Strikes* (1937). "The first screen star I can remember is La Rocque," he said. "I was a day-dreamer, which most directors are, and I would always think in theatrical terms. I liked movies, and I saw a lot of them when I was in high school. I'd think about them later, won-der how they were put together."

The family's financial recovery was short-lived. No sooner had they begun to relax into their restored status than the ground shook, twice — first from an earthquake, which caused a gas leak and fire that destroyed their Berkeley home, and then from bad savings-and-loan investments. "Money was no particular problem because Mother was fairly well off,"

Sturges told a film periodical in 1969. "But then the Depression hit. It seemed that every savings and loan that failed had Mother as an investor." Later, he added, "We were wealthy until 1929, and then—boom!—we were broke."

Sturges had dreamed of attending the University of California-Berkeley. He now had to lower his sights. Jack English, a neighbor who had played football at Tulane University, became his mentor and "taught me how to survive." He steered John to Marin Junior College (now College of Marin) in Kentfield, where he majored in science "with a heavy emphasis on math." English got him a $14-a-week football scholarship. Because of his size, he played center and was "knocked down by some of the finest football players on the West Coast." At night, he waited tables. The school was "this little-bitty place," he recalled. "I never had to study. I was an A student. So I corrected papers for the professors. I just generally made my way."

To supplement his part-time jobs and meager stipend, Sturges moonlighted for the Arts Guild of Marin County, which produced weekend shows at the Tamalpais Theater in San Anselmo. During the 1930–31 season, the company did *Quality Street, Alice in Wonderland,* and *The Sky Train,* an unusually ambitious mystery set aboard a dirigible. Though usually credited as stage manager (his name often misspelled in the program and local paper as "Sturgis"), he was encouraged to step in for the company's director, who was habitually tardy.

"[The stage manager job] didn't pay much," Sturges told *Action* magazine, "but I liked the work. . . . It wasn't terribly good, I suppose, but we did a lot of plays, old standbys." Later, he added, "I wound up directing most of 'em. It didn't seem to me very difficult. I never had any inclination to act, only to be technically skillful. Mostly, I just wanted to make some money, stay out of the bread lines."

While at Marin Junior College, Sturges recalled in the commentary for *Bad Day at Black Rock,* he drove to the Russian River with some friends "in an old, broken-down car." At the summit of a mountain, disaster: "On this very steep, winding road, we run out of gas. This guy comes along and says, 'I'll push you.' It turns out he's drunk, and he pushes us faster and faster, and we're ready to go over the edge. Finally, we drive off the road into a pasture to get rid of this lunatic." Years later, when Metro's Dore Schary wanted an additional action scene in *Bad*

Day at Black Rock, Sturges recalled this harrowing experience and had Ernest Borgnine ram Spencer Tracy's Jeep, running him into a ravine.

In 1931, at twenty-one, Sturges left Marin Junior College and joined his brother and mother in Los Angeles. To pool the family resources, they lived with Jean and her husband, William Stufflebeem, a retail-credit inspector. John did odd jobs and took engineering classes at Santa Monica City College, which gave him the equivalent of two years of college. Grace taught grammar school in San Fernando Valley. Jean worked as a social worker and, later, as assistant to then–District Attorney Earl Warren. Sturge parlayed his degree in architecture into an assistant art director job at RKO.

"I came down to Los Angeles during the Depression," recalled John Sturges. "I got a job for a dollar a day at this boatyard, chipping paint. And then I got a job at a gas station pumping gas. Starvation jobs. My mother was just able to stay alive on what little money she earned teaching."

Sturges's account, which glossed over life at the Stufflebeems, and the "family story" as recounted by Deborah Wyle, who got it from her mother and Aunt Jean, differed slightly. But then, said Deborah, her father's stories and family recollections seldom jibed. "You have to understand my dad was a brilliant storyteller. I'd take trips with the man, and we'd come back and his trip was so much more interesting than mine. I'd wonder, 'Was I there?'"

Sturges worked several menial jobs before being offered full-time employment at a gas station. The catch: he had to pay a then-considerable $20 for two uniforms. "The family, careful about new expenditures, raised the money because they felt it was a good investment," said Deborah. "But once they purchased the uniforms, Sturge announced there was an opening at RKO in the blueprint department."

As was the custom, a family meeting was called, and it was put to a vote. "It was a big decision," said Deborah, "because they had invested the $20, and the RKO job paid less than the gas station job." Ultimately, the family decided that there was more potential in movies than pumping gas, and they forfeited the money.

3

RKO

The curly-haired young man entered RKO Radio Pictures through the Gower Street gate and found his way to the personnel department. "I've come about a job. My brother, Sturge Carne, works in your art department—I'm John Sturges," he announced to the immediately befuddled receptionist. Sturges had no way of knowing it, but over the next eight years his life would take on new purpose. It was mostly dumb luck, he insisted—"right place, right time."

In 1932, RKO—or "the little major," as it was affectionately known—was about making movies, not family fortunes, and because the studio reins changed hands with such regularity—from Charles Koerner to David O. Selznick to Pandro S. Berman to Howard Hughes—there was no rule book or codified chain of command. This attracted such idiosyncratic talents as George Cukor, King Vidor, John Ford, Katharine Hepburn, Fred Astaire, and Orson Welles. You worked at the upstart studio—already a pioneer in sound technology and now toying with three-strip Technicolor—if you wanted to try something new, like *King Kong* (1933) or *Citizen Kane* (1941).

Director Richard Fleischer (*The Narrow Margin*, *20,000 Leagues under the Sea*) got his start during the Berman-Hughes regimes and knew Sturges. "The place was a revolving door," he said. "It was perfect for mavericks and up-and-comers like John."

It helped that Sturges had a connection. Brother Sturge—whose pencil-thin mustache gave him the appearance of Duncan "The Cisco

Kid" Renaldo — called in a favor and got John a night job in the art department. He earned $20 a week inking blueprints. The hours were long and mind-numbing, but the work appealed to Sturges's analytical bent. The key, he soon discovered, was to make yourself indispensable. He devised a ridiculously complicated filing system that no one but he could crack. For this, he received a promotion to office assistant.

"I started working at RKO doing blueprints at night," he recalled later. "And then I was promoted to office boy in the art department, keeping track of drawings and stuff. I must have been twenty-two, twenty-three. . . . On my own time I would hang around the sets all day long, watch John Ford and George Stevens, and imagine the way each scene would look."

Selznick, who had just been named head of production, was on the lookout for anyone who could help streamline the day-to-day operation. He was attempting to decentralize production and give more control to individual filmmakers. He welcomed the kind of creative problem solving for which Sturges was gaining a reputation. So when Selznick invited Broadway designer Robert Edmond Jones to conduct experiments in Technicolor and apply his findings to a musical short, Sturges was assigned to the New Yorker. "Jones, who looked a little like Groucho Marx, had never been in a studio in his life," Sturges recalled. "It was my job to steer the guy around, tell him who did what and so on. I was his office boy."

RKO's *La Cucaracha* (1934) — directed by Lloyd Corrigan, who would later star in two Sturges programmers (low-budget, hastily assembled B pictures, usually the second attractions on double bills) — earned an Oscar for best comedy short and paved the way for Technicolor features. Sturges assisted Jones on *Becky Sharp* (1935), the first three-strip feature, and *The Dancing Pirate* (1936), the first dancing musical in "100 percent color." The latter, which took gallows humor to new lengths with a scaffold tap dance, drew catcalls when previewed and was soon shelved. Jones returned to New York, making Sturges RKO's de facto color expert.

Selznick was about to shoot *The Garden of Allah* (1936) in Technicolor and, because of the stringent contractual demands of the new process, required a consultant on the set at all times. That person, Selznick stressed in one of his famous memos, would oversee technical matters pertaining to the film stock and not have a hand in the "creative side of our pictures." The job went to Sturges, who was paid $300 a week. "They tracked me down and offered me the job," he recalled. "I wasn't about to say no. I was made 'technical color consultant,' and got my first screen credit." (Actually, Lansing C. Holden received sole credit as color designer.)

Truth be known, Sturges was making up the rules as he went along. "Nobody knew too much about color in those days," he said. "They just went around dying pieces of cloth and talking mysteriously."

As entertaining as this story is, brother Sturge probably had a hand in helping John secure his first production job. Sturge was a set designer on *The Garden of Allah* and was helping establish what would become RKO's signature baroque style. In 1935, he graduated from assistant to associate art director and earned three credits, including Cukor's *Sylvia Scarlet*. The following year he was made art director on *Little Lord Fauntleroy*.

The Garden of Allah, starring Marlene Dietrich and Charles Boyer, went where no color production had gone before—the Yuma Desert in Arizona. As Selznick's memos regarding Dietrich's tantrums and too-perfectly coiffed hair poured from the teletype machine, Sturges drew on his engineering skills and, literally, kept the production from blowing away. "Nobody could get the Arab tents right," he recalled. "God knows how the Arabs do it. We had ropes and new canvas, but still couldn't manage it. I went to the construction guys and said, 'Build a framework like a lath house in the shape of those goddamn things.' David said, 'At last, somebody who knows how to do something!' And all of a sudden I jumped up a notch and thereupon was referred to as David's assistant, which I really wasn't."

More interested in learning a viable trade than working as Selznick's errand boy, Sturges took a cut in pay and began a four-year apprenticeship in RKO's editing department, working his way from film carrier to assistant sound editor to full editor. "I started in the cutting room, working my way up, because that was one of the best ways to learn how to direct," he said on the laserdisc commentary for *Bad Day at Black Rock.* "I swept floors, kept track of trims and outtakes; put them together on a machine. . . . Eight years [after arriving at the studio] I was a cutter."

Working in the editing stalls on either side of him were Mark Robson, Robert Wise, and Robert Parrish, who described the career path in his autobiography: "They taught me how to splice, clean reels, carry cans, file trims and keep my mouth shut in the projection room." Once he had mastered this, added Parrish, the would-be cutter would then learn how to "'bloop' sound tracks (paint out extraneous noises), to do synchronization (work the numbering machine that put matching code numbers on each foot of sound track and picture), to lie to producers, and to, finally, begin to edit sequences."

Wise, who worked his way up from the mailroom, called the RKO apprenticeship "one of the best routes for someone starting from scratch to learn the whole process of filmmaking." Like Sturges, his training was hands-on. William Hamilton (*Cimarron*) or another top editor stood at the Moviola and marked the cuts; the assistant, standing at the sync machine, did the actual cutting and splicing. If the editor was busy on the set assisting the director, an assistant might be entrusted with the first rough cut. Hamilton would then, said Wise, "come down and look at the sequence and improve it, and the last three films I did with him, I was doing so much of the work, he insisted I share credit."

Wise and Robson shared their dreams of someday calling the shots as director. Sturges liked the sound of this, and the three assistant cutters soon became the lot's horn-rimmed Athos, Porthos, and Aramis, "bumming around" together, according to Wise. At a costume party, they posed with Hank Berman (the editor brother of Pandro Berman) in vintage football uniforms. Sturges, easily the tallest, reclined in the foreground on a bearskin rug, with Wise, sporting a walrus mustache, kneeling behind him.

Sturges even talked landlubber Wise into building a twenty-one-foot sloop called *Partners' Choice*. "Johnny and I built the boat in a loft in the valley—hull and everything," recalled Wise. "We worked on it every weekend for almost two years." And when it was finished, save for mast and sail, they hauled it to Balboa Marina in Newport Beach. "We would go down every weekend and sail it. It was John's idea; he got me into sailing. He knew what he was doing. He grew up around boats . . . learned to sail as a kid."

Tellingly, the Sturges whom Wise remembered was "well-educated" and from "a quite well-to-do family back East." He added: "I remember Johnny as a tall guy with a great sense of humor. We were very close for six, seven years, until the war came along. He went into the service. I didn't. They were good times."

As an assistant cutter making $85 a week, Sturges worked on John Cromwell's *Of Human Bondage* (1934) with Bette Davis and George Stevens's *Gunga Din* (1939). The Davis vehicle, Sturges recalled, had "a disastrous Santa Barbara preview, laughed off the screen," but it was salvaged later in the editing room. He also assisted the sound editor on several Astaire-Rodgers musicals, such as *The Gay Divorcee* (1934). It was on these films that he learned about click tracks (cues for the composer and conductor), playbacks, and lily horns (directional mikes).

Gunga Din, shot on location in Lone Pine and the Alabama Hills, provided more opportunities for advancement. Besides serving as editor Hank Berman's assistant, Sturges doubled as "troubleshooter," racing from second unit (the Scottish regiment's approach through the valley) to inserts (men pitching headfirst off rocks) to sound effects (for the hand-to-hand combat). Of the latter, Sturges recalled, "We got a watermelon and hit it with a bat, and over-cranked the sound so it came out 'ka-RACK!' It was horrifying. We had to get rid of it. Too gruesome."

Impressed by his young assistant's versatility and initiative, Stevens invited him to work side by side with Berman during post-production, more as co-editor than assistant. "My official title was assistant cutter," recalled Sturges, "but, believe me, I did a lot of cutting on it."

When it came time to test *Gunga Din,* Sturges rode along in the studio limousine. There were four sneak previews, the most important taking place in Santa Barbara and Whittier. "*Gunga Din* would never have been the smash hit it became without those previews," he said. "We had enough film to make six pictures, and there was no way we could have cut it and committed ourselves to it without those test runs. You wouldn't believe the changes we made. We screened a dirty print with black frames in it and temporary dubbing—the whole ball of wax. Santa Barbara was safe, but we made one big boo-boo. *Gunga Din* is a violent picture, and Whittier is 90 percent Quakers. They were very polite to the picture, but after the show, when they asked to see the director, we said, 'I think he went the other way,' and we disappeared into the night."

Sturges was in awe of Stevens, whom he cited as a singular influence, the man who taught him the most about storytelling. "I was the student, George the master," he said.

Indebted to his young protégé, Stevens sang his praises to James Wilkinson, head of RKO's editing department. Wilkinson made

Sturges principal editor on Garson Kanin's adaptation of Sidney Howard's Pulitzer Prize–winning play *They Knew What They Wanted* (1940). Sturges's responsibilities were liberally defined by the inexperienced Kanin: he doubled as editor and assistant on the set, helping with camera setups "to be sure he got enough coverage." Unfortunately, *They Knew What They Wanted* proved beyond anyone's help. Besides endless tussles with the Production Code (over the title and a third-act pregnancy), it starred a hopelessly miscast Charles Laughton as an Italian immigrant vintner and Carole Lombard as his mail-order bride. The results played like "Cyrano de Bergerac Meets Desire under the Grape Leaves." Kanin knew Laughton's over-the-top performance and muffed takes would be a challenge for the most experienced editor. "Now starts the hard part, putting it all together," he told Laughton at the wrap party.

Sturges couldn't do much with Laughton's performance, but he was able to mold the footage into a cohesive, mildly diverting melodrama. His most impressive contributions included a letter-writing montage and a quick succession of close-ups to underscore the mounting sexual tension.

Kanin showed his appreciation for the salvage job by requesting Sturges for his next picture, *Tom, Dick and Harry* (1941), starring a Ginger Rodgers who can't decide among three very different suitors. Fast paced and quite racy for its day—in the style of a minor Preston Sturges farce—the *ménage à trois* relied heavily on editing, especially during the dream sequences, which start out giddy and become increasingly manic.

"Editor—John Sturges" appeared on two other films during this period. Neither did anything to advance, or impede, his career. *Scattergood Meets Broadway* (1941) was a low-budget programmer about a hayseed philosopher who outsmarts crooked city folk; *Syncopation* (1942), directed by William Dieterle and released after Sturges had enlisted in the army, was a well-meant attempt to trace the roots of New York boogie to Bourbon Street jazz and beyond. Looser, more abstract in execution than the other assignments, this novelty attraction afforded Sturges opportunities to cut to music. At least one Mississippi River montage brings to mind *Porgy and Bess* and begs the question: Why didn't Sturges try his hand at a musical? His final feature as editor demonstrates, if not a predilection, at least an affinity for the genre.

Looking back, Sturges said he became a cutter because he needed a career path and editing was the fastest route to directing. "Everybody's got to figure out their angle," he explained. "I wanted to be in the cutting room. I knew I didn't have literary merit, and I'd never been a deal maker or hustler. But I understood cutting. And if you know how to cut pictures, you know how to make 'em."

In time, the Wise-Robson-Sturges triumvirate lost its third member. Unlike his slightly younger, more gregarious friends, Sturges seldom attended studio functions or built relationships with executives. He kept more to himself, which would exact a toll years later when *The Great Escape* was being considered for Oscars. "John wasn't a salesman," said Robert Relyea, his longtime assistant director. "He didn't play the game." Consequently, as Sturges drew lesser films, Wise and Robson were assigned *Citizen Kane* and *The Magnificent Ambersons*. Because of family and medical problems (Wise was diagnosed with an enlarged prostate), they were ineligible for the draft and able to work for producer Val Lewton. Robson made his directorial debut on Lewton's *The Seventh Victim*, and Wise took over *Curse of the Cat People*—as Sturges reported for more hazardous duty overseas.

4

War & Wyler

By December 7, 1941, Grace Sturges had moved to a garden apartment in Westwood. John, however, continued to board with Jean and her husband, William Stufflebeem. Their son, Jon, vividly recalled that day. He was eight years old. "Our neighbor, Reg Keller, leapt over the four-foot fence between our two driveways, calling out to my father. 'Bill, Bill—turn on your radio! The Japs have bombed Pearl Harbor!'

"Uncle John wasn't around very much, but he was there that day, and we went in and listened to the bulletin on the radio, one of those big floor models. He was intensely patriotic, and nothing would do but that he must enlist."

Thirty-two and extremely nearsighted, Sturges was an unlikely candidate for military service. But these were minor impediments. The opportunity to serve in any capacity, said Sturges, was not to be passed up. On February 22, 1942—thanks to the relaxed definition of 1-A ("normally healthy") and a need for experienced filmmakers to help sell the war at home—he was inducted into the U.S. Army. In the space designated "civic occupation," he listed airplane-engine mechanic, film cutter, PR man, playwright, reporter. Sturge Carne, forty-three, returned to service as a lieutenant in the Army Corps of Engineers.

Unlike William Wyler, John Huston, George Stevens, and Frank Capra, all established filmmakers who were commissioned as officers so they could command film units, Sturges went in as a corporal without

25

any trade-paper fanfare. Major Capra was even granted a six-week delay to finish *Arsenic and Old Lace* before he donned an army surplus uniform and boarded the *Super Chief* for Washington, D.C. "The Army," Capra wrote in his autobiography, "was a welcome out for me, a clean, respectable way to turn down enslaving million-dollar contracts."

Sturges, by contrast, saw the military as an opportunity to serve his country while continuing to hone his skills. But there was no doubt about his primary motive: he wanted to join what Lt. James Stewart called "the biggest All-American Team we've ever had" to help "lick the Axes." Recalled Stufflebeem, who lived vicariously through his uncle, "He couldn't wait to get into uniform."

Sturges reported to the Recruit Reception and Training Center at Fort MacArthur in San Pedro. The base had been built during World War I to handle the assault on Los Angeles Harbor that never came. What he discovered reminded him of a studio façade—palm trees, neatly tended geranium beds, row after row of khaki-tan barracks. (Indeed, Fort MacArthur was a popular backdrop for such movies as *This Is the Army*.) Over the next several weeks, while drawing $75 a month, he completed basic training—endless drilling broken up by calisthenics and KP. On the basis of his RKO experience and test scores, he was then sent to Officers Candidate School at Fort Monmouth, New Jersey. In October, he received his second lieutenant commission in the Signal Corps and was stationed at Wright Field, Dayton, Ohio, which quickly became his least favorite spot. "I still despise Dayton and Ohio in general," he wrote Grace in 1943, during an especially muggy summer.

While based at Wright Field, Lt. Sturges—now attached to the Signal Corps' Army Pictorial Services and drawing $245 a month—directed informational shorts for the Army Air Corps (how to ditch a crippled Flying Tiger) and Army Intelligence (how to read aerial photographs). His greatest challenge was making the nose turret of the B-24 bomber appear cinematic. In all, Sturges worked on forty-five training and orientation films, several of which, including *The Operation and Maintenance of the B-51*, utilized the most expensive and realistic "props" any director could have desired. During the making of *The Great Escape* and *The Eagle Has Landed*, Sturges would wish he had access to a fraction of the ordinance at his disposal during the war.

"These training films," he explained, "ran all the way from ten-minute things that were ordered by the operational unit to something like 'IFF' [Identify Friend or Foe] on a transponder [decoder] that would tell you whether you had a friendly or hostile aircraft in your sights."

Though family lore has it that Sturges directed personal-hygiene films (such as how to avoid venereal disease), he said he didn't. "I skipped all those. I learned a trick from George Stevens: Don't just sit around with your thumb up your ass, do some detective work. That's how I got some of the better films at MGM later. Same thing in the army. I'd find out what all the projects were, and put in for the best ones."

After completing the B-51 short, Sturges had some fun at the military's expense. He made a parody of an army training film called *The Care and Maintenance of the M-1 Potato Peeler*. As a hand appears holding a potato peeler, the booming voice of the narrator explains, "This is the M-1 Potato Peeler. Method of operation: Firmly seize the base with your right hand, thumb locking over your fingers and scrape with a downward motion." The second half dealt with the maintenance of the peeler, how to wash it in salt water. "If it wears out, forget it—throw it away because"—cut to a shot of a warehouse with crates as far as the eye could see—"the Army's got millions of them!"

"Hilarious! We went through the whole ridiculous procedure," recalled Sturges, obviously still tickled by the prank. "We had some scrap film and put it together in the base cutting room. But, Jesus, somebody saw it, and there was hell to play. We all said, 'Gee, we don't know where that came from.'"

Sturges, known to embellish a good story, said the short almost got him court-martialed for wasting government supplies.

When several legitimate training films were completed, Sturges would travel to Washington, D.C., and screen them for General Henry "Hap" Arnold and his staff. His report (in a letter home) on one such screening: "Ran the Army Intelligence picture in final form in Washington last week, and it went over with a big bang. The turret picture looks good too, though not as susceptible a subject. Both of them quite elaborate for this place, what with sound, sets, actors, music, etc."

During the summer of 1943, Sturges wrote his mother that as a result of internecine competition between the Signal Corps and the Army

Air Corps, his unit was being split up, and he would, henceforth, be a member of the Air Corps. The transfer meant that in two months he would be coming home—"to be stationed, at least for a while, at the First Motion Picture Unit, Culver City, California. What do you think of that?"

The irony of going away to war and, eighteen months later, winding up a few miles from home was not lost on Sturges, who chafed at the cushy reassignment. "Of course it will be wonderful to see you and be home again," he wrote Grace, "but the idea of being in uniform in Hollywood doesn't appeal to me at all." The East Coast alternative— working out of Astoria Studio in Queens—"gives me the creeps too." Like Lt. Huston and others, Sturges was itching to record actual combat conditions, go "out where the work is."

After completing those films already in production, Sturges reported for duty in Hollywood. He didn't have far to drive. The First Motion Picture Unit (F.M.P.U. or "fum-poo") was stationed at Hal Roach Studios, a.k.a. Fort Roach, in Culver City. Its mandate, as outlined by General Arnold, was to train, recruit, and whip up support for the war. Further, pounded home a 1943 informational short, these films would "graphically illustrate what we're fighting for, what we're fighting against, and what we're fighting with."

"We made some great films in the army," Sturges recalled later. "We had these great props—huge airplanes—and top cameramen and actors. How could you miss? I made a picture with Lee Cobb and Arthur Kennedy. Pretty good actors. It was photographed by Ted McCort, for God's sake! It's gotta look good." (A contract cinematographer at Warner who specialized in Westerns, McCort went on to shoot *The Treasure of the Sierra Madre* and *The Sound of Music*).

It was at Fort Roach that Sturges met Major William Wyler, who was, next to Capra and Stevens, the unit's most illustrious director. The "Old Man," as the wiry forty-one-year-old was known, could pull strings and get Sturges assigned to a combat unit overseas. Sturges staked out the stage where Wyler was recording the narration for what would become *The Memphis Belle: A Story of a Flying Fortress*. "I made a point of hanging around watching, and finally Willy came over and said, 'Hello.' We chatted, and he said, 'How would you like to come over to Italy and do a film about a new kind of bomber squadron?'" Like others in the unit, Sturges would have to undergo "modified commando training . . . under simulated combat conditions." He assumed his role would be that of editor.

In June 1944—the month Rome was liberated by the Allies—Sturges and Wyler prepared to join the 57th Fighter Group on Corsica. Their assignment as members of the 12th Camera Combat Unit: to tell the public about the brave men who flew P-47 Thunderbolt dive-bombers. The single-seat, torpedo-shaped planes—or "seven-ton milk bottles," as the pilots called them—were used in Operation Strangle to cut off supplies and reinforcements to German-occupied Italy and break the stalemate at Anzio. The five-reel documentary, like *Memphis Belle*, would be written by Technical Sergeant Lester Koenig and scored by Corporal Gail Kubik. It would be shot silent in 16mm Technicolor by Wyler and Technical Sergeant Karl H. Maslowski, a wildlife photographer in civilian life. Only this time—because director and photographer could not ride along—the cameras would be attached to the wings, cockpit, and wheel wells of the planes, affording the movie-goer a pilot's eye view of the perilously low bombing runs.

On June 6, while awaiting his flight out, a nervous but excited Sturges wrote his mother: "Have seen a lot of people I know here in New York, including [*Gunga Din* editor] Hank Berman, who looks fine. Even took in a couple of shows and in general has been a fine trip. . . . Looking forward to the flight over with great interest. You wouldn't believe how little time it takes."

Wyler, Sturges, and a camera crew flew to Naples and crossed the sixty miles to Corsica in an LST landing craft. The 57th's Alto Air Base, on the north shore of the recently liberated island, proved to be a dust-choked tribute to American ingenuity, with steel-mat runway, flight tower, crude cabins, jury-rigged washing machine, and a barbershop called Jerry's Clip Joint. The Hollywood crew set up a Quonset hut "studio" (dark room, editing bench) and got to know the pilots, ground crews, and Group Operations officers. Sturges wrote in microfilmed V-mail: "All of these fellows in complete charge of an enormous organization with field and operation equipment and planes costing way into the millions." The stunning sunsets and mostly "swell weather," he added, were offset by the "primitive" living condition that included B-17-size mosquitoes and water "that tastes of that damned disinfectant."

There was also, he wrote, a strong anti-U.S. resentment among the locals who saw the Americans as "interlopers . . . chiseling in on all the credit!!!"

Not wanting to sound like he was complaining, Sturges stressed that he was "mighty active and having a fine time . . . with a very famous outfit, and a world of things going on that are swell for our picture." He closed on a more somber note: "Very interesting to meet the men here. They are the ones who are actually fighting the war. Most have been overseas for two years and have brought their planes all the way from El Alamein to here."

In early July, Wyler and his camera unit flew to Rome to document the Allies' triumphant arrival and waving crowds. Sturges's responsibilities by this time had broadened considerably: He doubled as writer, grip, sound man, and cameraman. He also played liaison, clearing potentially sensitive footage with field commanders. In two nearly identical letters home (the first missed the mail bag and was delayed), Sturges called the tour "quite an experience" and added that because of his "feeble Italian," he had been capable of only "small-time conversation." There was no mistaking public sentiment, a mix of respect and fear. "Being in the Air Corps and bomb damage all over the place they looked us over with considerable awe. . . . Of course they blame all their part of everything on the Germans." Letter two elaborated: "Now that they've lost they're very friendly of course, and the whole thing was the Germans' fault. Baloney." In still another letter, this time from France, Sturges called southern Italians "really as crummy a race as you could ever find. . . . Italy was the place that was really bashed into pieces. Which of course is the way it ought to be."

As for the documentary, Sturges (careful not to name Wyler or other members of the crew) reported that "some preliminary stuff" had been shot, and the basic outline of the story was in place. However:

> the real work isn't under way yet. Lots to arrange and plan, but we are enthused over the prospects and have a pretty good idea of the stuff we are going to shoot. We're telling the story of how a Tactical Air Force (strafing supply trains and troop movements behind enemy lines) operates which is wonderfully new and very effective stuff. There is a lot of their technique made to order for movie presentation and all of them are interested in giving us all the help we need.

The "made to order" technique was a reference to the wing- and fuselage-mounted cameras. They, however, provided only the pilot's perspective. Also needed were contextual shots — of the ground damage and the P-47s in midflight. For proof of how deadly the bombing campaign was, Wyler and Sturges flew to Naples and drove by jeep to the front, where, according to Wyler's biographer, Axel Madsen, they came within range of enemy artillery fire. They returned with shots of roadside corpses, mangled cars and tracks, downed bridges and aqueducts. The additional aerial footage was taken from a twin-engine B-25, whose doors and side windows had been removed, making communication all but impossible. Wyler blamed his near-career-ending hearing loss on the "deafening" drone of these flights. He usually sat up front with the pilot as Sturges bounced around in the tail and Maslowski darted from one side of the plane to the other with his camera.

In a V-mail from Corsica dated July 18 — well after the Normandy invasion — a sleep-deprived but jubilant Sturges asked his mother, "How did you like the little show that went on over here to hop up Adolf's headache a little more?" Purposely vague for the benefit of War Department censors, he wrote that he had a "mighty fancy operation to cover" and that the aerial photography should look great, but not to worry because "our part was on the interesting rather than the dangerous side."

During wartime, everything is relative, he pointed out. Life on Corsica seemed like the Waldorf Astoria "after munching K rations on the floor of a plane and getting a nap draped over various kinds of vehicles and equipment." The airbase came with a swimming hole and what was jokingly referred to as "a beach club." On movie nights, the filmmakers and the fliers stretched out on the ground before a makeshift screen, hooting and wolf-whistling at Rita Hayworth and Betty Grable. Their main concern, Sturges wrote, was the rain. The slit trenches that doubled as latrines were now filled with six feet of water, and "everybody hopes the Krauts won't scrape anything together that would send us diving into those things in the middle of the night."

Sturges was uncharacteristically emotional when it came to the heavy price paid by the young fighter pilots, some of whom were barely twenty-two.

Have gotten to know lots of the men here very well and they are quite a bunch. It's difficult to realize the terrible hazard of the constant missions they fly until you've had breakfast with a fellow and two hours later his squadron comes back minus him and with the story of his death. This happens all the time, not only out over enemy territory but in crackups right around us. I wish a few of the people who listen sympathetically to Italy's yelps that the Armistice terms are unfair and who already talk about not being vengeful towards misguided Germans could watch this awhile.

In September, Sturges and Wyler joined the army's southern offensive along the Rhône River, where they lived off the land and slept in barns. Bivouacked in a "fancy" château whose windows were blown out—"Jerry blew up ammunition train nearby"—Sturges wrote that he could see the end in sight and that "being with the French is almost like being in America." In stark contrast to the landscape and the French hospitality were "the firsthand stories and material evidence of the wanton and brutal killing of civilians by the Germans. . . . The things they have done are simply staggering and it's almost impossible to think of any just solution or retribution short of capital punishment for the whole nation."

Weighted down with film canisters, Wyler, Koenig, and Sturges flew to London to transfer the footage to 35mm film and splice together an early assemblage. En route, they came under enemy fire. "The flight was almost their last," according to Wyler's biographer. "The unarmed transport was flying low over liberated France when it was fired upon from the ground. When they landed in London, they were told there were pockets of Germans around the Normandy peninsula that still had food and, obviously, ammunition."

Satisfied with the rough cut, Wyler ordered Sturges and Koenig stateside to write and record the narration. Wyler flew to Paris, where he and George Stevens continued to document the Allies' advance through France. In Wyler's absence, Sturges took over the project, shaping it as a more immediate day-in-the-life vignette. Screenwriter Philip Dunne might have been referring to Sturges when, in a 1948 essay, he noted: "Give a good documentary editor an idea and he will express it for you in film: pictorial image, mood and tempo. His function is more often creative than editorial."

In early 1945, Sturges wrote that more aerial footage of Corsica and Rome was needed to smooth narrative gaps. Wyler went aloft for what he called "atmosphere shots." This time, however, he manned the open doors himself and took the full blast of wind and droning engine. Once again, he lost his hearing and equilibrium. But this time he was told at a Naples hospital, "You're being sent home—you're deaf." (Wyler sustained permanent nerve damage in his right ear. He regained some hearing in his left ear but from then on directed wearing headphones.)

On top of this, the footage was worthless. Wyler, it turned out, was a better director than photographer. "He just fired a camera like a water hose—in all directions," said Sturges. The footage might as well have been "exposed in a camera mounted on a rapidly revolving egg-beater," groaned Maslowski. "I've never seen a more disgusting waste of valuable film in all my days."

Stateside, Wyler agreed that Sturges's contributions went well beyond that of editor and, indeed, were extensive enough to warrant a co-director credit. At war's end, he would further reward Sturges by recommending him to Harry Cohn as a bright new directing prospect.

Conceived as anti-fascist propaganda, *Thunderbolt* would not be completed until the war was over and such combat missions were, to quote James Stewart's 1947 on-screen introduction, "ancient history." Sturges and Wyler joked, "The damn war stopped on us." In the weeks following the Armistice, the War Department offered the documentary—with "Actual World War 2 Color Footage!"—to theaters as a free short subject. There were no takers, probably because Lloyd Bridges's voiceover for the trigger-happy pilots ("Give her a few squirts—might kill somebody") came off as glib and bloodthirsty in the postwar climate. An independent producer finally picked up the film and released it through Monogram.

To pound home its authenticity, *Thunderbolt* employed a grim, *Dragnet*-style narration: "This picture was photographed in combat zones by cameramen of the Mediterranean Allied Air Forces and by pilots of the 12th Air Force . . . who, during missions against the enemy, operated automatic cameras in their planes . . . behind the pilot, shooting forward and back . . . under the wings . . . in the wings, timed with the guns . . . in the wheel well . . . in the instrument panels, photographing the pilot himself."

Thunderbolt, which earned Lieutenant Colonel Wyler and now-Captain John Sturges the Bronze Star, is more accurately described as a pseudo-documentary in the tradition of Huston's *The Battle of San Pietro* (1945). Some of it is sickeningly real, like the arbitrary strafing of farmhouses and the attempt to pull the charred remains of a pilot from twisted wreckage. Other scenes are obviously staged, like the recreational vignettes and "country club" sing-along to "Little Brown Jug." Elsewhere, to pound home a point, the filmmakers intercut material taken at different locations. Two children are seen picking through the debris, looking at "things not meant for children's eyes." Cut to: rotting corpse of a German soldier.

The *New York Times* reviewed the forty-three-minute version of the film in October 1945 and applauded its graphic depiction of tactical air power as well as the "vivid portrayal of how fighter pilots lived, fought and died." A year later, upon its commercial release, the *Nation* critic James Agee raved: "A good many incredibly fine air shots, well organized; by a long shot, the best of the movies reviewed above." No mean endorsement: Agee had covered Michael Powell and Emeric Pressburger's *Black Narcissus* in the same column.

Today, *Thunderbolt* is held in high regard as a war documentary on a par with *Memphis Belle* and Humphrey Jennings's London-under-siege dispatches. *When Hollywood Ruled the Skies* author Bruce W. Orriss considers it "one of the best documentaries to emerge from World War 2." This may be overstating the case. While jarringly blunt, the Wyler-Sturges collaboration is neither as focused nor as suspenseful as *Memphis Belle,* which succeeds in humanizing a B-17's crew on its final mission over Germany. *Thunderbolt* borrows the earlier documentary's narrative progression (from sunrise briefing and big-picture maps to mission and return flight); but where *Memphis Belle* uses the matter-of-fact daily rituals to create an ever-deepening sense of dread, the Corsica-set documentary feels patched together, desultory. Pilots joke with their ground crew, take off, strafe trains and farmhouses, return to base, enjoy R&R at the beach and bar—but without our ever feeling the cadence of life in this remote outpost. The juxtaposition of stirring music and glib, staccato voiceover makes up for some of this, but the uneven quality of the aerial footage suggests the filmmakers lacked sufficient coverage.

In Sturges's opinion, the film's saving grace was its matter-of-fact narration, which underscored the gallantry by shrugging it off.

"It's a trick I learned working with Willy," he said. "When we were in Italy, he explained why *Memphis Belle* worked so well. He said, 'See, these guys are all wrong about heroes. They come on like a booming "March of Time" newsreel. *These are our heroic men going over to face unbelievable odds!*' He said, 'You don't do it that way. You want the audience to say they're heroes. So what you have the guys say is: This is just a milk run. You get in the plane . . . you take the goddamn bombs . . . you fly them over there . . . and you drop 'em and you come back home. That's all there is to it.'"

This way, the audience becomes visibly upset and sings the praises of men too humble to toot their own horn. Sturges never forgot Wyler's lesson. He would call on this emotional sleight-of-hand later for his two most popular films, *The Magnificent Seven* and *The Great Escape*. "It's reactive," he explained. "You don't want your actors crying, you want your audience crying. You want the audience telling the pilot, 'What do you mean that's all there is to it? Jesus, they're shooting at you!'"

Though Sturges stressed how much he owed Wyler professionally, he was unhappy with his billing on the documentary. "'Directed and cut by William Wyler and John Sturges'—that sounds like it was directed by Wyler and cut by me. That wasn't the case. But he was a lieutenant colonel, I was a captain. And that's how the credit reads." (There was no confusion within the industry, where Sturges's rise in the ranks was frequently attributed to his wartime stint as co-director.)

Unlike Lee Marvin, James Garner, and others with whom he would work, Sturges did not shoulder a rifle in battle or sustain combat injuries. His later images of war were inspired by memories of events viewed as front-row spectator, not participant. Still, he was especially proud of *Thunderbolt* and kept a 35mm print in the hopes that it would someday be restored. The film stood apart because of its imperfections. "It's a real documentary—isn't a fake piece of film in the whole thing," he said, pounding his palm. "A lot of these new war movies, like *Memphis Belle* (1990), aren't very good. They're made by people who have never been in a war. Willy was in the war, I was in the war. You have to have the experience. It's curious that nobody has ever made a good picture about the war who wasn't in the war."

5

Columbia Years

Unlike the returning soldiers battling survivor's guilt and post-traumatic stress in William Wyler's *The Best Years of Our Lives*, Capt. John Sturges had no trouble slipping back into civilian life. He knew what he wanted; he had had plenty of time in the service to contemplate his next step. In November, he signed with Columbia to direct his first feature. On December 1, in less than twenty-four hours, he collected his discharge papers and married Dorothy Lynn Brooks, a secretary at Warner Bros. who had left her screenwriter husband, Charles Grayson, for the aspiring filmmaker. Following a simple ceremony in Glendale, the couple drove to Death Valley and honeymooned at the Furnace Creek Inn.

They rented a bungalow in Laurel Canyon for a couple of years, but after Deborah was born they purchased hillside property in Studio City. Their redwood ranch house, designed by Sturge, opened onto a patio and kidney-shaped pool and blended with the eucalyptus trees. It afforded a panoramic view of the valley. A veranda with mahogany bar, brick barbecue, and poster of Picasso's *Guernica* opened onto the pool. John—his back to the wall, gunfighter fashion—often read here as Stan Getz and Charlie Byrd's *Jazz Samba* poured from the patio speakers. The couple would become known for their poolside brunches. Sunday guests might include Spencer Tracy, Gene Autry, director Mel Shavelson, and, from across the street, William Roberts, who would be brought in for rewrites on *The Magnificent Seven*.

Sturges, however, was in no mood to relax; there was ground to be made up. In his absence, Robson and Wise had both directed four features and were about to begin their fifth. Sturges had no way of knowing it at the time, but he was fated to play a frustrating game of catch-up with his old friends for much of his career: He would do the routine boxing melodrama *Right Cross* as Robson landed the powerful, Oscar-nominated *Champion* and Wise the gritty, innovative *The Set-Up*. Sturges would go against his better judgment and make the indifferently received soap operas *A Girl Named Tamiko* and *By Love Possessed*, as his old friends raked in millions with *Peyton Place* (Robson) and *Executive Suite* (Wise). Tellingly, the genres in which Sturges bested Robson and Wise were the Western and large-scale war epic. (Robson's *Von Ryan's Express* was little more than *The Great Escape* in miniature.) Sturges had seen men in combat; they hadn't.

Harry Cohn, Sturges's famously coarse boss at Columbia, also knew what he wanted. With television threatening Hollywood's hegemony and ticket sales beginning to reflect the public's divided allegiance, King Cohn—or "His Crudeness," as Capra called him—was determined to take his studio up market with pricier star vehicles. The year Sturges reported for work, *A Song to Remember* and *Counter-Attack* filled this niche. Such titles were the exceptions, however. The rule: B Westerns, Three Stooges shorts, new installments in the Jungle Jim, Blondie, and Boston Blackie series. These films paid the rent and kept such novice directors as Budd Boetticher and William Castle busy. Now joining their ranks was the slightly older war veteran in the Harold Lloyd horn-rims.

Cohn was intrigued by Sturges. He was everything the studio chief wasn't—patient, soft-spoken, urbane. The big fellow might have a future in the picture business, Cohn told Sam Briskin, who oversaw Columbia's "B" slate. Even more to Cohn's liking, "the kid" had yet to receive his first directing credit, which meant an entry-level salary, and Cohn—known for "short-term contracts, tight budgets and limiting directors to one take"—was on the prowl for bargains. He signed Sturges for a rock-bottom $300 a week.

In retirement, Sturges was philosophical about this. He had to start somewhere, and the second-tier but scrappy Columbia, like RKO, offered something better than remuneration: on-the-job training and the opportunity for speedy advancement. "This was a time when studios were making 30 to 40 pictures each a year," he recalled. "By attrition, if nothing else, you're going to wind up getting a crack at directing." He still had to pay dues, and this meant making the best of the decidedly limited material thrown at him. "Hard to believe they even did stuff like that," he said.

Understandably, Sturges was reluctant to talk about these early assignments, dismissing them as "fifteen-day wonders." Most combined down-on-their-luck Hollywood vets, such as George Meader and Aubrey Mather, and young contract players, including Gloria Henry and Terry Moore, and were shot for less than $100,000 in twelve to fifteen days at the studio or Columbia Ranch in Burbank, then mostly orange and walnut groves.

Sturges jockeyed for the best of what was available, and with the exception of Charles Vidor's steamy *Gilda* and the Oscar-winning *The Jolson Story*, Columbia's 1946 slate was hardly what one would call noteworthy. Sturges's contribution consisted of three budget productions — a tepid courtroom drama-exposé, a lighthearted murder mystery that owed more than a small debt to early Hitchcock, and a Damon Runyon-esque caper comedy (released in 1947).

Sturges made his directorial debut with *The Man Who Dared*, a mystery-cliffhanger that went into production as "One Life Too Many." It was a remake of 1935's *Circumstantial Evidence*. George Macready starred as newspaper columnist Don Wayne, whose plot to discredit the use of circumstantial evidence in death-penalty cases nearly has calamitous consequences. Leslie Brooks and Forrest Tucker played Wayne's fiancée and sportswriter buddy. A forerunner of sorts to Sam Fuller's *Shock Corridor*, the mystery was set primarily in a cramped courtroom and D.A.'s office slashed with noir-ish shadows. It climaxed with a lively rooftop chase obviously shot on the backlot. In typical programmer fashion, things were tied up with a laugh and a knuckle rap: "Don, no more crusades!"

Although "nothing much" in Sturges's estimation, *The Man Who Dared* confirmed the studio's faith in the new hire as someone who was fast and efficient. According to the production log, Sturges — up before dawn and braced with plenty of hot coffee — completed thirty setups on the first day before the dinner break. As intended, the bargain-basement release, which ran just over an hour, filled the bottom half of double bills.

Shadowed, Sturges's second Columbia assignment, attempted a mix of humor and suspense à la Hitchcock's prewar thrillers, *The Lady Vanishes* and *Young and Innocent*. Originally titled "The Gloved Hand," this minor mystery introduced Sturges to John Haggott, who would produce five of the director's films at the studio. It starred the amiably bumptious Lloyd Corrigan—whom Sturges knew from *La Cucaracha*—as Fred J. Johnson, a widowed farming implements salesman with two daughters (Anita Louise and Terry Moore, née Helen Koford). Johnson's passion for golf gets him in trouble as an errant ball lands in a ravine, next to a murdered showgirl. The culprits turn out to be counterfeiters, who kidnap Johnson's younger daughter Ginny (Moore).

The sixteen-year-old Moore, who had played juveniles in MGM's *Gaslight* and *Son of Lassie,* was being groomed by Cohn for ingénue roles. She remembered the *Shadowed* shoot as fast and economical, and her role as marginally more adult (Cohn allowed her to wear lipstick for the first time onscreen). "It was a B picture that would play with an A— we did nearly everything in one take." What made it stand out, she said, was Sturges's enthusiasm and genteel manner. Indeed, she recalled him as being British. "He was rough and tumble, but eloquent, a real gentleman. Not many directors were like that. You had your real screamers in those days, like John Ford and Henry Hathaway, and directors who used actors as scapegoats, like Daniel Mann. Sturges was the opposite."

Moore recalled her audition. "I just walked into his office and read for him. When you're an unknown and somebody asks you to audition, they usually make you wait. He didn't. He knew exactly what he wanted."

Shadowed—shot primarily at the Columbia Ranch—opened promisingly with "duffer" Johnson alone on the fairway, driving a ball and— "Holy mackerel!"—scoring a hole-in-one. Unfortunately, the film then settled into a formulaic rut, with the killers closing in and with Ginny and Lester, her adenoidal boyfriend, inadvertently implicating Dad in the crime. Sturges attempted to make more of the programmer than was there by investing the later scenes with a *Desperate Hours* intensity and grouping characters in inventive ways. Such care, however, only highlighted plot contrivances (the signed and dated hole-in-one ball is, improbably, returned to play) and mawkish heart-to-hearts on the living room stairs. Still, Sturges managed a moment or two worthy of Hitchcock, such as the overhead point-of-view shot from a (sound-stage) trestle bridge and the use of an incriminating anklet chain as a McGuffin (a plot device that turns out to be immaterial).

The caper-comedy *Alias Mr. Twilight* reteamed the director with producer Haggott and scenarist Brenda Weisberg, here adapting a story by Arthur E. Orloff called "I Don't Want to Die." Trudy Marshall and Michael Duane played the love interests, Corrigan a professional con artist, and Gi-Gi Perreau his six-year-old granddaughter, described as "bubbling over with good spirits." A writer himself, Corrigan phoned Sturges at the last minute to say he had misgivings about the script. The elaborate stings didn't make sense. The director agreed. Moreover, he found the story sappy, old-fashioned. "The (original) script was so awful it wasn't even a script," said Sturges, who rewrote dialogue and scribbled diagrams of camera positions and angles in the margins of his script. "I threw it in the ashcan and wrote a new script. Next picture, same thing—the ashcan."

As more than one critic noted, *Alias Mr. Twilight* felt like a Damon Runyon fable, minus Shirley Temple. Corrigan's Geoffrey Holden is "a bunco artist *par excellence*" whose specialty is sleight-of-hand stings. He must pull one final job to keep his recently orphaned granddaughter out of the clutches of a blackmailing cousin (Rosalind Ivan). The increasingly elaborate cons include a "double-jewel swindle," a phony delivery and pickup, and a dockside switch, which leaves the cousin holding $5 million in counterfeit money as the cops arrive. Each illustrated a lesson Sturges learned early in life and would return to in *Best Man Wins* and *The Great Escape:* "You can't con anyone who isn't larcenous to begin with." The director added: "I've always liked con men. As a kid I had a whole collection of books on them. And that one was a good story. It's the first picture that brought me attention."

Alias Mr. Twilight bowed in February 1947 at the Pantages Theater. Sturges missed the opening: he and Dorothy were skiing in Aspen. The trades were split. The *Hollywood Reporter* dismissed the film, while *Variety* applauded its "excellent plotting" and predicted big things for the producer-director team. "The entertainment is simply a supporting item, but it is all entertainment," the critic effused.

Cohn, who screened *Alias Mr. Twilight* for guests at his home, saw promise in the former cutter, and Briskin assured him that Sturges was someone who could get the job done on time and budget—with a certain panache. That Monday, Sturges found himself being buzzed through the knobless door to Cohn's office.

"You're pretty good," Cohn told him. "Who wrote that picture?"

"Well, I did—I invented the characters."

"What else you got?"

Amazed by his good fortune, Sturges gathered a few ideas and marched into Cohn's office a week later, prepared for a pitch session.

Cohn was as usual preoccupied when Sturges took a seat in front of his massive, semi-circular desk. He had a listening device up to his ear and kept opening and closing a desk drawer.

"What the hell are you doing?" Sturges finally blurted out.

"I'm listening to the results at Santa Anita," Cohn said. "When you're as old as I am, you'll be able to listen to some goddam story like yours and the race results at the same time."

Cohn had given them the same treatment, Boetticher and Charles Vidor assured Sturges. Just when you thought you were in the boss's good books, he would knock you down a peg by handing you a programmer or series episode. Sturges's turn came later that year when he was assigned *For the Love of Rusty*, the third in what would be an eight-segment series set in Lawtonville, Illinois, and featuring Ted Donaldson and a German shepherd named Flame. Gloria Henry, who appeared in a later Rusty segment, as well as Sturges's *Keeper of the Bees*, likened the series to "a poor man's Lassie." She added, "They were sub-B pictures, to pair other things with and keep the kids happy. But they must have made money for the studio; they kept making them."

The formula: Danny, a mildly rebellious teenager, tests the limits of his parents and various town eccentrics; dog saves the day in the fifth reel; moral (usually having to do with sanctity of the family) is imparted. Sturges's segment—co-starring Tom Powers and Ann Doran as parents Hugh and Ethel—considered Lawtonville's brewing generational conflict. To address this problem, Hugh stages a father-son dinner. When it backfires, Danny falls under the spell of a wily old veterinarian/philosopher (Aubrey Mather) camped outside of town. Father frowns on the "unusual attachment." Ethel's response: "Hasn't it struck you that Danny's looking for a father?"

The project resonated with Sturges, who was about to become a father himself. (Daughter Deborah was born that year.) He treated the $200,000 production as if it were a prestige assignment, rehearsing his players before each shot and working out elaborate camera setups with his cinematographer. The installment opened with a crane shot that would have pleased Orson Welles: as voices are heard inside the Mitchell home, the camera glides down the garden path, past a dog house, peers in the kitchen windows, climbs up the pergola to Danny's second-floor room, descends to a boy's wagon with coffee-pot headlights, and stops at the garage.

"Sturges had the best script of any of the Rusty films," said Donaldson, who was thirteen at the time. "And he treated it as if he was directing an 'A' project, a major film. He respected the story; he respected the characters; he respected the actors. Usually on these things you rehearsed a bit, did one take, sometimes two—if someone forgot a line or a light blew—and then you moved on to the next scene. It was twelve to fourteen working days. With Sturges we would rehearse a scene three or four times and then do three or four takes. We all felt, 'My God, this is a helluva lot of rehearsal for a film like this.' It was unheard of on the seven other films I made in the series."

Of course a programmer treated as an "A" did not endear Sturges to the front office. Briskin began calling the set. "John, what's going on down there? You're behind schedule." To which Sturges would respond in his laconic fashion, "Uh-huh, uh-huh. Hmm, OK. Yes, right."

Then he would hang up and continue at his own pace. "At least I learned how to direct animals on that picture," he said later, shrugging. "Animals don't know what the hell they're doing. By cutting, you make the audience think they do."

The care lavished on what should have been one more studio programmer was not lost on reviewers, who warmed to Sturges's backlot Americana when the film shared a double bill with Randolph Scott's *Gunfighters* in 1947. "Good little pictures have long been the rule from the producer-director team of John Haggott and John Sturges at

Columbia," the *Hollywood Reporter* pointed out. *For Love of Rusty* "will do extremely well in its bookings, partly because trouble has been taken to develop interesting minor characters and characterizations. . . . Very pleasurable is the manner in which [Sturges] uses his camera for storytelling purposes, especially in the opening reel that introduces the Mitchell household." *Variety* was equally impressed by a "low-budgeter" that was "up to top billing in many spots, with good box office prospects."

Though annoyed by the director for going over budget and ignoring his one-take dictum, Cohn was impressed enough by the reviews to entrust Sturges with slightly more prestigious literary adaptations. The first would be an update of naturalist-author Gene Stratton-Porter's already twice-filmed chestnut *Keeper of the Bees*. This was followed by a musty variation on Hitchcock's *Rebecca* and a bit of rustic whimsy inspired by Mark Twain's "The Celebrated Jumping Frog of Calaveras County."

Keeper of the Bees, published in 1925 (after the author's death in a traffic accident), has not aged well. It is a sugarcoated allegory about a doomed doughboy's miraculous physical and spiritual rebirth in a California Shangri-la awash in sunshine and pollen. It was adapted as a vehicle for Clara Bow and then again in 1935 as what the *New York Times* called "an ideal defense of the sunshine school of thought." His version, Sturges vowed, would be less preachy. Now, instead of a wounded World War I veteran who stumbles upon the Bee Master and the holistic benefits of nature, protagonist Jamie MacFarlane was closer to Charles Strickland in *The Moon and Sixpence*, a disillusioned New York painter who, in turning his back on his wife and career, finds new purpose. Sturges regular Michael Duane played MacFarlane; Harry Davenport was cast as the beekeeper/matchmaker and Jo Ann Marlow his tomboyish assistant, Scout; Gloria Henry was tapped to play Alice, the orphanage worker and love interest; and, in a change of pace, Jane Darwell appeared as Mrs. Ferris, the town busybody who tries to sabotage the romance. Stratton-Porter's messy unwed mother subplot was dropped altogether.

Sturges did what he could with the dated, hopelessly contrived material, making the dialogue more colloquial and easy flowing. Wherever possible, the "re-dictated" script played against the intrinsic sentimentality of the piece. The new ending was less about getting the lovers together than making sure the town gossip got her comeuppance: MacFarlane now sics the bees on Mrs. Ferris, who, swatting madly, confesses her meddling.

Henry remembered the three-week shoot at Columbia Ranch as "one big picnic," where the old pros—Darwell and Davenport—sat around telling dirty jokes or regaling the young actors with tales of the good ol' days. "There was a feeling of camaraderie," she said. "It was a marvelous, gentle movie because Sturges stood out among the 'B' directors. He took his time and went for the nuances, listened to you, and gave you just the right hint."

Columbia trailers trumpeted *Keeper of the Bees* (1947) as "a new and tender telling [of] One of the World's Best-Loved Love Stories!" Only too aware of the book's reputation as a turgid Sunday school lesson, the critics showed up at the Egyptian Theatre premiere expecting the worst. They were pleasantly surprised by the filler feature's refusal to wallow in bathos. Sturges's direction, *Variety* observed, was leisurely but assured and appropriate to the material.

Sturges accepted the assignment as "another step up," but he would later dismiss it as a lesser *Lost Horizon* or *The Razor's Edge*, a hit at 20th Century Fox the previous year.

"Ah, Jesus!" he groaned when reminded of the sixty-eight-minute film. "It's an old funky story that they used for quiet reading in school [about] some old character who keeps bees and children who come to him with their problems. He's a sage and a philosopher. All I remember is I had an awful time trying to get those bees to fly away!"

The Sign of the Ram (1948), Sturges's next assignment, was a modern Gothic based on a Margaret Ferguson best-seller and set along the craggy coast of a backlot Cornwall. Because the principal character, Leah St. Aubyn, was confined to a wheelchair, Susan Peters, who had been paralyzed two years earlier in a hunting accident, snatched up the property and promoted it as "my comeback." Her embittered Leah attempts to wreck the lives of her tweedy, all-too-accommodating husband (Alexander Knox) and his children from a previous marriage. Phyllis Thaxter played Sherida, Leah's secretary-companion, who narrates the odd doings at Bastions, a seventeenth-century cottage overlooking the sea. Others in the cast included Dame May Whitty as the meddlesome neighbor and Peggy Ann Garner (*A Tree Grows in Brook-lyn*) as Christine, Leah's youngest stepchild and unwitting accomplice.

The film opens economically enough with train sounds and a depot billboard establishing the seaside setting, and then dissolves to a car and stock footage of a coastline and crashing waves. For a moment we're reminded of vintage Hitchcock—a comparison furthered by the participation of scenarist Charles Bennett (*Sabotage, The 39 Steps*). Once at Bastions, however, the plot reverts to hothouse Val Lewton with shadows, lighthouse, and mournful foghorn forecasting bad times ahead. An obvious source of confusion: multiple characters are quickly introduced, leaving one to sort out names and relationships. Sturges attempted to compensate for the problem with deep-focus compositions, but on the cramped set these groupings come off as cluttered, like a drawing room with too many suspects milling about waiting for the inspector. If Christine's slow ascent to Sherida's room with doctored milk felt familiar to audiences at the time, there was good reason: it echoed Cary Grant's stair climb in Hitchcock's *Suspicion*. In the end, thanks either to a bored screenwriter or the Production Code, Leah wheels herself to the edge of the cliff and, as the fog envelops her and piccolos intone "*Lee-ah, Lee-ah,*" pitches forward. Not a moment too soon. Peters, twenty-six, was clearly too young for the conniving matriarch and, much to Sturges's horror, played her as a full-blown gorgon with arched brow and clawed fingers forever raking the air.

The Sign of the Ram, Sturges's first top-of-the-bill, was promoted as a prestige women's picture and "The Return to the Screen of Miss Susan Peters." The newspaper ads teased, "*You may hate Leah . . . or love Leah . . . but you'll never forget Leah!*" The reviews, as prompted, played up Peters's travails but dismissed the movie as "flat and fatuous" (*New York Times*) and "a leisurely-paced meller slanted for the femme trade" (*Variety*). James Agee in the *Nation* described it as "a vapid 'psychological' melodrama in which Susan Peters polishes off a hearty histrionic banquet at her leisure while several other likable players . . . snap forlornly at scraps."

Sturges in retirement agreed. He dismissed the picture as "not very good—a talky vanity production." In retrospect, the studio curio—not that far removed from the "sickly-sweet" Victorian novels Ferguson attempted to parody—deserves a footnote as the valiant but unsuccessful return of Peters, who would die four years later. It is also notable as the only credited collaboration of Sturges and his brother, Sturge, whose Columbia assignments ranged from Sabu programmers to Orson Welles's *The Lady from Shanghai*. Carne finished out his contract with *All the King's Men* (1949), but because of his chronic alcoholism he found future employment difficult. "Sturge was a sweet, sensitive guy, and a good artist," said nephew Jon Stufflebeem, "but he walked off a set in a rage, and Hollywood blackballed him." (Carne died of cirrhosis at the Motion Picture Home in 1964. He was sixty-five.)

On paper, Sturges's next assignment, *Best Man Wins* (1948), looked almost promising. It was based on Twain's "Jumping Frog" stretcher, which Sturges had read as a child. Unfortunately, the script wasn't so much an adaptation of the tall tale as a sentimental re-imaging, with only incorrigible gambler Jim Smiley and the final barroom wager/con (champion frog is filled with buckshot pellets) remaining of the story. Twain's mining camp became Dawson's Landing, Missouri, "the kind of town where everybody knows everything about everybody else—a dangerous place to live." Edgar Buchanan was cast as Smiley, who, after a lengthy absence, returns home to discover his wife (Anna Lee), divorce decree in hand, about to marry a judge (Robert Shayne) to provide their son (Gary Gray) with "a decent future." Smiley wins his family back by foreswearing gambling, even as he devises clever wagers involving a gumdrop-eating rabbit and his "educated" frog, Daniel Webster, who jumps to the command "Flies, Dan'l, flies!"

Another variation on the father-son bonding theme that would run through many of the director's films, including *Jeopardy* and *Chino*, this exercise in backlot Americana alternated crowd-pleasing cons with bedside bromides. Twain most likely would have run screaming for the exit. The $400,000 budget necessitated stock footage of a riverboat intercut with Columbia Ranch exteriors. Well-known black actor Mantan Moreland appeared uncredited pushing a hokey-pokey wagon. When the comedy opened in the summer in front of William Wellman's *The Iron Curtain*, the reviews were surprisingly kind.

His contract about to lapse, Sturges found himself being courted by top independent producers impressed by his resourcefulness and no-nonsense approach. Randolph Scott and Harry Joe Brown offered *The Walking Hills*, which they were developing at Columbia as the maiden project for Scott-Brown Productions. Written by Alan LeMay and initially announced with William Holden as the lead, it was a tale of greed and betrayal in the modern-day Southwest. The film's title came from the ever-drifting sand dunes of Death Valley, which, along with Lone Pine and Mexicali, Baja, would provide the backdrops. Sturges, by now familiar with every hillock and rock formation on the Columbia Ranch, leapt at the opportunity. "Anything to get me away from that damn backlot," he said. An added incentive: a gunfight that took place in a sandstorm so fierce it could take the hide off a pack mule.

Besides the middle-aged but still fighting-fit Scott, who replaced Holden, the large ensemble included Ella Raines, Jerome Courtland, Edgar Buchanan, Russell Collins, Arthur Kennedy, Charles Stevens, William Bishop, blues singer Josh White, and John Ireland, who won over the director with his candor. "I'm starving—I need a job," he said, confronting the director in the street. "You got it," replied Sturges, who elaborated later, "John was a likable guy, and I knew that he could do the role."

Like Huston's Oscar-winning *Treasure of the Sierra Madre*, the story opens in a Mexican border town. In the backroom of a cantina, over cards, Old Willy (Buchanan) tells of a lost shipment of Spanish gold. Coincidentally, the lanky kid at the table (Courtland) has just found a wagon wheel in that very vicinity. He thinks he can backtrack to the spot. Also at the table and quick to join the impromptu expedition: a horse breeder named Jim Carey (Scott) and his Indian wrangler (Stevens); a hard-boiled private eye (Ireland) tracking a murder suspect (Bishop); the cantina's entertainer (White) and bartender (Collins, the telegraph operator in *Bad Day at Black Rock*); and a shady customer called Chalk (Kennedy). On the wall of the backroom: a calendar with a pin-up girl on a cake of ice. Marilyn Monroe, under contract to Columbia, posed for the picture.

As the party traverses the dunes—which "lean and crawl and swell, like they was alive"—Christy (Raines), once romantically involved with Jim, rides into sight and announces, "I'm cutting myself into this. Anybody mind?" The treasure hunters make camp and, as those thrown together in blast furnace heat invariably do, proceed to taunt and suspect one another. The kid is shot in the back. Will he survive? And who among the ten will make it out of the desert before the gathering storm?

It is becoming increasingly apparent that this is a fool's errand, that the buried wagons are remnants of another train.

While Death Valley is less than three hundred miles, as the crow flies, from Hollywood, the production company might have been on the far side of the moon. The mercury by mid-afternoon hovered at 120 degrees, which meant, according to a studio communiqué, if you wandered off without water and salt tablets, "life expectancy would be about three hours." Sleds with steel runners were used to transport the wind machines and cameras; trailers and trucks were fitted with oversized airplane tires; air hoses were always ready to blow sand from the sensitive camera mechanisms. After three weeks, the cast and crew returned to Columbia Ranch, where, for continuity purposes, sunlamps and tons of Death Valley sand awaited them.

"It was a murderous shoot," recalled Courtland. "Extremely hot—in the 130s, even up to 140. We'd get up early, rehearse in the dark and shoot until 11 o'clock. We'd break until 3 or 3:30, and then we'd shoot again in the late afternoon."

Having finally escaped the backlot, Sturges was determined that this would be one stranded-in-the-desert movie that made filmgoers sweat. The cast, he decreed, would not wear tanning makeup; they would be darkened by exposure to the sun. Further, each day he had Ireland, Courtland, and the others mount up at the hotel and ride behind the camera truck. That way, they arrived on the set caked in dust.

"Here he was doing this film about these guys out in the desert dying of thirst and exposure—you've got to see sweat on our faces or it doesn't look believable," said Courtland. "John would tell the makeup man, 'OK, spritz 'em' and they'd squirt a little water on us. But before they could roll the cameras, it would evaporate. So the only way they could get sweat was to put glycerin on us, because it wouldn't evaporate. We all had a look like we'd been powdered down from the salt that was caking. It was one of those cases where reality didn't look right on screen. So John had to find a different way of making it look real." (The lather on the horses was actually shaving cream.)

Leading lady Raines at the time was married to an ace fighter pilot who had a novel way of saying hello: he would fly over from a nearby field and, dropping to an altitude of twenty to thirty feet, buzz the set. Furious, Sturges shook his fist at the sky. "The roar stampeded the horses, scattered them all over the desert," said Courtland. "It took hours to get them all."

The Walking Hills opened in February 1949 and rode the slipstream of *Treasure of the Sierra Madre,* still in theaters. Like *Sign of the Ram,* it received top billing in some markets. The ads promised location authenticity mixed with risqué romance: *"Alone in the desert . . . Nine men and a woman!"* The campaign worked. The Western became Columbia's top-grossing release of the year, and the first indication that Sturges could be commercial. The reviews were mixed, praising the striking cinematography and "tight direction" (*Variety*) while criticizing the messy storyline, which tended to drift, like so much sand. There was certainly little of the psychological complexity or savage irony that distinguished Huston's prospecting drama. Still, the movie was a breakthrough for Sturges: It pointed up his early affinity for rugged outdoor adventures. It grabbed the viewer immediately, cutting from cantina to the desert vistas of the title. It also benefited from Scott's generous underplaying. The music by Arthur Morton, reminiscent of Hugo Friedhofer's fanfare for *The Best Years of Our Lives,* underscored the natural grandeur of Death Valley National Monument. Further, there was little of the ethnocentrism that characterized studio action pictures of the period. White's saloon singer, who performs "Blow My Blues Away," and Stevens's Native American are clearly the conscience of the group. The film's pièce de résistance remains the climactic sandstorm, which, with its shovel fight between Bishop and Ireland, brings to mind Erich von Stroheim's silent classic *Greed.* Sturges photographed the ensuing shootout between Scott and Kennedy in long shot, thereby adding to its suspense and believability.

Sturges downplayed the film's success. "It's all right, I guess," he said. "Not bad for its type." He was unduly harsh. Besides being a precursor to the macho ensembles in which he would later excel, the Western served as his passport from eager apprentice to respected studio hand— only now at MGM.

6

MGM

Sturges arrived at MGM in the fall of 1949, the year of the studio's Silver Jubilee. Leo the Lion, however, was not in a celebratory mood. Like its competitors across town, the sprawling Culver City lot was busy fending off a three-pronged assault—by television, the courts, and the House Un-American Activities Committee. In the monopoly-busting *U.S. vs. Paramount Pictures,* the Supreme Court had just decreed that the studios must sell their theater chains. Though the postwar economy was booming, overhead at the studios continued to soar as ticket sales declined. In this climate, MGM performed a tricky balancing act: It promoted a record $100-million production slate as it slashed in-house expenses. Sturges likened the situation to "a revolutionary shake-up." The word from above, he said, was "Cut, cut, cut—until it hurts." He added, "The front office had to approve everything, even minor things like mimeographing scripts." Directors were told to sketch camera set-ups in advance and eliminate elaborate crane and tracking shots; editors on Technicolor productions worked from black-and-white prints. One bean counter estimated that by limiting coffee-shop hours to the afternoon, the studio could recoup $22,000 a year.

"Television hit exactly the moment John Sturges arrived," recalled actress Polly Bergen, who would star in two of Sturges's MGM films. "The studios were scared to death, dropping people left and right. They wanted to make a lot of product but didn't want to spend money on it. All those big musicals were just a nightmare; they required big orchestras and months of rehearsal. That's the reason they created a special 'B' unit."

"Still," Bergen said, "there was nothing like being at MGM. You would be going in the gate the same time as Ava Gardner was walking in with no makeup and so beautiful you wanted to die. And you'd run into Deborah Kerr on the street. It was a magical, magical place."

Dore Schary, who had gone from boy wonder at Metro to beleaguered head of production at RKO, was lured back to MGM with a fourteen-year contract and virtual carte blanche. He became Sturges's boss and mentor. What Schary inherited as vice president in charge of production, he said later, was a studio "fallen into disarray." His job was to economize without appearing to economize. MGM, Louis B. Mayer never tired of reminding him, personified glamour: it was the studio with "More Stars than There Are in Heaven"—Tracy, Gable, Garland, and both Taylors (Robert and Elizabeth), among them. To humor Mayer, Schary remained outwardly dedicated to Metro's stock-in-trade, the Arthur Freed musicals (*Take Me Out to the Ball Game, Annie Get Your Gun*) and epic costume dramas (*Quo Vadis*)—while he shepherded cheaper, left-leaning "problem pictures" that tackled racketeering, anti-Semitism, racism, and the exploitation of migrant labor.

If Hollywood was to survive, Schary argued, such edgy stories would have to buttress the frothy star vehicles. At RKO, he had personally green-lighted *Crossfire,* a murder mystery with an anti-Semitic message. "Don't be afraid of [the] term—social background," he told a New York sales meeting. "*Crossfire* had social background, and did fine. So did *Gentleman's Agreement, The Farmer's Daughter,* and *The Best Years of Our Lives.*"

These message films were primarily made by the studio's Schnee Unit, run by producer-writer Charles Schnee. They were budgeted at under $500,000, shot in fifteen days and, therefore, could take risks. Sturges's *Jeopardy* and *Fast Company* (1953) were Schnee productions. So was Mark Robson's *Trial,* starring Glenn Ford and Arthur Kennedy as attorneys defending a Latino youth charged with murdering a white girl. The future, Schary said, lay with B productions by new producers and new directors like Sturges, Zinnemann, and Richard Brooks, who could work quickly and economically but still turn out high-quality entertainment. During Schary's eight-year tenure—he was ousted after too many poor-performance pet projects such as *The Next Voice You Hear*—MGM's per-picture cost went from $2.2 million to about half that amount.

Schary and Armand Deutsch, the Sears heir who had just graduated from Schary's assistant to producer, got their first look at Sturges's work at evening screenings at Schary's Brentwood home. They were especially impressed by early footage from *The Walking Hills* and *The Capture*, an independent production directed by Sturges between studio assignments and released by RKO in May 1950. "Somebody in the room said, 'God, he's good,'" recalled Deutsch. "He seemed to have a great deal of ability. I called him, and he came to my office at MGM. I took him upstairs to Schary's office. Schary liked him immediately because he was down-to-earth, quite unlike most Hollywood directors. They must have hit it off because he soon left Columbia and came to work for Metro. . . . Schary had a great deal to do with steering his career."

At the most hierarchical of the studios, Schary was surrounded by sycophants and yes-men. Everybody had an angle. Sturges was different. He spoke his mind, but only when pressed. "It wasn't that he was naive, as some suspected," said Deutsch, "it was just that he couldn't care less about studio politics." He was also an unpretentious storyteller who could fold social issues into mainstream entertainment. *The Capture*, written and produced by Niven Busch (*Duel in the Sun*), appealed to Schary's sense of moral rectitude. Though set in Mexico, the modern-day Western about second chances was shot northeast of Los Angeles in Pioneertown and Yucca Valley. Lew Ayres and Teresa Wright, Busch's wife, co-starred. Ayres played Vanner, an oil-field superintendent who accidentally shoots an unarmed man suspected of stealing the company payroll. To atone for his mistake, Vanner accompanies the man's coffin by train back to his ranch and signs on as a hired hand. When the widow, Ellen (Wright), discovers the truth, she works Vanner mercilessly. Predictably, the two fall in love over dirty dishes, Vanner bonds with Ellen's son (Jimmy Hunt), and Vanner tracks down the real thief.

The Capture—which unfolds as a confession to a taciturn priest (Victor Jory)—benefited from its rugged locations but was, overall, dry and uninvolving. RKO stressed the forbidden love angle in ads that teased, "Killing a Man is One Thing, Loving His Wife is Another . . . both are DYNAMITE!" The *New York Times* found it "static, pretentious . . . full of high-sounding talk, short on action."

Still, Schary was impressed enough by what he saw and, in the fall of 1949, agreed to a trial employment. Sturges was ecstatic. He would be working alongside such veterans as George Cukor, Clarence Brown, and Mervyn LeRoy. After the meeting with Schary, he raced home to share the news with Dorothy and Grace, who, even at seventy-seven, remained as a force in her son's decision making. Suddenly, the budgets and resources that had been out of reach at RKO and Columbia were now available. And Sturges planned to make the most of them, working in a variety of genres with such top stars as Barbara Stanwyck, June Allyson, Elsa Lanchester, and Ethel Barrymore, who bore more than a passing resemblance to his mother.

Depending on how you look at it, Sturges's arrival at MGM was either ill-timed or fortuitous. Yes, production costs were being slashed (27 percent by 1955), but so too was the studio's stable of directors (down to thirteen from thirty-five), which meant more opportunities. Also, as actor James Lydon (*The Magnificent Yankee*) pointed out, MGM was the Holy Grail—"the epitome of everything we all aspired to." During the next ten years, six of which were spent at MGM, Sturges would direct twenty features, including on loan-out *Gunfight at the O.K. Corral* and *The Old Man and the Sea*. For Schary, he did *Jeopardy* and *Bad Day at Black Rock*, which would bring him his only Oscar nomination.

Sturges's MGM movies were studio collaborations in the classic sense. His ascendancy to the rank of producer-director who could pick and mold material according to his own likes and dislikes was still more than a decade away. Under the very much hands-on Schary, the "chief architects" of a movie were the producer and the writer. Schary saw the director as a field commander who marshaled the forces and devised a plan of attack. "Today's directors have more authority and control," he wrote in his autobiography. "We had neither the time nor the funds to hand over a script to a director who might then decide to junk it and invent a new one. The director would function closely with the writer, the producer, and me. Once a decision was made regarding the thrust and form of the picture . . . we shared a common image and goal." (Sturges's shooting scripts from this period reflect this—they have far fewer revisions than his scripts at Columbia.)

Added Richard Anderson, who appeared prominently in three of Sturges's MGM pictures, including *The People against O'Hara* and *Escape from Fort Bravo*: "There were still remnants of the studio system at

MGM, and the producers were the ones pretty much calling the plays; they had the real power, particularly someone like Arthur Freed. John was a director who was given assignments. That's how it worked."

Mystery Street—about the investigation into the murder of a B-girl—was originally discussed as a project for Robert Wise or Joseph Losey. It became Sturges's MGM tryout. If he liked what he saw, Schary said, he would reward the director with a multipicture contract. Van Heflin and Dick Powell were seen as possible leads, but Ricardo Montalban landed the role of Portuguese-American police lieutenant Pete Moralas. The twenty-nine-year-old Mexican actor—who had just appeared in *Battleground* and *Border Incident*—leapt at the opportunity to again break with the Latin lover/Fernando Lamas stereotype and prove "I could do something besides dance." Early drafts of the script, which bore Losey's thumbprint, played up Morales's ethnicity and showed how his investigation was hampered by prejudice in the predominantly white community. This angle, while not eliminated altogether, was reduced to a raised eyebrow and patronizing retort, which pleased Montalban.

"I had something of a following in those days," recalled the actor, "but I was still playing Hispanic characters. The Sturges film was a definite breakthrough for me. It was a well-written scenario that just told it like it was and made no apologies for my character having an accent. It was the first time that had happened for me, and, I think, one of the first times it had been done in a Hollywood movie."

Weekly minutes of MGM board meetings show *Mystery Street*—scripted by Sydney Boehm and Richard Brooks and originally called "Murder at Harvard"—in development for much of 1949, along with Sturges's follow-ups, *Right Cross* and *The People against O'Hara*. The project was budgeted at a healthy $1 million and closely supervised by Schary, who saw it as an efficient police procedural in the tradition of *Kid Glove Killer* and *The Naked City*. Cinematographer John Alton (*He Walked by Night*, *T-Men*) was assigned to shoot the "atypical" MGM noir in his signature low-key lighting style, and Ferris Webster, beginning an association with Sturges that would last almost a quarter of a century and include *The Magnificent Seven* and *The Great Escape*, was hired as editor. Cast opposite Montalban were Jan Sterling as the murder victim, Bruce Bennett as the scientist who reconstructs the crime from the victim's skull and bones, Marshall Thompson and Sally Forrest as the murder suspect and his distraught wife, Betsy Blair as a waitress friend of the victim, and — "the woman of a thousand faces" — Elsa Lanchester as the crass, blackmailing landlady.

Production got under way in November on Soundstage 3 with a reduced budget of $830,000. The Beacon Hill, Trinity Station, and Harvard Medical School exteriors were done on location in December, which assured an appropriately overcast hue. Brooks, about to make the transition to directing, was a constant presence on the set.

Shooting in Boston and on the Harvard campus "added a whole new dimension," said Montalban. "It lent a sort of realism to the performances, and gave the story a certain veracity. Of course, John Alton contributed quite a bit to the realism of the piece. John Sturges respected him and listened to his suggestions. I remember it being an easy shoot. The Boston weather cooperated and — though Elsa Lanchester exerted her personality the minute she walked on the set — everyone got along fine."

Montalban described Sturges on location as "a gentle giant." "He wasn't an Anthony Mann or John Ford. He didn't shout, 'Do this! Do that!' He guided you without your knowing you were being guided." Further, he helped Montalban "tone down" his performance. "I'm inclined to approach roles too flamboyantly," he wrote in his memoir, "and that's why I need a director who will help me to simplify, simplify, simplify."

Mystery Street opened in the summer of 1950. The poster — a torn photo of a female corpse — exploited the story's salacious elements and unique participatory structure. "No Clue to Begin With . . . Not Even a Body . . . A Story of Love and Crime is Pieced Together . . . Bit by Bit . . . You'll See What Happens When a Lonesome Man Meets a Girl at a Bar!"

The reviews took the reverse tack, praising the film's tastefulness. The *New York Times* and *L.A. Times* called attention to its rich investigative detail and singled out Montalban's cop and Lanchester's landlady for praise. "There is more science than mystery in this cops-versus-killer number," opined *New York Times* critic A. H. Weiler, "but it is an adventure which, despite a low budget, is not low in taste or its attention to technical detail, backgrounds and plausibility." *Time* magazine's review could have been written by Schary: "Sturges and scripters Sydney

Boehm and Richard Brooks have treated the picture with such taste and craftsmanship that it is just about perfect. All the performers seem to be working on the theory that there should be no difference in quality between a B picture and its budgetary betters. Montalban is natural and likable as an eager small-town detective on his first case . . . and Elsa Lanchester is a delight as a snooping, gin-drinking landlady with genteel airs."

Though less intense or stylized than Dmytryk's *Crossfire* and Mann's *T-Men*, two better-known noirs, *Mystery Street* provides its own perverse pleasures and can be seen as the first important picture in the Sturges oeuvre. In some ways, it is a precursor to *Silence of the Lambs* and the hit TV show *CSI*. Among its strengths: Alton's moody, deep-focus photography, especially well utilized for the rooming house and Cape Cod diner sequences; the sharp dialogue ("fresh air couldn't get in here with a permit") and morbid humor (a fussy ornithologist stumbles upon a skeletal foot protruding from a sand dune); and the catty badinage between Montalban's gung-ho Boy Scout and Lanchester's greedy snoop. The pacing only slackens during a talky third-act parlor sequence and contrived (off-screen) prison break, but it picks up again for a chase through Trinity Station and the surrounding railroad yard.

Even today, Sturges's direction seems remarkably adult. How, one wonders, could he have gotten away with Sterling's pregnant call girl or the anything-but-oblique references to extramarital sex? Forrest to Thompson: "About that girl . . . Did you?" Thompson: "You know I didn't kill her." Forrest: "I didn't mean that." Thompson: "I made lots of mistakes. Not that one."

The usually self-critical Sturges was, for a change, pleased with the results. "That was a good picture," he said later. "It had a script by Dick Brooks—the last thing Dick wrote before he started directing. It opens with the skeleton of a girl in the sand at the beach. The real cop assigned to the case was Portuguese. He took the skeleton to a department at Harvard's Medical School that was endowed by a woman whose husband was murdered. They reconstructed all kinds of things [about the girl's disappearance], told him she had been a ballet dancer—that she was this, she was that. They gradually tracked the guy down and caught the murderer. Good script. Good performances by Montalban and Lanchester. Good movie."

Schary agreed, making Sturges a full member of the studio's direct-ing team. "On the success of *Mystery Street*—boom!—they signed me to a contract at Metro, which I managed to get out of four or five years later."

Without a break, Sturges was tapped to replace Roy Rowland on *Right Cross,* a boxing melodrama written by Schnee and shot almost en-tirely on the backlot. The picture—produced by fight fan Deutsch and scored by David Raksin (who would go on to do four more Sturges films)—reteamed the director with Montalban, this time third-billed after MGM's popular husband-wife team Dick Powell and June Ally-son. Montalban, a natural athlete who had once played jai-alai, pre-pared for his role by working out with Johnny Indrisano, a former boxer and the film's technical adviser. Montalban's Johnny Monterez is a light-heavyweight champ who, like Robert De Niro's Jake LaMotta, proves his own worst enemy. Having escaped the barrio, Johnny be-lieves a "gringo conspiracy" means to send him back.

The thirty-two-year-old Allyson, sporting a girlish pageboy and filmed through a Vaseline-smeared lens, played Johnny's girlfriend, Pat O'Malley, and Powell drew the thankless role of the heartsick sports-writer buddy, Rick, whose cynical bravado fools no one: he's really in love with Pat. MGM warhorse Lionel Barrymore, in his seventies and acting from a wheelchair because of arthritis, appeared as Sean O'Malley, Pat's father and Johnny's fight promoter. Sean discourages the romance between the boxer and his daughter, but not because he's a bigot, like the opponent who calls Johnny "a greaser." In an odd reversal—given Hollywood's advocacy of the Good Neighbor policy—Sean argues that Johnny is shadow-boxing himself, that he has a cultural inferiority complex.

"I understand him, [but] I don't like him," Sean says. "I don't like any man who's ashamed of the blood that's in him." Pat responds lamely: "Johnny isn't ashamed of being a Mexican. It's just that he doesn't like some of the things that have happened to him . . . *because he's a Mexican.*"

In the end—after losing to a gringo and fulfilling his own gloomy prophecy—Johnny says he wants to leave Pat and return to "my own world." Rick, who earlier serenaded Johnny in Spanish with "El Ran-cho Grande," replies, "What are you going to do? Wear a sombrero?"

Shot for $900,000 and pitched as "The Love Story That Pulls No Punches," *Right Cross* (1950) turned a slight profit but failed to impress either sports fans or romantics. Sturges called it "a mild, nothing picture"—a leaden hybrid that can't decide if it's a screwball comedy, a fight picture, or a civics lesson. Most of the ring action takes place in an upstate New York training camp, and the climactic title fight—diagramed by Sturges in the margins of his script—packs little of the sting of such pugilistic standards as *Body and Soul* and *Champion*. The film deserves a footnote for its then-daring intercultural romance and a one-scene cameo by Marilyn Monroe, who would make more of an impression the same year in the studio's *Asphalt Jungle*.

Right Cross composer Raksin found Sturges "involved but easygoing . . . I saw a lot of him when I was scoring. He was imposing but didn't impose himself, he wasn't a prima-donna type. He had a job to do and he did it with as little fuss as possible." Montalban recalled being embarrassed doing "love scenes" with Allyson as her husband looked on and "brown-bagging" lunch with Barrymore, a fight aficionado. He talked with Sturges, who was almost fluent in Spanish, about life in Mexico. Even then, well before *The Old Man and the Sea* and *The Magnificent Seven,* Montalban pointed out, the director had an affinity for Latin culture and "was very receptive to my ideas about Monterez. We were dealing head-on with racial issues, and my self-hating character was controversial to a certain extent. But the movie was considered a step in the right direction."

Sturges never thought of himself as a "political" director. During the McCarthy witchhunts, as left-leaning writers and directors such as Joseph Losey and Jules Dassin were hounded into exile, he kept a low profile out of self-preservation. "I was anxious for a chance to direct—that's all I thought about during that time," he admitted. "And the 1950s turned out to be a busy time for me." Secretly, he detested Screen Actors Guild (SAG) president Ronald Reagan, whom he later called "an FBI stooge and informant." The record shows that Sturges did take a stand against Cecil B. DeMille, who favored a compulsory anti-communist loyalty oath and a network of studio informants. In October 1950, DeMille attempted a recall of Screen Directors Guild (SDG) president Joseph L. Mankiewicz, who bitterly opposed the oath. When DeMille's recall petition came to light, John Huston and twenty-four other guild members signed a counter-petition to force an emergency meeting. "We've got to block this thing," Huston told Sturges, whom he knew from the First Motion Picture Unit. Sturges became the tenth signatory, after Robson and Brooks. He also attended a strategy meeting at Chasen's and helped man the phones to gather other names. Wyler, Wise, Zinnemann, Wilder, Losey, Jean Negulesco, and Nicholas Ray were among those who also came onboard.

The upshot was a historic, four-hour Sunday meeting in the ballroom of the Beverly Hills Hotel.

"It was a really nasty affair," said Don Mankiewicz, who would write *Fast Company* and later dramatize the brewing crisis in his play *The Battle of Hollywood*. "The meeting, which went from 8 until midnight, was called at the request of these twenty-five to make charges against the people who had circulated the recall. The principal architect of the argument was George Stevens, who kept track of everything in a yellow notebook. He documented that the ballots had been improperly sent to some people and not to others, and that the SDG staff had been subverted."

DeMille stood and said, "I've behaved honorably here and nobody can say I haven't."

An anonymous voice standing in the vicinity of Sturges responded: "No, you haven't."

At this DeMille flew into a rage. "So, this is what's it come to." He waved the petition and said that most of the twenty-five names were affiliated with subversive groups and known to the California Un-American Activities Committee in Sacramento. "Strange waters brings strange fishermen," he said, and then began reading names. But instead of starting at the top of the list with Huston, he jumped to the foreign-born Jewish signatories—Wyler, Wilder, and Zinnemann. "*Mr. Villy Vyler. Mr. Villy Vilder. Mr. Freddy Zeen-a-MOND . . .*"

This brought boos and Rouben Mamoulian's tearful rebuke, "For the first time in my life I feel ashamed because I speak with a foreign accent." John Ford surprised everyone by denouncing DeMille, admitting his own culpability in the affair, and then motioning for all board members to resign. The motion was carried, whereupon DeMille and his faction walked out, and Joseph Mankiewicz received a unanimous vote of confidence with four abstentions.

Did DeMille believe Sturges was a subversive? "Probably," said Don Mankiewicz. "But he didn't include him because he had an American name. You can't say, 'With a name like Sturges, he must be a commie.' That didn't work. DeMille only named the names he could mispronounce."

"That was the only time I saw McCarthyism close-up," said Sturges. "C. B. DeMille, miserable bastard, tried to kick Joe Mankiewicz out as president by labeling him a 'fellow traveler.'" And two days later at the Beverly Hills Hotel, "they took DeMille apart. Wanted to kick him out of the Guild. Jack Ford of all people said, 'No, we have to stick together.' We agreed to let bygones be bygones. Told the press nothing. That was McCarthyism rearing its head."

Grace Sturges feared for her son. When Jon Stufflebeem visited, she cautioned him to be careful what he said about HUAC because his Uncle John was "walking a very thin line." "John was clearly not involved with communism," said Stufflebeem, "but as Grandmother pointed out, a word could ruin anybody's career."

During this period, as Hollywood's patriotism was being scrutinized, Sturges was assigned to two unabashed flag-wavers. *It's a Big Country*, developed and co-written by Schary and budgeted at more than $1 million, was an omnibus celebrating America as melting pot. Sturges directed the second segment, starring Ethel Barrymore. *The Magnificent Yankee* was an adaptation of the hit play about Supreme Court Justice Oliver Wendell Holmes, with Louis Calhern reprising his Broadway performance. An actor impersonating F.D.R., Schary's hero, spoke off-camera in both films.

It's a Big Country was a big—make that bombastic—declaration of the MGM family's commitment to the American spirit—individualism, diversity, tolerance. Lest there be any question of its intentions, Schary, in a 1950 preview reel, proclaimed, "This is a propaganda picture. Yes, sir, we won't attempt to hide it from you. This picture has a message. The message is: Hurray for America!" Following a shot of the Statue of Liberty and a full brass medley of "Stars and Stripes Forever" and "God Bless America," narrator Calhern poured on the sea-to-shining-sea platitudes. The opening credits listed "citizens" Ethel Barrymore, Gary Cooper, Gene Kelly, Fredric March, Van Johnson, Janet Leigh, William Powell, and Nancy Davis. Behind the camera were seven directors

(Clarence Brown, William Wellman, Charles Vidor, Don Hartman, Richard Thorpe, Don Weis, and Sturges), four cinematographers (including John Alton and William Mellor), six art directors, two editors, and seven composers (including Raksin, Bronislau Kaper, and David Rose).

Subtitled "An American Anthology" and proudly stamped "a stirring panorama of the American way of life and the throbbing rhythm of a country at work and at play," the film consists of eight episodes of varying length and quality. It opens with a conversation between James Whitmore and William Powell aboard a transcontinental train and segues to a montage salute to prominent blacks ("the other Americans"), a farcical romance between smitten immigrants (Leigh and Kelly), and a sly Will Rodgers–like monologue (delivered by Cooper) that plays on Texas's reputation for bigness.

Sturges's thirteen-minute episode—"The Lady and the Census Taker"—is by far the best. It features a delightfully understated Barrymore as Mrs. Brian Patrick Riordan, an elderly Boston widow who, to her consternation, has been overlooked in the latest government census. "I wasn't counted," she tells the managing editor (George Murphy) of the local newspaper. "I suppose they forgot me." After first trying to con the old lady with a reporter posing as a census taker (Keenan Wynn), the editor champions her cause, phoning all the way to the White House. Finally, a real census taker arrives at her doorstep. (The *New Yorker* source story, "Overlooked Lady," ended on a sour note with the editor and reporter pulling off the ruse.)

From all reports the director was intimidated by his leading lady, whom, even in retirement, he referred to as "Miss Barrymore." Her gaze, recalled Katharine Hepburn, "scared you to death sometimes." It was Medusa-like, always demanding, "What next, young man?" (Sturges would learn more later about her rumored alcoholism.)

"How do I tell Ethel Barrymore what to do?" Sturges asked Joel Freeman, his assistant director and Schary's nephew. "She's a sweet lady," said Freeman, who had worked with Barrymore before. "Just tell her what you want."

Sturges finally sought out Ethel's older brother, Lionel, whom he knew from *Right Cross*. Lionel assured the director that his sister was quite easy to work with. "What she wants," he said, "is for you to tell her what *you want*—in simple, straightforward terms. Spell out the actions she needs to do."

The first shot called for Barrymore to retrieve a newspaper. Sturges explained, "I'd like you to open the screen door, walk down the steps, pick up the newspaper, look across the street, and walk back up the steps to the front door."

After carrying out these instructions to a T, Barrymore—who saw something genteel in the young director—walked over to him and said, "You know, John, I think we're going to get along just fine."

Sturges shot the segment on a soundstage and in front of a small, wood-frame house in L.A.'s factory district. The script called for an aerial shot of the house. Sturges saved the $280 rental for helicopter and pilot by making do with a crane. The only interruption: a real postal worker walked onto the cordoned-off street, nodded to Barrymore, and dropped a letter in her mailbox.

Though it went into production before *The Magnificent Yankee*, Schary's civic lesson tested poorly and did not reach theaters until January 12, 1952, the same week as DeMille's circus extravaganza *The Greatest Show on Earth*. The public wasn't in the mood for Schary's blatant "message picture." The *New York Times* called it a "cheery, sentimental estimation of life in these United States," which, due to the "shallow chauvinism" of the narration, came off as a commercial. Sturges's contribution was described as "a wistful little tale." *Variety*, while predicting "far from socko" business, singled out Barrymore for praise.

The Magnificent Yankee, scripted by Lavery from his own play, and *Kind Lady*, a remake of the Edward Chodorov conspiracy thriller based on a Hugh Walpole story, were seen as a step up for Sturges. The Chodorov adaptation, a natural after the success of *The Spiral Staircase* and *Gaslight*, reunited him with Ethel Barrymore, whose health had deteriorated since their last meeting and would now cause production delays.

Deutsch saw Louis Calhern in the 1946 Broadway production of *The Magnificent Yankee*, which co-starred Dorothy Gish as the fiercely protective wife, Fanny Holmes. During the course of the evening, Calhern, sporting a lavish Guardsman's mustache, had aged thirty years, from sixty-one to ninety-two. Impressed, the fledgling producer spent the next four years selling Schary and MGM management on the project. "I hit the jackpot with that one," he said later. "I loved the play, just loved it, but there were doubts about it as a picture." Translation: Even for a stage production, the show was unusually talky and claustrophobic (it took place entirely in Holmes's Washington study). Also, the title posed a problem. People would line up expecting the Babe Ruth story.

Deutsch countered that it was a crowd-pleasing character study, overlaid with not one but two love stories—between Wendell and Fanny, and between Wendell and his thirty surrogate sons/secretaries. Given the political climate, what better than a nonpartisan reaffirmation of democracy through dissent? Holmes is a Republican appointee but disapproves of many Republican rulings. And in the end he is seen standing at wobbly attention for a Democratic president.

When MGM announced Calhern would reprise his Broadway performance, the New York gossip columnists wasted little time reminding Schary et al. that the actor's penchant for boozing and womanizing had nearly cost him the stage role. His bouts with the bottle were almost as legendary as those of John Barrymore, and in one of his black "moods," Calhern could devour a timid director. His optimum working hours, he announced, only half-joking, were noon to 3:30. Recalled James Lydon, who played the lovesick secretary Clinton and knew Calhern from New York, "Louis was a rascal and a ladies' man, a wonderful bad boy."

Not to be swayed, Deutsch and Schary agreed the project only made sense with the original Holmes, who, they also pointed out, would take home a fraction of Tracy's or Gable's salary. Deutsch, fingers crossed behind his back, vouched that the show was his old friend's comeback, a declaration of newfound sobriety: The bad boy had learned his lesson and was now, if not dried out, at least under control. For insurance they would entrust Calhern to the quietly forceful Sturges. Besides sharing Holmes's Yankee temperament, his belief in discipline and hard work, the director was descended from a long line of New England jurists. Schary's first choice for Fanny Holmes was future first lady Nancy Davis. Deutsch obliged by testing her, but Sturges held out for Ann Harding.

Production got under way at the studio in early July 1950. Tackling his rare movie lead—after memorable turns in *Notorious* and *The Asphalt Jungle*—Calhern was a jumble of nerves and flubbed speeches he had delivered hundreds of times onstage. "Sturges watched as we rehearsed, and then moved the camera around accordingly," recalled co-star

Richard Anderson. "He was fast. He did one or, at the outside, two takes and then said, 'Let's move on.' But Louis had troubles with his lines, and we had to do some scenes six or seven times. But Sturges kept quiet."

Budgeted at just over $600,000 at a time when the average MGM release cost $1.4 million—Lydon called it "a small 'A'"—*The Magnificent Yankee* was shot in six weeks on two sound stages, with a few days allocated for location inserts (of the Capitol building, Arlington Cemetery, and Lincoln Memorial). Sturges, determined to make it more than a filmed stage play, tracked and dollied wherever he could. But the material still came off as stage-locked and mawkish. It didn't help that Schary encouraged Lavery to beef up the already blatantly patriotic speeches while trimming the quieter moments with Fanny. As an afterthought, voiceover narration was added. It was delivered by Holmes's novelist friend Owen Wister (played by Philip Ober, who bore a strong resemblance to Sturges).

With *The Magnificent Yankee,* Sturges's stock climbed. This film, unlike his Columbia programmers, was treated as an event. It premiered in late December at Radio City Music Hall, on the same program as the Corps de Ballet and the Rockettes. While acknowledging that this was a budget, no-star production from a studio known for its all-star casts, *Variety* hailed Calhern's booming, tour de force performance and Sturges's direction and predicted a brisk box office. More significantly, the trade paper pointed to "the 'Positive Americanism' that many in the business have been clamoring for." Crowther of the *Times* found the movie, like the play, to be overly sentimental, but he was impressed by Calhern's ability to age three decades in ninety minutes. "There is generally great taste and deep affection in the actor's performance," he wrote. "If Justice Holmes were not like this we feel sure he would not dissent."

Sturges was embarrassed by MGM's attendant fanfare. The critics had, for the most part, overreacted. "Jeez, they called it a masterpiece!" he recalled. "It was terribly overrated and received a special running. It wasn't a masterpiece. Wasn't bad, but wasn't good."

The public agreed. *The Magnificent Yankee* flopped at the box office, earning less than $500,000 worldwide. Deutsch's faith in Calhern, however, did not go unrewarded: the actor was nominated for a best-actor

Oscar. (He lost to José Ferrer in *Cyrano de Bergerac*.) The nominated top hats and tails, Sturges recalled laughing, were bested by the lion pelts and loincloths in *Samson and Delilah*. Still, the filmed stage play revealed a different side of Sturges and helped him ascend another rung on the studio ladder. Recalled Deutsch: "The picture was very prestigious but wasn't expensive—I mean it wasn't an 'A' picture. So MGM didn't expect much of it. But it got great reviews and was nominated for some Oscars. It helped both John's career and mine."

But had Sturges in the bargain become Schary's stooge? Did he unwittingly help sell his boss as John Q. Patriot? The answer is no, not entirely. Determined to rise in the ranks—and dodge the Carne Curse, which had destroyed his father and was threatening his brother— Sturges knew exactly what he was doing. Unlike his soon-to-be blacklisted colleagues, Dassin and Losey, he had agreed out of professional expediency to mount a soapbox in defense of bedrock Americanism.

Schary rewarded Sturges's loyalty. The director's next assignment was an adaptation of the play *Kind Lady,* described as "a story of subdued horror." MGM had done the Victorian London thriller in 1935 and still held the rights. The original version starred Aline MacMahon as wealthy do-gooder Mary Herries and Basil Rathbone as the street artist/scoundrel who holds her hostage in her own home and, with the help of his gang, sells off her art treasures. The remake could be done quickly and cheaply on the backlot, and, as noted in a studio memo, updated to the present, making it possible "to cast the principal role with a young woman" à la Dorothy McGuire in *Spiral Staircase*. Schary said no to a modern-day heroine and cast the venerable Ethel Barrymore—at seventy-one more than twice MacMahon's age when she had played Herries. With only fond memories of their first collaboration—she loathed bullies and shouters—Barrymore OK'd Sturges as director. Deutsch, though told that the film was intended as "a tax write-off," agreed to produce.

Sturges and Deutsch wanted Ray Milland for Henry Elcott, the starving artist who insinuates himself into the Herries household. They had to make do with Shakespearian actor Maurice Evans, notorious for what Deutsch called his mumbled delivery. Even so, the British actor managed a more refined and, consequently, more sinister version of Elcott. Also cast were Betsy Blair as Elcott's sickly wife, Angela Lansbury and Keenan Wynn as Elcott's "servants," and John Williams as the bank clerk who comes to Miss Herries's rescue. Behind the camera were Webster, Raksin, and cinematographer Joseph Rottenberg (*Gaslight*), a master of hazy, atmospheric lighting. Chodorov and Charles Bennett collaborated on the new adaptation, condensed from several years on stage to just one. Other significant changes: Elcott's wife, Ada (Blair), was made a more sympathetic victim; the abuse to Herries was more graphic; and a trick ending was added that involved a wheelchair and a corpse presumed to be that of Herries.

After two weeks of rehearsal, the film got under way in late November 1950. Sturges threw himself into the production, starting on Lot 2 with sixty extras, three horse-drawn hansom cabs, and exteriors of the townhouse and adjacent London square. But what was supposed to be a snappy twenty-four-day shoot—scheduled to wrap two days before Christmas—took two and a half months. The sign posted on the soundstage door explained: "This production closed due to Miss Barrymore's illness." Barrymore suffered from a kidney infection, traced to her binge drinking as a young woman. She "liked to dip into the bourbon," said Lydon. "She loved the sauce—even more than her brother, John." Whatever the reason for the delays, they were expensive. With cast and crew on full salary, Barrymore's illness cost the production almost a quarter of a million dollars and pushed the budget to $900,000.

"I would not say it was an easy shoot or a hard shoot," said assistant director Freeman, who still has the plaster replica of the Benvenuto Cellini doorknocker that Elcott uses as a pretence to enter the house. "But Barrymore was never 100 percent. We were all very conscious of that."

In January, Sturges celebrated his forty-first birthday and the birth of his second child, Michael Eliott. Barrymore returned from sick leave to help cut the birthday cake as cast, crew, and Schary looked on. (Though he would be considered middle-aged by today's standards, MGM billed Sturges as "one of Hollywood's youngest directors.")

Anderson recalled bumping into Sturges in the commissary. The actor was appearing in *Kind Lady* on stage in Santa Barbara and asked about the movie. Sturges scowled. The "subdued horror" that had raised goose bumps in the 1930s, he grumbled, now seemed terribly dated and, worse, uncinematic. "I've got to get this thing moving," he said, shaking his head. "It's such a staid period piece."

Production resumed in February with Barrymore, now battling bronchitis, tied to the upstairs bed. Her appearance worked to the film's benefit: She looked exhausted and pale, like someone who really had been sedated and held captive. Her delivery—"a pronounced wheeze . . . that sounded like a train whistle"—was another matter. It would be fixed in post-production, said Sturges, who treated his leading lady like royalty while pushing the crew mercilessly. Eighteen-hour days were not unusual.

Faced with a creaky set piece that would be obligatorily "opened up" with park and cobblestone-street scenes that looked like exactly what they were—the Metro backlot—Sturges was desperate to breathe life into the project and up the suspense quotient for an audience familiar with all the old parlor tricks. He accomplished this with low-key lighting and long shadows, and Raksin's creepy electronic score, which accentuated references to Elcott's murderous past. He also experimented with mise-en-scène, positioning players to suggest the unfolding power struggle. In one of the best sequences, Elcott, Edwards, and his wife drop the masquerade and slowly encircle Miss Herries.

"This is monstrous! What is it you want of me?" she demands.

"Sit down, old lady," Edwards (Wynn) snaps.

While Herries's abuse is only alluded to in the 1935 movie and play, Sturges takes us into the upstairs bedroom where he shows the old woman bound and gagged in bed, and then, in grim counterpoint, he cuts to horses in the street masked by feedbags. Dissatisfied with the knock-at-the-door play ending, Sturges reshot it, twice. The third ending has the police, accompanied by Foster (Williams), taking Elcott and the Edwardses into custody as his star looks at the Cellini door knocker and flashes, per the screenplay, "That Barrymore look."

Principal photography was completed in February. In lieu of a wrap party, Sturges and Deutsch retired to Deutsch's office and got roaring drunk. The sound department then went to work on Barrymore's wheezy delivery. The melodrama, paired with a Tom and Jerry cartoon and travelogue, opened in late summer 1951. The ads, which featured Lansbury in silhouette, played up both the suspense ("80 Minutes in a House of Mystery!") and New York pedigree ("MGM presents Broadway's Dramatic Thunderbolt"). Exhibitors were encouraged to fan interest with lobby games, such as "Open This Lock! Win $1." The critics found the period drama a polished improvement over the original adaptation. Sturges's direction, observed *Variety*, starts out slow but "builds to a strong mood of suspense." Barrymore was called a shoo-in for an Oscar nomination. But at the Academy Awards the following March, her name was nowhere to be found. Everybody was talking about Vivien Leigh in *A Streetcar Named Desire* and Katharine Hepburn in *The African Queen*. George Stevens's *A Place in the Sun* was also a frontrunner. *Kind Lady* had to make do with a single nomination—for black-and-white costume design.

Still, Sturges was pleased with the movie, a precursor to such lady-in-distress classics as *Sorry, Wrong Number* and *What Ever Happened to Baby Jane?* "It was a very good picture," he said. "Most titles in those days weren't very perceptive. This one was—it's a *quiet* thriller, but a good one. It got good notices and did very good business. Barrymore was marvelous in it, and wonderful to work with. She was very fond of me, and she endured a great deal—they grabbed her, tied her to her bed, as she tells everyone, 'I'm not crazy.' Of course, if you're crazy that's the first thing you say."

Spencer Tracy, a friend of Barrymore, had, unannounced, visited the *Kind Lady* set. He was struck by the director's composure and requested him for his next feature, *The People against O'Hara*. Based on a popular novel by Eleazar Lipsky, this crime thriller was a gutsy move for MGM's reigning star. Tracy, an alcoholic, played James Curtayne, a New York attorney attempting a comeback after being hospitalized for alcoholism. Because Curtayne has fallen so far in the eyes of his daughter (Diana Lynn) and the assistant D.A. (John Hodiak) and he still gets the shakes when he approaches a jury box, this is a story of redemption. For Sturges it would be further proof that he was becoming one of the industry's most reliable action directors, as well as a strong judge of talent. Cast in a bit part—for which he received $110 for two days' work—was a brooding, hatchet-faced actor of Polish descent named Charles Buchinski. A decade later, as Charles Bronson, he would reteam with Sturges on *The Magnificent Seven* and *The Great Escape*.

After the success of Edward Dmytryk's *Crossfire* and Elia Kazan's *Boomerang!*, few in Metro's front office could deny the importance of location shooting. The public knew the MGM backlot like its own backyard, Sturges insisted. They wanted real people on real locations, such as Rossellini and the postwar Italian neo-realists had offered. And with a budget in the $1 million range, *The People against O'Hara* cried out for gritty shots of New York's Lower East Side. Tracy, however, wasn't buying it. He hated leaving Culver City, particularly when there was so much money to be made at home. Besides the Sturges project—which would net him $124,000, or almost $6,000 a week—Tracy was committed to *Father's Little Dividend*, *Pat and Mike*, and *Plymouth Adventure*, with, per his contract, "four weeks rest between pictures."

Sturges persisted. He sugarcoated the New York shoot as a paid vacation. They would stay at the Pierre Hotel. All that would be required of the star was a couple of street scenes—done in long shot. Tracy finally relented, and in late February, after four days of rehearsal, Sturges, Tracy, and James Arness—cast as murder suspect Johnny O'Hara—flew to New York for five days of street and skyline shots, which included the Criminal Courts Building, the East River, and, for the opening chase between O'Hara and the cops, the George Washington Bridge. These would be intercut later with backlot nightscapes, where shafts of light pour from windows and doorways. (In 1994, *The People against O'Hara* was included in Film Forum's ambitious two-month "NYC Noir" retrospective.)

"We went to New York and did quite a bit of stuff there, including going down to the Fulton Fish Market," recalled Arness, who earned $4,000 for sixteen days of work. "At the time I was a minimal actor, struggling to get any kind of job. *O'Hara* was a big break for me, and I was trying my hardest to hold it together. I recall John as friendly and professional, but preoccupied. Not surprising—he had a lot of responsibility in guiding that whole thing along."

William Campbell, who played a stoolpigeon in pompadour and flashy striped suit, had a street-savvy that appealed to Sturges. "He cast me as a smart-aleck kid because that's what I was—a smart aleck from Newark, New Jersey," Campbell said. "But I was intimidated by Tracy and told Sturges I'll never get through the courtroom scene."

"I can't say my lines," Campbell, struggling to catch his breath, told Sturges.

"Don't be afraid of Tracy—he's an actor, you're an actor," Sturges reassured him. He might have added, "Besides, Tracy is just as insecure as you are."

It was not unusual to find the star—who said the secret to acting was "learn your lines and don't bump into the furniture"—seated on a bench outside Stage 25, mumbling to himself as he committed the entire script to memory. During the office sequence with O'Hara's distraught parents, Tracy muffed a speech and looked furtively over his shoulder. "*Uh-oh, Uh-oh,*" he clowned, feigning schoolboy concern. "Someone's going to call Mr. Mayer and tell him Tracy's blowing his lines."

Was Tracy drunk on the set? Depends on whom you ask. Campbell recalled Tracy as being on his best behavior. "I heard rumors that he was still drinking, but I never saw it. Hepburn kept him in line most of the time, but he was starting to get older, and [the drinking] was starting to show on him. Whatever damage was done was done before *O'Hara.*"

Co-stars Lynn and Richard Anderson, however, saw a different side of the actor, who, oddly, wore a white doctor's coat to rehearsals. After a scene with Tracy, Lynn complained, "Jesus, he didn't throw me a single right word." But it didn't matter. Tracy would mumble something, and if it was in the ballpark, Sturges would yell, "Print it!"

The shoot, said Anderson, "went like butter. . . . There were no major delays. John had a lot to do with that. He understood when Tracy 'wasn't feeling well' and made allowances because at that point the alcohol helped his acting."

The People against O'Hara, which reteamed Sturges with cinematographer John Alton, opens in classic noir style with rain-slick streets, an all-night café, and the flash of gunfire. Since the abandoned getaway car belongs to Johnny O'Hara, he is hauled downtown, where the assistant D.A. is waiting with Johnny's "partner," Frankie Korvac (Campbell), a mouthy pretty boy. Johnny's immigrant parents (Arthur Shields and Louise Lorimer)—old friends "from the neighborhood"—beseech Curtayne to come out of retirement and take the case. Curtayne's daughter Ginny and the district judge think it's a bad idea, but Curtayne, itching to get back in the courtroom, ignores them and assumes the dual role of investigator-counselor, interviewing Korvac's brothers and Johnny's boss, mobster Knuckles Lanzetta (Eduardo Ciannelli). The strain proves too much, and in one of the film's strongest sequences, prosecution snitch Korvac verbally ties Curtayne in knots as Johnny and his parents look on. "I was groping for questions . . . I couldn't remember," Curtayne tells his daughter. Humiliated, he begins drinking again and attempts to bribe the D.A.'s star witness—with a $500 check, no less.

When Johnny is found guilty, Lanzetta's young wife comes forward to supply his alibi and, inadvertently, the real reason for the shooting: a cheap suitcase molded from $200,000 in pure heroin. Facing indictment for bribery, Curtayne is, improbably, allowed to play bait in a dangerous stakeout that leads the D.A. to the real killer, Korvac's older brother. In a stroke designed to please both the Production Code and temperance crowd, Curtayne pays the ultimate price for falling off the wagon. Wisely, Sturges dropped the obligatory death speech. He had Curtayne die off-camera as the D.A. and a prosecutor friend (Pat O'Brien) discuss what to do with the incriminating check.

Though a definite improvement over Sturges's other courtroom drama, *The Man Who Dared*, *The People against O'Hara* is still a minor noir in which Alton's bravura camerawork is at odds with the antiseptic studio interiors and plot contrivances, such as Curtayne's phone call from the stakeout to give Ginny and her boyfriend his blessing. To their credit, Sturges and screenwriter John Monks Jr. refused to follow the novel's lead and soft-sell Curtayne's "condition." Ginny and Jeff discuss the lawyer's addiction with a candor that had to have disturbed Tracy.

Jeff: "If he wants to drink, he's gonna drink—just like any alcoholic."

Ginny: "He's not an alcoholic, he's not!"

Jeff (resigned): "Alright, he just drinks."

Later, after Curtayne falls off the wagon and loses the case, Lanzetta taunts, "Couldn't beat it, could you? Just a worn-out old lush."

The People against O'Hara opened on the top half of double bills in the fall of 1951, when *Kind Lady* was still in theaters. *Variety* predicted the mystery's "unnecessarily downbeat" ending and "cluttered" plot would dampen the box office but praised Sturges's handling of the suspense. The *New York Times* applauded the "smooth and level-headed direction" while shrugging off the picture as "curiously old-fashioned." The *Times* was impressed by the panel-truck stakeout, which combined crosscutting and the latest surveillance equipment.

Sturges agreed that the "downer" ending hurt the box office, but he was proud of the film, calling it "a different style of picture-making, like

Blackboard Jungle and *The Set-Up.*" Wise, Brooks, Zinnemann, and he were being hailed as "a kind of new wave," he said.

Sturges jumped quickly now from one assignment to the next. *The Girl in White,* taken from the Dr. Emily Dunning (Barringer) memoir *Bowery to Bellevue,* began production in late October with June Allyson as Dunning, the first woman to intern at a New York hospital. *Jeopardy,* a modest but soundly constructed thriller co-starring Barbara Stanwyck, Barry Sullivan, and Ralph Meeker, went before the cameras the following July, and *Fast Company,* a knockabout farce with Howard Keel and Polly Bergen, was shot three months later at a San Fernando Valley horse track. (Sturges also was mentioned for "See How They Run," a McCarthy witch-hunt allegory eventually released as *Talk about a Stranger* in 1952.) Of the three completed films, *The Girl in White,* budgeted at $1 million, was the most ambitious, utilizing much of the MGM backlot to approximate New York at the turn of the century. *Jeopardy* was the most commercial, a disaster thriller in miniature that demonstrated Sturges's talent for solving logistical problems—in this case, a race against the rising tide to save a man trapped under a pier.

Grace Sturges spoke often of her sister, Mary, a Suffragette and one of the first women to graduate from Columbia Medical School. Mary went on to practice pediatrics in Boston, where the teenage John visited her in the summer. This "family connection," he said, attracted him to the Emily Dunning project. He would regret the decision. The script turned Dunning's autobiography—which documented the grim rounds at Gouverneur Hospital on the Lower East Side—into a sanitized, Currier and Ives romance, *Meet Me in St. Louis* without the songs.

The tenements Dr. Dunning recalled reeked of "overcrowded humanity; crime in every form, robbery, murder, rape; insanity, alcoholism in all stages: I was to meet the budding gangster, the prostitute and to visit dives where the underworld held out and one reeled under the nauseous opium-laden air." None of that made it to the screen. As technical adviser, Dunning was lucky to sign off on the ambulance uniforms. The studio, it soon became clear, had purchased her story, only to develop cold feet. The public, Deutsch explained, was not ready for something this controversial, or clinical (the book contained graphic descriptions of ulcerated veins and suicide by carbonic acid). After all, the American

woman had only just relinquished her place on the assembly line and returned to her presumptive role as homemaker. Consequently, Dunning's story became a formulaic biopic, with Allyson a marginally scrap-
pier version of her plucky ingénue, only now facing such life-or-death
dilemmas as how to take a bath in an all-male dormitory and what to do
when your petticoat shows during ambulance duty. At the heart of the
film is Emily's career-versus-matrimony quandary. Will she or won't
she see her internship through as the handsome Dr. Ben Barringer (Arthur Kennedy) pitches woo? Ben, like Walter Pidgeon's Pierre Curie,
carries out hands-on experiments with radium; and the hospital's glum
director (Gary Merrill) argues that women are too emotional to become
physicians—that is, until at a staff party he sees Emily in a skirt.

   To achieve what the studio called its "semi-documentary style," the
director deployed camera units to Cornell University in Ithaca, New
York, and Oxnard, California. For the only real action sequence—a
breakneck race to an accident scene, with Emily clinging to the back of
the horse-drawn ambulance—Sturges combined process shots, spectator cutaways, and driver's point of view. He worked fast and efficiently,
making up the time lost to constant script revisions and what production charts referred to as "Miss Allyson's illness" (she was pregnant).

   Given the studio's nervousness over the commercial viability of the
project, it was a minor miracle that any of the book's feminism found its
way to the screen. The film's ending attempted to have it both ways
with Ben and Emily professing their mutual love but going in separate
directions—he to a sabbatical in Paris, she on her nightly rounds. If there
were any doubt about the ultimate outcome, the ward corridor, lighted
to suggest a church altar, quashed it.

   Never more disgusted with the limitations of the backlot, Sturges
demanded his next picture take him on location. He was assigned a race-
against-the-clock—or in this case, rising tide—thriller titled "Riptide."
It was set along a remote stretch of Baja. The catch: to save money, Dana
Point, near Laguna Beach, and Yucca Valley would sub for the Mexican
peninsula. A second unit would do inserts of Pacific Coast Highway and
Tijuana. But even with these restrictions the shoot meant a holiday from
the studio, and the director was determined to make the most of it.

   The screenplay by Mel Dinelli (*The Spiral Staircase*) was expanded
from a radio play called *A Question of Time*. When broadcast in 1950, the

half-hour drama was narrated by Anne Baxter's Mary, who, on vacation in Baja, seeks help when her husband becomes pinned beneath a derelict pier. She's taken captive by an escaped convict who finally listens to her plea—and redeems himself. Stanwyck, who had just gone through a very public divorce from Robert Taylor, was cast as the victimized wife, now called Helen Stilwin; Sullivan played her husband, Doug, a smug veteran rendered helpless by the accident, and eight-year-old Lee Aaker, who would star in TV's *The Adventures of Rin Tin Tin,* appeared as Bobby, the son. (Billy Curtis, a Munchkin in *The Wizard of Oz,* stood in for Aaker during the more hazardous pier shots.)

A modest B picture—budgeted at $500,000—*Jeopardy* would become much more in Sturges's hands, a minor classic of its kind and a forerunner of such disaster thrillers as *The Last Voyage* and *Earthquake.* Production began in early July with the casting of Latino actors as Tijuana locals and Federales who man the roadblocks. Sturges and assistant Joel Freeman drove to Pioneertown, a façade Western town built for Gene Autry and the Cisco Kid. Behind them, a caravan of trucks, loaded with cameras, cables, walkie-talkies, and portable toilets. Stanwyck and the other principals arrived a week later.

A memo by Sturges prepared everyone for what lay ahead: "Travel will be by bus. Crews will be gone approximately two weeks, [and] will proceed from desert location to [Dana Point] beach location. Desert days are hot and desert nights cool. The work at the beach will include wet work. The accommodations at the desert are adequate but limited. The accommodations at the beach are the same."

Recalling those childhood road trips with Grace, Sturges approached the assignment like any good Boy Scout. He drew up two location maps—one of the real Baja, with corresponding plot points marked on the roads heading south; the other of the Yucca Valley "Baja" with roads also assigned specific events ("roadblock," "meet Indians," "flat tire," "crackup"). To assure continuity, he contacted a Coast Guard substation in San Clemente for information on Dana Point tides. The pier rescue—which starts with a jack and progresses to a beam/fulcrum lashed to the family car—was carefully orchestrated to assure maximum viewer interaction. It was shot partially on location and, for the close-ups, partially on a soundstage with wave machine.

"Shooting at Dana Point was a wild experience," recalled Freeman. "We were in the water in swimming trunks and tennis shoes, planting these phony beams and rocks, and a tsunami occurs. This huge wave! It threw us all over the place. John looked up, and said, 'Where did everybody go?'"

Jeopardy opened in March 1953—a few months before RKO's similarly plotted *The Hitch-Hiker*. It did reasonably well at the box office. How could it not, given the budget and coolly executed cross-cutting for suspense? Also, like MGM's *The Long, Long Trailer* with Lucille Ball and Desi Arnaz, it plugged into the near-giddy postwar Zeitgeist. Filmgoers identified with the vacationing Stilwins: With Dwight D. Eisenhower in the White House and Swanson TV dinners in every freezer, Americans had taken to the road in droves to become a nation of tourists. And the voiceover narration by Stanwyck—backed by Dmitri Tiomkin's deceptively carefree score—captures this, albeit with more than a hint of sarcasm.

> Vacation time in the United States means traveling, and traveling in the United States is wonderful. Fill your gas tank and hit the road. The big rolling freeways and the fantastic traffic patterns—monuments to a civilization that moves on wheel. . . . There is a turn off to everywhere, and you can go straight ahead, too—if you only know how. Some people go to the mountains or the shore. We packed two weeks camping equipment in a trailer and headed south, to a place I'd never seen.

The tone and now-Latin-flavored music become more ominous as the family crosses the border, past a "Warning" sign. Tijuana is fun, like a conga, Helen tells us. "It's a boom town, with tourists for oil wells." A policeman bids the family "*bienvenido*," and Helen translates dryly, "That means 'welcome.'" Once again Sturges relies on visual aides—a gas-station map of Baja establishes the distance from Ensenada to La Paz (four hundred miles). Helen continues:

> Nothing but names. Oh, picturesque names. Ancient settlements and missions no longer existing. Ghost towns. Ruins. Below Ensenada, it's a road of dirt and desolation . . . a road of shifting sand and bruising rocks, of quail that scoot through clumps of cactus, and doves that rise

in soft whirring clouds. High adventure beckons down this road . . . but never again will it beckon to me.

MGM, inexplicably, sold *Jeopardy* as a salacious melodrama with titillating shots of Stanwyck's bare thigh. One ad promised: "A woman in 'Jeopardy' . . . A Shocker that makes others sound like baby-talk!" Another leered: "She did it . . . and no woman in the world would blame her! She did it . . . because her fear was greater than her shame! She did it . . . and it was bad! She did it . . . *Would you?*" *Variety* found the film "unpretentious, tightly-drawn," and went on to congratulate Sturges for "no wasted motion or budget dollars in the presentation." The *New York Times*'s Crowther—fast becoming the director's nemesis—found the ending contrived, but conceded: "The settings are strikingly authentic, the situation is coolly credible and the visual laminating of the story perceptibly tightens the suspense."

Over the years, *Jeopardy* has gained in stature. Alexander Payne (*Sideways*) remembered seeing it as a film student and admiring its taut construction, and novelist Wallace Markfield sang its praises in a memorable essay on B movies "made on workhouse budgets under coolie conditions" by "modest, movie-wise, endlessly inventive craftsmen who would take a hopelessly hack assignment and turn it into 95 fast minutes of sharp detailing, understated performing and hard-nosed truth." Placing *Jeopardy* with *Gun Crazy, He Walked by Night,* and other "shoestring miracles," Markfield marveled at the "plain, pure physicality" of the rescue operation and added, "Director Sturges loves, as a 5-year-old cave dweller would and a Hitchcock sometimes does, the banal, beautiful reality of bumper jacks, tow ropes, lug wrenches, crowbars, joists, grapples." Meeker and the climactic rescue "wind the movie up like a tight spring; a rough equivalent to the last half hour might be watching the invention of the wheel."

Fast Company—shot close to home at Devonshire Downs and Northridge Farms in the San Fernando Valley—followed. The comedy ran into winter weather and went four days over schedule. Though he showed little enthusiasm for the material, Sturges made up for the delays by minimizing takes and maximizing setups (ten to forty a day). When it was overcast or rainy and he lost half of a day, instead of falling behind he tore pages from the script or had his Studio City neighbor,

William Roberts (who later worked on *Underwater!* and *The Magnificent Seven*), write him out of the jam. Sturges delivered the feature for under $471,000. Now earning $1,250 a week in salary, he would be a bargain at twice the price, all agreed.

Writer Don Mankiewicz said he intended *Fast Company* as an amiable tribute to bush-league horse racing or the "gyp" (for gypsy) circuit, but the script was retooled as a comedy romance for MGM baritone Howard Keel and Stanwyck, who eventually backed out. Mankiewicz was well-acquainted with the "leaky-roof race tracks" where "the money distributed in the purses was less than what it took to keep the horses alive. But it was the perfect subject for a movie—races that were easy to follow, promised lots of excitement and built to a fine climax eight times a day."

The rewritten version, which owed an obvious debt to Damon Runyon and Frank Capra, featured Keel as Rick Grayton, a down-and-out trainer whose horse, Gay Fleet, always runs dead last—on purpose. Grayton wants the horse, which leaps out in front when serenaded by her jockey, to be disparaged as a "deadbeat" so he can buy her. Vying for Grayton's affections are Carol Maldon (Polly Bergen), Gay Fleet's dim-but-feisty owner from back east, and Mercy Bellway (Nina Foch), a wealthy breeder whose stable has more men than horses. Besides a number of comedy veterans, the track regulars included Marjorie Main and Iron Eyes Cody, whose mute Cigar Store Indian must have struck someone as funny at the time.

The twin rap on Sturges, then as now, was that he was uncomfortable with comedy and uptight around women. *Fast Company* did little to assuage either perception. He was a good storyteller, said son Michael, but he wasn't "a jokey guy" who would pal around with the cast and crew after hours. "Everything about him was serious, his demeanor, his face, which was always set. When he smiled, it would startle people, scare them, because it happened so infrequently and was so incongruous."

Added Freeman, "I don't remember John being easy around Stanwyck or women in general. He came off as aggressive, sometimes harsh—very much a man's man. I think that's why, as his career progressed, he did fewer movies with women."

Bergen, a singer with little acting experience who would go on to *Escape from Fort Bravo* and *Cape Fear* (1962), said the director provided no guidance whatsoever. "That part was the lead, and I did not get any help from Mr. Sturges, thank you very much. He was one of those directors who had a very short attention span for beginners."

Today, *Fast Company* can be seen as a harbinger of *The Hallelujah Trail*. It is a painfully overdone farce that combines pratfalls, running jokes (the chaw-chewing track bugler who always blows sour), whinny-ing reaction shots (à la Francis the Talking Mule), and quasi-naughty seductions, which, in one instance, involves lowering and raising the zipper on Carol's sleeping bag. Bergen is hopeless as Carol, who, drunk or sober, mugs appallingly, like a Carol Lombard in training. Her love taps are more like haymakers: she knocks Rick unconscious twice and sends his trailer, with him and Mercy inside, careening down a hill. She is so unappealing that later, when she gets socked in the eye by her new trainer, you can almost hear a collective cheer. Such material clearly cried out for that other Sturges, Preston.

Mankiewicz, who left the production early to concentrate on an-other assignment, now wishes he had made the time for what he calls a "lost picture" among the Sturges oeuvre. "If I had been there, I would have hollered. My story was more raffish, realistic, because horse racing at this level is not a glamorous game. It became a shabby little semi-musical, a 'B' picture. Horses do not run faster in response to music; they go faster in response to the whip or drugs. But nobody wanted realistic. MGM was more for gloss and less for gritty."

The ads for *Fast Company* played up the low-down habitués of the gyp circuit. "A Fast Buck! A Fast Kiss! . . . and you're traveling in 'Fast Company'!" ballyhooed one poster. "Blackmailers! Hustlers! Schemers! Fast Dames!" promised another. The film opened in April 1953 to generous reviews. The trades called it "likable" (*Variety*) and "good-humored" (*Hollywood Reporter*), while acknowledging that it was a low-budget programmer that ran just over an hour.

Anxious to begin initiating his own projects, Sturges approached Sam Goldwyn with *The Great Escape,* Paul Brickhill's nonfiction ac-count of a massive breakout from a German POW camp. He had read an abridged version of the book in *Reader's Digest*. "What the hell kind of escape is this?" Goldwyn demanded. "Nobody gets away!" As a con-solation prize perhaps, the director was given *Escape from Fort Bravo,* a blend of Civil War prison break and Indian skirmishes. It was unusual fare for Metro, more comfortable with prestige musicals than horse operas. Shot in Death Valley National Monument in MGM's pre-CinemaScope aspect ratio (1.66:1) and featuring an A-list cast headed by William Holden and Eleanor Parker, the film would become Sturges's biggest money-maker to date. The original Michael Pate-Phillip Rock story, titled "Rope's End" after the lead character, Captain Roper, was purchased for $15,000 with the understanding that it would be tailored as an action-romance for Holden. The actor, however, didn't like the changes, which included having Roper tend roses behind his quarters and let down his guard when in the company of Parker's Wild West Mata Hari. He backed out of the project until he was reminded of his contractual obligations to the studio. The versatile Robert Surtees—whose credits would eventually encompass *Mogambo, Ben-Hur, The Graduate,* and *The Last Picture Show*—was named cinematographer. He shot in Ansco Color, marking the director's escape from black-and-white programmers.

Fort Bravo takes place in Arizona Territory, 1863. Captain Roper is second in command at the titular garrison, which doubles as Union stockade. Third in command is Lieutenant Beecher (Richard Anderson), a principled West Point graduate engaged to the commandant's daughter (Polly Bergen). Corralled on the parade ground and planning their escape are Confederate prisoners led by Captain Marsh (newcomer John Forsythe, whom the director found through Robert Wise). The Confederates include such types as the crusty old-timer (William Demarest), the hothead (William Campbell), and the sensitive kid (John Lupton) who fears he's a coward. Roper—a softy at heart, like Wayne's Captain Brittles in *She Wore a Yellow Ribbon*—is easily conned by Carla Forester (Parker), a new arrival who turns out to be a Confederate spy and Marsh's fiancée. While mooning over the pretty stranger, Roper relaxes his guard, and Marsh and the others escape in the back of a wagon. Angry over being played like a lovesick puppy, Roper quickly chases down Carla and the Johnny Rebs. En route to the fort, they are attacked by Mescalero Apaches.

What follows is Sturges's most impressive pre-*Magnificent Seven* action sequence, a desert standoff inspired by the Battle of Agincourt in *Henry V.* It begins with Roper and his party being observed by Indians in extreme long shot. When they realize they have been spotted, they make a break for it, only to be pinned down in a dry creek bed. After several fruitless charges, the Indians turn to classic battlefield strategy. They throw spears to establish the target, and then shoot arrows to measure distance, angle, and trajectory. "Like artillery," says Lieutenant Beecher in admiration. "We're bracketed."

Sturges said he was drawn to the project because of its logistical challenges: it appealed to the frustrated engineer in him. He triangulated the climactic standoff, using semi-circle, dots for characters, LR/RL directional notes. He also exploited the Death Valley locations for panoramas reminiscent of *Fort Apache.* Sturges's debt to Ford is most evident in the opening and closing tableaux, which utilized swelling music and silhouettes of cavalry formations, shot against "billowy clouds" and "great expanse of sky." During an early patrol, Roper finds a supply wagon in flames, with the drivers staked to an anthill. After the burial, composed much like the hilltop funeral in Stevens's *Shane,* the patrol enters a canyon. The horses' hoofs and command to "Check carbines!" echo off the walls, adding to the suspense.

To his credit, Sturges played up the anachronistic dialogue, which was weirdly hip and, at times, morbidly funny. During the standoff, two of three Indians fall from their horses. Campbell to Demarest: "You musta missed." Demarest: "Nah, we just killed the same one twice." Campbell, spying a circling buzzard, asks Demarest, "Friend of yours?" Demarest: "He don't want me. He's looking for you—all soft and young, like a nice quail." Later, Demarest tells Campbell, "Why don't you take a nice nap, and I'll wake you when you're dead."

"Buddy and I were Western buffs, and the original story was written from a young person's point of view," said Pate, an Australian character actor who, after co-starring in *Hondo,* would be typecast as Native Americans and Western heavies. (Ironically, he was cast as an Indian elder in Sturges's *Sergeants 3,* while being passed over for an Aussie POW in *The Great Escape.*) "It didn't have that gravitas of some of the more orthodox Westerns of the day by Louis L'Amour and W. R. Burnett. It was more down-to-earth."

Known around town as an expert in Old West military procedures, Pate was summoned to MGM for advice on an as-yet-untitled cavalry picture. Pate met with Sturges in his bungalow. They talked about the West during the Civil War and how the underdefended Fort Bravo would be at the mercy of Indian raiding parties. They also talked about the Apache's hit-and-run strategy. Chief Vittorio's vainglorious charge at the end of *Hondo* was all wrong, Pate said. The Apaches were experts at guerrilla warfare and would attack the Blue Coats at their most vulnerable, in this case as they made their way through a canyon or were trapped in an arroyo.

"You seem to know a helluva lot about this script," Sturges said after twenty minutes.

"I should, I wrote the original," Pate replied.

Embarrassed—and aware that further discussion would mean retaining Pate as technical adviser—Sturges looked at his watch and remembered he was late for a meeting.

Production got under way in April in Death Valley, moved three weeks later to Gallup, New Mexico, down wind from the government's A-bomb test site, and wrapped in late May on the backlot and Ray Corrigan Ranch in Simi Valley. In Death Valley, the mercury at times hovered around 104 degrees. "It was a tough movie to make, because of the weather and the action," said Anderson, who narrowly missed getting a hoof in the face when his horse threw him in the canyon sequence. "In one scene, we had to go full gallop down a hill. If one horse had fallen, we'd all have gone down. John never said a word."

For authenticity, Sturges had the cast do as many of their stunts as possible and use wood-hard Civil War saddles. Holden, however, wanted none of this: he picked out a thoroughbred horse and a softer pommel saddle. "I rode with Holden quite a bit, and he did great things with that horse," said Anderson. "He drank, but never on the set, only in the evenings when he was playing poker with the guys. . . . Bill was married to Brenda Marshall at the time, but that didn't stop him. He loved women and he loved to drink."

The ride through Yellow Canyon was done at Zabriskie Point. The gulch standoff—with its shower of arrows—was staged in Gallup. "It was the hook—the reason Sturges and [producer Nicholas] Nayfack wanted to make the film," said Anderson. "If it didn't work, there was no movie."

In preparation for the action set piece, Sturges diagrammed camera angles on the reverse side of his script. A semi-circle encasing seven dots connoted the trapped characters. He left the actors to their own devices and huddled with Surtees and the effects team, which, for maximum impact, had rigged hollow arrows to travel down a wire into boards hidden beneath the costumes. (Kurosawa would borrow this trick for *Throne of Blood*.)

"Anderson got hit by two arrows during the film—one in the shoulder, one in the leg," recalled Campbell. "It was interesting but frightening, because they were shooting them from a ladder down the line into this cork board that they put under your pants. Each time they shot an arrow, I thought, 'Don't make any mistakes, or we're going to have to carry one of these people out.'" They did not undercrank the camera to increase the speed of the arrows, said Campbell, because "they were going extremely fast without that."

Because of the complicated action sequences and the problems matching color exteriors and soundstage inserts (of the fort, a campsite with waterfall), the production went eight days over schedule and the budget ballooned from $800,000 to $1.5 million. Nayfack constantly battled with production manager Walter Strohm for "just one or two more days." The additional time wasn't wasted on rehearsals or dialogue sequences, said Bergen, who, as Anderson's love interest, was not required to go on location. "Eleanor Parker was very insecure so most of the scenes we played together were all played over my shoulder onto her. But Sturges didn't seem to mind. We had very little give-and-take, which in my opinion made him a not very good director of actors. It was obvious even then that he preferred male ensembles and big action scenes with very little personal intrusion."

Countered Anderson: "John was not a dramatic coach. He was like William Wyler: He assumed you knew what you were doing." Campbell's take: "Sturges was not the most talkative guy," but even when things got testy on location, "he didn't yell or carry on."

Escape from Fort Bravo—promoted as an epic outdoor drama with a "cast of hundreds"—opened in December 1953. *This Is Cinerama* and the first CinemaScope release, *The Robe*, were already in theaters; *Hondo* in 3-D was due at Christmas. The reviews, as Sturges had hoped, played up the spectacular backdrops and his handling of the climactic battle. *Variety* called it a "cut above" the standard Western and cited Sturges's "meticulous direction." *Time* raved that the Agincourt-inspired siege lifted the film from usual program fare. The *L.A. Times* said the finale was so vivid it might have been in 3-D. The *New York Times* dubbed it a "class horse opera" and praised Sturges's "professional smoothness, particularly in the sweeping, headlong Indian battles."

The box office was equally gratifying. *Fort Bravo* earned $1.4 million in a little over a year, or $200,000 more than *Quo Vadis,* which because of its prohibitive running time, was forced into fewer bookings. "Sturges went off and made his film," said Pate. "And it's always been recognized as a very good film of its kind." A decade later, the director, recalling the Reb prisoners' jeering rendition of "Dixie," would orchestrate a second prison break, only on a much grander scale. In 1965, a Sturges fan named Sam Peckinpah would oversee a similarly plotted Civil War Western called *Major Dundee.*

"Allies" John and mother Grace, a.k.a. "the grande dame," in Santa Monica, California. (courtesy of Deborah Sturges Wyle)

Top left: John Eliot Carne as an infant in Oak Park, Illinois. (courtesy of Deborah Sturges Wyle)

Bottom left: Jean (née Alice) and Sturges Carne, John's older siblings, in front of the Oak Park house. (courtesy of Deborah Sturges Wyle)

John "saddles up" at an ostrich farm in South Pasadena, California, circa 1922. (courtesy of Deborah Sturges Wyle)

The early entertainer: John in a sophomore-year Berkeley High School production as King Tut's Mummy in 1925. (courtesy of Deborah Sturges Wyle)

Sturges (reclining in foreground) clowns around at a costume party with RKO editing buddies, from left to right, Mark Robson, Robert Wise, and Hank Berman. (courtesy of Deborah Sturges Wyle)

How to ditch a crippled Flying Tiger: 2nd Lieutenant Sturges (behind cameraman) directing an Army Air Corps training film in Orlando, Florida, in 1943. (courtesy of Deborah Sturges Wyle)

Sturges celebrating his forty-first birthday on the set of MGM's *Kind Lady* as crew and cast—including Ethel Barrymore, Maurice Evans, Angela Lansbury, Keenan Wynn, and Betsy Blair—offer their congratulations. Studio boss Dore Schary (fourth from Sturges's right) looks on. (courtesy of Deborah Sturges Wyle)

"The gorillas have taken over." Sturges confers with Spencer Tracy and Robert Ryan on the Lone Pine, California, set of *Bad Day at Black Rock*. (courtesy of Deborah Sturges Wyle)

Dorothy and the children, Deborah and Michael, in 1951. (courtesy of Deborah
Sturges Wyle)

Playing Hemingway, with Dorothy in Mazatlan, Mexico, in 1955. (courtesy of Deborah Sturges Wyle)

7

A Walk in the Sun

Flash forward. Late summer, 1968. Following the release of *The Hallelujah Trail*, John Sturges went on a fishing trip to Lake Tahoe with his seventeen-year-old son, Michael. The director—now divorced and, in the eyes of some, "on the ropes" professionally—wanted to take stock and reconnect with his children. To this end, he chose the scenic route out of Los Angeles—Highway 395 toward Bishop. He was at the wheel of his white Porsche, pushing it well over the speed limit but still cautious. He was wearing a red windbreaker, aviator glasses, and racing gloves (affectations lifted from McQueen). His eyes seldom left the road. He wasn't a great talker who would point out landmarks or old movie locations, Michael remembered, but there was a bond there, and every so often a comment would pass between the two, or Sturges would have his son grab the wheel as he flipped open his Zippo and lit another Camel.

"There'd be cycles of talking," said Michael Sturges. "He'd ask me about school or whatever. Then silence for another half-hour. He was not one of those guys who dwelled on the past. 'This is where I did this. This is where I did that.' We could drive past a street corner where he shot something and he wouldn't even mention it. On this trip it was just father and son, hanging out."

Sixty miles from Bishop they passed through Lone Pine, and Sturges asked, "Would you like to see where we shot *Bad Day at Black Rock?*"

Michael, who had seldom heard his father reminisce about anything—the war or the early studio years—leapt at the opportunity. "You bet, Dad."

They drove north toward the Alabama Hills and Mt. Whitney, which, to young eyes, never seemed to arrive. About a mile from town, they turned east onto Narrow Gauge Road, past an abandoned depot. The asphalt became white gravel. "We drove forever. He knew where he wanted to go, but how to get there was a little problematic. We went down a lot of what must have been agricultural roads." They came to a wire fence and a gate marked Department of Water and Power. Michael got out and unlatched it, and his father drove through. They kept to the river and soon crossed what had once been a raised grade.

"This is where Tracy got off the train," Sturges said, rolling to a stop.

The façade town was long gone. So, too, were the tracks, torn up by Southern Pacific in 1961. It was scrub country, dry and desolate. All you could see was the barest of outlines for Main Street and where the jail, hotel, and gas station had stood. Only a few charred two-by-fours and scraps of tin and burlap marked the spot. But that was enough.

Sturges talked his son through the plot. "This is where Spence walked into the hotel. . . . This is where Borgnine got into a fight with Tracy and got all gummed up in the screen door."

"He described all these things," recalled Michael, who briefly followed in his father's footsteps as an assistant director before becoming a software systems engineer. "He talked about the problem of using the anamorphic Panavision lens and not making it look like the cast was artificially raked out to fill up the screen. He laid out the geometry of the set and explained how the story always moved further into the town. You were always looking at what you would see next—the hotel, the gas station, the hills. There wasn't anything there, but he saw it all clearly."

Appropriately, the town of Black Rock blossomed, mean and ugly, out of postwar paranoia. Actor-writer Don McGuire, who later directed Jerry Lewis in *The Delicate Delinquent,* found the original story, "Bad Time at Honda," in a 1946 issue of *American Magazine.* Written by Michael Niall (a pseudonym for Howard Breslin), it dealt tangentially with something Hollywood had yet to tackle: the mistreatment of Japanese Americans during World War II. McGuire optioned the story for

$25,000 and banged out a script. Don Siegel read it at Allied Artists and enticed Joel McCrea out of retirement to play the lead. Unfortunately, the front office didn't share his enthusiasm. In 1953, McGuire went to Dore Schary, who, after *The Boy with Green Hair* and *Crossfire*, had a reputation as "a message guy." Schary had taken a stand against internment camps during the war. Here was a chance to combine exposé and lean, one-against-many yarn in the tradition of *Shane* and *High Noon*.

"Schary saw it as a great opportunity to make this thing public," said Millard Kaufman, who would inherit the project as screenwriter. "He liked the idea of dealing with the persecution of Japanese Americans in the so-called Wild West, that stronghold of democracy where the deer and antelope play."

The source story by Breslin is hardly more than a vignette. It unfolds in and around the southwestern town of the title, where the "glaring sunshine has baked everything, thoroughly, into one color—sepia. Even the dust that swirls up as the Streamliner passes is the same thinned-out, tired brown." Peter Macreedy, in rumpled black suit, steps off the train that usually blows by Honda. He's a former Chicago cop, "a big man, bulky." The townspeople are immediately suspicious. "He ain't no salesman, that's sure," says Doc Velie. Macreedy, accompanied by a pretty garage owner named Liz, drives out to Adobe Wells, where he finds the charred remains of a house that had belonged to a Japanese American farmer named Kamotak. A shot rings out from the rocks; Macreedy pulls a revolver. Kamotak, we learn, is the father of a young soldier who died after saving Macreedy's life. Macreedy promised to visit the boy's father, but the locals boast they ran off the "old Jap squatter."

Trimble, the voice of the mob in the short story, explains: "Other places settled it other ways. Camps. Things like that. We only had the one. We ran him out. Burned him out. That's all." There's obviously more. Kamotak, Macreedy learns from Liz's ex-boyfriend, died from a heart attack the night his place was torched. Disgusted, the ex-cop confronts the conspirators in the town saloon with the truth about Kamotak and his war-hero son, who died for their freedom. "Macreedy looked the crowd over with his calm gaze. Then he spoke, and the word crackled like an insult: 'Honda!'" He then walks to the station and boards the Streamliner for home.

Charles Schnee was assigned to the project as producer; Richard Brooks, a former marine who had written the novel *The Brick Foxhole*, replaced the originally announced George Sidney as director. Brooks was on a roll with the Oscar-nominated *Take the High Ground!* (1953) and a couple of successful Humphrey Bogart pictures. He had a reputation for tough issue films. (Schary also discussed the project with Vincente Minnelli.) And since Metro had Spencer Tracy in a "pay or play" contract and was desperate to get him back before the cameras, why not make Macreedy older and proffer the role to the two-time Oscar winner?

Schary rejected McGuire's formulaic script—called "Bad Day at Honda"—out of hand. (After a contentious negotiation, McGuire would receive an "adaptation" credit.) Schary wanted Kaufman, another ex-marine, who, he said, was "a combination of toughness and hard intellectuality." Kaufman had teamed with Brooks on *Take the High Ground!* and earned an Oscar nomination. Kaufman found Breslin's story "pat and flat," but agreed it might be the basis for something more provocative.

"Nothing is ever solved in the original story," Kaufman said. "This guy—tough, moss on his teeth—arrives, confronts the town in the bar, and then storms out, takes the train to Never-Never Land, where he came from. We changed everything except the basic idea of the Nisei farmer."

For starters, the hero's former profession was changed. The retired cop angle had been milked by Dick Powell and others. "Because every writer is the hero of his own plot," Kaufman, a marine platoon leader in the South Pacific, made Macreedy a platoon leader in Italy. Now, however, he was from Los Angeles, not Chicago. Then there was the problem of the McGuire title. "Bad Day at Honda" sounded too much like *Hondo*, the Warner Bros. 3-D Western with John Wayne. The year remained unchanged—1945, two months after V-J Day.

Kaufman, inspired by Zinnemann's *High Noon*, adhered to the Aristotelean unities and—instead of the two days covered by the Breslin story—compressed the action to "a period not to exceed 24 hours." Sturges, also a fan of *High Noon*, took this a step further: He borrowed the Western's clock conceit. The script began with John J. Macreedy stepping off the Streamliner at a railroad station described as "abandoned, in an extreme state of dilapidation." The setting—"a wasteland of the American Southwest, a gigantic bruise from which heat waves like bloodshot arteries spread themselves over the poisoned sky"—was clearly meant as a break from the pastoral clichés of the traditional studio "oater."

The town as memorably described in Kaufman's script:

> Minute and forgotten, crouching in isolation where the single line of railroad track intersects a secondary dirt road. The twin strips of steel glisten in the fierce sunlight, fencing the dreary plain from the false fronts of the town. In b.g. is the bluff of a black stony mountain. . . . The town and the terrain surrounding it have, if nothing else, the quality of inertia and immutability—nothing moves, not even an insect; nothing breathes, not even the wind. Town and terrain seem to be trapped, caught and held forever in the sullen, abrasive Earth.

Macreedy was given a new mission: to deliver the fallen comrade's medal to his father. Trimble was demoted to a town thug and replaced as head conspirator by Reno Smith, another rancher. Kamotak became Komako, and then Komoko. Liz and Hastings, the "spineless" station agent, remained basically unchanged, while Doc Velie, the mortician-veterinarian, was promoted to the story's sardonic conscience. The town's name—already changed from Honda to Parma—came to Kaufman during a road trip with Arthur Lowe Jr., scouting Arizona locations for a B Western. "We stopped for gas at one of those way stations the Russians used to call 'populated places.' It had a post office and a gas station and a place where you could buy a Milky Way. It was called Black Rock, and I called it in to Dore, who liked it."

It was settled, then. The new title was *Bad Day at Black Rock,* which, besides entering the lexicon as shorthand for worst-case scenario, would be an apt description of the production snafus to come.

As important to the production as a star was the gleaming red-and-silver passenger train that would deposit Macreedy in the god-forsaken town. Consequently, whatever location was selected had to connect by rail to Los Angeles. Lone Pine, wedged between the Sierra Nevadas and Mt. Whitney and the backdrop for *Gunga Din* and *Lives of the Bengal Lancers,* had a stretch of unused track, and Southern Pacific said it could get a train there for $5,500, plus the price of 265 round-trip tickets. The train would have to run backward, however, because some of the trestle bridges were in disrepair and needed to be tested. Seven miles north of Lone Pine—but never mentioned or visited by the cast—was Manzanar Relocation Camp, where ten thousand Japanese Americans had been interned in 1941-45.

"We shot [for 21 days] near Lone Pine, back of Mt. Whitney," said Sturges. "That's the oldest movie location in the world. Goes back to 1914. Tom Mix, Hoot Gibson, William S. Hart—all those old silent Western guys used to go up there. Running the train backwards, light cars over the bridge first, it took them 18 hours to get the train up there."

Production was scheduled to start in late June 1954, and wrap in July, thereby avoiding the most oppressive heat. In August, Lone Pine's temperature jumps from 105 to around 115 degrees. It's the worst month—ungodly hot and, because of "monsoonal flows" from Mexico, humid and oppressive.

Though dismissed as "just another Western" by the studio, *Black Rock* was budgeted at a healthy $1.3 million and would be shot by William C. Mellor in Eastman Color. Following Fox's lead on *The Robe* (1953), the studio commissioned two answer prints: one in standard 35mm (1.37:1 aspect ratio) and one in the new anamorphic CinemaScope process (2.35:1). This was done, Sturges later groused, to appease the "anti-CinemaScope group" who saw the wider screen as a fad, like 3-D. As in *Executive Suite*, ambient sounds (klaxon, clock chimes, prairie wind) would sub for conventional background music and underscore how utterly alone the hero is.

"Next, I decided not to have any music. Only sounds," Schary wrote in his autobiography, *Heyday*. "First the quiet of the speck of a station in the heart of desolation. A wind blowing, a yowl of a coyote, the far-off-horn of a diesel engine, then the roar of the train. The music department hated me." MGM president Nicholas Schenck, already fuming over Schary's endorsement of Adlai Stevenson for president and his leftist politics in general, ordered Schary to cease pre-production. Schary's response: "I refused to take the picture off the schedule and told Schenck he could fire me or I would quit if he went over my head and ordered the studio not to do the picture." (How reliable Schary was on the subject is debatable. He called *Black Rock* an "original story" by Maguire and misspelled the main character's name.)

"To my knowledge there was no resistance to the film being made," said Sturges later. "Most people by that time sort of recognized the snap judgment of interning the Japanese Americans was wrong and done without justification: there were no known examples of spying or sabotage."

Then Tracy backed out. He wasn't feeling well, he said, and didn't want anything to do with an arduous, uncomfortable location shoot. Besides, who would buy him as a platoon leader? Platoon leaders just out of the service were in their twenties. He was more than twice that age. "Not knowing about the pay-or-play clause, I would have hesitated to put Spence in that part," said Kaufman. "He was an older man—kind of pot-bellied, arthritic, tired. Christ Almighty, when I was a platoon leader I was twenty-five years old, and I would have been too old for the role."

They had to make Macreedy more appealing. Maybe by adding an intriguing backstory or some distinguishing characteristic that would appeal to the ham in every actor. "What would happen if he had a para-lyzed arm or something like that?" Schary asked Kaufman during an all-night story session. "Jesus, it can't hurt—why not?" Kaufman replied.

Tracy liked the idea of the one-armed paladin who rides into town and, his voice no more than a whisper, demands justice for a war hero and his father. His answer, however, was still no. Why not, then, cast the original Shane—Alan Ladd? Schary put in a call to Ladd's office and was told the actor was in Europe and had left instructions he was not to be bothered "under any circumstances." Unfazed, Schary sent Tracy the revised script, adding nonchalantly, "Thought you might like to read it, but don't worry—we have Alan Ladd."

The ruse worked. Tracy phoned back, "Get rid of Ladd—I'll do the picture."

Now it was Brooks's turn to throw a wrench in the works. Still smarting over the Academy's recognition of Kaufman for *Take the High Ground!*, the director laid down the law during their first story confer-ence. Like John Huston, with whom he had worked on *Key Largo*, he would participate in the writing and, therefore, expect co-screenplay credit. "Sure," said Kaufman, "if you contribute half the screenplay, of course you get credit." Brooks then did something Kaufman would never forget. He picked up the phone, dialed Tracy's home, and began to denigrate the project.

"Look, this is a piece of shit, but Millard and I are trying to do something with it," Brooks told Tracy. "So don't expect anything."

Kaufman couldn't believe his ears. "What the hell are you doing?" he screamed as Brooks hung up the phone. "We're trying to get this guy to play the part!"

Before Brooks could answer, the phone rang. It was Schary. "You two, get your asses up here!" Tracy had called Schary and demanded, "What are you giving me here, Dore? The director says it's a piece of shit."

Schary, joined by Schnee and associate producer Herman Hoffman, wanted an explanation. Schnee, who barely came up to Brooks's shoulders, went further. "He challenged Brooks to a fistfight in Dore's office," recalled Kaufman. "'*Step outside!*' he shouted. That kind of nonsense."

Schnee quit on the spot, and Schary stepped in as producer. His first order of business: replace Brooks, who really wanted to make *Blackboard Jungle* anyway, with Sturges, whom Tracy knew and trusted. Given all that had transpired, it was not surprising that the trade press wrote off the picture as "hopelessly stalled." Kaufman was determined to prove them wrong. "I wrote the damn thing in three weeks because I thought it would never be made," he said. "Not because of its political content, which I thought was negligible, but simply because it had this history of fights and giving bad luck a workout."

Kaufman was not sorry about Brooks's departure. "I disliked Brooks intensely from the moment I met him," he said. "He was constantly and brilliantly kissing Dore's ass. And then when Dore was fired (by Metro), Brooks was afraid to talk to him or be seen with him." Sturges, on the other hand, was a standup guy, said Kaufman, who added, "He had that kind of sociality that was lacking in so many who were protecting their rears in the business."

Less admirable was Sturges's tendency during pre-production to tune out those closest to him. He was able to "completely disassociate" himself from family when working, said daughter Deborah. "You could sit down with him at dinnertime, and it was like he wasn't there. . . . His ability to focus was scary." On *Black Rock*, he wouldn't let Kaufman out of his sight. He even took the screenwriter shopping with him. "He walked into my office, introduced himself and said, 'Why don't you take the afternoon off and come with me. I want to buy a pair of khaki pants.' So we went to Beverly Hills and shopped for those khakis he favored. That way we could talk about the picture from the time we left my office until we got back."

Sturges credited the Brooks-Schary-Schnee team with coming up with the paralyzed-arm idea and changing Macreedy from an ex-cop to an ex-G.I. on a peacetime mission. His contributions were the Spartan performances and the multi-planed widescreen compositions. He had little patience, he said, for the behind-the-scenes jockeying. "They spent more money not making that picture than I spent making it. After Brooks left, Spence said he'd do it if I did it. I told Schary, 'I'll do it if you leave me alone.' You can do anything if they leave you alone."

Most of the cast was in place before Sturges came onboard. Robert Ryan, the former Dartmouth boxer who was so memorable in RKO's *The Set-Up*, was cast as chief heavy Reno Smith; newly signed contract players Anne Francis and John Ericson were announced as Liz Brooks, the femme fatale in dungarees, and Pete, her weak-kneed brother. Oscar-winners Walter Brennan and Dean Jagger were cast, respectively, as Black Rock's cagey, philosophical Doc and the rummy sheriff. Going by the rule your hero is only as strong as your villain—or in this instance, villains—MGM announced two of the meanest-looking character actors in the business as Reno's henchmen: Ernest Borgnine, "Fatso" in *From Here to Eternity*, was cast as the vicious, child-like Coley, "a gross behemoth of a man," and Lee Marvin, the coffee-hurling thug in *The Big Heat*, was cast as the rangy, calculating Hector, distinguished by his "insolent gaze."

The shooting script called for "loafers" or incidental onlookers. Before the fight between Macreedy and Coley at Sam's Sanitary Bar & Grill, four men seated at the bar—Krool, Murtry, Bentham, and Lenard—agree that they want nothing to do with whatever is in store for the stranger. A boy called T.J. (Mickey Little) also had a few lines outside the garage. Both sequences were shot, but as Sturges worked out the logistics and blocking, the microcosm that was Lone Pine became fixed. His mantra: "No people. Cast only."

Recalled Sturges: "A poor assistant put some lady in the background hanging out her wash. I said, 'Get rid of her.' Then he had somebody drive by. 'Get rid of him.' Nobody is ever seen arriving or leaving town, except a clump of cops at the very end. There's almost nobody there except the principals. Few extras. It's the most unrealistic staging ever. It's like a Greek tragedy: theatrically true but realistically false. I sometimes wonder how I pulled that off."

Breslin must have had Lone Pine in mind when he described the "dry, breathless furnace heat" of Honda. The town's exact location is never given in the movie, but Kaufman placed it in the desert, 156 miles from Phoenix and 211 miles from Los Angeles. Close enough. Lone Pine is 220 miles northeast of L.A. and a Hades on Earth in late summer. The cast and crew caravanned in limos, buses, and "monster" panel trucks so weighted down with lights, sound equipment, and cable that there was always the danger of becoming mired in sand. They bivouacked at Lone Pine's Dow Hotel. Area residents—some of whom were old hands at movie work and already members of the Screen Extras Guild—were retained as needed for "walk-bys." Five miles away, the studio bulldozed a dirt road across the tracks and erected a seven-structure façade town.

Tracy—who had no intention of "sweating [his] balls off"—backed out of the production a second time the Friday before shooting was to commence. The threat of a lawsuit and stiff fine—he would have to make good on the $480,000 already spent on cast and sets—had the intended effect. To save face, Tracy decreed that instead of the six-day workweek SAG allowed on location, they would have to make do with five in his case.

Finally, in late July, the man in black detrained and sauntered down the world's least hospitable street. The month-long delay had meant a ten- to fifteen-degree jump in temperature. By midday the thermometer read 125—ten degrees hotter with the brute lights needed for Technicolor. Sturges's assistant had a ready supply of salt tablets. He also laced the water with dry oatmeal, a supposed cure for dehydration. "Boy, that was a hot one, I mean really hot—a scorcher all the way!" said Borgnine, exhaling loudly. "But it worked in a way. We looked irritable and about to pass out. And that's the look John wanted."

The fifty-four-year-old Tracy, whose blood pressure was already alarmingly high, especially minded the heat and altitude. "He obviously wasn't feeling well; he seemed nauseous some of the time," recalled Anne Francis. "You have to remember he was also on the wagon at the time, and that would have added to his irritability."

Sturges likened Tracy to Moses in the wilderness. "He would go out in the desert by himself and read the whole script aloud. He'd do this two or three times, he told me, until he understood what the picture was about."

During the second garage sequence between Tracy and Ryan, Sturges called for a second take. Tracy turned to the crew. "How was that for you? Did you understand me?" The crew, taken aback, shook their heads yes. "That's it, then," Tracy said. "I don't want to do another take."

"As good as he was in the film, Tracy was the only one on the set who didn't give John full cooperation," confirmed Freeman. "He'd say, 'I don't want to do another take,' or — because he was getting old — 'Don't do close-ups.'"

As he had on *The People against O'Hara*, Sturges made accommodations. "With Spence," he said, "you could print his first rehearsal."

The heat left the cast so exhausted there was little energy left for hell-raising. In Borgnine's words, "It was too damn hot to party." Still, Tracy invited everybody to his hotel room for the cocktail hour and, as studio receipts vouch, much scotch and bourbon was consumed. "Spence," recalled Francis, "wanted everybody to come in and have drinks at his place — while he drank his 7-Up." As was his custom, Sturges would have a Tom Collins or a gin and grapefruit juice as he reviewed the next day's setups with Mellor and Freeman. "I have wonderful memories of those sessions," said Freeman. "John was always prepared — unlike Peckinpah and others."

With this mix of seasoned actors (three of whom could lay claim to six Oscars) and Young Turks, is it any wonder there was tension on and off the set? Tracy and Brennan, political opposites, sparred throughout. During one cocktail hour, Brennan, an archconservative, made the mistake of segueing from Tracy's liberal leanings to Katharine Hepburn's very public outbursts against the McCarthy hearings.

"He said that Katie didn't have 'good judgment' or common sense, and that topped it for Tracy—he went icy cold," said Francis.

The next day, as Sturges blocked out the all-important meeting on the tracks, the two actors—allies in the movie—weren't speaking. Tracy said to Sturges, "Would you ask Mr. Brennan to not get in my key light?" Brennan replied, "Tell Mr. Tracy if he hit his mark, I wouldn't be in his key light."

Later, Brennan got his revenge. As he passed Tracy running lines with Ryan, he whistled and held up three fingers, code for: "I've got three Oscars, you've got two." Brennan "loved to see him scorched," said Sturges.

Francis remembered Tracy as a moody "taskmaster" who would give you the cold shoulder for days if he felt you did not pay him the proper respect. One night, Francis and Ryan borrowed Tracy's car and went for hamburgers. The next morning he complained that the car was parked crooked. "He would flare up about little things, and I got the silent treatment because he felt Bob and I were having an affair, which we weren't."

Later that day, Francis and Tracy shot the scene where Liz, pretending to be on Macreedy's side, drives him to the Adobe Flat. She gunned the accelerator, took a rise at full speed, and almost dumped Tracy, who had to keep his left hand in his pocket at all times. "When I took off, I really took off. By the time we were done with that scene, he was talking to me again."

The most complex action sequences in the Alabama Hills were shot first. The car chase, where bumpers scrape at full speed, was inspired by Sturges's college story about almost being pushed over the edge of a mountain by a drunk driver. The movie version, including the plunge into the ravine, took two days; stunt driver Cary Lofton doubled for Borgnine, Roger Creed stood in for Tracy. The nighttime ambush of Liz and Macreedy—which ends with Reno's immolation by Molotov cocktail—took a day and a half.

The night before, Sturges shook his head. "I know what we're doing tomorrow, but I'm not sure how it will work. Anybody got any ideas?" Freeman, who had been a driver in the Air Force, pointed to the tap cock under the jeep. "If Macreedy gets under the jeep, he can get gasoline and still be protected," he said. Sturges liked the idea and used it. "I was his assistant, but after four films we were also friends. And for him, picture-making was always a collaborative effort."

The sequence, photographed night-for-night with every available light, utilized squibs and explosive caps to ignite Reno's stunt double, who was smeared with petroleum jelly and protected by asbestos suit and gloves. The stuntman made the mistake of inhaling and scorched his lungs.

"Get me! Get me! Come and get me!" he screamed.

"It was pretty scary," said Francis. "They extinguished the fire and drove him to the hospital. His arms, chest, and part of his neck and face had received third-degree burns. Nothing that scarred. He was around the next day, but obviously in pain. I think he was more frightened about being suffocated."

As scripted, Macreedy returns to town in the jeep. Liz's body is under a tarp on the backseat; Reno, his shirt scorched, is tied to the front fender. It was an attempt at black humor: Reno the hunter, introduced with a deer lashed to his fender, has been "bagged." Sturges shot the scene, looked at it, and decided it was "too self-conscious."

The company returned to the studio in early August for interiors of the jail, hotel lobby, switchboard office, and Doc's office. The show-down between Macreedy and Coley—a brutal forerunner of fights in *Billy Jack* (1971) and *Witness* (1985)—was staged by Johnny Indrisano, who had worked on *Right Cross*. To accommodate the CinemaScope lens, Sturges shot the sequence in full frame with a minimum of cuts and reverse angles. Tracy delivered the terse dialogue but refused to do his own fight choreography. "When Spence plays a scene it's happening," Sturges explained. "Twice he meant to miss a guy and hit him—broke one guy's jaw, knocked another guy's teeth out. He was so contrite. He came to me and said, 'Believe me, I can't do it, I feel these things. I'll hit him for real.'" So Lofton doubled for Tracy, and Ted Pavelic, a former boxer, stood in for Borgnine. (Later, Sturges would complain that Tracy's double was "not very good.")

In the cathartic, crowd-pleasing sequence—52 minutes into a lean 81-minute film—Macreedy comes in, sits down at the counter, and orders a bowl of chili. Hector and three others are seated at tables. "Buy Bonds!" and Army recruitment posters line the walls, mocking this town's cowardice. Reno and Coley enter, and Coley, chewing on a tooth-pick, attempts to provoke Macreedy.

Macreedy's reply: "No comment."

"No comment and all the time he's got my stool," snarls Coley as Macreedy moves down two places.

Coley moves with him and then douses his chili with half a bottle of ketchup.

"Your friend's a very argumentative fellow," Macreedy tells Reno.

"Sort of unpredictable, too. Got a temper like a rattlesnake."

"That's me all over—half horse, half alligator. You mess with me, and I'll kick a lung outta you."

Still unable to goad the laconic stranger into a fight, Coley goes for the jugular.

"You're a yellow-bellied Jap lover. Am I right or wrong?"

"You're not only wrong, you're wrong at the top of your voice."

As Macreedy stands to leave, Coley also stands, unstraps his wrist-watch (a bit of business that originally belonged to Hector), and grabs the stranger's useless arm. Macreedy chops him in the neck. Coley gasps and falls against the wall as Reno and Hector look on in disbelief. As scripted, Macreedy "brings the heel of his hand hard against and slightly under the tip of Coley's nose. The cartilage shatters. Blood spills down his face. . . . Coley shuts his eyes and falls unconscious." End of fight.

The Production Office and Catholic Church's Legion of Decency would never countenance such violence. Therefore, Sturges gave Coley a slight nose bleed and had him revive long enough to rush Macreedy, who delivers chops to the stomach and neck that send Coley staggering through the screen door and onto the (soundstage) road. The sequence, like many others, was done in one take. Borgnine's befuddlement is genuine: He expected the door to swing open. Instead, his momentum tears it from its hinges, and he ends up wearing it like a picture frame.

Brennan, standing just off camera awaiting his entrance, gave Borgnine a thumbs up. Man, he thought, did that ever look realistic. Borgnine in a fury extracted himself from what was left of the door.

"What happened to that damn door?!" he demanded.

"Don't you know?" Sturges replied. "I nailed it shut."

Shaking his head, Borgnine could only flash a gap-toothed smile. "I should chase you all over hill and dell, you rascal," he said, realizing he'd been conned, good and proper. "Borgnine has never forgiven me for that," Sturges laughed. "He hadn't planned on going right through the door, and I knew it couldn't hurt him."

Sturges's explanation for why the fight held up over the years: "You care who wins or loses. That's the formula behind every successful fight scene. You can have guys forty stories up, fighting on a six-inch ledge, and if you don't care who wins or loses, it's not much of a fight. The thing that makes that a great fight is the five minutes of needling that Tracy endures before he hits Borgnine. We went right up to the point where the audience, in disgust, is about to say, 'Oh, for Christ's sake!'"

When Tracy saw the fight in rushes, he thought it preposterous. "How could an old guy make such short work of a gorilla like Borgnine?" he said. Sturges explained that the character's karate skills gave him an edge. Tracy didn't buy it. So they showed the footage to a Marine drill instructor from San Diego. "The way you executed that chop to the larynx, the guy would be dead," he assured Tracy.

"Tracy is great in that scene," enthused the director. "Up until he hits Borgnine, he's polite, apologizes for things. He's purely reactive. I learned that from George Stevens's *Giant*. James Dean didn't do anything but react to all the things that are done to him. *Shane,* too. Ladd doesn't do anything until the end of the picture when he's forced to return. . . . Spence knew all this. That's why he was such a good actor."

Black Rock wrapped at the studio in late August. The final sequence was the opening exchange between Macreedy and the train conductor, who, staring at the good citizens of Black Rock, says, "Man, they look woebegone and far away."

Sturges felt good about the shoot—the second of what would become five in Lone Pine. He gave full credit to screenwriter Kaufman. He had made so many flawed films at Columbia and Metro, he was beginning to doubt that he would ever see the perfect script. "If you've got a script, making a picture is really fun. *Black Rock*—best script I ever had. It was a walk in the sun." In the laserdisc commentary, he added: "With *Bad Day at Black Rock* I never doubted it would be a good film. I always knew it would play. . . . Spence [was] so hep. I don't think I ever told Spence how to play a scene. . . . I had less to do with this script than any other script. We had 85,000 feet of negative. Only a handful was Take 2. Scene after scene was Take 1."

Kaufman returned the compliment. "John had a lot of good ideas. For example, whenever Spencer faces this horde of villainy, John set the camera so that one or another of them is always above Tracy, looking down. That happens on the porch of the dilapidated hotel—Borgnine and Marvin are above Tracy, looking down. In what is probably the most interesting scene in the picture, when Ryan confronts Spence in front of the garage, Bob is standing beside a gas pump and Spence is sitting down. There was stuff like that throughout the script that John saw that I never wrote into the script."

This included the layered reflections in the hotel window and the gathering of conspirators on the tracks. In the script, these moments are all but thrown away ("Doc looks out the window," etc.), but as staged they represent a startling validation of the new widescreen process.

Sturges, typically, waved off these compositions as serendipitous, improvised on the spot. "One of the best things you can learn, George Stevens taught me. He said, 'Always have a backup location, don't commit. Stage according to what you see.' I see some guys inside the hotel reading newspapers, I see my own reflection. And then Brennan walks out on the porch as Spence walks by. You have three levels. It's not in the script, it's just there. All you had to do is photograph it. That's why I never used storyboards, like Hitchcock. You do that, you're committed to a shot." (He did, however, rough out actor and camera placements and, in his script, diagram the meeting between Reno and the others at the railroad crossing.)

Fighting an ulcer but still very involved, Schary looked over Sturges's shoulder in the editing room. "The film, as I cut the first rough version, discussing it each day with John Sturges, came to exciting life," he said, conveniently forgetting Sturges was a former editor.

Bad Day at Black Rock received three preview screenings—two in October, one in December. The fall screenings were held at the Picwood in West L.A. and, two days later, the Encino Theatre in Encino. The film was initially previewed without music or aerial opening. It began with Tracy stepping off the Streamliner and, accompanied only by the sound of the wind, walking down Main Street. There was also a cutaway to the depot clock à la *High Noon*. Many in the audience at the first preview found the opening too abrupt. A full quarter of those in attendance said they would not recommend the film to a friend. (This figure increased to 30 percent when just women were considered.) Tracy and Borgnine received the most favorable comment; Francis received the most "fair" and "poor" ratings. Predictably, more males than females rated the ensemble cast "outstanding" or "excellent." To the question "Which scene did you like most," many answered "café fight." Among the suggestions were calls to speed up the "draggy" pacing, change the title, and add a conventional score.

A sampling of comments: "Tracy too old to have returned from war." "The death of just one man seemed poor excuse for the picture as a whole." "If you're trying to start a new fad with no music, don't." "The absence of a musical score heightened the realism, but the sound of the wind and the rattling of doors and loose boards, etc., etc., don't have to be deafening. . . . That wind hardly stirred up dust, but it was as loud as the hurricane in 'Caine Mutiny.'"

Schary recalled, "We died for the first ten minutes because the picture fought like the devil to capture the audience, who were, because of the opening silence, puzzled as to what kind of film they were watching. Once they found out, the picture moved, but then faded out again without music."

The Encino screening, which targeted an older demographic, fared better. Over a third of the 225 in attendance rated the film "Excellent," and a majority of these viewers said they would recommend it. Again, there were calls for a better title and complaints about the glacial pace and lack of background music. Only one viewer seemed to pick up on the film's anti-racism message, observing, "The Japanese who fought for us have need of a champion." To Sturges's relief, a couple of viewers understood what he was after, calling the film "*High Noon* with grenades," and "Tense, realistic and hot!" His frustration over having "just missed" with a different kind of action picture was echoed by a viewer who wrote, "Seems like an adult, offbeat drama. . . . Can't make up my mind if I really liked the picture or not."

Obviously revisions were in order.

"We went to Chasen's to get a drink and read the exit cards," recalled Kaufman. "They were terrible. All about how slow the picture was in getting started. Problem was the damn clock. It had nothing to do with the progression of the story. John—who had a marvelous eye but was not very good on story—loved *High Noon*. He wouldn't let it go."

It was associate producer Hoffman, Sturges freely acknowledged, who conceived and executed the new opening with the Streamliner tearing across the desert. Hoffman, a fan of Robert Parrish's *Cry Danger* (1951) and Fritz Lang's *Human Desire* (1954), knew how a cannonballing freight could galvanize an audience. At the second preview he approached Sturges. "You ought to start on that train going like a bat out of hell," he suggested. "The train is a character."

Sturges and Schary agreed. Because Sturges had moved on to the Revolutionary War adventure *The Scarlet Coat* (1955), Hoffman was dispatched with helicopter to Lone Pine. The idea was to shoot the train, 3D-like, hurtling into the audience. But how could a helicopter shadow a charging locomotive? The pilot would be pulled into the slipstream. Stunt flier Paul Mantz (killed on the original *The Flight of the Phoenix* in 1965) had a solution: Run the train backward and have the helicopter hover over the retreating engine; then move up and away, and fly the length of the train. Print the film backward, and the train would appear to be barreling toward the camera. "Movie tricks," said Sturges. "Of course you can't fly into a moving train. It's a helluva shot, but I didn't make it."

For the score, MGM's music supervisor Johnny Green suggested André Previn, who had started at the studio at age sixteen as an arranger. He was now twenty-four and something of a musical chameleon, having composed the scores for *Kim, Border Incident,* and *Kiss Me Kate*. For *Black Rock,* Schary wanted something that would grab the viewer and not let go—"something loud, throbbing and martial in undertone." Pantomiming a slide trombone, he added, "I want it to sound military. Lots of French horns." From this, Previn extrapolated "lots of brass instruments." Sturges approved. Unlike Schary, he never bought into the idea of the "creative sounds" score; he found it gimmicky—"any trick that will evoke emotion." Previn attended a studio screening and jotted down ideas for what he called "a vaguely dissonant and sinister score." Francis, also at the screening, saw Previn sitting in the dark, taking notes. "My God, by the end of the film he had the whole thing worked out, musically choreographed."

In early December, the new version of *Bad Day at Black Rock*—with train credits and hard-driving symphonic score—was previewed to a young, predominately male audience at the Egyptian Theatre in Hollywood. The changes seemed to work. Out of 168 viewers, only 13 said they wouldn't recommend the film. The men in attendance liked it more than the women. One woman quipped: "Terrific movie for men. Would play up in ads—'It's a man's movie.'" There were still complaints about the pacing, and now the music was "too loud" and "too modern." Also, one viewer found it odd that "throughout the whole picture there was no one in the town but the cast. At the end there were many other people to wave goodbye to him." Freeman chalked this up to a typically jaded Hollywood audience. "They think they're critics."

Two days later, the film was previewed at Lowe's 72nd Street Theatre in New York. Market Research reported: "Audience spellbound last night. Literally, the suspense was so terrific you could have heard a pin drop. . . . 92 percent will recommend as against an average for dramatic picture of 86 percent. . . . All very happy that the company has fine attraction to start off new year releases."

Predictably, the censors and Catholic Legion of Decency took exception to the karate fight and Molotov cocktail sequence, where Reno becomes a human torch. The Legion of Decency gave the film an A-II (adults and adolescents) classification. Studio executive Robert Vogel used the positive preview response to the café fight and "burning of Robert Ryan" to undercut the censors, who, he said, had trouble with the "alleged excessive brutality in this picture." W. D. Kelly in Metro's home office talked to the New York Censor Board about the violence and reported, "Every censor group in the United States approved of this picture, including the various church groups of the various denominations, and I have just been advised by the Director, that they will give us the seal, but they are going to write us a letter cautioning us to be careful on certain types of violence, as evidently there are many pictures coming through from Europe that are combining violence with sex."

The café fight remained a sticking point. Macreedy's karate blows looked lethal. What if young people emulated the character and were injured? Kelly countered this with a report on the sport's growing popularity. Even America's most popular TV host, Arthur Godfrey, had had a demonstration on his morning show.

"There are judo instruction places all through Los Angeles," said Kelly in an interoffice memo. "It is of course taught in all branches of the armed service, and what is shown in *Bad Day at Black Rock* is elemental judo. . . . The opening wallop on the neck is really no different than a blow by the fist to the Adam's apple." Exasperated, Kelly concluded, "I do not understand why the censor board in New York can be opposing this struggle for the right by an unarmed man against a monster like Coley."

By year's end, the film had cleared its final hurdle, the notoriously unyielding Australian censors. They passed it without a cut. Schary forwarded the news to Sturges and Kaufman. "Dear Fellas: Cut yourselves a piece of cake and enjoy it with me."

Bad Day at Black Rock opened in early February 1955—first in Manhattan, then Los Angeles. The ads declared it a "Masterpiece of Suspense" and splashed the CinemaScope logo. The critics drew the encouraged *Shane* and *High Noon* comparisons and applauded Sturges's taut, economical direction and creative use of the new widescreen process. *Newsweek* adjudged it "that rare but rewarding thing, an 'intelligent' Western," adding: "With CinemaScope and Eastman Color [Sturges] makes Black Rock by turns ugly and attractive, and, at each turn, quite out of any civilized world. His drama is cool as a knife blade." The *New York Times*'s Crowther, true to form, was less effusive. He liked Sturges's "patient, methodical pacing" but found the premise implausible. "Why these small-time tyrants . . . should assume it necessary to murder the stranger . . . is a point that the script never makes reasonable." The blazing sun, however, left an impression. The cinematography, Crowther conceded, captured "the gritty, dry-hot feeling of a rough-plank desert town, lying bare beneath the sun and a mountain backdrop." Novelist John O'Hara, writing for *Collier's*, didn't mince superlatives. He called *Black Rock* "one of the finest motion pictures ever made."

In March, the film crossed the Atlantic. Again, the reviews were exemplary, praising Tracy's laconic turn and Sturges's dynamic depiction of a "primitive community under the spell of guilt and fear" (*London Times*). In late April, *Black Rock* and *East of Eden,* also in CinemaScope, became the official American selections at the Cannes Film Festival. *Black Rock* drew "enthusiastic applause," reported Metro's European publicist. "Five hundred newspapermen gathered from all European countries unanimously considered 'Bad Day' as one of the great American pictures in years and a tremendous step forward in CinemaScope technique."

More kudos at year's end. The National Board of Review named *Black Rock* one of the ten best pictures of 1955. Crowther, who had dragged his feet on the first go-round, took a second look and decided it was one of the best of a "not tremendous" year, along with *Marty* (also with Borgnine), *Mister Roberts,* and *Oklahoma!,* the first CinemaScope musical. (*East of Eden* and *Blackboard Jungle* were among Crowther's "second ten.")

While some agreed with Tracy that he was too old to be a recent platoon leader, author Breslin diplomatically applauded his casting. A week after the opening, Breslin—who as Michael Niall would novelize Kaufman's screenplay—wrote Schary that he had seen the film in New York and enjoyed it immensely. "It was particularly pleasant to see my imaginary town, characters and situation brought to life on the screen with taste, tautness, and rare skill. Mr. Tracy, strangely enough, I had mentally cast as Macreedy while the yarn was still in my typewriter, and his terrific performance was a writer's dream come true."

All the plaudits, however, did not help the box office, which Sturges described as "so-so. . . . It was not a huge financial success." After twenty-five weeks in release in the United States and Canada, it had posted $1.2 million in ticket sales in three thousand theaters and still had not broken even. A year later it had earned $1.9 million, less than Metro's *The Prodigal* and *Love Me or Leave Me.* The new social-problem films, such as *On the Waterfront, Blackboard Jungle,* and, from France, *The Wages of Fear,* were popular with the emerging art-house audience. *Black Rock* had the misfortune of occupying a middle ground. It was too pessimistic and allegorical for some, too glossy and old school for others. Just days before the opening, Schary announced a sequel that would reteam Tracy and Brennan and show "the restoration of morale" to the town. It was quietly dropped.

Writing ten years later in *I Lost It at the Movies,* Pauline Kael acknowledged the Sturges-Schary collaboration as the first Hollywood film to dramatize the government's mistreatment of Japanese Americans during the war. "Though *Bad Day at Black Rock* is crudely melodramatic," she wrote, "it is a very superior example of motion picture craftsmanship. John Sturges is an excellent director—each movement and line is exact and economical."

Spencer Tracy may have gotten the better of the bullying Borgnine in the diner, but Borgnine, who signed to play the lonely schlub in Paddy Chayefsky's *Marty* while on location, had the last laugh when the Academy Awards nominations were announced. *Marty* received eight—including those for best picture, best director (Delbert Mann), best screenwriter (Chayefsky), and best actor—to *Black Rock*'s three—for Tracy, Kaufman, and Sturges. (Brooks could also chortle: He drew nominations for directing and adapting *Blackboard Jungle*.) At the awards ceremony in March, *Marty* bested *Black Rock* across the board. "None of us won," laughed Kaufman. "Everything went to *Marty*."

A decade after the film's release, Kaufman was invited to Japan to receive an award for treating the Japanese with uncommon dignity. "The whole thing was absurd because there were no Japanese in the movie. But I knew what they meant."

Sturges found special satisfaction in *Bad Day at Black Rock*. Not because of its box office, but because of the understated performances and storytelling technique. It was that rare occasion, he said, when all the pieces slid into place. In time, it replaced *Shane* as the archetypal action film about a lone figure in an inhospitable setting whose combat skills are underestimated by conspirators—to their lasting regret. Akira Kurosawa's *Yojimbo* (1961) and Tom Laughlin's *Billy Jack* had similar heroes. So did Norman Jewison's *In the Heat of the Night* (1967), which turned the premise inside out. Like Macreedy, Sidney Poitier's Virgil Tibbs steps off a train in a southern town blinded by bigotry. In Peter Weir's *Witness*, another variation, Harrison Ford's outsider takes refuge in an Amish community and brings the violence with him.

"I can't remember them by name, but it's been used in a TV series at least four times and at least three pictures I know are essentially the same story," Sturges said. "It has a seminal kind of plotline. A stranger comes to town. Everybody acts mysteriously and hostile. He figures out gradually what's going on. You learn it as he does."

For Sturges, *Black Rock* was as important an experiment in classic Kuleshovian montage as Hitchcock's *Rear Window*. Film at its best is about reacting, not acting, he said. That's why Tracy was so powerful: he picked his words carefully and reacted to the mounting threat around him. "Spence played the reluctant hero, trying to avoid trouble."

The premise is so basic, Sturges added, that "you could update it," replacing World War II with Vietnam, Korea, or the Middle East. That thought has occurred to more than one producer. James T. Aubrey, former head of MGM, considered remaking *Black Rock* in the early 1990s, until Freeman, now a producer, talked him out of it. "Jim, you're crazy," he said. "It's a period piece and would be close to meaningless." In 2003, Ron Howard, like Spielberg a Sturges fan, said, "I just saw *Black Rock* for the first time a few months ago. Pretty cool. You could put it out today and it would work."

William Friedkin (*The French Connection*) agreed, adding, "I love everything about that film—the little guy in the black suit with his hand in his pocket, the aura of dread . . . the bar fight. That's probably the best bar fight ever. It's a thriller that's about something."

The debate over *Black Rock* being an allegory for the McCarthy witch hunts continues to this day and, if anything, has gained momentum in recent years. Sturges himself shot down the theory. Kaufman, who had been accused of being a communist sympathizer by the pamphlet "Red Channels," saw it as a latter-day *High Noon* and another chance to demonize HUAC. Recalling Macreedy's line "The rule of law has been suspended in this town—the gorillas have taken over," he inscribed a copy of the script: "So it was—so it seemed to me—in Hollywood during the McCarthy Captivity when this screenplay was written. It is dedicated to those men and women who inspired it, who courageously held their ground against the onslaught of the gorillas."

Kaufman did not place Richard Brooks in this heroic company. He firmly believed that Brooks, the nominal "tough idealist," attempted to sabotage *Black Rock* because he thought the story's political stance would come back to haunt him. This seems doubtful. *Blackboard Jungle*, according to Brooks, was condemned as "a lousy commie movie" because of its pioneering use of rock 'n' roll. The falling out probably had more to do with Schary's personal interest in the project. The producer would not have tolerated Brooks's admitted need to make "every screenplay mine."

"This picture will always be one of my favorites," wrote Schary in his leather-bound copy of the script. "The concept of the film was largely mine but Millard Kaufman wrote a terse and powerful script and John Sturges directed it with enormous skill."

While *Black Rock* was still in production, Sturges, the history buff, announced his next project would be a warts-and-all portrait of George Washington, based on the president's letters and diaries. Described as a "mammoth venture" developed by the director over the last five years, the biography in the end proved too ambitious and was replaced by *The Scarlet Coat*, a Revolutionary War swashbuckler that recounted "history's most treacherous plot": General Benedict Arnold's thwarted attempt to hand over West Point to the British. Produced by Nicholas Nayfack and budgeted at a mid-level $1.5 million, the eighteenth-century period adventure was shot in CinemaScope and Eastman Color and starred a mix of contract players and stage actors, including Cornel Wilde as Continental Army spy Major John Bolton; Michael Wilding as his willing dupe, British Major John Andre; George Sanders as a suspicious doctor; and Robert Douglas as the one-note turncoat, Arnold. Anne Francis, who described the film as "another of MGM's colorful costume epics," appeared as a Tory wench who plays both sides: she's betrothed to Andre but attracted to Bolton. She strolls in and out of the proceedings, registering as neither vixen nor victim.

Production began in late November at West Point, the Old Dutch Church in Sleepy Hollow, and Philipse Castle near Tarrytown, New York. Sturges boasted that the locations included "the exact spot where Andre was captured, tried as a spy, and executed." *The Scarlet Coat* wrapped on the backlot in December. After disappointing previews, it was double-billed with the re-released *The Wizard of Oz* and became the third Sturges film to open in less than a year. Unfortunately, the director's penchant for widescreen groupings couldn't compensate for the lethargic pacing and talky script (the battles take place off screen). The *New York Times* was more impressed by the Hudson Valley exteriors than the "dogged literacy" and "excessively sentimental finale" in which Andre marches smartly to the gallows. "It'll be but a momentary pang, Jack," he assures his betrayer. (Today, Andre's blind affection for Bolton suggests a homosexual attraction. His insistence on "crossing swords" on two occasions with the handsome spy furthers the impression.)

As unlikely as *The Scarlet Coat* now seems when viewed in the context of Sturges's career—Francis registered surprise when reminded who directed it—the costume adventure deserves a footnote as the last film in Sturges's indentureship at MGM. It would be his last movie as a studio contract director.

8

At Sea

When Peter Benchley's *Jaws* was still in galleys, Universal approached John Sturges about the rogue shark adventure. At age sixty-three, he may have been too old to handle the physical demands of such a project, but as one of the few Hollywood "old-timers" who enjoyed working on water he was a logical choice for, if not the job, at least pre-production discussions. He was known for his sea legs. He had survived Howard Hughes's *Underwater!* salvaged Warner Bros.' *The Old Man and the Sea,* and piloted a (miniature) nuclear submarine beneath the Arctic ice pack in *Ice Station Zebra.* Sturges the boating enthusiast understood the exigencies of a protracted sea shoot as few in the industry did.

In the summer of 1953, RKO's front office circulated a frantic memo. Howard Hughes needed a script for Jane Russell, who had not made a picture at the studio since *The Outlaw* (1943). Requirements: It had to incorporate extensive underwater footage à la Fox's new *Beneath the 12-Mile Reef* and it had to be shot in 3-D to take full advantage of Russell's generous cleavage. Harry Tatelman, head of RKO's story department and an aspiring producer, dug up a treasure-hunt story called "The Big Rainbow" (as in chasing the impossible dream). Russell, who had inordinate creative input, said yes to the project, which, over the next six months, would undergo twenty-one rewrites. Besides Robert Bailey and Hugh King, the original authors, and Walter Newman, who would receive sole screenplay credit, Niven Busch, Jack Leonard, and Charles Lederer submitted drafts. Leonard's 3-D version—whose awed take on the undersea world owed much to Jacques Cousteau's just-published *The Silent World*—opened in Santa Monica Harbor and included dives off Mexico, madness on the high seas, and an octopus "stretching into the audience, embracing everyone in the front row." It climaxed with the treasure ship rising from the depths, exploding, and sinking from sight. Newman's rewrite moved the action to Havana. The plot now revolved around a Spanish galleon teetering on a ledge and the race to retrieve its cache of gold bullion.

Without mentioning that Russell was attached to the project, Tatelman showed an extended treatment, "barely sixty pages," to Sturges. Schary—pleased with how *Escape from Fort Bravo* had turned out but lacking a follow-up assignment—sent Sturges along with his blessing. "Enjoy the vacation," he said, only half joking. After conferring with Newman, the director was satisfied. "The Big Rainbow" could be a fun B picture, but only if shot quickly and cheaply off Catalina. They didn't need a name star because the star would be the still-novel Aqua Lung or, as it would soon be known, SCUBA (self-contained underwater breathing apparatus). Richard Haydn and William Bendix would be sensible choices.

Hughes had something gaudier in mind. The underwater sequences would be shot in Hawaii, and the focus would be Russell, sporting Aqua Lung and a couple of brawny co-stars, yet to be named. "With Jane the emphasis was always on her bust line; she was very voluptuous," said Lori Nelson, who co-starred in the picture. "Hughes was just enamored with her figure. He accentuated it in every film he put her in."

Sturges felt blind-sided. "After working with Newman on the story, I'm informed that Jane Russell wants to play the female lead," he said. "She told me, 'I've got to do a picture, and I like the sixty pages.'" She assured the director, "Howard will give you anything *I* want."

Sturges tried to dissuade her, pointing out that Theresa, the wife of the treasure hunter, wasn't much of a role.

"I know it's a little part," she said coyly. "But don't worry, I'll build it up."

Though Russell had ceded control to producer Tatelman, she was still calling the shots. "Harry hired this other writer, and we both talked to the writer about what we thought it should sound like," she recalled. "He'd write and then Harry would hand me the next hunk. If I had any suggestions, well, that's what we did."

Sturges was furious. He called Burt Allenburg, his agent at the William Morris Agency (who also represented Sinatra and Richard Brooks), and complained that things were spiraling out of control.

"I fail to follow you," Allenburg said.

Sturges explained that the "little picture" he agreed to do had suddenly become a star vehicle with an extended shooting schedule and costly Hawaiian locations. "Oh, Christ, I just think it's a terrible idea," he moaned, adding, "I didn't get into this business to make bad pictures."

Allenburg couldn't believe his ears. "Let me see if I've got this right, John. Instead of unknowns, Hughes wants to give you his star? Instead of a low-budget, he wants to give you a big budget? Instead of faking it someplace, he wants you to go to the right place?"

Allenburg, Sturges enjoyed recounting, didn't wait for a reply. "Don't ever call and bother me again!" he said, and hung up.

This got back to Hughes, who summoned Sturges to the front office, where, Sturges recalled, "These jerks in management, the guys with the cattle prods, are all sitting around a desk, staring at a phone."

Rather, they were staring at the red light on the phone.

When the light illuminated, Sturges grabbed the receiver.

"Hello," the voice said.

"Hello?" Sturges repeated, before launching into a prolonged story pitch, building up to what he referred to as "my big finish."

The voice said, "Go ahead—" and Sturges, taking this as Hughes's blessing, hung up, much to the horror of everyone in the room.

"I guess I sort of cut him off," Sturges said, sheepishly.

"Yeah, you did—you cut off Mr. Hughes."

Back on the line, Hughes said, "Why don't we just get any writer you want, spend any amount of money you want? I want to make a picture with you and Russell. See what happens. If it's no good, it doesn't work out, we'll still have some fun."

After the cost-cutting at Columbia and MGM this sounded promising. He had never been given carte blanche. He passed the word to Newman, a former reporter who had written *Ace in the Hole* and had tailored dialogue for Russell on Josef von Sternberg pictures. Together, they reworked the script into a lively mix of narrow escapes and south-of-the-border romance. Former navy divers Johnny Gray and Dominic Quesada were now based out of Cuba and scouring the ocean floor on an experimental "sea-sled." Johnny is married to Dominic's sister, Theresa. Ironically, after Dominic "salts" another wreck site to prolong the search, the trio stumbles upon a Spanish galleon laden with gold bars and Madonna statue. The rotted hull rests on a constantly shifting rock formation and is in danger of breaking up. Topside: Father Cannon (Robert Keith), the expedition's elderly historian; Gloria (Nelson), Dominic's girlfriend and the owner of the schooner *Sans Souci;* and the shark hunters (Joseph Calleia, Eugene Iglesias, Ric Roman), who are intent on stealing the booty.

There would be one more story conference with the disembodied voice. "I never met Hughes. It was all done over the phone," said Sturges. "But I knew we shared one thing in common: he was nuts for all this kind of mechanical stuff and fascinated by the scuba gear."

Consequently, as work continued on the script, Hughes summarily approved the mounting pre-productions costs. These included 3-D tests in Catalina's Emerald Bay, camera sled ($1,000), matte paintings ($8,000), underwater makeup and hair-dye tests, scuba gear (masks, weight belts, spare tanks), boat and crane barge, interviews with expert divers and marine biologists, location trips to Florida's Marineland and Weeki Wachee Spring, whose general manager wired back, "The conditions are perfect for underwater photography—in fact, all the underwater scenes for *Mr. Peabody and the Mermaid* and *Crosswinds* were filmed here." Republic Studios proffered its underwater tank at $3,000 a week. RKO decided to construct its own 500,000-gallon tank.

Estimated final budget: $1.75 million. Sturges's salary, a portion of which would go to MGM: $93,560.

By October, it was decided that 3-D was more trouble than it was worth. The film would be shot in SuperScope, RKO's in-house anamorphic process, and, despite reports of poor visibility, the second-unit work would be done off Kona and then matched and intercut with close-ups of the stars in the studio tank. Sturges, photographer Harry Wild, and veteran set designer Albert S. D'Agostino, responsible for the mock-ups of the sunken ship, flew to the Big Island. They were joined by famed underwater photographer Lamar Boren and film loader–assistant cameraman Fred Koenekamp (who would go on to photograph *Patton* and *Islands in the Stream*). A small armada awaited at the wharf, including the World War II patrol boat *Oinah*, a pair of flat-bottom skiffs, a tugboat, and a 175-foot barge with crane. Besides raising and lowering the galleon prow, the latter would double as camera platform and scuba changing station. Sturges posted orders on everything from "coral shoes" (high-top canvas with quarter-inch rubber soles) to après-dive sustenance (hot bouillon). His instructions for the barge were precise:

> Half-tarped to cover equipment and as shade from sun. Be sure you build a dark room on deck so you can load film during the day as you will be away from land and you won't carry enough magazines . . . be sure plenty of blankets and towels aboard. . . . Also, important to have hot bouillon or soup or coffee for divers, some crackers with jam and peanut butter and cans of fruit juice as you get awfully hungry working below water. You will find the boys drinking soup every time they come up. It gives them strength and they will work better. . . . Never allow one man below water alone as he may get a cramp and there will be no way of knowing about it unless there is someone with him.

Accompanied by local divers Wally Young and Jack Ackerman, whose early experiments with scuba had been documented by Cousteau, Sturges and his party scoured the coast, north and south, for potential sites. They were looking for just the right combination of sand, coral, rock formations, visibility, and depth (less than thirty feet, so decompression stops would not be necessary).

After five days of "heavy swells and murky water," the *Oinah* rounded Mano Point, eighteen miles north of Kona. "It was flat and calm, exactly what we were looking for," said Ackerman. Sturges strapped on a tank and went below. He found himself gliding over a spectacular canyon with glistening bottom, the perfect spot for the opening sled ride. Farther out, a rock formation with a ledge that dropped fifteen feet. It was made to order for D'Agostino's galleon prow. Another nine miles up the coast, Makaiwa Bay—secluded, mirror smooth, teeming with coral and other marine life. Markers were dropped at all locations. An assistant cabled back: "Moderate swells, water clear, BEST YET!"

For the next month, Sturges and his crew worked these spots, casting off at 8 a.m., suiting up around 9:45, and staying as long as the weather permitted, which was usually early afternoon. Stunt woman Pat Deane Smith doubled for Russell; Ackerman, Young, Frank Donahue, and Mickey McNab doubled for the yet-to-be-named leading men. Young also watched for sharks. Ackerman, who called himself "the kingpin of the whole ballgame," laughed at the sea sled. "It was kind of a phony damn thing—all that resistance when you're towed behind the boat." At the start of the shoot, Sturges joined the divers below, even riding the sea sled. Later, he donned only mask and snorkel and directed from the surface.

The production log provides a snapshot of conditions:

> Unable to shoot due to bad weather, strong surge and murky water. . . . Unable to shoot all day due to heavy dark clouds, with exception of one shot when sun came out. . . . Ground swells from 12 ft to 15 ft high. Light wind, and cross chops. About to move to another location when Coast Guard warning came of a tidal wave approaching. Ordered back to port. . . . Camera raft damaged by rough sea during night. . . . Galleon prow at bottom but unable to make secure on account of heavy surge. Prow hauled back aboard barge. . . . Camera sled problems, overcast. . . . Water condition very dirty, with heavy ground swells. . . . Underwater shots of Johnny traveling on sled . . . require refilling aqualungs between shots, resting divers. Light now not good.

Among the daily annoyances: a concrete prow that weighed so much it could not be positioned underwater; corroded tripods and camera heads; engine malfunctions that, more than once, necessitated a tow to shore.

"It was incredible!" said Sturges. "We had to make our own cameras and find our own underwater photographer, Lamar Boren, who worked for the Scripps Institute of Oceanography. He showed up, and the union said, 'You can't use him.' I said, 'Just try to stop me.' So they gave me the [union] card. . . . We built one set underwater, but it wasn't very good. D'Agostino, our art director, was in his fifties and couldn't go underwater. But we got all this gorgeous stuff . . . and then the water got all burnt up with algae."

Recalled Young, "It was one of the worst fiascos ever. The Spanish galleon weighed tons, but the base was made of lathe and plaster, which crumbled when it was positioned by crane. It was taken back to

Honolulu and re-built. Amazing that a Hollywood effects team could not make a Spanish galleon."

RKO cabled that Haydn and Bendix were no longer in the running as Russell's costars. This made shooting with doubles tricky. Russell wanted the six-foot-two Richard Egan for Johnny because, she said, he was one of the few men in Hollywood who "looked like he could throw me around." Hughes favored Richard Widmark. Widmark's response: "Hell, no. I made *The Frogmen* with that goddamn Hughes. Worst picture I ever did."

"Hughes was enough to drive you nuts," Sturges said. "In his inimitable fashion, he let me sit over there. He would not make up his mind who the leading men were. So I got as close to the divers as I dared without letting you see their faces. Later, in the RKO tank, we shot close-ups and interiors of the wreck. But when we edited them in, they looked funny, staged. Reality was destroyed."

Finally word arrived that Hughes had OK'd Egan and Gilbert Roland, who had just appeared as a sponge diver in *Beneath the 12-Mile Reef* but was petrified of the water. Egan was known for his deep voice and barrel chest. He was also a steal at $3,000 a week. "Jane's leading men— Mitchum, Victor Mature, Bob Ryan—were big men," Egan said. "So when my name was submitted, Hughes said, 'I want to see a picture of Egan with his shirt off.' That's how I got the part. I'd been working out like a demon."

Russell was wild about Egan—"like a big brother," she was quick to add. "I had seen footage on Richard, serving drinks behind a bar," recalled the actress. "I said, 'If we could lighten his hair, he would be great.'" Egan's hair was bleached "right to the core," and he and Russell worked on their tans on the studio roof.

Christmas Eve, Sturges flew home to meet his stars and spend the holidays with Dorothy and the children. The gregarious Ackerman came along as technical advisor and dive instructor. Four days later, they passed a "NO VISITORS, PLEASE" sign and entered Stage 10, now home to a massive steel tank. Bobbing on the surface like bath toys, the *Sans Souci* and shark boat. On the bottom, fifteen feet down, the interior of the galleon hull, designed to separate on cue. When everything went as planned, which wasn't often, Boren and Koenekamp donned scuba gear and photographed Russell, Egan, and Roland picking their way through the barnacle-encrusted innards. (The majority of the underwater shots in the completed movie are of Smith, Ackerman, and Donahue—the unsung stars of *Underwater!*)

Unimpressed by the project, which she dismissed as a "turkey," Russell was chronically late for her 9 a.m. call and kept cast and crew waiting as she changed bathing suits and had her body makeup retouched. (There are numerous "Wait for Miss R" entries in the production log.) More than once Russell's doctor phoned to say she was suffering from acute sinusitis. The nervous Roland gashed his head on a ladder as he popped to the surface. "He was deathly afraid of the water," said Young. "After that accident, they put him in a 'hard hat' diving helmet. With filters on the camera, they found they could shoot him that way." The actors frequently slipped and went into the tank. They laughed it off. Not so the grip who fell from a catwalk and was taken away by ambulance.

The most infuriating problem for Sturges was the cloudy water. It meant the tank had to be drained and cleaned periodically. When this happened, Sturges moved to Newport Pier for the Havana harbor sequences. Ventura's Sequit Point served as the island where Johnny and Dominic strand the shark hunters, but not before their rowboat capsizes. Again, everything that could go wrong did. Besides heavy fog, the waves proved too formidable for Egan and Roland, who were replaced by doubles. Then, the outboard motor on the camera launch died, and the current carried the boat dangerously close to the breakers. By midday, crew and doubles had to be rescued.

The trickiest tank scenes were left for last. These involved Theresa being trapped by a fallen beam, and Johnny and Dominic setting the blast that blows the strong-room door and eventually causes the wreck to slide over the ledge. These effects were accomplished with electrical charges and breakaway beams. The morning of the blast, however, signals got crossed and two effects men were caught in a "premature explosion (that) caused multiple puncture wounds to upper and lower extremities."

Sturges and editor Stuart Gilmore—known for his collaborations with Preston Sturges—assembled the picture as they went along. Each night, Hughes secretly screened their work. "Finally, I got my spy system going," said Sturges, laughing. "We started putting a little piece of paper in our cut stuff. If the paper was missing, someone had run it in the middle of the night. Hughes was a weird guy: He was always second-guessing you."

Luckily, Sturges had an out. Schary needed him back at MGM for *Black Rock*. When he heard this, Hughes, right on cue, ordered new scenes and endless retakes of Russell. "Hughes said he wanted Jane's footage all reshot," the director said. "I wanted off the picture."

Sturges's theory: Hughes purposely held up the film because he didn't want to let Russell out of her contract. "This big blast comes out: Jane Russell is injunctive. She can't get out of her contract because the picture has to be almost entirely reshot, and retakes are necessary all the way through it."

Sturges told Tatelman, "If it's that bad, get another director." Sturges then confronted Russell, who told him, "Howard wants to make trouble with the contract. He doesn't want to lose me. Just keep making the film."

In June, after Sturges had returned to Metro, Boren flew to Nassau in the Bahamas to photograph sharks that had been corralled in a pen. This expedition, which called for $300-a-day "shark catchers," cost RKO an additional $428,000 and resulted in little usable footage. Back in Hollywood, the team tried a different tack. It purchased three blue sharks and released them in a tank at Ocean Park Pier. The unfortunate predators—$4,500 each—were, per the agreement, "disposed of after completion of photography."

Hughes, the consummate micromanager, would tinker for another eight months, pushing the budget to more than $2 million. Nelson, on loan from Universal, ended up staying a year at RKO. She called the production "jury-rigged" to serve Russell. "No wonder Sturges was frustrated. It was always another little scene, another this, another that. And then this huge promotional campaign and endless round of photographs." Bit player Iglesias, earning a career high of $750 a week, welcomed the delays. "You lucked out, kid," his agent told him.

The posters and ads for "The Big Rainbow," as it was still called, promised "Jane Russell as you've never seen her before!" in revealing two-piece bathing suits; but the star wore only one-piece suits onscreen and participated in fairly chaste kisses and embraces. Hughes had obviously learned his lesson from the protracted battle with the Breen Office over Belle Starr's plunging neckline. In September, the film went before the Production Code Administration. Not only did the panel approve the picture but it predicted that the film would have "wide family audience appeal and, because of its unique underwater story, will do as good at the foreign box office as it will on the domestic market."

Asked about the salacious ads, Russell shot back, "What else are you going to do to publicize it?"

A different kind of adventure, *Underwater!*, as it was now known, warranted a different kind of sendoff. "How about an underwater premiere, the first in history?" hazarded publicity director Perry Lieber, not expecting to be taken seriously. Hughes loved the idea, and the underwater grotto at Silver Springs, Florida, was selected for the January press junket. At the resort, following an initial "dry" run of the film, Russell and a handful of the reporters strapped on fins, facemasks, and tanks and dropped eighteen feet to the bottom of the pool, where they perched on iron benches before a blurry screen. The projector, in a waterproof case, was suspended from a boat. The less intrepid watched from a glass-bottom boat. More for show than insurance, firemen stood by with respirators. Russell called it "publicity nonsense."

"Generally, it was thought of as Hughes's idea," said Egan. "He flew in reporters from all over the country. There were hundreds of people down there. They had seats underwater and they projected it underwater, but you couldn't very well sit there all the time or you'd run out of oxygen. Plus, people weren't that familiar with the Aqua Lung. I was because I'd just done a fifteen-week picture. I was somewhat waterlogged."

In attendance, besides Egan and Russell, who ushered people to their seats, were Debbie Reynolds, Tab Hunter, Rory Calhoun, Gordon Scott (the new Tarzan), and a buxom blonde named Jayne Mansfield. As photographers pivoted and flashbulbs popped, Mansfield's bikini came loose on cue. Furious, Russell stomped off. Newspapers and fan magazines played up the rivalry of the sexpots. Among the tabloid headlines: "Jayne Out-Points Jane."

"The whole thing was a mess," said Sturges, who, along with Roland, refused to attend. "You can't project a picture underwater. They never figured that out. And then Mansfield showed up and upstaged Jane, and she got mad and wouldn't appear. And Dick Egan got drunk and fell in the pool. But it got space. We're even talking about it today. A bad idea can get you space."

Underwater! premiered in New York in February and Los Angeles in March and, despite the cost overruns, was a box-office hit. RKO's new SuperScope aspect ratio (2:1) wasn't on a par with Fox's CinemaScope, but it did, as *Variety* noted, enfold the viewer and add to the "big event" nature of the movie. "Amazingly enough," wrote Russell in her autobiography, "*Underwater!* has the distinction of racking up more bookings than any other RKO picture in the preceding decade." She added later, "It was the first of its kind. If it made a lot of money, it's because people wanted to see it." (The delayed release meant audiences were treated to a triple dose of Sturges: *Bad Day at Black Rock* and *The Scarlet Coat* were playing across town.)

Given the nature of the shoot, Sturges was not surprised by the notices. Reviewers generally enjoyed the underwater footage, hated the topside romance. "One is carried with the swimmers into a world of twilit beauty, of coral and cliffs and waving seaweed," rhapsodized the *L.A. Times*. *Variety* praised Sturges's direction and predicted brisk box office with Russell "mermaiding in the ocean depths." Crowther, harpoon poised, carped: "Seldom has anything so trifling as this story of delving for treasure beneath the seas been dished up as feature entertainment. . . . Even the underwater action is on the lethargic side, with the actors merely swimming around in wreckage and giving out bubbles instead of words." Russell, Crowther concluded, "does nothing underwater that she hasn't done better above."

Today, thanks to the stars flexing their pectorals and Russell affecting a bad Spanish accent, *Underwater!* has attained a justifiable reputation as high camp. Observed playwright-filmmaker Luis Valdez, "Roland playing opposite Jane Russell in brown face—what we called 'Mexican Makeup No. 10'—was ludicrous, but it was very much in keeping with the way Hollywood did business at the time." As Sturges had feared, the footage from Hawaii, the Bahamas, and the studio tank did not match. Some of it was murky, some blue- and aqua-tinted, some crystal clear (as if taken in a fresh-water spring). The process work is obvious and subpar even by 1950s standards; and for a film that underwent so much last-minute tweaking, *Underwater!* is full of technical glitches, such as an "open water" shot where you can clearly see the lip of the soundstage. The prop galleon, which Sturges always hated, still rests on a reef close to shore. "Every now and then it's discovered as a wreck," he said.

Despite its generally unfavorable reputation—one Sturges family member dismissed it as "boobs swimming at a camera"—*Underwater!* remains a pioneering work in underwater cinematography. New lenses were ground and new cameras and camera housings developed. More than a third of the film's 99-minute running length takes place below the surface, a record held by a theatrical feature until Peter Yates's *The Deep* (1977) and then James Cameron's *The Abyss* (1989). More important, without the Hughes "fiasco," as Wally Young called it, it is unlikely that, four years later, Sturges would have been approached about a decidedly nobler maritime venture.

In June 1956, the director signed with Warner Bros. to take over the adaptation of Ernest Hemingway's 1952 novella about God, hubris, and a Cuban fisherman's marathon battle with an eighteen-foot marlin. To say that *The Old Man and the Sea,* starring Spencer Tracy as the white-haired Santiago, was the *Waterworld* of its day would be generous. Before Sturges signed on, the film had been in development for two years— with Humphrey Bogart and Anthony Quinn lobbying for the lead, and Fred Zinnemann beating out Nicholas Ray and John Huston as director. It would take another two years to reach the screen. The delays cost the studio $3.5 million and were attributed to numerous factors, including Warner's attempts to appease an author who held Hollywood in open contempt; the inability of the studio machine to "think small" and produce what cried out to be a simple man-against-the-sea parable; and Tracy's "health" problems and reluctance to go on location to Havana.

"They went to Cuba and went right on their ass," said Sturges. "They spent three times as much not making the picture as I spent making it. Disaster. So they closed it out, and came to me."

Initially, the reunion of Zinnemann and veteran photographer James Wong Howe, collaborators on *High Noon,* sounded inspired. Their filmmaking style, stark and unfussy, mirrored the author's prose. Unfortunately, Zinnemann obsessed over the smallest detail. He imagined the allegorical, heavily symbolic story as an Eisenstein-like study of Cuban fishermen struggling to eke out a living. And this led to the kind of nightmarish logistical problems that had plagued Orson Welles's Brazilian segments in *It's All True* and, much later, the Martha's Vineyard sequences in *Jaws.* In fact, the fate of the Hemingway adaptation was at

one point, like the Benchley adaptation, tied to the success of a mechanical behemoth.

Sturges likened passages of the novel to the Old Testament—"just
beautiful, like poetry"—and recalled how the production grew from the
idea of Tracy touring in a one-man show. "At the time," Sturges said,
"Charles Laughton went around reading the Bible. Standing Room
Only. Someone said, 'Jeez, Spence, you ought to read *Old Man and the
Sea*.' 'I'm not going on the road 250 days a year!' So they said, 'So why
not make a movie then that's just atmospheric—clouds and the sea and
a little boat in the distance—and you read over that?'

"They hired Freddy Zinnemann. Freddy's not an atmospheric director; he's literal. Somehow, the thing grew into a literal movie."

A fish tale to rival Hemingway's own, the story of the movie is one
of greed, ineptitude, and clashing egos. It began well before Sturges
came onboard with playwright-screenwriter Paul Osborn (who had just
adapted *East of Eden*), assuring producer Leland Hayward he could
"lick" the Hemingway story, provided he was allowed "a free hand." By
this he meant that Hemingway, who lived outside Cojimar, Cuba,
should be kept out of the writing process and then brought in as adviser
because "he knows (about fishing) and we don't." Hayward agreed that
Hemingway would "probably only get in our hair."

Osborn "reshaped" the material by dropping Santiago's dreams of
Africa and the marathon arm-wrestling contest, and creating "a story
that would eliminate all flashbacks (which I feel would be deadly because they would serve no purpose)—and would eliminate the use of
the [narrator's] Voice, which is merely a device and I feel would tend to
make the story unreal and 'arty.'" Osborn also beefed up the role of the
boy, Manolin, with "Meanwhile, back on shore . . ." cutaways. This
turned the epic struggle between Man and Nature into something more
mundane, a "love story" between the Old Man and the boy, complete
with lovers' spat, Coast Guard search, and reconciliation. As Osborn
saw it, the Old Man goes out too far to prove himself to the boy and win
back his favor. "The trick," said the screenwriter, echoing Hayward's
concern, "is to be able to follow the long tiring fight the Old Man puts
up, without having just to remain with the Old Man alone in the boat."
He solved this with a "delirium sequence" in which the boy materializes
in the boat and talks to the Old Man.

Hemingway, who had more input than Hayward let on, hated Osborn's changes and insisted he be replaced by Peter Viertel, who had adapted *The Sun Also Rises* and could be trusted to act as liaison with the studio. He wanted Huston, Viertel's friend and collaborator on *The African Queen,* to direct. Huston shared Hemingway's passion for marlin fishing. Hayward, however, wanted someone in *his* camp, which fed the author's disdain. "Although Ernest liked to watch movies in his living room in Cuba, the only ones he went to see in New York were those based upon his books and stories, and then he went in a spirit of self-imposed duress," wrote A. E. Hotchner in his Hemingway memoir. The author hated the Rock Hudson–Jennifer Jones version of *A Farewell to Arms* (1957). He bolted after thirty-five minutes. *The Killers* (1946), starring Burt Lancaster and Ava Gardner, was more to his liking, though he regularly nodded off during the first reel. Of *The Sun Also Rises,* he cracked, "Any picture in which Errol Flynn is the best actor is its own worst enemy."

Still, the author wasn't above hobnobbing with the steady stream of visitors from Hollywood and soaking Warner Bros. for everything he could get. Besides consenting to a cameo—he is glimpsed at the back of a thatched-roof bar—he was retained as technical adviser and his boat, the *Pilar,* rented for $5,000 a week to hook a giant black marlin for a camera crew. When the conditions proved unfavorable off Cuba, he talked Hayward into trying the waters off Cabo Blanco, Peru. For the trip, which would cost $75,000, he required new khaki outfits for his crew, "top quality" fishing gear, two chartered fishing launches (owned by friends), hotel and meals, and personal insurance for eight crewmembers. Anxious to begin his all-expenses-paid adventure, he wrote Hayward:

> Have been careful to hold expenses down but have had to buy a lot of stuff to outfit the old timers and also a lot of big line that can be used on my big reels to hook fish and then transferred to a rowing boat when out away and fastened to a hand line and be large enough to be used by the fisherman as a handline. Would like assurance from you that all these expenses will be re-imbursed. Everything used in actual fishing has to be of the absolute top quality or your whole thing collapses. We can always be beaten by weather or by absence of fish. But you cannot allow yourself to be beaten by faulty gear.

Hemingway's fishing off Havana resulted in seven reels of "various scenes of sea life" but no usable footage of a monster marlin breaking the surface. His largest catches were well under five hundred pounds, about half the size of the fish in the story, and even these refused to jump on cue. In April, the Hemingway flotilla made for Peru. Their efforts there proved just as futile. The fish, complained Zinnemann, were "camera-shy and behaving in a totally unpredictable way." Not true, said Hemingway. They hooked a huge fish and began to bring it in when the unit director yelled "Abort!" "Hemingway was incensed," said Hotchner. "It was always the light. After eight hours out, this is not going to endear you to him. He quit in disgust and went back to Havana."

As insurance, the studio ordered special-effects composites (traveling mattes) and began negotiations for spectacular marlin footage shot by a Texas sport fisherman. The technical department also designed a prop fish, which Zinnemann called "a miraculous dummy." He added: "It had a motor inside and could wiggle its fins and tail. It was so big that it had to be shipped—on two railroad cars—from Burbank to Miami. Hemingway hated it at first sight and christened it 'the condomatic fish.'"

Hayward and Zinnemann arrived in Havana in March to finalize locations, cast the boy (the role went to eleven-year-old Felipe Pazos), and, most important, clear the shooting script with Hemingway. Principal photography was set for mid-April—in hopes of beating the rainy season. Tracy, who needed to acclimate to the heat and humidity, arrived two weeks early. Zinnemann would have just as soon he stayed home. He thought the actor a poor choice for Santiago, described in the book as "thin and gaunt with deep wrinkles in the back of his neck. . . . Everything about him was old except his eyes and they were the same color as the sea and were cheerful and undefeated." Tracy had the furrowed neck and sparkling eyes, but he was anything but gaunt, and Zinnemann felt this would ultimately doom the production.

The story was "about the triumph of man's spirit over enormous physical power, personified by a frail old fisherman and an immense fish locked in a battle for existence," Zinnemann wrote in his autobiography. "To dramatize the odds I wanted the old man to look weather-beaten, just leathery skin and bones, and to seem bereft of all strength. Spencer Tracy liked the idea; he agreed gradually to lose a lot of weight during the six months before the start of shooting."

Ensconced in the luxurious Hotel Nacional, Tracy gained, rather than lost, weight. He missed wardrobe fittings. He refused an insurance physical. And, in contrast to his behavior on *Black Rock*, he became drunk and belligerent in the hotel bar. Steve Trilling, Jack Warner's assistant, described the actor in a memo as "no joy to work with." Worse, he was becoming paranoid; he felt everyone was laughing at him behind his back.

"After discussing wardrobe, Tracy again brought up the subject of the first night he arrived and of his drinking," said assistant director Don Page. "He stated that all Hollywood knew about it and that I must have done a lot of talking. . . . He feels no one in the company likes him and *he* doesn't like anybody connected with us.

"As for his promise to lose weight, it seems to me that he is as heavy now as he has always been, and I recall Mr. Zinnemann's statement to Mr. Hayward that if Tracy did not lose the necessary weight that he would not start the picture with Mr. Tracy, as he would be laughed right out of the theater." (Ernest Borgnine recalled receiving a telegram from Tracy, begging him to take over the role. He ran into Tracy later at the studio. "Goddamn it, now you come!" Tracy said. "I sent you a telegram and you never responded.")

Zinnemann the perfectionist presented his own set of problems. He and Howe vetoed out of hand anything that smacked of phoniness, including motorized fish and blue-screen process shots. Howe, who had just done *Picnic* at Columbia, sought to convey the "intense heat and sunlight" that the old man endured. This meant shooting without lens shade or polarizing filter. In three days in June, with a crew of 120 sitting idle, Zinnemann and Howe photographed Tracy rowing into the harbor, Tracy unfurling a sail in the harbor, and a close-up of the sun. Their approach was so painstaking they could have been doing a Robert Flaherty documentary. Zinnemann wanted to fly to Yankee Stadium for the incidental daydreams of the great DiMaggio. Exasperated, Hayward ordered the director to use stock footage or deploy a second unit. The opening and closing dream sequences of the lions at play on African beaches, the producer pointed out, could also be "tricked" with stock footage and special lens. In May, six motorized sharks malfunctioned and sank to the bottom. Frogmen were dispatched to Bimini to shoot real sharks in an underwater pen.

After screening the Havana footage, Hayward realized the company was spinning its wheels. Because of the island's fast-moving clouds, there were lighting and continuity problems. There was also the "very distracting" bobbing up and down of the camera in the rowboat. "I told you shots shouldn't be done [in Cuba]," he chastised Zinnemann. "All three of these shots are absolutely perfect examples of the ideal U.V. [ultraviolet] or process shot. I would guess that you could do the three shots in a maximum of two hours in the studio. . . . Freddie, it is impossible to ever match backgrounds in Cuba for more than 15 minutes at a time. This is why I keep getting at you to take keys every time you get a master shot."

Hayward ordered the company back to Burbank. The close-ups of the Old Man at sea, he decreed, would be done in a soundstage tank, the long shots with a double in Hawaii. Zinnemann fired off his letter of resignation. "Shooting most of the movie in the studio tank seemed to be the only way out; unfortunately, I could not see how this could be done," he wrote in his memoir. "Meanwhile, Tracy had arrived in Havana not having lost one ounce of weight. Suddenly the story seemed pointless. It made little sense to proceed with a robot pretending to be a fish in a studio tank pretending to be the Gulf Stream with an actor pretending to be a fisherman."

For weeks, Soundstage 7, where the tank awaited, was posted "Closed Down." Then the *Los Angeles Times* reported, "John Sturges will check in May 15 at Warner to direct *The Old Man and the Sea,* which will resume shooting in June in Hawaii. . . . The film has been a long time in the works." Sturges was an inspired replacement. He knew Hawaii, was more flexible than Zinnemann, and, most important, had a track record with Tracy. Still, he had to be talked into it. Memories of the Hughes shoot were all too vivid. And as much as he loved and respected Tracy, he agreed that the actor was a poor choice for Santiago.

"Spence is no more a starving Cuban fisherman than FDR. Just ridiculous," he grumbled. "Secondly, the Gulf Stream is a very rough place, and sharks, I learned from experience, aren't easy to catch. And it's not easy to fake one."

Sturges craved adventure, but not at the expense of his career. "If Freddy can't do it, I'm not about to try."

"Fine, but first take a look at the scenes Zinnemann shot," Hayward said.

Sturges met Hayward and Tracy at the executive screening room and, fully prepared to beg off after a polite interval, wound up being floored by the Zinnemann-Howe footage.

"There wasn't much of it, but what there was—exquisite! Much of it was out in the ocean. God, it looked beautiful. Jimmy Howe was a helluva cameraman. So I got tempted. I thought, 'Well, I can't go through my life just cranking out mechanical stuff. Have a go at something that has potential, but do it your way.'"

Sturges was less impressed by the script. "There was no screenplay," he said. "How Peter Viertel could have accepted an [Oscar] nomination for what he did on that script I'll never know." Why not have Hemingway provide the scene bridges? "I wrote him and said, 'We've got to make a compression in time. We can't just go from one speech to another.'" He offered some recommendations, adding, "Don't even dream of using this." Hemingway wrote back criticizing the director's prose. "He said, 'It's like a watch that runs part of the time. Good writing has to run all the time.' I thought it was kind of funny. I was just suggesting a mechanical requirement of length. In the end, he wrote something for me." (Sturges eventually lost Hemingway's letters—"I never kept stuff; I just never really took myself that seriously.")

Tracy, who could not understand how he could play the fisherman and also narrate, was told by the director, "The beauty of the words read by you is our No. 1 asset." The actor agreed, after hearing "insurance" narration by Joseph Cotten.

The two-month shutdown gave Sturges time to regroup and talk Hayward into trying "quieter" waters off Hawaii. He envisioned Tracy pulling at his oars in mid-sea. "I told him, 'We either do that or forget it.' No further discussion."

In mid-June, Sturges and underwater cameraman Boren returned to Kona. Though it was announced Tracy would join them for two weeks, he never materialized: Tracy's double did the rowing. The company hired a barge equipped with crane, lights, dressing room, and generator. A boat with a mock-up of the giant marlin was attached to the barge. Jack Ackerman once again guided them to calm waters. "I could hold my breath a long time, so they strapped a fin on my back and had me play a shark," he recalled.

Still dissatisfied with the shark footage, Sturges and Boren flew to the Bahamas. Here, they photographed the Old Man's boat from below, the three shark attacks and the eerie tableaux of the boat being "brought in" by the head and skeleton of the ravaged marlin. The mechanical fish that Hemingway had hated was crated up and shipped back to the studio. In its place: a 350-pound frozen marlin that was thawed and tied to a scaled-down boat. The entire rig was fastened to the bottom by a monofilament line. "It looked like a 1,500-pounder from below," the director said.

Dreading a repeat of the *Underwater!* experience, Sturges had locals corral about fifty tiger, leopard, and thrasher sharks in a 2,500-square foot pen in six feet of water. Boren, protected by a shark cage, photographed the sharks ripping into the marlin as they were being stabbed from above. "It was so dangerous the shark guy quit," Sturges said. "So one of the members of the crew said, 'Christ, I'll do it.' He's up there stabbing them with swords. . . . They're biting each other. Real thing. Unbelievable!"

Sturges estimated that "maybe about a tenth of the sea stuff" was done in the studio tank. This sounds unlikely, given the number of process shots in the completed film. Matching the tank footage with the location footage was "a run-of-the-show headache," said the director. Howe's solution: a wall of bright, ultraviolet lights to approximate the harsh glare of the sun. "Batteries of studio flood lamps, using a total of 40,000 amperes, enough to service a town of 25,000 people, supplied artificial sunlight for the simulated Gulf Stream," reported an observer. Tracy's eyes became red and irritated, and this caused further delays. "This picture is becoming my life's work," the actor complained. "If I'd known what trouble it was going to be, I'd never have agreed to it." Tracy "suffered severely from the stress of the shooting," added Hepburn biographer Charles Higham, "and at the end of each day Kate was shocked to find him utterly exhausted." The rolling of the sea was approximated by gently rocking the camera. To make a bird light on Tracy's finger—in a sentimental reworking of a Hemingway passage— Sturges and Howe taped BB pellets under its wings. The "money shots" of the giant marlin breaking the surface finally did come from Peru. However, they were purchased for $22,500 and the credit line "Some of the marlin film used in this picture was of the world's record catch by Alfred C. Glassell, Jr. at Cabo Blanco Fishing Club in Peru." Glassell also finagled the "special adviser" credit that Hemingway turned down.

Dmitri Tiomkin—who had won Oscars for *High Noon* and *The High and the Mighty*—was commissioned to compose the score, now considered an integral part of the production. Used to writing big orchestral themes, Tiomkin assumed his music this time would be used sparingly, to fill the gaps between Tracy's monologues. Sturges said he wanted something more ambitious—a veritable tone poem. The lush orchestral theme, which has the exhilarating feel of crashing waves, was recorded in nine days with Ray Heindorf conducting sixty-seven musicians. "He delivered a beautiful score," said Sturges. "But you have to talk to these guys, lay out a challenge. You have to put the empty spaces there." Tiomkin also argued for a title song, to be sung by Mahalia Jackson. It was deemed inappropriate. (Twenty years later, for *Islands in the Stream*, easily the best of the Hemingway adaptations, Jerry Goldsmith would draw inspiration from Tiomkin's score.)

As post-production droned on, Hayward called upon Sturges to help out on another troubled production: Billy Wilder's *The Spirit of St. Louis*, starring James Stewart as Charles Lindbergh. Jack Warner hated the film. He found it dark and dreary and, worse, sacrilegious. (Wilder talked openly of being an atheist.) Because Wilder was "unavailable" (he was in Paris editing *Love in the Afternoon*), Sturges did three days of what were diplomatically referred to as "bridges." He reshot the Garden City hotel sequence, where Lindberg spends a sleepless night waiting for the fog to lift, and shot the famous St. Christopher medal insert where Lindbergh, battling exhaustion, cries out, "Oh, God, help me!"

After screening a rough assemblage of *The Old Man and the Sea*, Sturges called for a number of "small changes." These included routine continuity fixes, sound tweaks (such as the rope "burning out over the gunwale"), and lab work that would eliminate the fishing line in the Glassell footage. He also informed Hayward that "the cat meows too much" in the village scenes, and, per Hemingway's request, "the tourist scene is being shortened so as to eliminate you-know who." (The grizzled Hemingway in white fishing hat can still be seen at a table at the back of the Terrace café.) "The music must be softened in scenes between the old man and boy," he said. "The key is to play against the poignancy [we hope] of this part of the picture." He ordered more optical effects (black flashing spots, distorted and wavering fish shots) to approximate the old man's growing fatigue and delirium. These would be perfectly acceptable "theatrical liberties," he said, adding: "They have a quality of hallucination or a disturbed and nightmarish feeling. . . . These effects work better if they're motivated. By this I mean the distortion of the fish stems from the Old Man's tiredness and progresses easily in degrees." Hayward agreed wholeheartedly. "In the case of this picture," the producer said, "[the effects] are a matter of life and death."

In January 1958, more than four years after Hayward had approached Osborn about the adaptation, the $5.5-million, barely eighty-six-minute *The Old Man and the Sea* previewed in Pasadena. On the same bill to get the audience in the Hemingway mood was Selznick's remake of *A Farewell to Arms*. According to a studio report, the preview cards ran about 75 percent excellent, 20 percent good, with the balance "somewhat critical." Much of the praise went to Howe's cinematography. Observed one viewer, "Would like to have stopped the projector at least 40 times to hold certain scenes motionless on screen." The preview report reflected this bias: "Scenes of the Caribbean with sunlight, moonlight, clouds, rain; of the Old Man in boat; of the giant Marlin breaking water all made for deep impressions."

"It was the most extraordinary preview I've ever had of a picture," recalled Sturges. "The theater held eight hundred and we got seven hundred cards back—and 90 percent of these were good. They didn't run the other picture again. Nobody came back. They just hung around outside talking to me. They loved it."

Jack Warner still had his doubts, as did composer Tiomkin, who continued to lobby for a theme song to make the picture "more palatable to the general audience." Sturges and Hayward hated the idea, but the composer persisted, "Although our preview went very well, I definitely feel that the song which I composed at your request would bring the end of the picture to a spiritual climax very fitting to the story—especially if the song is sung by Mahalia Jackson whose renditions are of tremendous power and style. The same song could also be used in the trailer and surely would help from a promotion and box office angle. . . . There are some people who, due to nearsightedness, do not see the value of this idea, but I want to quote they have raised the same objection to my treatment of *High Noon, The High and the Mighty* and *Friendly Persuasion,* among others." Sturges was adamant: No song.

Buoyed by the preview cards, Warner Bros. positioned *The Old Man and the Sea* for Oscar consideration by opening it in the fall. Its box-office competition included *The Vikings, South Pacific,* and Wyler's *The Big Country.* The ads had critics' blurbs ("a film masterpiece!") and assured viewers they were getting "a cinematic epic" that was "years in the making" and shot on location in Cuba, Peru, and Hawaii. To lend an air of solemnity, there were no opening credits, only "Ernest Hemingway's *The Old Man and the Sea.*" For salvaging what was thought to be an unsalvageable production, Sturges was acknowledged with the closing credit "This picture was directed by John Sturges." In violation of guild guidelines, Tracy demanded his name appear last, and that to "cover the confusion about the narration," he receive the credit "The story was told and the Old Man played by Spencer Tracy." Hayward's name appeared last; Tracy was billed simply as "the Old Man."

The trailer was simple but effective: a series of pastel drawings of the fisherman and the Cuban coast, and the promise of a "motion picture that explores New Horizons in entertainment . . . from the finest work by one of the Greatest Writers of Our Times." The Old Man in the drawings was closer to Hemingway's original concept: tall and gaunt, like Don Quixote. Reluctantly, Tracy agreed to a European promotional tour. He got as far as New York, where he contracted Asiatic flu and was unable to do any press. Hayward, citing disappointing tickets sales in Europe for *Around the World in 80 Days*—"because of stinking lousy dubbing"—asked Warner to spring for "prominent" foreign actors to dub Tracy—Vittorio De Sica in Italy, Charles Boyer in France, and so on. Respected actors—"as against the miserable reading that you get from the average dubbing actor"—would increase box office by 25 to 50 percent, he said, adding in desperation, "When we have as much money as we have in this picture, it seems to me that we should fight very hard for everything that we can do to give the picture a better chance." Jack Warner, refusing to spend another cent on what he considered, at best, a limited release, never got back to Hayward.

"Now in step the geniuses," fumed Sturges. "They put the film into a 2,000-seat house on Broadway, following *Around the World in 80 Days*. What insanity! It's a little picture—only an hour and twenty-some minutes. It had to fail. No way you could sit in a 2,000-seat theater and look at that little postage-stamp screen up there and have this thing work. And since it wasn't long enough, they got some tired short about ballet dancers to put with it. If they had put it in a little theater, as they subsequently did, it would have run forever."

Crowther at the *New York Times* praised Tracy's "brave performance" and the music but found the tank process shots too obvious and Viertel's slavish, word-for-word adaptation largely missing the book's allegorical shadings. Tracy, continued Crowther, was a one-man show, "a soloist with a symphony. . . . He looks convincingly ancient with lank white hair and stubbly beard, and he performs with the creaky painful movements of a weary, stiff-jointed old man." Also singled out were the shots of the coast and village and the fisherman returning in the red glow of dawn—Zinnemann's footage. Howe, Tracy, and Tiomkin all received Oscar nominations; Tiomkin won, beating Jerome Moross (*The Big Country*) and Hugo Friedhofer (*The Young Lions*). The National Board of Review named Sturges's "little art film" best picture of the year.

Despite everything—the erratic production schedule, the indifferent public reception—*The Old Man and the Sea* has grown in prestige over the years. It is talked about now as "a cinematic classic" and, though too calculatingly poetic for some tastes, is taught in high schools (along with Huston's *The Red Badge of Courage*) as an example of the successful novel-to-screen adaptation. It is also often referred to as the preeminent Tracy performance, a tour-de-force and the capstone of a career devoted to naturalistic underplaying. The actor had to sustain three levels of narrative—Santiago's public and inner voices and that of omniscient Narrator who comments matter-of-factly on life's harsh lessons—and, abetted by Sturges's expert pacing, he pulled it off. While his Portuguese fisherman and paisano con artist in, respectively, *Captains Courageous* and *Tortilla Flat* were more popular in their day, they remain caricatures beside Santiago, who is tired and resigned but still capable of expressing wonderment at the fight and majesty of the great fish. It is a minimalist, no-frills performance, as calloused as Santiago himself. And there is a pronounced, singsong-y lilt to Tracy's narration, which, as in the book, seems both wise and sardonic. Even the boy played by Pazos, whom Hemingway oddly fixated upon and blamed for the film's failure, has his moments. His flat line readings work as counterpoint to Tracy's sometimes dewy-eyed delivery and render him the disapproving "parent" in the relationship. He is certainly less cloying than the children in *Best Man Wins, Jeopardy,* and *The Magnificent Seven.* (In general, Sturges, who grew up with the adult companionship of his mother and older siblings, was not comfortable around young children, his own or those encountered on the set.)

The worst aspect of *The Old Man and the Sea* is also its best—the cinematography. There are wonderful shots of the island fishermen—forming a lantern processional in their march to their skiffs, rowing slowly out to sea in the morning dark—and there are shockingly sloppy process shots with telltale white halos. Sturges and Zinnemann were right to be concerned. The chore of matching open sea to tank shots *was* insurmountable, at least for the day scenes (the nighttime shots are fine and, bathed in lantern glow, conjure a Winslow Homer–like lyricism). The film is also hurt by its heavy-handed religious symbolism. It is one thing to read about the old man shouldering his mast like a cross and slowly making his way up the path to his hut, but to see this Cuban Via Dolorosa as you're being told that "the old man had to sit down five times before he reached his shack" imposes a stupefying literalness that must be laid not at Zinnemann's feet but Hayward's and Sturges's. In his *New Republic* review, Stanley Kaufman complained, "I could almost hear a voice whisper, *'Get it? Station of the Cross!'*"

What did Hemingway think of the film? It depended on whom you asked. Some said he hated everything about the adaptation; others said that he liked the film, hated the boy. In press interviews, he was far from complimentary—"Tracy," he sneered, "looks like a fat, very rich actor playing a fisherman"—and in the end, the author refused to give the studio what it wanted most: his personal endorsement.

Warner Bros. announced that Sturges would sit down with Hemingway in Key West to discuss "The Fighter," expanded by Hotchner from his teleplay of the author's story "The Battler." Why not then hand-deliver a print of *The Old Man and the Sea?* The studio said no, and the trip fell through. (In 1962, "The Fighter" was folded into

Hemingway's Adventures of a Young Man, directed by Martin Ritt.) "Warner was afraid if I took the picture back there and ran it for him, he'd hate it and refuse to let them release it. All sorts of things could go wrong, and at the time I wasn't a powerful enough director to insist on the trip. I didn't get that kind of power until I did pictures like *Ice Station Zebra.*"

Hayward finally screened the film for Hemingway in Key West, and in a carefully worded memo, Steve Trilling, Jack Warner's personal assistant, reported back: "Hemingway ran the picture last night with his wife. He liked it very, very much . . . said it had a wonderful emotional quality and is very grateful and pleased with the transference of his material to the screen. He thought Tracy was great (in light of his quarrels with him, this is quite a compliment) . . . the photography was excellent . . . the handling of the fishing and the mechanical fish very good. Had some minor dislikes such as did not like the boy (Felipe Pazos); however, this dates back to the very beginning of the picture and he did not like him even then . . . did not like the lions at the end. . . . Thought they should be lions, not cubs, cavorting on the beach . . . felt that the shots of the shark underwater were too small, they should have been larger sharks. But all in all, he was terribly high on the picture and very pleased with it."

Regarding Hemingway's personal testimonial, Trilling added, "Leland did not think the timing was just right to press too much for the letter(s) . . . so he will wait until the reaction penetrates and then go after him again and get the letter(s) you want within the next week."

The letter(s) never materialized. According to Hotchner, Hemingway hated the film. "He said, 'Spencer Tracy looked like he was playing Gertrude Stein as an old fat fisherman.'" Hemingway sent Zinnemann a picture of himself posing with the marlin that had eluded him in Peru. The caption read: "One small, edible, non-rubber fish."

Four years later, Sturges told the *L.A. Mirror-News,* "[Hemingway] keeps saying in press interviews that he didn't like the film, but I know he did. He wouldn't let us publicize what he really thought about it, though. He said that Hollywood had brought the Hemingway touch to the screen only twice—in *The Killers* and in *The Old Man and the Sea.* . . . He objected to only one thing in the film—the little boy. But he even backed down on that complaint when I talked to him about it. He finally said, 'I guess there's no little boy in all the world who would satisfy me as I visualized him.'"

In retirement, Sturges elaborated: "Hemingway got so mad at Warner Bros. he wouldn't have anything to do with the picture. But he told Leland that Leland could tell me that he liked the picture. He said whatever it is that I have that makes my work successful is in that picture. How do you like that for a quote to sell a picture? But he wouldn't let them use it. He said, 'I didn't like the boy. I have in my mind the kind of boy to play it, and it's not that kid.'"

Asked about the coincidence of author and director both hailing from the Oak Park suburb of Chicago, Sturges waved it away as just that, a coincidence. "I don't think I was fated, as you say, to direct that picture. I read all of his stuff long before I knew he was born there."

In 1965, the director called *The Old Man and the Sea* "my biggest disappointment . . . a financial failure." A quarter of a century later, in a poorly received TV adaptation, Anthony Quinn played the fisherman who is "defeated but not destroyed." This "freer translation" went beyond Osborn's proposed liberties to give Santiago a grown daughter and a dramatic foil in an American writer modeled on Hemingway. Quinn took the opportunity to tell reporters that Sturges and Hayward always saw him as the real Santiago, but that their hands had been tied because Tracy was the bigger star.

9

Gun for Hire

Like Richard Brooks and Robert Wise, the forty-six-year-old Sturges was now officially a gun for hire who could demand creative input and more money, if not a percentage of the profits. Appropriately, four of his next six freelance assignments would be Westerns, including the box-office triumph *Gunfight at the O.K. Corral* (1957) and the grim, unheralded *Last Train from Gun Hill* (1958). Both films starred Kirk Douglas and were produced by Hal Wallis, whom Sturges called "one of the brightest producers that ever was."

During this almost four-year interim, besides *The Old Man and the Sea*, Sturges directed *Backlash* (1956), with Richard Widmark and Donna Reed; *The Law and Jake Wade* (1958), with Widmark and Robert Taylor; and the guerrilla-warfare saga *Never So Few* (1959), with Frank Sinatra, Gina Lollobrigida, and Steve McQueen. In early 1958, as MGM sorted through the logistical challenges of the latter—should it be done on location in Burma or on the backlot?—Sturges performed an uncredited patch job on Universal's *Saddle the Wind*, a psychological Western scripted by Rod Serling, directed by Robert Parrish, and co-starring Robert Taylor and John Cassavetes as brothers. Sturges was brought in for two days of retakes and blue-screen inserts, which now made it appear that the trigger-happy Cassavetes commits suicide in the climactic face-off with his brother. Sturges waived his fee as a courtesy to the film's producer, Armand Deutsch.

Sturges's hard-fought freedom would prove bittersweet. In the winter of 1955, Grace, who had miraculously survived a massive heart attack four years earlier, died in a San Fernando nursing home. She was eighty-two. The *L.A. Times* identified her as "the mother of film producer Preston Sturges." (The next edition corrected the error.) Grandson Jon Stufflebeem remembered visiting Grace in the hospital after the first heart attack. She was emaciated, confined to an oxygen tent, but still a presence to be reckoned with. "She made me go to her purse and take out $20 to buy a pair of shoes," he recalled. "She wasn't supposed to survive, but she fought her way back, and they put her first in an assisted-care facility in Santa Monica and then a nursing home full of famous Hollywood people who were all 'old soaks.'" So he could be close by, John had gotten his mother, a teetotaler, a suite in the Motion Picture Retirement Home in Woodland Hills.

In February 1956, Sturges signed with Universal-International to direct the "vengeance trail" Western *Backlash,* developed by Widmark and Borden Chase (*Red River*) from a novel by Frank Gruber. Sturges's salary for the thirty-four-day shoot was $56,800, plus a generous per diem. There was also the allure of Arizona locations, some of which he had visited as a child. After studio interiors, the company moved to a ranch in Nogales and the façade town of Old Tucson, whose Main Street figured prominently in *Arizona* and *Winchester 73*. The location shoot was hot (107 degrees at one point) and not without mishap. A stagecoach overturned during a tricky maneuver, resulting in broken bones and contusions, and a light reflector fell from a roof, sending the cinematographer to the hospital. The $1 million production came in three days behind schedule and about $25,000 over budget.

Originally titled "Fort Starvation"—which sounded more like a box-office forecast—the mystery-Western played on viewer expectations from the opening shot: the archetypal lone rider turns out to be a woman, Karyl Orton (Reed). What follows involves lost gold and the search for the mysterious "sixth man," whom Jim Slater (Widmark) believes left his father and four others to be massacred by Indians. His investigation leads to the cavalry, warring Apaches, a gunslinger named Johnny (William Campbell of *The People against O'Hara*), and a range war between a former Civil War major (Roy Roberts) and a slick cattle thief named Bonniwell (John McIntire), who turns out to be Slater's father, setting the scene for a showdown with Oedipal overtones. (As originally written, after the ranchers shot it out, the father, son, and girl-friend walked off into the sunset, presumably to a life of crime. This was changed to Bonniwell being killed—first by his son in a shootout, and then, after some fancy editing, by a stray bullet from the major's posse.)

The Western was obviously meant to further distance Widmark from psychos and second-tier heavies. Lest there be any doubt about this, scenarist Chase, tongue firmly in cheek, reminded the reader in his character description: "This is the lead, to be played by Richard Widmark. He looks like Widmark, talks like Widmark, acts like Widmark." He might have added "and laughs like Widmark" because the distinctive chortle that introduced Widmark's Tommy Udo in *Kiss of Death* echoed through the canyons. By film's end it was a toss-up as to who had the more demented laugh, Widmark or Campbell, whose "eccentric" gunslinger was closer to Liberace than Jack Palance.

Campbell recalled Widmark as intractable, "a bit of a son-of-a bitch" who seemed to come unglued when it was suggested that Johnny and Slater might be kindred spirits, both seeking father figures. "I think we're missing something," Campbell told Sturges. "It's a love affair between the kid and the wanderer." Sturges liked the idea; Widmark found it weird, suggestive. "I want it this way, and that's the way it's going to be!" he sputtered.

Pitched by U-I as a cowboy movie "in the classic tradition," *Backlash* was really intended as an adult Western in the Anthony Mann–Delmer Daves mold. It was even more adult before the Production Code had its say. Besides the ambiguous arm-in-arm fadeout, the original script had a shooting suicide, a knifing, an attempted rape, and Karyl's confession of prostitution "to keep alive" during the Civil War. Much to Sturges's disgust, the PCA's Geoffrey Shurlock asked for, and got, reductions in profanity ("expression 'damn good' should be eliminated") and violence ("too many killings dramatized in detail"; the gun-whipping "unacceptably brutal and should be handled by the merest suggestion"), and a toning down of the sadomasochistic overtones when Karyl ministers to Slater's injury ("the searing of the wound seems unduly gruesome . . . we ask that it be handled more by suggestion"). Further, the PCA stated, Sturges should refrain from "any undue exposure when the girl removes her blouse" and "any unduly intimate embracing while these people are reclining." (Laughing up his sleeves, Sturges complied by having Karyl take off her blouse and use it as a bandage, and then slip the still-frisky Slater a "pain pill" that leaves him delirious in her arms.)

An early cut of the film—with Slater killing his father in the climactic shootout—was previewed with the Audie Murphy story *To Hell and Back*. More than a third of the Huntington Park audience said it would recommend the film to a friend. The campfire sequence in which Karyl tends Slater's wound was a clear favorite, though one viewer asked quite reasonably, "How come she had to take off her blouse? She had an extra one in her saddlebag." The scene in which Bonniwell, dying, tells his son, "You're good with a gun—real fast. You got that from me, son. It's kind of nice to know I've got a good man for a son," was found "sentimental" and "hammy."

Backlash—minus the death speech and now edited to make it appear a stray bullet killed Bonniwell—had its premiere in Houston in March and opened a month later in New York. The unusually ambitious ad campaign exploited the very elements the PCA had red-penciled. "He knew her lips . . . but not her name . . . nor the reason she followed 'the trail of empty graves'! SUSPENSE THAT CUTS LIKE A WHIP!" Widmark, who took a cut in salary for profit participation, complained bitterly that his name and image were not, as contractually obligated, large enough in the ads. "One look at the ads, and all you see is Widmark!" Sturges said, shaking his head. *Variety* called *Backlash* a "regulation Western" and faulted Sturges's direction for being "not always surehanded . . . [allowing] characters to wander to the ludicrous side." Widmark, however, was "tough enough to please those who like him best when he's mean." The *New York Times* dismissed the film in a five-paragraph notice, calling it picturesque but familiar.

Wallis shrugged off the notices. He had responded to the "gutty quality" of Sturges's work on *Bad Day at Black Rock* and, therefore, issued the director a return ticket to Old Tucson. The former head of production at Warner and now representative of a new breed of independent producer, Wallis had just struck out on his own at Paramount with a string of Martin and Lewis comedies and torchy women's pictures, such as *September Affair* and *The Strange Love of Martha Ivers,* which introduced Kirk Douglas to movie audiences. Wallis now wanted to make what he described as "hard-hitting," myth-debunking Westerns.

He optioned a 1954 *Holiday* magazine article by George Scullin called "The Killer." It purported to tell the true story of Dr. John "Doc" Holliday, who, on October 26, 1881, allied with the Earp brothers against the Clantons and the McLowerys in a field behind the O.K. Corral in Tombstone, Arizona.

In many eyes, this was hallowed ground: John Ford had already staged the shootout in *My Darling Clementine* (1946), taken from Stuart N. Lake's "Frontier Marshal" and starring a mustachioed Henry Fonda as Wyatt Earp and Victor Mature as the consumptive Holliday. As spectacular looking as that film was, it was still, in Wallis's eyes, "romantic fiction, fantasy," starting with the bushwhack murders of James and Virgil Earp prior to the shootout and including Doc's sacrificial death in the shootout. Sturges put it more bluntly. "Crap—the whole thing!"

"When John came in for discussions, I liked him at once," recalled Wallis. "A tall, powerfully built man who could have been a Western hero himself, he was an expert on Western history and contributed a great deal to the success of the picture."

Said Sturges: "I didn't have to do a lot of research. I knew quite a bit about it. I had read all the books on the subject, as well as the *Tombstone Epitaph*. And when I was a kid, I visited a working ranch in Wilcox, Arizona, forty miles east of Tombstone. It was a cow town with real cowboys. Still is."

Sturges insisted he was not at all nervous about mining the same material as Ford, who, late in life, became an acquaintance. *My Darling Clementine* was shot in Utah, in the shadow of Monument Valley, and turned the by-all-accounts ruthless Wyatt into something of a choirboy. "I thought Jack Ford was a hell of a director and *Clementine* an interesting movie," Sturges said. "But it's ridiculous to say it had anything to do with Earp and Holliday. For Chrissake, Holliday was played by Victor Mature as a surgeon from Boston who tries to save his Mexican sweetheart's life by operating on her in a saloon. And the way the Earps acted in that picture didn't remotely resemble the real thing."

He added, "Ford's picture wasn't competition at all. Nobody had ever told the gunfight as far as I was concerned."

Scullin's "The Killer," a sort of backstory essay, described Holliday, a dentist from Philadelphia, as a racist and a drunk with a nasty tubercular cough, and the legendary shootout in which thirty-four shots were fired as a "bit of homicide, lasting just thirty seconds." When the gun smoke cleared, Billy Clanton and Frank and Tom McLowery lay dead or dying. Holliday, according to the article, was "a dude" who wore a felt sombrero, string tie, and black frock coat. "Just about everyone who knew him hated him, if he lived long enough," said Bat Masterson. The Scullin piece presaged the revisionist Westerns of the late 1960s and early 1970s, such as *The Left-Handed Gun, Doc,* and *Dirty Little Billy.*

Stuart N. Lake, Wyatt Earp's by-then-ancient biographer, submitted an early script. Wallis rejected it out-of-hand as preposterous and fawning and brought in ex-marine Leon Uris, who had just adapted his best-selling *Battle Cry* as a hit movie. Uris provided an unusually frank and complex treatment, which focused on the feud between the Earps and the Clantons, the love/hate relationship between Earp and Holliday, and the proud/self-contemptuous contrast in their women. The film would be shot by veteran Charles Lang Jr. (*The Man from Laramie, The Big Heat*) in Technicolor and VistaVision, which provided a deep-focus clarity and the burnt-umber cast of a Frederic Remington painting. (Ron Smith, who oversaw the film's restoration in 2003, traced "the more shadowy, true-to-life look" to the studio's *Shane.*) Sturges asked Dmitri Tiomkin to compose the score and, as he had on *High Noon,* collaborate with Ned Washington on a title ballad to be sung by Frankie Laine (who would later spoof the song in Mel Brooks's *Blazing Saddles*).

Humphrey Bogart, Burt Lancaster, and Barbara Stanwyck were mentioned as possibles for Holliday, Earp, and Holliday's masochistic mistress, Kate Fisher. Bogart and Lancaster begged off; they had never felt comfortable in the saddle. Stanwyck said no because, at age forty-seven, she was not ready for supporting roles, no matter how colorful. Wallis contacted Kirk Douglas, whom he had found on the New York stage and initially signed for $1,250 a week. His asking price was now $200,000. Douglas, who just immersed himself in *Lust for Life,* eyed the role hungrily as a fun change-of-pace—provided Lancaster, who still owed Wallis two pictures, played Wyatt Earp. Lancaster again turned down the role, and Van Heflin, Richard Widmark, and Jack Palance were briefly considered. Then Wallis sweetened the pot—play Earp, and you can do Starbuck in *The Rainmaker*—and Lancaster said yes.

Rhonda Fleming and Jo Van Fleet, who had just won an Oscar for *East of Eden,* were announced as the female leads, "lady gambler" Laura

Denbow and prostitute Kate Fisher, known in the penny dreadfuls as "Big Nose Kate." Fleming was cast for her striking beauty, Van Fleet for her Method intensity. Lyle Bettger, barely forty, was tapped for Ike Clanton, the murderous patriarch played by Walter Brennan in the Ford version. The impressive supporting cast included Earl Holliman, Dennis Hopper, Martin Milner, Jack Elam, DeForest Kelley, Kenneth Tobey, Lee Van Cleef, and John Ireland, who was the reckless Billy Clanton in *My Darling Clementine* but now vied for Kate's attention as Clanton's hired gun, Johnny Ringo.

Sturges's script contains numerous reminders to "talk to Kirk and Burt" about costume and action changes, confirming the impression of a star-driven project in which Douglas and Lancaster demanded, and received, inordinate input. "From the start, both stars asserted themselves," said Wallis. They "tried to override Sturges, but John was a match for them." Sturges said he got along fine with Douglas but clashed frequently with Lancaster, who was "tough to handle" and a frustrated director who insisted on rewriting his scenes, elaborating on Wyatt's motivation. By one account, he attempted to insert a speech immediately before the gunfight, hammering home Uris's subtextual references to the duality of Doc and Wyatt. To humor Lancaster, Sturges shot the windy self-analysis with no intention of using it.

"Burt hadn't seen *Black Rock*," Sturges said, "but Kirk had and was a big fan. Burt told me he didn't think I was much of a director at all. He thought *Gunfight* was nowheresville—until he saw it. Then he decided I was one of the greatest directors of all time."

Notorious practical jokers, the stars enjoyed ribbing the straight-laced Sturges, recalled Holliman, who would also appear in *Last Train from Gun Hill*. "They gave him a rough time. When approaching a scene together, one would say, 'I think we should play this this way, have me do such-and-such,' and then the other would say just the reverse. So it put John in the middle. Of course they were having a wonderful time."

After the curmudgeonly Ford and Howard Hawks (*Red River*), Ireland found Sturges a welcome change. "I liked John a lot, and thought his take on O.K. Corral was very good—different from *Clementine*, but just as good," Ireland said. "Like Ford, he told his stories with the camera. But unlike Ford, who was one moody SOB, John was always respectful. He had this way of telling you everything you needed to know in a few minutes."

Holliman found Sturges imposing but approachable. "I once asked him about his method. He said, 'I try to get the best actors for the part and turn them loose, and when they find the scene, I find the best place to put the camera.'"

Van Fleet, who had trained at the Actors Studio, needed help getting "into the moment." Her Kate was an abused woman, and Van Fleet wanted to feel that abuse. "Slap me," she told Douglas. "Go on, hit me!" Douglas, no slouch in the mind-game department, obliged with a crack across the face. "I hauled off and whacked her. Her head spun," he recalled in his autobiography. "Burt stood there with his jaw dropping, watching this sadomasochistic ritual."

It was that very sense of danger that made Van Fleet and Douglas's scenes together so electrifying. "The two of them together were so full of steam and energy," Holliman said. Fleming envied the complexity of Van Fleet's role. "It was a good part, but she had to get herself revved up," recalled Fleming.

During their first sequence, the bitter Kate mocks Doc's southern heritage. Outraged, he throws a knife at her, narrowly missing her head. Sturges called for a trick knife. "But Jo insisted they not 'dummy it up,'" said Holliman, "and that the knife-thrower throw a real knife in her direction. Because she wanted that reaction, that look of shock and fear."

Fleming confirmed what Polly Bergen and others said about Sturges: when it came to his female leads, the director who had once charmed Ethel Barrymore was now almost indifferent. "Sturges was soft-spoken, but he had two strong male stars, so he had to be strong himself to handle them," said Fleming. "He allowed me to play the elegant lady gambler in a natural way, but he didn't give me a lot of direction. He just let me go."

Had she been more observant or career-savvy, said Fleming, she would have realized that the colorfully garbed (in various shades of green) Laura Denbow was fast becoming window dressing. An early tip-off: When Denbow arrives by stage, she doesn't rate a close-up. Later, when Wyatt kicks Laura out of the Long Branch Saloon and a fight breaks out with a cowboy defending her honor, there are no reaction shots of Laura. "Sure I felt left out," said Fleming. "Sturges assured me I was going to be in some wonderful scenes. Those close-ups would have enhanced my role in what has become a classic."

Sturges's shooting script reveals that the Denbow character as originally conceived was more forthright. During her parting with Wyatt at The Bluffs, she delivers an ultimatum: "What makes you think [your brother Virgil] needs you anymore than I do? We're not going to start a life together with a gun in your hand. Either you make a clean break or—" This speech and others were cut, and as Fleming noted, Laura was finally "pushed aside." "I always felt I was left with a horse," she said, still smarting from the slight.

Gunfight at the O.K. Corral, budgeted at just under $2 million, proved a long shoot—fifty-six days, from mid-March to mid-May. Sturges returned to Old Tucson and other southwest Arizona locations for the Fort Griffin and Dodge City exteriors, barbershop, and Cosmopolitan Hotel interiors, the Clanton ranch, and the rutted road leading to the corral and the final shootout. "It was a bone-dry spring, perfect for our purposes," Wallis said. "The look of bare, scorched earth helped establish the fact that people lived here at the mercy of the elements." Sturges considered shooting where it happened, at the actual Wells Fargo livery stable and O.K. Corral, but as Douglas noted, it was "[too] small and we would have been cramped for angles." Also, it had become a busy tourist attraction.

The Long Branch Saloon interiors and street scenes were shot on the backlot and at the Paramount Ranch. In April, Sturges returned to Old Tucson for the climactic gunfight. Taking a page from Anthony Mann, he labored over camera placement and logistics. In his shooting script, he diagramed the action, showing exactly where Cotton, Ike, Ringo and the others stood when Doc and the Earps approached on Fremont Street. "The gunfight was choreographed like a ballet," explained Wallis. "John and I drew up a map plotting every move Burt and Kirk and the Clanton boys made." The producer added: "We wanted the audience to clearly understand the geography of the scene, to know at any given moment exactly where Earp and Holliday and the Clanton boys were." Such preparation paid off: Sturges was able to complete twelve to thirty setups a day.

The history books report that the gunfight took place around 3 p.m. on a wintry October day and was over in a flash. "The real gunfight," allowed Douglas, "was smaller than ours, and duller: 30 seconds, 34 shots, three men dead." Ford staged the battle at dawn, as the new day is announced by the rising of Ike Clanton's head, and expanded it to a little more than three minutes. Sturges's more theatrical re-enactment, which took three days to shoot, involved stampeding horses, a burning wagon, and thunderous shotgun blasts as Wyatt and his brothers dive for cover. Also staged at daybreak, Sturges's battle was less a metaphoric resurrection in the Fordian sense than a reaffirmation of brotherly love. Douglas recalled the shootout lasting five minutes; Wallis said eleven. Using the first shot and the death of Billy Clanton (Hopper) as parameters, the gun battle runs a little more than seven minutes. (In *Hour of the Gun*, his O.K. Corral sequel, Sturges would rely on eyewitness accounts and compress the battle to a mere thirteen seconds.)

Of course, *Gunfight at the O.K. Corral* was no more a documentary of the event than *My Darling Clementine*. For all Uris's and Sturges's research, the film was a flamboyant embellishment that benefited from Douglas's craven Doc and Tiomkin's soon-to-be-hit theme song: "*O.K. Corral—O.K. Corral / There the outlaw band / Made their final stand / At O.K. Corral! / Guns blazed—guns roared / Men fell—Dear Lord!*" Sturges himself called it "a slick horse opera with the accent on opera." Little wonder the French championed it and Uris disowned it, he said. It was the kind of escapist entertainment that only Hollywood, going full tilt to distance itself from television, could manufacture. It was to the Western what Douglas Sirk's *Written on the Wind*, released a year earlier, was to the melodrama. The real love affair was not between Wyatt and Laura, who is abandoned midway through the narrative, but between Wyatt and Doc—the brooding, by-the-book marshal who is chided for being so self-righteous (he even dresses like a preacher) and the embittered gambler-gunslinger who wears ruffled shirts, swills lilac water, and frequents the bad side of town.

"You know, we're playing two pre-Freudian fags," Lancaster told Douglas. "We're in love with each other and we don't know how to express ourselves that way—so we just kind of look at each other and grunt and don't say very much, but you know we love each other."

Doc and Wyatt represent two sides of the same tormented persona; and, as such, they can be seen as precursors to the antagonistic buddies in *Never So Few*, *The Magnificent Seven*, and *The Great Escape*. By the time they are called out by the Clantons, their roles have been reversed:

Doc is the more reasonable one; Wyatt, funereal solemn, cloaked in shadow, is bent on vengeance, the bloodier the better. He makes amends over the corpse of Billy Clanton by discarding his badge. "They shared a common sense of values, a common sense of integrity," Sturges pointed out. "Earp was a very straight-on guy. He discovered to his amazement that so was Holliday. Doc didn't lie. He didn't kill without cause. He never pretended to be anything he wasn't. Wyatt liked him for that reason. Each was kind of amazed by the uprightness of the other."

At the last minute, Sturges asked Uris to write two speeches to underscore where Hollywood stood on vigilante justice. One would be delivered by Doc to Wyatt, standing over the body of his slain kid brother; the second would be delivered by Virgil's wife, Betty (Joan Camden), at a family meeting. Uris refused. He wanted no part of what he saw as a civics lesson. So Sturges, using Macreedy's "rule of law" speech as his model, restructured the moments leading up to the gunfight and wrote the inserts himself. Doc now said, "Don't let them push you into a personal fight. You're a lawman, Wyatt. Don't throw away a lifetime's work. Where's your logic?" Wyatt responded: "To hell with logic. It's my brother lying there." Moments later, Betty lectures the downcast brothers: "You are lawmen, all three of you. You have no right to put yourself above the safety of this town. Your duty is to the people, not your own pride."

"Leon hated those scenes and, though it added to his reputation, told everyone he hated the picture," said Sturges. "He told me, 'I'm glad you don't make your living as a writer; you don't write so good.' That's the only thing I contributed to the script." (In an earlier interview for *American Film*, Sturges stated Uris agreed with the changes and, however reluctantly, wound up polishing what he had written.)

Gunfight at the O.K. Corral—promoted as "The Strangest Alliance This Side of Heaven or Hell"—opened in late May 1957. It was a box-office hit, grossing $4.7 million on its first run and another $6 million in re-release, and earned Oscar nominations for editing and sound. *Variety* credited the film to Wallis and called it "a strong money picture" with a topnotch cast. Sturges's direction, the trade added, "captured the stirring spirit of the period." Echoing Fleming's sentiments, *Time* likened Wyatt's decision to leave Laura for Doc to that of a "man who is heading for nothing better than the electric chair." Crowther raised an eyebrow over a title sequence lifted almost verbatim from *High Noon*, but conceded that, overall, the film was a rugged, energetic return to the Westerns of yore.

Though the film is generally referred to as Sturges's first hit, the director downplayed its importance. "*The Magnificent Seven* and *The Great Escape*—they're my pictures," he said. "I'm the one who put the imprint on them. On *Gunfight*, I was a director, period. It was a Hal Wallis Production." Further, in his eyes, the Western was too self-consciously pretty and suffered from a weak antagonist in Lyle Bettger. Brennan, the prototype for the murderous patriarch, should have reprised the Ike Clanton role. "When I look at it now," Sturges said, "it doesn't hold up like *Black Rock* and *The Magnificent Seven*. It looks 'movie-ish' and arty, the sets look too clean, and I think it's staged in a mechanical manner."

The film's success translated into industry kudos (a Directors Guild nomination) and the number 9 spot (after John Huston and Vincente Minnelli) on the exhibitors' poll of top moneymaking directors. Sturges now was linked to a number of hot properties, including *The Sons of Katie Elder* with Charlton Heston (ultimately replaced by John Wayne) and *The Wreck of the Mary Deare* with Gary Cooper and Heston. He turned down these projects to pursue his dream of remaking *Mutiny on the Bounty*. He wanted Lancaster for Fletcher Christian, Anthony Perkins for the midshipman, Montgomery Clift for the ship's doctor, and—in what was seen as either brilliance or sheer lunacy—Tracy for Captain Bligh. Schary, who shunned remakes, said, "My God, it will cost $5 million!" Sturges laughed and replied, "More, because we have Tracy, Lancaster, and Clift." Later, the director challenged, "Top that cast! Spence had no ego as an actor. He didn't care whether Laughton had played the part. Can you imagine how he would have been as Bligh and Burt as Christian? But Dore was very small-picture minded."

In 1958, MGM announced a remake of *Mutiny on the Bounty* with Marlon Brando as Christian and possibly Orson Welles as Bligh. Sturges was involved, until he received a call from Brando. "This picture isn't really about the mutiny on the Bounty," the actor told him. "It's really about racism. If black people and white people can't get together, we're all doomed." Sturges replied, "Fine, Marlon, if that's the picture you want to make, make it. But not with me." (Sturges was replaced by Carol Reed, who, mid-shoot, was replaced by Lewis Milestone.)

In October 1957, a full year before Warner would premiere *The Old Man and the Sea*, Sturges accepted *The Law and Jake Wade*, another Western at Metro. "I'm off to Lone Pine to get back in the saddle again," he told Hayward, happy to be away from sharks and corroded studio tanks. The new project starred Robert Taylor and Richard Widmark as former outlaw buddies now on opposite sides of the law. The trick opening had Jake (Taylor), all in black, riding into town with a spare horse and saving Clint Hollister (Widmark) from the hangman's noose. Clint insists Jake tell him where he buried $20,000 from their last bank job; Jake refuses and returns to his new life—as upstanding town marshal with a fiancée, Peggy (Patricia Owens). He thinks he killed a child during their last robbery; hence, the conversion. By kidnapping Peggy, Clint and his men (Henry Silva and DeForest Kelley among them) force Jake to lead them to a ghost town where the money is buried. A Comanche raiding party and the obligatory shootout follow.

Shot in CinemaScope in the Alabama Hills and snow-capped High Sierras, where the temperature hovered around zero and the crew breakfasted on hot soup, *Jake Wade* fused elements of *Gunga Din* and William Wellman's *Yellow Sky*, also set in a ghost town. Among the film's assets are Sturges's typically rugged locations, a strong supporting cast, and Widmark back playing the wild-eyed desperado with hyena laugh. The action set pieces: Jake and Peggy's attempted escape (played against the howling mountain wind) and the Indian raid on the ghost town, which included stunt gags that would be recycled for *The Magnificent Seven* and *Sergeants 3*. Unfortunately, even with upturned collar, Taylor came off as stiff and remote, and the script lacked a third act. "Trust me to do what I have to do," Jake tells Peggy as he rides back to settle the score with Clint.

Like *Backlash*, much was made of *Jake Wade* as one of the new breed of "adult Western" in the tradition of *Jubal* and *The Naked Spur*. Silva's Rennie is an obvious psychotic, a preacher's son who leers at Peggy and brags about gunning down his own father. Next to Anthony Mann's stock-in-trade, however, the film feels both muddled and conventional.

Silva, who described his character as "a mean-spirited cowboy," related to Sturges, who shared a love of fast cars and good stories. "Sturges was a strong guy, but he wasn't a macho bullshitter," said the actor, who would later appear in *Sergeants 3*. "He had experiences that were just phenomenal. He could invite you over to his house and keep you entertained for weeks." Taylor took an instant dislike to Silva. "The first day on the set he stared daggers at me. What the hell was he pissed off about? I didn't have many scenes with him. Later, I figured out it was my height. Before I got the job they asked me how tall I was. I'm only five-eleven, but still taller than Taylor, and this must have bugged him. He was the total opposite of Sturges, who I never saw angry once."

Released in June, four months before *The Old Man and the Sea* and just ahead of *The Bravados* and *The Big Country*, both with Gregory Peck, *Jake Wade* did mediocre to average business. Crowther at the *New York Times* dismissed it as clichéd and predictable but liked the locations, which he found "authentic and awesome." He also acknowledged that Sturges was carving out a niche for himself as an action director. "It is in the nightlong running battle, fought out in a creaky old ghost town that director John Sturges has the opportunity to make the best, in visual terms, of those clichés. He does rather well, considering how many times he's stood off Comanches. . . . Needless to say, the hatchets come right at the camera and miss."

Widmark's terse appraisal: "bad picture, good part."

Often referred to as a downbeat, overtly psychological companion piece to *Gunfight at the O.K. Corral, Last Train from Gun Hill*— developed by Kirk Douglas's Bryna Productions and reuniting the star, Wallis, and Sturges—can also be seen as a hybrid of *Bad Day at Black Rock* (outsider versus evil town), *High Noon* (clock on the wall ticks down, this time to 9 p.m.), and the Delmer Daves–Elmore Leonard Western *3:10 to Yuma* (hero and prisoner wait in a hotel for the next train). This time, instead of the Clantons, Marshal Matt Morgan (Douglas) battles a former-partner-now-cattle-baron named Craig Belden (Anthony Quinn), whose son Rick (Earl Holliman) and a ranch hand (Brian Hutton) have raped and killed Morgan's Indian wife. Morgan rides to Gun Hill and confronts Belden, who, though emotionally torn, refuses to hand over his son. Morgan waits for Rick in town and holds him at the Harper House as Belden and his hands gather on the street below, debating their next move. Belden's mistress, Linda (Carolyn Jones), an entrepreneurial madam like Katy Jurado in *High Noon*, allies with Morgan.

Last Train, from a story by Les Crutchfield, went into production as "Showdown at Gun Hill." The Arizona locations included Old Tucson and—for the rolling prairie leading to Belden's adobe ranch house—the historic Empire Ranch, southeast of Tucson. The opening rape was staged in the same wash and "tunnel of trees" used for Laura and Wyatt's courtship in *Gunfight at the O.K. Corral.* The Belden ranch, saloon and hotel interiors, and the depot shootout were filmed at the studio. James Stewart had climbed the main staircase of the Harper House the year before in *Vertigo.*

Wallis described the Western as "a powerful tale of revenge, just the kind of story I like." Though the script was by James Poe, Douglas went behind the producer's and Sturges's backs to the blacklisted Dalton Trumbo for rewrites and additional scenes. It should come as no surprise, then, that the most powerful monologues drip with glib bitterness, a Trumbo trademark after his dealings with HUAC. The first is delivered by Gun Hill's pragmatic sheriff (Walter Sande, the café owner in *Black Rock*), who prides himself on taking "the long view." Staring into the street, just as Sheriff Cotton Wilson does in *O.K. Corral,* he tells Morgan, "Forty years from now the weeds'll grow just as pretty on my grave as they will on yours. Nobody'll ever remember that I was yellow and that you died like a fool. That's your long view, son."

Trumbo's present to Douglas was a speech about slow justice "the white man's way" and swinging one cold morning at the end of a noose. It was delivered through clenched teeth by Morgan to Rick, handcuffed to a hotel bed and near tears.

> You'll hit the end of that rope like a sack of potatoes, all dead weight. It'll be white hot around your neck, and your Adam's apple'll turn to mush. . . . You'll fight for your breath, but you haven't got any breath. Your brain will begin to boil. You'll scream and holler. But nobody'll hear you. You'll hear it, but nobody else. Finally, you're just swinging there. All alone and dead.

Politically, this would appear the antithesis of Douglas's courtroom plea to save three soldiers from the firing squad in Stanley Kubrick's *Paths of Glory.* Trumbo, who opposed capital punishment, intended the words to point up how far Morgan had sunk in his pursuit of vengeance.

"The speech added a whole new dimension to the character," Holliman said. Sturges, however, saw capital punishment as a deterrent. He used the speech to underscore Morgan's righteous resolve. It was shot from a low angle, Rick's perspective, with Morgan in half-shadow, looming over the kid.

"It was a mystery where those speeches came from," said Sturges. "All I knew is they were powerful stuff, and that Douglas said we could have them for $3,000. I called Wallis. 'Here are two things Kirk gave me.' He asked, 'Are they any good?' I said, 'They're terrific.' So we gave Kirk the money and later learned they came from Dalton."

Like *Gunfight*, the new Western was shot by Charles Lang Jr. in Technicolor and VistaVision. Unlike *Gunfight*, which has a burnt, autumnal look, *Last Train* was shot in midsummer and, therefore, has much richer hues and an almost surreal pictorialism. Sturges took his time on the depot shootout, which was diagramed from all angles and photographed at night in deep focus. "Unfortunately, the tracks were laid just under the office windows of Paramount boss Y. Frank Freeman and the noise drove him crazy," recalled Wallis. "We had to reroute the railroad."

Douglas and Quinn had costarred in the Van Gogh biopic *Lust for Life*, which had brought Quinn a supporting-actor Oscar for his Paul Gauguin. Douglas was still fuming over not winning for best actor, said Sturges, and was determined to upstage Quinn whenever possible. No "mystery speeches" by Trumbo went to Quinn. And when it came time for Belden to storm the hotel, Quinn rubbed his head. Wouldn't the town's most powerful man kick in doors, rather than stand around deliberating?

They rehearsed the scene. Quinn shouted to Douglas in the hotel, "I've got twenty men down here. Now, you turn Rick loose." But Quinn, who had just directed *The Buccaneer* for Cecil B. DeMille, his father-in-law, couldn't make sense of the exchange. He told Sturges, "With all these gunmen I've got, and this whole town on my side, why don't I just go up there and shoot the place up and spring him?"

"Because you're paid not to," Sturges said.

"What?"

"This is reel four, Tony. We've got five reels to go."

"Tony was a bright guy, a good actor," Sturges acknowledged later. "But he could never direct a picture. After seeing *Last Train,* he came to me and said, 'You're a genius. My God, the way it all works. That thing where I'm looking out the window and I see my kid up there and I see Douglas—it's great!' I said, 'What the hell did you think you were looking at, Tony?' He hadn't a clue." (At certain points, Quinn's voice is dubbed by another actor, suggesting he left before post-production was completed.)

Holliman, who attended the film's San Francisco premiere with Sturges and Dorothy, said he was impressed all over again by the director's easygoing decisiveness. He would do just about anything to get a shot. For the scene in which Belden orders his son to take a swing at the ranch foreman (Brad Dexter) there was a long-horned steer rack over the fireplace and little room to maneuver. "I was supposed to be emotionally hurt, and Sturges wanted a close-up," recalled Holliman. "But Lang couldn't get his camera in close. 'I can't get in there, I can't shoot it.' Sturges told him, 'Cut the set in half. Cut it.' He had that kind of clout."

Last Train from Gun Hill opened in July 1959. The critics this time praised Sturges's assured pacing. Crowther called the suspense Western "valiant," adding, "Director John Sturges is experienced at this sort of thing, having done *Bad Day at Black Rock* and *Gunfight at the O.K. Corral.* It shows." *Last Train,* however, did not fare nearly as well at the box office as *Gunfight* because, like Raoul Walsh's grim *Pursued* (1947), it was less about blazing six guns at high noon than Freudian subtext and psychological scars. The opening rape—which unfolds behind the spinning wheel of an overturned buggy—provoked more than one Production Code memo. (The ripping of the victim's blouse came from, of all places, Roger Vadim's *And God Created Woman,* starring Brigitte Bardot.)

Linda's confession to a lifetime of prostitution—"I haven't been lonesome since I was twelve years old"—escaped the censors because Linda by film's end appeared rehabilitated. Though she peers longingly after Morgan following the shootout, she is at the slain Belden's side. The script ended more cynically. Linda, trance-like, wandered back to the bar, now doing "a whooping business."

Salesman: "All right, missy. Now how about that little drink?"

Linda, hearing a mournful train whistle, forces a smile. "Sure, honey. Why not?"

"I was pretty adroit at getting away with as much as I could," said Sturges, whose sense of Victorian decorum would never allow him to wander into more graphic Sam Peckinpah or Don Siegel territory. "*Last Train* was done in good taste. Very mild compared to now. We didn't use the word *rape*. We just implied that he killed her."

In 1963, to tap unrealized profits, Wallis re-released *Last Train* on a double bill with *Gunfight*. The ad campaign was obviously an attempt to improve upon the star power of Sturges's 1960 release, *The Magnificent Seven:* "The fiery brilliance of eight great stars in the mightiest double-barreled excitement to blaze across the screen!" The press book for the "quality Westerns" played up Wallis but barely mentioned Sturges, who was persona non grata now with the producer, annoyed by his defection to the Mirisch Company. Seeing the films back-to-back, audiences had a chance to study their marked differences in tone and execution. *Last Train* opens with a bravura sequence played with almost no dialogue and, despite Sturges's refusal to acknowledge an agenda, tackles the treatment of Native Americans in the "civilized" West. Morgan's wife, Catherine (Israeli actress Ziva Rodann), is referred to as "squaw missy" and "Cherokee squaw" by her killer. A townsperson tells Morgan, "Hereabouts, we don't arrest a man for killing an Indian, we give him a bounty." The sheriff replies with a forearm to the face. (This theme would be treated in a more heavy-handed manner the following year, in John Huston's *The Unforgiven*.)

Sturges, in attempting another tightly plotted variation on *High Noon* and *Black Rock,* also demonstrated a growing reliance on mise-en-scène. Like Hitchcock in *Shadow of a Doubt,* he used the train's black smoke to announce Morgan's arrival and dark intentions, and later, as the drama at the Harper House unfolds, he uses the "O"s in saloon to accentuate disapproving eyes. As a possible nod to the director of *High Noon,* Zimmerman Bros. Grain and Feed Sales is one of the more prominent buildings in Gun Hill.

Appropriately, the film's pièce de résistance is the depot shootout, from buildup to execution. A model of its kind, it is played in close to real time, utilizing the parallel tracking and cross-cutting that Sturges would utilize later in *The Magnificent Seven*. Morgan and Rick, shotgun beneath his chin, depart the burning hotel standing in a buckboard; Belden, Linda, and Smithers, bent on rescuing his partner, fall in behind the rig, along with townspeople hoping to witness Morgan's death. As the train pulls in and cuts off the buckboard from Belden and his men, Smithers draws on Morgan and accidentally kills Rick. Morgan returns fire, killing Smithers. Having administered swift rather than slow justice, Morgan prepares to board the train. Belden, distraught over his only son's death, calls Morgan out. The ensuing gunfight makes superb use of deep-focus VistaVision, with the depot platform slicing the frame diagonally. Unlike the shootout at O.K. Corral, however, this outcome is anything but cathartic. Morgan's victory is a Pyrrhic one, at best. To gain "justice" for his family, he has destroyed his friend's family.

10

The Rat Trap

It sounded like a contradiction, given their antithetical work ethics, but John Sturges was seduced as much by Frank Sinatra's bad-boy image as his talent. "Frank never took anything off anybody and I admired the hell out of that. Maybe because I was like that myself, but in a less out there way." Their different notions of machismo, what it meant to be a "man's man," brought them together twice—first for the World War II melodrama *Never So Few* and then, two years later, for an ill-conceived Western remake of *Gunga Din* called *Sergeants 3*.

"Sturges and Sinatra? They *were* a weird team," agreed Robert Relyea, the director's assistant. "John was so square we used to say he was cubed; everything had to be proper and straight. If you held your cards out, John wouldn't look at them. He was one of those kinds of guys." The entertainer, on the other hand, could be mischievous and inconsiderate. "What can you say about Frank?" said actress Ruta Lee. "He liked to play—and do things on 'Frank time.'" Added Henry Silva, "There were fireworks on *Sergeants 3,* but most of the time Frank respected the hell out of Sturges because Sturges was so well prepared."

With the critical acclaim of *From Here to Eternity* and *The Man with the Golden Arm*, Sinatra had evolved into a credible dramatic lead and reliable box-office draw. But it was well known that, for all his ambition, he had trouble concentrating on a project very long and was always anxious to move on to the next thing, be it a recording session, a club engagement, or another movie. "If Frank said, 'I won't work beyond such-and-such date,'" recalled Relyea, "that was it—you had better adjust your calendar." Not surprisingly, then, he gravitated to filmmakers who got things done quickly and efficiently. When MGM optioned Tom T. Chamales's best-selling *Never So Few*—about Kachin rebels trained by American and British O.S.S. operatives in the jungles of northern Burma—and announced Sinatra as Captain Tom Reynolds, the lead, Sturges's name came up. Sinatra liked the idea: He was a fan of *Bad Day at Black Rock* and *The Old Man and the Sea*. But he needed reassurance because, at least initially, the project would mean a trip to remote, potentially dangerous locations. He called Spencer Tracy, and Tracy confirmed that Sturges was all right—"a no-bull kind of guy."

"Frank," explained Sturges, "had no tolerance for people in the industry because they had steered him wrong so often, and he had made a lot of pictures he thought were crap because he needed the money to pay his income tax. . . . On that first picture, I had no trouble with him. He had heard from Spence that I was the kind of director he'd get along with."

Sturges accepted the project provided he could retain members of his team, including Millard Kaufman and Ferris Webster; shoot on location in the jungles of Burma and Ceylon, where David Lean had shot *Bridge on the River Kwai;* and, most important, have Sinatra's undivided attention. Sinatra, between record deals and concentrating more on movies, assured the director of his commitment, even as he promised roles to buddies Peter Lawford and Sammy Davis Jr., who, because of ill-timed comments about Sinatra, would be fired before principal photography began.

Sturges liked Chamales, who was retained as technical adviser. The swarthy, curly haired author, fast earning a reputation as a brawler, reminded him of a cross between Johnny Cash and James Jones. Indeed, Chamales acknowledged that his novel would "never have been written had I not read Jones's *From Here to Eternity*. . . . Jim's subsequent aid, his highly valued friendship have been a great part of my incentive." In his early twenties, Chamales had commanded a battalion of northern Kachin tribesmen against the Japanese in defense of the Burma Road, China's lifeline. His experiences were the inspiration for the 1957 bestseller, which took its title from Churchill's quote about home-front resolve during the Battle of Britain. With its frequent shifts from the jungle to the boudoir, the book echoed the pulpy excesses of *Battle Cry* and *The Naked and the Dead.* Further, the climactic raid into China to punish a renegade warlord played on Cold War paranoia. (Though blamed on Chiang Kai-shek in the book, the raid would become, in Hollywood's hands, a less-than-veiled warning to Chairman Mao.) Chamales received $150,000 for his book and another $10,000 to coach Sinatra, who, in goatee, was essentially playing the author.

Sturges's mandate to Kaufman: Lose the flashbacks and foreground the jungle action and R&R romances with Margaret, the nurse from Reynolds' past, and Carla, "a lovely, Madonna-like" Austrian refugee who travels in ritzy circles. "Sacred and Profane," as the project was originally titled, included several graphic battles with Japanese soldiers "eager for the kill" being impaled on punjis and dying in a hail of bullets. For the action set piece, a nighttime assault on a Japanese airfield, Kaufman had "a Jap soldier covered with oil . . . burning like a live torch" and shrapnel careening "across the sky" like a comet and "great splinters of steel ejaculate, hitting planes and hangar." These and other vignettes (including a Kachin scout having his leg amputated) were eventually dropped to shave costs and placate the censors. The action sequences that remained, all taken from the book, included an opening jungle ambush, a surprise attack by the Japanese (acting on information supplied by a Kachin traitor), and Reynolds's mission into China, which brings rebukes from the U.S. high command. The original script, like the book, ended with Reynolds being killed by a grenade blast.

Sturges returned to Metro in 1958 to oversee pre-production. He now occupied an office in the Thalberg Building. Relyea reported to "this very distinguished, very impressive man who you just respected to begin with, partially based on his work, partially based on his presence." Sturges had misgivings about the project, however. He had never made a picture in such a remote location and, though he traveled throughout his career, never liked living out of a suitcase. "He wanted to make everything in Lone Pine . . . or on Santa Monica Boulevard," said Relyea, who after that first meeting accompanied Sturges to purchase a passport holder.

Instead of celebrating Christmas Eve with Dorothy and the children, Sturges spent it with the film's producer, Edmund Grainger, screening movies shot in Ceylon and Thailand, including *Bridge on the*

River Kwai, Elephant Walk, and *The Purple Plain,* starring Gregory Peck. A longtime Lean fan, Sturges had production manager Ruby Rosenberg fly to Ceylon to find key backdrops from *Kwai,* including the waterfall and the summit overlooking the bridge. Rosenberg was then dispatched to Burma to scout jungle locations and strike an agreement with the government to shoot "Kachins in traditional dress and other local color." He wired back from Rangoon that, although MGM had the approval of the Ministry of Information and stories had been planted in the local paper ("Burma will be richer by $100,000 and movie fans will have the pleasure of seeing Frank Sinatra in person if the government approves MGM's request to film sequences here"), the country was racked by political corruption and could not guarantee the actors' or the crew's safety. Further, written approval of the project would be granted only "on condition all strips of film taken in Burma be pre-censored by government before they are released for showing."

Things were worse the farther north you went, wired back Rosenberg. The Kachin State was beset by "holdups, shootings, etc. . . . So far, what I have seen & heard, I am sure it is going to be real tough to operate in this country. The government is not reliable & unable to have law & order in the northern states. This is just a stopgap government. In six months, there will be a new bunch in power." (Another reason for the red tape: The production company planned to bring along enough artillery—M1 rifles, dynamite, 60mm mortars—to mount its own coup.)

Around New Year's, Sturges flew to Rangoon and then Kandy, Ceylon. He cabled Sinatra and Siegel: "Burma poor. Ceylon excellent. No need principals here. Will discuss upon arrival [at studio]."

Though MGM later insisted in press handouts that *Never So Few* was shot where the battles took place, the decision was eventually made to bypass Burma for Ceylon and Thailand and shoot "wild" (minus synchronized sound) with doubles, thereby saving money and maximizing studio time. In February, Sturges, Relyea, and cinematographer William Daniels returned to Ceylon. Here, over the next month they shot widescreen footage of rice paddies, pagodas and, in the Ratnapura Kalu region, the guerrilla forces snaking across jungle rivers. In the skies over Kandy—the first stop in what would be a 27,000-mile location shoot—Sturges relived memories of his flights over Italy. He and Daniels rode in the DC-3 that parachutes supplies in the opening sequence. It was a bumpy ride but resulted in some of the film's best footage. "He had spent a lot of time in 'puddle jumpers' and was very comfortable in the air," said Relyea, an experienced flier himself. (Relyea would double as a stunt pilot in *The Great Escape*.)

While Sturges was on location, Sammy Davis, who was set to play Sinatra's driver, Corporal Ringa, appeared on a Chicago radio show and said he thought he was a bigger, and certainly more approachable, star than Sinatra. "Talent is not an excuse for bad manners," he told host Jack Eigen. "I don't care if you are the most talented person in the world. It does not give you the right to step on people and treat them rotten. This is what [Frank] does occasionally." Sinatra was furious and, according to Peter Lawford, demanded that that "dirty nigger bastard" be kicked off the picture. Grainger welcomed the decision. In his first meeting with Sinatra, he committed the ultimate faux pas. "You know, we're not being accurate [about an integrated American platoon]," he said. "We don't want any of *those kind of people* in the film." Sinatra insisted the producer be barred from the set.

Siegel cabled Sturges with the official studio line: "Because of possible conflicting engagement, may have to recast role of Ringa. Therefore, essential in each shot you do with Davis double, you also do one with Caucasian double of medium height and build. Stop. Situation should be resolved by Tuesday or Wednesday." Three days later, a second cable: "Impossible to resolve conflict of engagements. Therefore, use only Caucasian double for remainder of work."

"Sammy's double was prominent in most of the jungle scenes," said Relyea. "We had been shooting for four weeks, and I had diligently trained this African American to walk with the funny kind of gait Sammy had. Then we got a coded telegram. 'Chicago out. Stand by.' I looked in my code book. 'Chicago' was Sammy. Then we got a telegram the next day saying, 'Chicago replaced by Detroit.' I look up 'Detroit,' and Detroit's Steve McQueen. So John yells, 'Get [Davis's double] in the back of the bunch!'" (The released film contains long shots of a short black man walking behind Sinatra's double as the column fords a river.)

The role as "rewritten" now matched the book's Corporal Ringa. He was cocky, blond, and, as Chamales wrote, "vigorously built with piercing icy eyes in the incongruous baby face." Stan Kamen of the William Morris Agency suggested a scruffy New York actor named Steve McQueen. McQueen had done a walk-on in Robert Wise's *Somebody Up There Likes Me* and had made a few B movies before landing the Josh Randall lead on the TV series *Wanted: Dead or Alive.* "He plays a bounty hunter, but with attitude," Kamen said. "He's Hollywood's next Bogie." Sturges wasn't impressed. He didn't watch television. But Dorothy did, and she and half the women in America were drawn to the twenty-seven-year-old's Method insouciance. Sturges recalled, "When he walked into my office, he had the same thing that you saw later in *The Magnificent Seven* and *The Great Escape*—brashness cut with insecurity. He was a bundle of contradictions. But he had an immediate 'scene sense.'" Sturges described McQueen's acting style as "reactive, like James Dean in *Giant.*" He signed the actor to a three-picture deal at $25,000 a week. (Davis would have gotten $75,000 a week.)

More problems arose when Sturges returned to Bangkok for pickup shots of hotels and a rubber-tree plantation. The Thai Ministry of Defense refused to allow its soldiers to double for Kachin tribesmen. It relented after some shrewd bartering by the director: MGM would build a schoolhouse outside the city in exchange for a hundred soldiers, some of whom would double as Japanese and Kachins.

The cables home to Dorothy were becoming increasingly terse, even for Sturges. Concerned, Dorothy alerted the studio that she planned to join her husband on location. After the tickets were purchased and hotel accommodations made, the trip was canceled, leaving some to conjecture that the relationship was in trouble.

"Dorothy was a helluva nice woman, bright and commonsensical," said Kaufman. "They got divorced because John was jumping around with other women. My first awareness of this came on *Never So Few,* when I went around to see him about something. He was in his office with a girl during work hours, and the door was locked. I thought, 'Oh, shit, if he's this overt about it, he's going to get in a terrible jam.' And that's what happened. His affairs weren't that difficult to uncover because of the way he was. Out in the open."

During downtime in Bangkok, Sturges played tourist, splurging on souvenirs for family and friends. He bought a twenty-foot teak canoe for his swimming pool and a collection of Burmese gongs for a singer friend in Hawaii. "John never saw a trinket that he didn't want," said Relyea. "I had to wait for two hours while he bargained with a guy for the gongs. Then he had to find somebody to ship these things back. . . . The canoe barely fit in his pool."

After a month on location, the director received a frantic telegram from Kaufman. In his absence, the studio had hired the husband-wife writing team of Irving Ravetch and Harriet Frank Jr., Sturges told Relyea at the hotel bar that night. "Listen, they're gutting the script. I'm flying out on the first plane tomorrow."

Sturges wanted the movie to end the only way that made sense dramatically, with the battle-weary Reynolds's death. Sol Siegel, MGM's head of production, had other ideas and signed Italian superstar Gina Lollobrigida to play Sinatra's love interest, Carla. (The Margaret character was all but eliminated.)

"It was a helluva movie at one time, but Siegel made ridiculous changes," charged Kaufman. "The only way I saw the film to end was to have Sinatra's character killed. You knew goddamn well he's gonna get killed. I threatened to quit, but Siegel convinced me to stay. After I was off the lot, they tacked on a new ending with Sinatra and Lollobrigida in a hot embrace. It was awful. The color didn't even match."

"The whole thing got changed on us," Sturges elaborated. "Kaufman's script stuck to the book, which was pretty factual. The idea was for Frank to play Chamales with a beard, which he shaved when he went into town. It was a character role, which Frank could do. Look at *The Man with the Golden Arm.* . . . But then the studio got the idea that instead of the girl just being a girl, which is all she was, co-star Frank with Gina Lollobrigida. The Ravetches rewrote the whole goddamn script and then handed it over to Frank and me. We were outraged by the changes. I was particularly astounded because you're continually accused by the front office of rewriting their stuff on the set, and here we're shooting the approved script and they're rewriting it up in the front office. Well, it changed the whole complexion of the picture."

As soon as he arrived in Culver City, Sturges collected Sinatra, and together they confronted MGM's head of production. "Will you excuse us for a second, John?" said Siegel, leading Sinatra into a side office. Ten minutes later, Sinatra emerged and sheepishly said, "I think we better go along with these guys." The director had been blindsided.

"I never knew what Siegel told him," continued Sturges. "Maybe Frank owed money to the government—income tax—or maybe he had borrowed some money from the studio. Who knows. I was angry enough to quit, but Frank asked me not to. See, if Frank wasn't on my side, I couldn't win and it wouldn't have been right to just quit."

Never So Few—the first of Sturges's three World War II movies—was shot in Metrocolor and CinemaScope and budgeted at just under $2 million. It had a liberal three-month shooting schedule, most of it spent on the backlot, which was dressed for the jungle bivouacs, hotel and mansion interiors, and Hibachi Airfield, site of the nighttime raid. The budget included everything from toupee tape to Japanese Zeroes leased from a nearby aviation museum. Sinatra received $200,000 a week and a share of the profits; Lollobrigida, making her Hollywood debut, was signed for a flat $300,000, but saw only $50,000 (the balance paid to Cinematografica and Howard Hughes, to whom she was still contractually obligated).

Sensing an aggravating shoot ahead, Sturges made sure he was well compensated. He was guaranteed thirty-three weeks at almost $3,500 a week, or a minimum of $114,500. Because the film would go several days over schedule—due to the stars' chronic tardiness—the budget ballooned by almost $1.6 million to $3.6 million. That meant an additional $40,000 for Sturges. It also meant cutting extras and location costumes ("do not dress anyone; if possible, shoot as they are").

Though significantly older than the book's protagonist, Sinatra gamely donned goatee and Australian bush hat as Reynolds, the guerrilla leader. Lollobrigida played the mysterious kept woman, Carla Vesari, who, in the end, appears to have something to do with Allied intelligence. After failing to sign Jack Hawkins and Trevor Howard, Richard Johnson was announced as Reynolds's British sidekick, who sports bandolier and monocle and refers to Carla as "quite a crock of curry." Charles Bronson was cast to type as the combative Sergeant Danforth, the Navajo decoder; Paul Henreid played Carla's worldly benefactor; and the Asian American character actor James Hong played General Chao, who is Red Chinese but treated as stereotypically as the film's "yellows" or "Japs." Veteran Brian Donlevy appeared briefly as an American general who faces down Chao with a defiant "In the words of an old hymn, you go to hell!" After years of heavy drinking, Donlevy's memory was failing, and the scene, scheduled for an afternoon, took two days, with Sturges patiently standing by as the actor read his lines from a blackboard.

Lollobrigida, unlike Carla, did not possess "a heart as big as the Himalayas." She flirted with her leading man one moment, cursed him the next. (The studio planted stories about a fiery romance.) "Sophia Loren! Sophia Loren!" she screamed when Sinatra mentioned his previous leading lady. "I'm a thoroughbred race horse next to that donkey." In addition to limousine service, Lollobrigida's contract specified jewelry and costume approval, and a dialogue coach. "English wasn't her first or second language," said Relyea. "This distressed Frank, who liked one take. He refused to hang around for Take 27 because she couldn't say 'transgression' in English."

The stars' contrasting work methods were a constant source of friction, Sturges acknowledged. Sinatra favored short days; Lollobrigida insisted upon long rehearsals. They wound up competing to see who could report late to the set most frequently. "Frank had no tolerance for people who weren't prepared," said the director. "He rehearsed and knew his lines. If he couldn't get a scene, he would apologize to the crew and come in the next day and reshoot. That whole business of him doing only one take is bullshit. Because I was organized, so was Frank."

Michael Sturges visited the set regularly. At age eight, he remembered feeling lost among the maze of lights and cables. His father was usually off in a corner with McQueen, who, in pegged pants and golf cap, couldn't decide if he wanted to be "hip" or anachronistic. Like Sturges, the actor never knew his father, and this made him preternaturally wary, like a feral cat. Because he was dyslexic, his wife, Neile, read him the script. John Ford would have poked fun at the disability; Sturges made allowances for it. "Steve was always looking for his father, and his sense of John was that he was a mentor-surrogate," said Neile McQueen. "Later, the role passed to Henry Hathaway. But it was John in the beginning. High praise from Steve, who didn't respect or trust many people."

Sinatra saw McQueen as a younger version of himself and generously ceded the spotlight. "He told Steve, 'It's all yours, kid—take it and run with it,'" said Neile. "We felt we'd been blessed by the pope."

They were on the same wavelength, said Steve McQueen at the time. "We dig one another. We're like minds . . . children emotionally."

No one had to convince Relyea of this. Sinatra and McQueen made life hell for him by tossing lit firecrackers behind crew members and lobbing cherry bombs into dressing rooms. Relyea sent a memo to the front office reporting "firecracker play" that had ignited a can of paint and caused "considerable damage." Sturges laughed at the memory. "You don't sign on with Frank and not expect a little horseplay."

In July, the pyrotechnics began in earnest as a large section of Metro's backlot, converted into the Ubachi Airfield, came under attack. "There will be fire and smoke from burning oil drums, tents and various set units," MGM alerted the Culver City Fire Department. Sturges promised to keep the "force of explosions to a minimum and not greater than those witnessed for the *Ben-Hur* sea battle," but an overzealous effects team turned the dummy oil drums into bazookas. Like burning Frisbees, lids sailed into the crowd of onlookers. No injuries were reported. (Ultimately, much of the airfield sequence was done with miniature trucks and Zeroes.) Lot 3 was then flooded for the raid on the Chinese garrison. During an attack on a hut, Sinatra sustained a minor eye injury. He returned the next day with his head swathed in bandages. "Frank had seen too many war movies," said Relyea. "He yells out, 'I'm hit! I'm hit!' It wasn't the wad in the blank that hit him—that can be dangerous—but a splinter from the bamboo."

Sturges lobbied for more location footage and additional screen time for his latest discovery. "We have trimmed too close where Steve McQueen sticks his gum on the jeep windshield. Chokes a good laugh," he told Siegel. He also argued in a memo for a more bittersweet, *Casablanca*-inspired ending: "As you know, I think we should use some of the air and ground stuff I shot in Ceylon and Thailand in the opening of the picture. . . . Has anyone thought about trying the airfield ending at the next preview? It might be just as effective as the present ending [and perhaps even more realistic]." He won the first battle, conceded the second. The MPAA was less conciliatory. The off-screen torture of the traitor must be muted, and "because of possible disrespectful interpretations," all references to Kachins as "gooks" and Japanese as "Japs or yellows" must be deleted. Also, out of concern for diplomatic relations, the Chungking government's role in border skirmishes should be downplayed.

Contrary to reports, the excessive consumption of alcohol— especially by the perpetually drunk Norby (Dean Jones)—was not added by Sturges and Kaufman to make the characters appear more macho. It was a key element of the novel, wherein scotch and laku (a native drink) are swilled by the bucketful for medicinal purposes and to anesthetize Reynolds and his men to the horrors of war. Chamales himself was a heavy drinker and died in 1960 in an alcohol-related fire. He was thirty-six.

Intended as a Christmas 1959 release, *Never So Few* had trouble finding theaters in the wake of MGM's *Ben-Hur* and didn't open until January, albeit at New York's Radio City Music Hall. It was afforded a flashy sendoff to capitalize on the fan-magazine gossip generated by the stars and fared well at the box office. "Fireworks! Combustion!" promised the press book. The lobby poster had Sinatra leaning over the supine Lollobrigida. *"He was one of the forgotten few fighting a forgotten war—and she gave the kind of love that no man ever forgets!"*

Sturges laughed at this. The war had indeed been forgotten—by Hollywood. "The picture was supposed to be about Reynolds, who goes into China and starts his own war by pursuing communism at its source," he said later. "They rewrote the whole goddamn thing for Lollobrigida, and the stuff about the hypocrisy and injustice of the warlords was lost. Here we were fighting the war, and these guys were taking our equipment and selling it to the enemy, who used it to shoot at us!"

Sturges felt he had betrayed Kaufman's trust. Their second collaboration, he said, had been rendered a melodramatic mishmash—a "phony-looking" soundstage romance interspersed with jungle action instead of the other way around. The revisions by the Ravetches and the appalling lack of chemistry between the stars resulted in some of the most memorably bad love scenes ever played. "I like mature men, Capt. Reynolds," Carla coos at one point. "They ripen a girl, if you know what I mean." When Reynolds has trouble seducing Carla, he reverts to the patented Sinatra approach: "Tell Nikki [Henreid] it's over. Finis. Tell him you're going down the social scale. Because you've taken up with a no-good G.I., who's gonna keep you barefoot and pregnant and on the edge of town."

The best material came from the location shoot: eerie panoramas of jungle shrines and the guerrilla army moving, ghost-like, through bamboo forests. The set pieces, as intended, were the nighttime raid on the airfield (an obvious influence on Aldrich's *The Dirty Dozen*) and the silent, economically staged infiltration of the warlord's camp, which, thanks to McQueen's improvised moments, could be seen as a run-through for even more outlandish scene-stealing in *The Magnificent Seven.*

The reviews for *Never So Few* were deservedly brutal. *Variety* found it a "gaudy . . . patchy affair" and questioned Sinatra's casting and his character's sketchy morality (he euthanizes a fallen comrade and orders the mass execution of the Chinese renegades). Bosley Crowther ogled Lollobrigida's cleavage while ridiculing the "juvenile brashness" of Sinatra's "hard-bitten . . . booze-guzzling buck." Going for the jugular, he added: "There is no way to measure this picture with a yardstick of pure intelligence. It is a romantic fabrication by which intelligence is simply repelled. The war scenes are wild and lurid, the dilly-dallying in the Calcutta bars and palatial hangouts of the wealthy is make-believe from an Oriental dream." Sturges, Crowther conceded, had managed to imbue the action with a "flashy flamboyance" and sustain a mood of "violent bravura." Most of the reviews acknowledged McQueen's "star quality." It was a little role, allowed Hillard Elkins, the actor's manager, but it "gave Steve an opportunity to make some real noise."

Following *Never So Few,* Sturges attempted to revive *The Sons of Katie Elder* at Paramount with Charlton Heston, Dean Martin, and Shirley MacLaine in the leads. When he lost Heston (because of re-shoots on *Ben-Hur*), Sturges suggested an all-star remake of Rudyard Kipling's *Captains Courageous.* He wanted Sinatra for Manuel, the Portuguese fisherman role that had won Tracy an Oscar, and Tracy for the boat's crusty-but-lovable captain, originally played by Lionel Barrymore. Sinatra and Tracy, who had been looking for a project, loved the idea. "I talked to Frank about it," said Sturges. "He said, 'And how!'" Sturges went to MGM with the idea. Schary's successor listened patiently before showing the director the door. "It was a marvelous idea, couldn't miss," insisted the director, shaking his head. "I expected to be knighted. Their response: 'Oh, too expensive.'"

Frustrated by the rejection of what he saw as another surefire hit, and no closer to realizing his dream of filming Paul Brickhill's *The Great Escape,* Sturges decided to follow the example of producer-directors Billy Wilder and Robert Wise and "make my own breaks." The Mirisch Company provided the opportunity. For a year now Harold Mirisch and his brothers had been packaging their own projects and releasing them through United Artists. "I thought [about Schary and the subsequent MGM regime], 'These people are through.' I knew the days of the studio system were over when they turned down those projects. We would have gotten the same double-talk on our remake of *The Seven Samurai.* That's why I became an independent."

In 1959, between *Never So Few* and *The Magnificent Seven*, Sinatra approached Sturges about *Ocean's 11*, a comedy caper set in Las Vegas and tailored for the Rat Pack. Sturges turned it down because there was no script, and Sinatra had begun to conform to his own bad press. He announced he would be available only after lunch and before cocktail hour—11 a.m. to 4 p.m. His dictum: "You can spend all the time you want setting up a shot. You get one take. I don't want to hear a light failed or a board creaked, or there was a hair in the aperture. One take." (Lewis Milestone wound up directing *Ocean's 11*, released in 1960.)

Sinatra changed his tune a year later, after seeing *The Magnificent Seven.* He had yet to appear in a halfway decent Western, and Sturges obviously had a knack for the genre. How about the two reteaming for a cavalry version of *Gunga Din* written by W. R. Burnett? It would be financed by Sinatra's Essex Productions and feature Sinatra, Dean Martin, and Peter Lawford in the Victor McLaglen, Douglas Fairbanks Jr., and Cary Grant roles. Sturges, who had just completed *By Love Possessed,* was easily seduced. He missed the raucous camaraderie of the Rat Pack. Set in the Dakota Badlands in the 1870s, *Sergeants 3*—originally called "Soldiers Three," after the 1951 remake of *Gunga Din*—was shot outside Kanab, Utah, and at the Samuel Goldwyn Studio. As producer-star, Sinatra made sure his and Martin's Las Vegas commitments were built into the shooting schedule. Depending on whom you ask, the arrangement made for "one long party—a piece of cake" (Henry Silva), or it was a source of constant friction (Bill Catching, Martin's stunt double).

"I know it was difficult because Sturges was trying to make a good picture, and Frank wanted to play and just do things on his time," said Ruta Lee, who, at twenty-three, had the token female role, Lawford's fiancée. "I felt sorry for the man. Trying to control this group was like wrangling rabbits. They were like children, attention-deficit children. Cherry bombs flying all the time."

Sturges—as his demeanor in a group portrait taken on location suggests—was in no mood for hijinks. During a reporter's visit to the set, he stood on the sidelines, looking miserable. To the question "Can you get them to take orders?" he barked, "Once I get them out there in front of the camera, yes." He did the picture to buy more time for pre-production on *The Great Escape*, he explained later. He also had pro-prietary feelings toward *Gunga Din* and felt, as a debt to Stevens, he should shepherd the new version. Three-time Oscar-winner Winton Hoch, who had photographed Ford's *She Wore a Yellow Ribbon* in Utah, was behind the camera. A perfectionist when it came to lighting for Technicolor, he labored over each setup, which made him "One Take" Sinatra's perfect alibi. Editor Ferris Webster—nicknamed "the Bear" because of his gruff demeanor and lumbering walk—was part of the package deal. After eight Sturges films, he liked to brag, he could read the director's mind and deliver a polished first cut.

Martin, Lawford, and Sinatra—billed as "happy-go-lucky, plucky soldiers of fortune"—attempted hip variations on the original charac-ters. Sturges's approach was more reverential. Sinatra called their com-promise a "balancing of grimness with comedy." Comedian Joey Bishop played the stone-faced sergeant major; Lee, a popular fixture on televi-sion, provided what she called "a piece of added fluff"; Michael Pate and Henry Silva appeared as the Sioux medicine man and his renegade son. Sammy Davis Jr., back in Sinatra's good graces and a bigger draw than ever on the nightclub circuit, was third-billed as ex-slave Jonah, introduced in the script as "genial, likable, happy-natured." In contrast to Sam Jaffe's regimental lackey, whose mascot was an elephant, Jonah came with a white mule and addressed Sinatra's 1st Sergeant Mike Merry as "Massa Mike."

Like *Gunga Din*, *Sergeants 3* revolves around a fanatical sect bent on the annihilation of all white men. In the original, set in colonial India, Grant and Jaffe are motivated by greed. They attempt to plunder a golden temple, where Grant is taken captive by a thuggee cult. Jaffe es-capes and returns with Fairbanks and McLaglen. In the less plausible Western, Martin and Davis track the murderous Ghost Dancers out of patriotic duty. Sinatra and Lawford, who like Fairbanks is conned into re-enlisting, return with Davis to rescue Martin. The wounded Davis grabs his bugle and warns the regiment of an impending ambush.

Davis, unlike Jaffe, survives and realizes his dream of becoming a trooper. (The inside joke: Davis, an antique gun collector and Hollywood's reigning quick-draw specialist, never got to fire a gun in the film.)

Cast and crew were bivouacked at the Parry Lodge in Kanab. Sinatra and the Pack took over an entire wing, where, according to Lee, they played poker and entertained "party girls." They commuted the thirty to forty miles daily by helicopter to Paria Canyon (nicknamed "Pyorrhea Canyon") and Bryce Canyon National Park. They arrived around 10 a.m. and were cued to pack up at 3 sharp by the *whoop-whoop-whoop* of revving blades. It was a spectacular ride. "We'd skim the fields chasing jack rabbits and then soar up into an eagles' aerie, and then come down and see beautiful long-horned sheep," recalled Lee.

Once on location, Sturges was all business. "He would sit off by himself and think," said Marshall Schlom, the script supervisor. "He was in sort of a cocoon." Sinatra kept to his trailer and, after a vodka martini or two, reemerged around lunchtime. Martin sunbathed so he wouldn't have to wear tanning makeup. Meals were served in a large white tent that could barely withstand the wind. When he noticed the crew was brown-bagging sandwiches from a local café, Sinatra decreed that their meals be flown in from his favorite restaurant, causing executive producer Howard Koch to crack, "If I had the money Frank spent on flying in spaghetti from Los Angeles, I could bankroll another three pictures."

Temperamental under the best conditions, Sinatra on location was a petty tyrant. He made it clear who was in charge. "Let me up on the crane—I'll set up the shot," he told the cinematographer. Sturges walked away.

"It was a very unhappy experience for John," said Relyea. "Frank under certain conditions could be abusive, and John's reaction was to draw back."

Things came to a head in June, when the production moved to the façade town of Medicine Bend, where the soldiers are ambushed by Silva and his braves. Martin was supposed to save Sinatra by shoving him aside just as an Indian leaps from a roof.

"Thanks, paley," Sinatra mugged on the first take.

"CUT!" yelled Sturges. "What the hell was that, Frank? This is the Wild West, not some Vegas saloon."

"Says who?" Sinatra shot back. "This is my show—I'll decide what goes."

"Sturges just flipped out—this isn't what he signed up for," recalled Bill Catching. "He stomped off the set and would have quit if Howard Koch hadn't gotten them together for a talk. . . . After that, Sturges relaxed and fell in with the more contemporary feel of the thing. Heck, half the dialogue on that picture was ad-libbed."

While Davis was deferential to an embarrassing degree on talk shows (see his "Person to Person" interview with Edward R. Murrow), Sturges said the performer was different in Sinatra's company, "always on." Davis even encouraged the watermelon-and-fried-chicken jokes and affected a stereotypical Negro dialect. "*I is here! I is here!*" he shouted as he arrived on the set. "Where's my steed?" He was led to a corral and shown a bronco mule named "Ceffie." On his bed in the motel was Frank's welcome gift—a watermelon. "Sammy thought it was funny. He almost wet his pants laughing," said Silva. "I thought, 'Is this something you do to your buddy, or someone you hate?'"

Every Friday afternoon, whether Sturges was on schedule or not, a DC-3 would shuttle Sinatra, Martin, Lawford, and Bishop to the Sands Hotel in Las Vegas. Davis, on call most Saturdays, was left behind in Kanab. The Western was worked into the Pack's Sands routine. Sinatra: "There's an Indian chief in our movie who dies from drinking too much tea." Bishop: "Yeah, he drowns in his teepee." Sinatra returned late Sunday afternoon to a dejected Davis, who had passed his evenings playing Monopoly with the script supervisor. "We would stay up all night until Sammy won," said Schlom. "He needed the companionship. He wanted to get his mind off the fact that he wasn't part of that group that went to Vegas."

Sturges may have seemed to submit to Sinatra's demands, but the tone of the completed film—often at odds with the knockabout humor—suggests otherwise. Indeed, some of the tableaux have an elegiac quality, bringing to mind *The Man Who Shot Liberty Valence* and *Ride the High Country*, released the same year. Sturges's annotated script may be seen as a record of creative differences. It contains Sinatra's ending, which could not have been in worse taste. After the medal ceremony at the fort, the foursome marches "straight into the camera" to a fife-and-drum rendition of "Camptown Races." The mule joins the parade, as Jonah does "a wild take, looks, then grabs Ceffie's bridle." The released ending, while less offensive, felt flat: Sinatra tells Bishop to arrest the departing Lawford for desertion.

Sturges would drop by the editing room once a week, scribble a few notes and disappear. His attention had shifted to one of his business ventures. Over the years he would speculate in real estate, commercial fishing, and German disk brakes. In 1961, he was bent on developing beachfront property just north of Kona. He had gotten the idea while scouting locations with Wally Young for *Underwater!* He planned to buy a thousand acres for $750,000 and turn it into a hotel-resort. "We flew to the Big Island, stopped at an army surplus store, and bought a $12 surveying kit," recalled Relyea, who, along with Young, accompanied Sturges. "It was the blind leading the blind. Wally took us to the spot, and we damn near drowned getting ashore. Then we tried to survey the land, which was really lava flows. Typical John."

Sturges had blueprints drawn up for the resort and attacked the project, according to his son, with the "same zeal and attention to detail he expended on movies." He was finally talked out of it by his wife and her lawyer, who were concerned about the pending divorce settlement. "Somewhere along the line cooler heads prevailed, and his advisers got to him," said Relyea. "My God, he would have been rich. Where he wanted to build was right where all those golf courses are today."

Sergeants 3 opened in February 1962. It did a robust $4.3 million, paving the way two years later for the Rat Pack's *Robin and the Seven Hoods*. The poster, by *Mad* magazine's Jack Davis, included caricatures of the stars flanked by piles of miniature Indians. Sinatra and Koch omitted any mention of the Hecht-MacArthur original in the credits and press handouts. *Variety*, not to be snowed, referred to the film as "warmed-over *Gunga Din*." The *New York Times* winced at the frequent shifts "from slapstick to slaughter" but allowed that the scenery was quite spectacular. Sinatra poked fun at the notion he had trod on sacrosanct ground by doing a TV spot with a reporter in trench coat asking people what they thought of a *Gunga Din* remake. "I can't accept that," each protests, stomping off. "Maybe we should have remade *Ben-Hur*,"

Martin suggests. "Next time," Sinatra deadpans. (A protracted dispute between Sinatra and UA over profit shares and distribution rights essentially kept the film out of circulation until 2008, when it was released on DVD.)

"Served 'em right," said Sturges. "It was a deliberate remake. They kind of minced around about it. I didn't."

Burt Lancaster as Wyatt Earp and Kirk Douglas as Doc Holliday in *Gunfight at the O.K. Corral*, Sturges's first real box-office hit. It was produced by Hal Wallis, who would reteam with the director on the less successful *Last Train from Gun Hill*. (courtesy of Kathy Sturges)

Top right: Spencer Tracy and eleven-year-old Felipe Pazos in *The Old Man and the Sea*. Sturges, who inherited the project from Fred Zinnemann, complained, "Spence is no more a starving Cuban fisherman than FDR." (courtesy of Kathy Sturges)

Bottom right: Sturges coaches Steve McQueen on his role in MGM's *Never So Few*. McQueen replaced Sammy Davis Jr. as Corporal Ringa in the 1960 release, the first of three increasingly difficult Sturges–McQueen collaborations. (courtesy of Deborah Sturges Wyle)

The King and I: Yul Brynner and the director on the Tepoztlan, Mexico, set of *The Magnificent Seven*. (courtesy of Kathy Sturges)

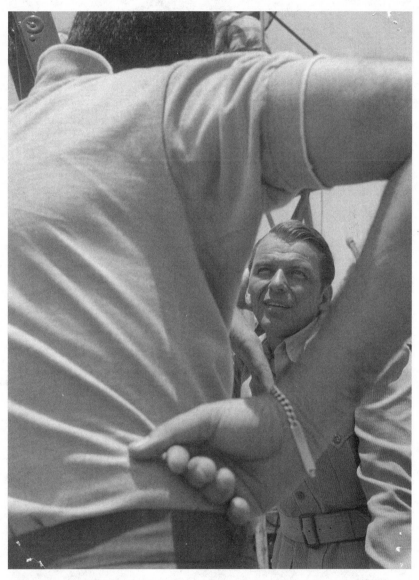

Frank Sinatra takes direction on a Utah location for *Sergeants 3*, the Rat Pack remake of *Gunga Din* co-starring Dean Martin, Peter Lawford, and Sammy Davis Jr. (courtesy of Deborah Sturges Wyle)

Sturges and "the cast of a lifetime"—James Coburn, Steve McQueen, and Charles "Weed Soup" Bronson—outside the POW compound built for *The Great Escape*. Much of the film was shot in and around Bavaria Film Studios in Geiselgasteig, Germany. (courtesy Kathy Sturges)

Sturges and his cameraman prepare a crane shot of Stalag Luft III as "Tunnel King" Wallace Floody (in white) recounts firsthand life in the POW camp. James Garner and Richard Attenborough (right foreground) look on. (courtesy of Curtis Wong)

Sturges shooting *The Hallelujah Trail* on an Indian reservation outside Gallup, New Mexico. (courtesy of Kathy Sturges)

James Garner and the director on location in Mexico for *Hour of the Gun*, a darker revisionist take on O.K. Corral and its aftermath. (courtesy of Photofest)

Final days: with Kathy, his adventurous second wife, in San Luis Obispo, California, in 1991. (photo by author)

Top left: The director at his most bankable shares a laugh with Rock Hudson on the nuclear submarine set of *Ice Station Zebra*, shot at MGM in 1967. (courtesy of Kathy Sturges)

Bottom left: Sturges and John Wayne take time out from production at a Seattle marina, one of the backdrops for *McQ*, a cop thriller dubbed "Dirty Duke." (courtesy of Kathy Sturges)

11

Seven the Hard Way

In September 1957, as the major studios awoke to the verities of the Television Age, the Mirisch brothers—Harold, Marvin, and Walter—announced the formation of a different kind of production company, one that would ultimately spark the director-as-auteur movement of the 1960s. Operating out of the Samuel Goldwyn Studio and underwritten by United Artists, the prime objective of The Mirisch Company was to attract the best directors in town by promising them more control over the tools of production and an opportunity to share financially in the fruits of their labors.

"It came down to personal relationships," said Walter Mirisch, the youngest of the brothers. "Who did you want to work with? Who did you want to spend time with? Who did you want to talk to about your pictures?"

The Mirisches wanted to go into business with the legends and near-legends: Billy Wilder, John Ford, William Wyler, Michael Curtiz, John Huston, Fred Zinnemann, Robert Wise, and John Sturges. Over the next seven years, Sturges would direct six pictures in partnership with the brothers, starting with *The Magnificent Seven* and including *By Love Possessed*, *The Great Escape*, *The Hallelujah Trail*, *The Satan Bug*, and *Hour of the Gun*, his grim revisionist take on the Earps and the aftermath of O.K. Corral. Later, Blake Edwards and Norman Jewison joined the company. Jewison, who directed *In the Heat of the Night* for the

Mirisches, recalled, "Once you agreed on a budget, the brothers offered artistic freedom, creative freedom; they were totally director-oriented." Walter Mirisch put it more succinctly: "We provided a buffer for the director against the interference of studio people."

The brothers' roles were clearly delineated: Harold, the eldest and president of the company, brokered the deals with UA and oversaw distribution, exhibition, and advertising. "He was the real go-for-broke fellow—a gambler spirit," said Sturges. "Harold was the king, the brains of the outfit," added Jewison. Walter provided the creative input: he approved projects and, depending on the situation, indulged or rode herd on the director. Marvin was responsible for the daily operation of the office, which was a model of efficiency, expanding and contracting with each new production. During *West Side Story* and *The Great Escape,* the office was a hive of activity. Between movies, it shrank to a core staff—production manager, business-affairs coordinator, accountants.

Shortly before *Easy Rider* and the dawn of the New Hollywood, what Peter Biskind and others have designated the "directors' decade," the Mirisches laid the groundwork by doing something that, at the time, seemed almost seditious. They spent money on the actual productions, rather than on padded pre-production costs. Further, by making those who spent the money—the directors—full partners, they ensured that budgets would not be inflated. It was textbook capitalism. (Vanity productions such as *The Hallelujah Trail* and *The Private Life of Sherlock Holmes* would prove costly exceptions.)

Since United Artists did not operate a backlot or hold contracts on between-assignment artists, it was more liquid and better able to withstand the growing competition from television. Stanley Kramer and Otto Preminger found a home at the upstart studio, run by Arthur Krim and Robert Benjamin. "I made an unprecedented contract with UA for *The Moon Is Blue,*" said Preminger, who would also make *The Man with the Golden Arm* and *Exodus* at UA. "I demanded and received complete autonomy and the right to the final cut. . . . I had at last the freedom I had always wished for."

The Mirisches had a similar dream of creative autonomy, for themselves as well as their directors. They struck a deal with UA whereby they would package the talent and UA would guarantee the loans, pay their salaries, and handle distribution in exchange for a 5 percent over-head charge and a third of the box office. Their goal was to produce four films a year.

"UA, in effect, financed our pictures," said Walter Mirisch. "We had an arrangement for very minimal overhead, actual overhead, rather than a percentage of the cost of the picture. In those days, the major studios were charging [independents] 30 to 40 percent of the cost of a picture as an overhead charge. This had to be recouped before the par-ticipant would get his share of the profit. And that was of significance financially."

In the summer of 1960, with *West Side Story* in production, the Mirisch Company celebrated its third anniversary by announcing a slate of fourteen films to be made for a combined budget of $45 million. Besides *The Great Escape,* the lineup included *Hawaii, Irma la Douce, The Haunting,* and *The Children's Hour.* "United Artists has given us the flexibility to hire creative people and put the responsibility on their shoulders — once we are agreed what the basic material is going to be," Harold Mirisch said upon the company's fifth anniversary. "It has been good business for this company to concentrate on tying up creative talent rather than actors."

Robert Relyea likened the Mirisches' recruitment campaign to an Attila the Hun raid. "The three brothers came on the MGM lot in their limousines one day and harvested all the key directors," he recalled. "Why MGM ever let them on the lot, I don't know. They roamed the stages, ravaging and pillaging. They went to all the directors and said, 'How'd you like to be your own boss? Come with us and we'll let you make your picture. You'll be a producer-director in the true sense of the word. We won't tell you how to make it. And if it works, we'll give you another bag of money.'"

And if it flopped, Harold would add with a wink, "We can be friends and play gin rummy, but we won't make movies together."

It was Walter Mirisch's idea to approach Hollywood's most proficient action director. Yes, he was older, almost fifty, but in the waning days of the studio system maturity still garnered respect "I want to make pic-tures with you," Walter told the director. "Let's look for material we both like." In 1958, Sturges agreed to a non-exclusive deal that would pay his going salary (around $4,000 a week) plus one-third of the profits. He would be billed as producer-director and oversee his own production company, Alpha Corporation.

Recalled Walter Mirisch, "I'd seen John's pictures before I met him. I was crazy about them. *Jeopardy*—a marvelous job of picture-making. *Black Rock?* Suspenseful, action-packed, and—though I was never one who bought into the HUAC thing—it had a certain amount of social significance. What else do you want for your $1.10 admission? I wanted to make pictures like that, only better." Further, Mirisch felt comfortable in the director's presence. "He was rather closed-mouth about his personal life, but you could tell he was a man of strength and humor."

In their first meeting, Sturges talked excitedly about Paul Brickhill's *The Great Escape,* which he had read in 1951. Mirisch said he would look into acquiring the rights. That process, Mirisch would later complain, proved "exceedingly difficult" because the Australian author, who had been a POW himself, was skeptical about how the details of the escape would be played. He didn't want it done as "an Errol Flynn picture." He was also concerned that the families of those killed in the escape would think he was capitalizing on the tragedy. Sturges invited Brickhill to Hollywood and, over a long lunch, won him over. "I convinced him it would be on the level," said the director.

633 Squadron, the first film announced in the Mirisch-Alpha pact, wasn't that far removed from *The Great Escape.* A variation on *The Dam Busters,* another Brickhill book that had been successfully adapted, it chronicled a daring raid by British Mosquito bombers on a German rocket-fuel factory hidden in a Norwegian fjord. It was an ideal choice for an ex-Air Force officer. However, when William Holden, Sturges's choice for the squadron leader, backed out, the project was temporarily shelved. (*633 Squadron* was resurrected four years later with another director and Cliff Robertson in the lead.)

In the fall of 1959—as the actors and writers guilds threatened to strike over television residuals—Mirisch found a project that seemed made to order for the director of *Gunfight at the O.K. Corral.* He called Sturges. "John, I've got something I think can be great, and I want you to be exposed to it." It was a cowboy remake of Akira Kurosawa's 1954 black-and-white epic, *The Seven Samurai,* about a ragtag band of mercenaries who rescue a village from bandits and, in so doing, reclaim their honor. "I arranged for us to see the picture together at a projection room at the studio," Mirisch recalled. "It was a marvelous screening, one of the most stimulating experiences I've ever had in this business. I can still see us sitting there, shouting back and forth. As it played out, we translated it into Western terms. We re-imagined it."

You have to work backward from Yul Brynner, who would ulti- mately star as Chris, the leader of the gunfighters, to figure out whose brainstorm the project was. Mirisch said he got the idea from Brynner, whose agent said, "Yul has had an interest in doing a Western version of *The Seven Samurai.*" Brynner got the idea from Anthony Quinn, his di- rector on *The Buccaneer* and announced costar in the ultimately aban- doned "The Gladiators." Quinn got the idea from screenwriter Lou Morheim, who, upon seeing the Japanese film in Los Angeles, told his wife, "This would make a classic American Western." In any case, it was hardly an original notion. Crowther in his 1956 *New York Times* review (of the shortened version of the Kurosawa film) pointed to numerous "touches that would do honor to Fred Zinnemann or John Ford" and added that the picture "bears a cultural comparison with our own popu- lar Western *High Noon.* That is to say, it is a solid, naturalistic, he-man outdoor action film."

Morheim optioned the remake rights from Toho Company for $250, wrote a script, and approached the actors, who, given their fire- and-ice personalities, seemed unlikely partners. (Quinn, in his memoir, described Brynner as "one of the most pretentious people in show busi- ness . . . a drearily insufferable man.") Morheim expected a producing credit and a piece of the action. Brynner—who had directed live TV and was a respected still photographer—announced that the project would mark his feature directorial debut; Quinn would play the Toshiro Mifune role, and Spencer Tracy—who bore a resemblance to Takashi Shimura, the samurai leader—was seen as a possible co-star. Brynner discarded Morheim's script and commissioned Walter Bernstein to start from scratch. Bernstein turned the mercenaries into disillusioned Civil War veterans and stuck closer to Kurosawa's tone and narrative.

"Originally, it was more of a direct copy or a pastiche, as you can tell by the idea of casting Tracy," said Bernstein, who flew to Paris to work on the script with Brynner, who was starring in *Once More with*

Feeling. "The tone of the thing was very different, more elegiac, like the original movie. What they eventually did—a shoot-'em-up Western—had nothing to do with what I had done, or had been trying to do. Theirs was totally different, except for the fact that there were these seven guys."

Tyrone Power's death from a heart attack on the Spanish set of *Solomon and Sheba* put everything on hold. United Artists needed a bankable star to step into the lead of the biblical epic and courted the Oscar-winning King of Siam, who said yes on condition UA bankroll *The Magnificent Seven.* Brynner now saw himself as a younger version of the leader. He asked Martin Ritt, who had been attached to "The Gladiators," to take over as director. Quinn, who had not been consulted about any of this, balked at the arrangement, and things quickly deteriorated into a very public feud. Brynner had his lawyer remind Quinn's lawyer that, although Quinn had brought the project to Brynner, it was Brynner, not Quinn, who held the remake rights. Suddenly, Brynner was negotiating with the Mirisches. "I asked Yul about how the thing came together and never got a satisfactory answer," said Walter Mirisch, picking his way through a minefield. "From what I can tell, Quinn felt he had been duped and painted out of the picture."

Enraged, Quinn sued Brynner, Brynner's production company, and UA for $1,150,000. The complaint said that the actors had verbally agreed to purchase the rights together. Since there was no signed contract, the suit was dismissed. "As it turned out," Quinn wrote in his memoir, "I did not have the same scheming head for business as my new associate. In the months ahead, Brynner would dupe me from my share of the picture." And set about rewriting history. "I don't know where all that hogwash came from," he fumed while on tour years later in *The King and I.* "It was totally me—I was behind *The Magnificent Seven.*" He also insisted that it was he, and not Morheim, who had sewn up the rights to *The Seven Samurai.* Countered Mirisch: "Yul deserves a great deal of credit for the film—that is not displaced—but *we* made the deal with the Japanese company to buy the rights. Nobody had that until we got it."

According to Sturges, Brynner now told the Mirisches, "I'd like to bail out of this thing. I'll just play the part of the leader, and you can reimburse me the $112,000 I've already got in it."

Walter Mirisch, whose credits included several Joel McCrea Westerns plus Anthony Mann's *Man of the West,* listened to Brynner's pitch
and said he would get back to him after screening the Kurosawa film. He
immediately saw potential. "Absolutely! I think it will make a wonderful
Western," he told Brynner. "But not with Ritt. I've got someone else in
mind." (Ritt would later direct Paul Newman and Laurence Harvey in
The Outrage, an unsuccessful Western version of Kurosawa's *Rashomon.*)

Starting virtually from scratch, Sturges and Mirisch agreed that a
less arty or cerebral approach was warranted, and that the film, to be
budgeted at $2 million, should be shot in widescreen color in Durango
and Mexico. Sturges reunited with Walter Newman for the script. A
former newspaperman, Newman specialized in terse, modern dialogue.
Charles Lang Jr., who had shot *Gunfight at the O.K. Corral* and *Last
Train from Gun Hill* as well as Wilder's *Some Like It Hot,* was announced
as cinematographer. He joined Ferris Webster and a fast-rising young
composer named Elmer Bernstein. Mirisch broke the news to Morheim that Sturges would be acting as his own producer. After contem-
plating a drawn-out suit that would invariably burn bridges, Morheim
agreed to "go away" for a finder's fee and nominal associate producer
credit. He had nothing to do with the project from that point forward.

The script arrived in early February, and Sturges knew he had been
right about Newman. It was edgy and economical, the best he had been
given since *Black Rock.* He closed his eyes and saw the seven riding in
single file. "It was like daydreaming, I could imagine the scenes," he said
later. "It was a good story, and the characters and ending rang true. I
liked the idea of the ex-gunfighters. Where do you go when you're
through, and nobody trusts or likes you? I especially identified with the
O'Reilly character, who was half Mexican, half Irish. He was a tough
guy who had a need for family life and children. I liked the scene where
he said, 'Your fathers aren't cowards, I'm the coward.' That struck me as
appealing."

"Jeez, this is good stuff," he told Newman. "This is going to work!"

The announcement of the Mirisch-Alpha production raised more
than a few eyebrows in an industry on the verge of a strike. The Writers
Guild of America (WGA) and Screen Actors Guild (SAG) contracts
were up for renewal on November 17 and January 31, respectively, and
the majority of the membership favored walkouts because they weren't

being paid for movies aired on television. Already in production—and in danger of being shut down—were 20th Century Fox's *Let's Make Love* with Marilyn Monroe and MGM's *Butterfield 8* with Elizabeth Taylor. Besides the Western, the Mirisches had Wilder's *The Apartment* on their plate. Should they rush into *The Magnificent Seven* and risk a work stoppage? Mirisch accelerated pre-production, signing agreements with both unions hours before their contracts expired, and made arrangements to film outside Cuernavaca and at Churubusco Studio in Mexico City. Like *The Guns of Navarone* shooting in Greece, the Western was now technically a "foreign" production, exempt from some domestic regulations.

Sturges—a stalwart friend of labor who held both Directors Guild and WGA cards—said he would rush the casting but not violate union rules. On January 16, WGA's two thousand members called a strike that would last five months. (The more powerful SAG joined them in early March, and stayed out forty-three days.) With an announced start of February 29, the director had a month to cast the picture and set up production offices in Mexico. "We have to do this right," Sturges insisted. "I want all the actors' contracts signed before the strike deadline." To expedite the process, blank contracts designating "role to be determined later" were sent out right up to the Sunday midnight deadline.

With Brynner, forty-four, committed to playing Chris—described as a man in his late thirties who has "been around (and) developed a manner best described as panache"—Sturges set about casting the other hired guns and the bandit leader, Calvera. Each man had to possess a distinct quality—be laid-back, wary, or overeager. He began by interviewing actors he knew: Charles Bronson, Brad Dexter, and Steve McQueen, who still owed him two pictures. McQueen, hungry for stardom, said yes immediately to Vin, who "takes things as they come." However, he was contractually tied to the TV series *Wanted: Dead or Alive*. As an incentive for McQueen to break his contract, Sturges announced Dean Jones as Vin. It worked. Four Star Productions granted McQueen a hiatus—after he staged a car crash and showed up for work in a neck brace. O'Reilly, who wears "a habitual mad-at-the-world scowl," was tailor-made for Bronson, who seemed to live under a dark cloud. Sturges said he cast against type. "Charlie as a rough, tough guy didn't interest me," said the director. "The fact that he had this tender interior, this need for family, that's what made it a good character." Dexter, the classic hail-fellow-well-met, was recommended by Sinatra. He would play Chris's crass, mercenary friend, Harry Luck, who refuses to believe the villagers aren't hording gold.

The seemingly absurd idea of casting German actor Horst Buchholz as Chico, the hot-headed romantic lead, came from Billy Wilder, who had the European idol under contract for his West Berlin–set satire *One, Two, Three*. At the time, Buchholz was appearing on Broadway in *Cheri* opposite Kim Stanley. His dream — *every* European's dream — was to someday star in a cowboy movie. He couldn't believe his good fortune when contacted backstage by Mirisch, who said, "I heard you like Westerns. We have an important part in a new one. Interested?"

Buchholz — the son of a baker who at age ten was forced to join the Hitler Youth — flew to Los Angeles and sought out quick-draw specialist John Derek for a crash course in handling a six-shooter. Trained in dance and already a skilled equestrian, he was soon twirling a gun on horseback. (Like Chico, Buchholz was a little too eager. On location, he discharged his gun in the holster, grazing his leg.)

"We talked to Horst and convinced ourselves that he could be believable as a Mexican," said Mirisch, who went along with UA's plan to promote the actor as "That European Sensation."

For the bandit chief Calvera — as crucial to the film's success as any of the seven — Sturges again went with his instincts and signed the unlikeliest candidate, character actor Eli Wallach, who had studied with McQueen at the Actors Studio. Sturges's models for Calvera, who frets about "the morality of this country" as he plunders the poor box: his bosses at Columbia and MGM. "I didn't want a big tough guy because the style of that part was not that of a big tough guy. Like Cohn and Mayer, he's a conniver, a negotiator . . . this hypocritical guy who sanctifies what he's doing by twisting things around."

Mirisch shook his head when Sturges suggested Wallach. "You're crazy! He's a New York Jew, only five-foot-four, and he's never been on a horse. What the hell are you talking about? How is that going to work?" (Wallach is actually five-foot-eight.)

But as they talked, Mirisch warmed to the idea. "I began to see it," he said later. "John deserves all the credit for casting Eli, who was wonderful. But it really came from leftfield."

Now Sturges had to convince Wallach, a Broadway actor who specialized in Tennessee Williams. "Initially I didn't want to do it," said Wallach. "I had seen *The Seven Samurai* and liked it a lot. But I only saw myself as the crazy samurai Mifune played. John said, 'That's the love interest. He's already cast. Horst Buchholz. We want you for the head bandit.' The head bandit? He arrives at the beginning wearing an eye patch, and all you see are horses' hooves. Dullsville. Same with Calvera. He comes in in the first scene, and then for the next forty-five minutes all they do is talk about him. 'Calvera's coming! Calvera's coming! Let's get ready.'"

Calvera was the star *in absentia*.

"Trust me, Eli," Sturges said. "I'll get you out there on location for a couple of weeks and you'll learn to ride. We'll double you here and there. You can handle the part, you're an actor. When you read the script you're going to see why this is not some jerk playing around being a tough guy."

Wallach liked the sound of that, but remained skeptical. He had dealt with well-meaning directors before. He knew that when problems arose it was the producer, not the director, who wielded the real power. "What will 'they' think?" he asked sheepishly. "Eli," Sturges replied, "there is no 'they.' It's just you and me."

Calvera is described in detail in the script. He is "a man who is an irresistible force and knows it and knows you know it. His self-assurance, therefore, is overwhelming and from it derives a certain bravura in manner and dress: expansive gestures, slightly exaggerated facial expressions, broadly striped pants, enormous rowels to his spurs." Wallach built on this, creating a character who is part father figure, part bullying narcissist who enjoys his plunder. "In all these Westerns, they break into banks, hold up trains, but you never see what they do with the money," he told Sturges. "I'd like to show what he spends the money on—the red silk shirts, the silver-studded saddle, the gold teeth."

"Do it," said Sturges, pointing the actor in the direction of Western Costume in North Hollywood. The two gold teeth that catch the sun so memorably when Calvera rides into view were purchased in Mexico City. The dentist recommended something more permanent. "Señor," Wallach remembered him saying, "I will drill two little holes in your front teeth, insert a diamond in each, and you will light up the screen."

Caps, it was agreed, would be less painful or invasive. "They cost me a lot of money," said Mirisch, recalling the $1,000 props.

Wallach still felt uneasy. Something was missing.

"I'll tell you what's missing," Sturges said. "Here, put these on." He handed the actor a pair of high-heel Mexican boots.

"He was four inches taller in those boots," the director recalled. "He said, 'I'm the man'—and he was." For his hat, Wallach deferred to Mexican director Emilio "El Indio" Fernández, who helped him pick out a cocktail-table-size black sombrero, later cut down to a more manageable size.

Sturges found Lee, the haunted gunslinger with a trace of southern gentility, in *The Young Philadelphians,* starring opposite Paul Newman. Robert Vaughn gave off a cultivated-but-cornered vibe that Sturges liked. What's more, the twenty-seven-year-old actor had just been nominated for an Oscar, which couldn't hurt the box office. Sturges called Vaughn to his office, which was plastered with production sketches, and said that based on what he had seen he would like to offer him something, "but I can't show you anything in terms of your role because it's still in the writer's mind."

Sniffing a once-in-a-lifetime opportunity, Vaughn said it didn't matter; he was excited by the project and would tag along and hope for the best. At Western Costume, he helped himself to striped vest, string tie, black leather gloves—what the script called Lee's "touch of elegance." "I just picked out whatever I wanted to wear," said Vaughn, "and that's what people have talked about for years because my costume was so unlike the others. I guess I was kind of a dandy."

Repeatedly checking his watch during Vaughn's interview—Sunday's strike deadline loomed—Sturges broke protocol and asked Vaughn, "Know any other good actors? We have another idea for a character—a Gary Cooper type who doesn't talk a lot. Kind of in the background. Know anybody like that?" Vaughn did. An acting-school buddy named James Coburn, who, it so happened, had worked with McQueen on three episodes of *Wanted: Dead or Alive.* Depending on whose story you believe, Vaughn either tracked Coburn to a Greenwich Village loft, where he was "shacked up with a black woman, smoking pot," or bumped into him leaving an L.A. supermarket. Coburn had his agent call Mirisch and arrange an interview. The next day, Sturges looked up from his desk at a lanky six-foot-three actor grinning back, a perfect match for the switchblade-throwing Britt, inspired by Kurosawa's master swordsman. Methodical, a doer not a talker, Britt is described as "silent, anonymous, complete in himself." He is introduced at a railhead cattle pen, stretched out on the ground, his hat over his face. Goaded into demonstrating his prowess with the knife, he pushes his hat back with one finger and "then, in one smooth motion, he is on his feet and moving toward a fence post 20 feet away."

Sturges said he would let Coburn know by three o'clock that afternoon. Coburn's phone rang at 2:30. The voice on other end said, "Come on over and pick up your knives."

Sturges had beaten the SAG deadline by nine hours. His hastily assembled cast also included Whit Bissell, Robert Wilke, Bing Russell, and Val Avery—all of whom had appeared in previous Sturges films. Veteran character actor Vladimir Sokoloff was selected for the village elder, and Rosenda Monteros, twenty-five, was cast as Petra, Chico's love interest. John Alonso, one of the three villagers who go in search of protection, had an ulterior motive for watching Sturges and Lang: ten years later he would become a cinematographer, eventually shooting *Chinatown* and *Scarface,* among other films.

That Monday, with the start date less than a month away, Sturges and assistant director Relyea flew to Mexico City, where, in a matter of hours on a grassy lot next to the studio commissary, they cast Calvera's men, key villagers, and background extras. In keeping with the government quotas, several jobs, including that of production manager and location doctor, went to locals. The notorious Emilio Fernández (General Mapache in *The Wild Bunch*) was made production liaison and second-assistant director. He also acted as an after-hours guide, for everything from cockfights to brothels.

Since he didn't know who would play what role, Sturges once again distributed blank contracts. "We'll sort it out and tell you in a few days," he assured the players, who were happy to have work.

Sturges, familiar with Mexico from his frequent fishing trips to Acapulco and Mazatlán, had a good idea of where to find Ixcatlán, his farming village under siege. It helped that it was described in detail in the script, right down to the volcanic-ash soil: "Remote and insignificant— a score of adobe cubes arranged in a square around a dirt plaza—it occupies the center of an irregular patchwork of farmlands, green with young corn or black with freshly turned earth, that contrast sharply with the rocky, sandy wasteland of the valley-bottom from which they have been wrested." Sturges immediately thought of Tepoztlán, known for its iron-black mountains and Aztec pyramid, and located outside Cuernavaca, about an hour from Mexico City. It was here that Eduardo Fitzgerald, the Mexican production designer, constructed the town plaza, adobe walls and dwellings, and a sixteenth-century chapel that looked so authentic locals crossed themselves when they passed it. Camarga, the border town where Chris and Vin ride shotgun on a hearse, was built at the same location to save time.

"I knew a little bit about Mexico. I'd been there a lot," Sturges said. "I also knew that we could get marvelous flavor from Tepoztlán—there wasn't even a highway into the thing until a year before we made the picture. We just hired the whole town. They were the extras. They had to look good, and the dance they do while Britt is waiting for the bandits had to look authentic. That's a real dance."

The villagers also had to appear self-sufficient and, according to Sturges, "Tide clean." Government censor Jorge Ferretis—still fuming over the Burt Lancaster–Gary Cooper Western *Vera Cruz* (1954), which doted on Emperor Maximilian's court while reducing Juárez's forces to cannon fodder—decreed the new production must not include anything "denigrating to the country." Consequently, the script had to be approved before the start of production, and a censor would have to always be on the set. This presented immediate problems because the villagers were described in the script as helpless and dirt poor, living in one-room adobe huts. Chris lectured Chico in an early draft, "You don't hate them, you come from just such a mud-heap yourself." This became: "Sure you hate them . . . because you come from a village just like that one."

"Overall," Mirisch explained, "the objection was to the basic situation, that the Mexicans couldn't solve their own problem and had to hire outsiders, American mercenaries, to deal with the bandits."

A partial solution was to make the villagers less demoralized, outfit them in spotless white tunics and pants, add a few speeches about the importance of family and land. Also, the roles of Chico and the half-Mexican O'Reilly were expanded. Sturges did some of this himself, as his much-edited shooting script attests, but it wasn't enough for Ferretis, who had become a Calvera-like tyrant, striking everything that might suggest the villagers were destitute or indecisive.

"This censor is an autocrat who lives in a dream world," Sturges complained bitterly to the press. "The regulations laid down by the Mexican government are practical and workable. But he operates on the basis of whimsy. He is confused, petulant and goes on the theory that anything debatable should be stricken out. . . . I think his only concern [is] that there must be nothing that someone in Mexico might conceivably consider anti-Mexican."

Desperate, Sturges asked Newman to join him on location to "appease the censors and further work out the characters, especially Lee, who we still can't get a handle on." Newman refused because, according to Mirisch, he had gone on to another project or was coping with a family emergency. (Despite the dispensations granted UA, he may also have been reluctant to cross his union's picket line.) Sturges turned to Studio City neighbor William Roberts, who co-wrote *Fast Company* and had just completed *The Sheepman,* a popular Glenn Ford Western.

"Come on down to Mexico and help me work up some stuff," Sturges suggested, picking his words carefully. "We'll do it together. You do the typing. Mostly, we have to find a part for Vaughn."

"Jesus, John, I can't tailor Newman's script," said Roberts. "Writers Guild rules."

"Don't do it for credit, then," said Sturges, who fully intended to submit Newman as sole screenwriter.

In late February, Brynner, McQueen, and the other principals arrived in Cuernavaca. They would be on location through early May, observing only Sundays and Mexican holidays. Brynner and Buchholz, accompanied by his wife Myriam, had adjoining villas; the rest of the cast and crew stayed at the Hotel Jacarandas, described by Vaughn as a "glorified motel." Producer Mirisch made a point of remaining in the shadows. "I was in Cuernavaca for a couple of weeks when we started the picture, but I didn't want John to feel I was looking over his shoulder." While Dorothy knew enough to stay away, Sturges's children, Deborah and Michael, were frequent visitors to the set. "We went down to Mexico eleven times, enough that the people at the border finally decided that we were smuggling drugs," said Deborah. "I missed more of seventh grade than Campbell High would have liked. Theoretically, I was learning Spanish."

The schedule called for exteriors and action sequences first, hotel and cantina interiors last. Sturges began with the border town and Chris and Vin's ride up Boothill. He made a note to himself: "Very few women. Heavy on cowboys." From here, he moved to the house on the plain where O'Reilly (Bronson) agrees to join the gunfighters. By week's end, he was filming establishing shots of the mountains and Calvera's unforgettable entrance.

> Silence. And suddenly. Rocketing birds burst up out of the trees like shrapnel, cawing and screeching in alarm. . . . Forty mounted men jog slowly and arrogantly out of the forest past a burial ground and through the fields toward the village. Indios, mestizos, a scattering of North Americans, they are a grimy, sweaty lot, ragged and unkempt, with cartridge belts Xed across their chests, rifles slanted across their backs and machetes flopping at their waists.

Week 2 included the festivities and procession on the plaza. Sturges took pride in the fact that the Yaki Indian deer dance—celebrating the tribe's hunting prowess—was authentic. "They actually ran the deer until exhaustion, grabbed it, and killed it. We needed one guy in deer horns, two in masks. I just said, 'Who does this dance best? Hire them.'" The bull dance, known as a *teredo*, proved trickier. The papier-mâché bull was strung with spinning rockets. "Those are real fireworks in that goddamn thing. When we started shooting all of a sudden a couple of rockets go by—a hundred miles an hour!—and set fire to the hut next to me. I hollered, *'Cut! What in Christ's name!* You can't have real fireworks in there.'"

Relyea conferred with the dancers and reported back. "They're glad to do it for you, but they don't want to do it if there aren't real fireworks in the bull."

"What if somebody gets burned?"

"They don't care—just so it's authentic."

The first battle—set in the plaza, where Calvera, taken by surprise, loses several men—was only a page and a half in the script. It was delayed until mid-March, when a wind machine could be brought in to fan the fire in the cornfields. Sturges, still fleshing out Vaughn's character, noted to himself, "Lee has been hiding, watching."

On Day 21, Sturges staged the climactic battle in which Calvera and four of the seven are killed. As scripted, Lee died as he made a mad dash for Calvera. The scene cried out for something flashier. After all, it was Lee's moment of truth. Sturges (in penciled notation) had Lee, in classic gunfighter fashion, walk up to a building where villagers are being held captive, holster his gun, kick in the door, and outdraw the guards. "Lee comes out carrying gun. Stops, straightens to full height. He has found himself—his courage is back. He is hit. DIES."

Vaughn suggested something even more theatrical, and Sturges went along with it, positioning a second camera to capture the actor in close-up. "I fell against the wall after I'd been shot, and I let my face slowly drag down this roughhewn surface," the actor recalled. "I told John I only wanted to do it once because it was going to scrape hell out of my face." The death, easily the most poignant in the film, made the final cut.

Britt's exit also became more flamboyant in the staging. As scripted, he raced behind the church and died off-screen. Chris found him "face down on the ground, his rifle pointed toward four or five of Calvera's men who lie dead a dozen yards away with their heads in his direction, like the ribs of an open fan." This was changed to Britt being shot on-camera and, as he pitches forward, throwing a knife into an adobe wall.

Sturges's instruction to Wallach as he lay mortally wounded was succinct but inspired. "I want the light to go out of your eyes," he told the actor, who accomplished this by staring so hard his eyes lost focus.

Sturges—looking like Britt's older brother in standard location attire (well-worn jeans, western shirt, aviator sunglasses)—was obviously at the top of his game. He worked quickly and efficiently, devoting most of his time to the big action set pieces, little to coddling his cast. The margins of his script were full of visual cues and notations. Even the film's coda was reworked on location. Chris originally said, "The Old Man was right. Only the farmers have won. We're the losers. Always." This became the more wistful: "The Old Man was right. Only the farmers won. We lost. We always lose."

Vaughn recalled, "As far as directing the actors, John seldom said a word to anyone. I guess once he got McQueen and Brynner, he figured they knew what they were doing. The only person John spoke to with any regularity was Charles Lang, the cinematographer. They'd set up the scene photographically, do the master shot until they got what they wanted, and then go in close." (Years later, the director boasted to Michael Caine, "*The Magnificent Seven* was entirely 'Take One.'")

When not on call, the cast frequented the local cantina, played poker and gin rummy, and just generally marked its ground. "There was a lot of testosterone floating around," said then-pregnant Neile McQueen. "Here were these Young Turks all on the brink, all competing with each other. It was wild. Steve got arrested a couple of times, once for stealing a bus-stop sign."

"Because they hadn't written my part, I didn't work for the first month at all," Vaughn recalled. "John told me to check under my door at night for the next day's pages. There never were any pages. So I played poker with the stuntmen, who'd drink until midnight and still be on the set by 7 a.m. . . . I drank a lot of margaritas and ate at lot of Mexican food. Fortunately, I was still able to get into my costume, which was tight to begin with."

As often happens on location, the cast split into cliques. Sturges encouraged the petty rivalries: he knew they would augment the on-screen conflicts. "Foreigners" Brynner and Buchholz gravitated toward one another. Sturges treated them like royalty. Oddly, he saw Buchholz, not McQueen, as the film's "find." McQueen, who coveted the Chico role, badgered the pair mercilessly, frequently complaining, "They're Europeans—what the hell do they know about horses and guns?" McQueen found a kindred spirit in Bronson, who addressed Horst as "Hoss." Coburn hung out with Vaughn, who occasionally discussed Russian theater with Brynner. The Buchholzes hosted poolside soirees. "I was cooking a very good mousse of chocolate, and Yul played the guitar," recalled Myriam. "The only one unhappy was Bronson."

Befitting his name-above-the-title billing, Brynner affected an imperious air. "Yul had a coterie," said Mirisch. "He was a very big star and the others weren't, and he never let them forget it." While the rest of the cast made do with director's chairs and a communal makeup trailer, Brynner had his own luxury coach, complete with potted palm trees, hammock, and fish pond. It was referred to as the Taj Mahal and "Yul's wickiup." He had cognac and cheese shipped from Paris, and steaks flown in from a ranch in Texas. Brynner's entourage included a personal secretary, two gofers, and a barber to make sure his head was always cue-ball smooth. You didn't just walk up to Brynner, said Coburn, you requested an audience. "He liked to have his cigarette lit for him at the snap of a finger—movie star treatment."

Brynner and fiancée Doris Kleiner were married during production on the plaza set. "It was like a king getting married," said Neile. "There was a platform for him and Doris, so people could stand at their feet and wish them congratulations." McQueen shunned the spectacle; Sturges made sure he had a spot on the platform.

Brynner and Dexter played gin rummy—rather, Brynner played as Dexter good-naturedly forked over large chunks of his salary. Bronson, the misanthropic narcissist, sat around shirtless, recounting ad nauseam his grim youth in the coalfields of Pennsylvania, subsisting on weed soup. When a local señorita passed, he would snap out of his funk, scurry up the cliff behind the hotel, and swan dive into the pool. Wallach, happily married, soaked up the local color and bonded with his *caballeros*. "They taught him enough about riding that he looked OK," said Sturges. "The only time he was doubled was on the first fight, where the bandits ride out on jumping horses through town. . . . But when he rode, his left hand kept flopping up and down. I told him, 'Eli, quit typing.'" (Sturges was less successful teaching the actor how to handle a pistol. The camera always caught him peering down to locate his holster.)

Sturges pushed Roberts for revisions. The censors, he said, still objected to the scene where the Old Man tells the frightened villagers to hire gunmen. A partial solution: Make the trip to the border about buying weapons, not mercenaries. "Buy guns. Go to the border. Guns are plentiful there," the Old Man now counseled. The idea of hiring gunfighters would come from Chris, who suggests, "Why don't you hire men? Gunmen nowadays are cheaper than guns."

"Most of us didn't think the film was going to come together because we didn't know what we were doing from day to day," confessed Vaughn, who by the start of the second month was receiving pages on onion-skin paper slipped beneath his door. "We'd ask, 'What are we going to shoot tomorrow?' The A.D. replied, 'They're going to shoot this scene over by the well.' We'd ask, 'But where's the scene?' 'It isn't ready yet.' So our feeling was how can you have a good movie when the scenes are being written at night that are being shot the next day? We were new to movies. We didn't know *On the Waterfront* was done essentially that way."

Mirisch dismissed the notion that the production was in trouble. "Yes, work was done on the script on location—that's why Roberts was there, to help us while we were shooting," he said. "We were professionals. We knew it was going to cut together. I've been on pictures where the amount of rewriting in production was much more extensive—*The Great Escape,* for instance."

McQueen counted his lines—barely six or seven in an early draft—and concluded that he was playing "second banana to the bald man." Only Coburn had less to say. He cornered Sturges and Roberts in the hotel and demanded an explanation. He saw himself as the romantic lead, but he didn't get the girl. Buchholz did. Indeed, the funny German who paraded around in madras shorts seemed to have all the big scenes—a drunken rant in the cantina, a bell-tower call to arms, a comic toreador routine. Sturges assured McQueen, as he had assured the others, that he would "give him the camera." Satisfied, McQueen set about improvising bits of business, what Sturges called "Steve catching flies." During the ride up Boot Hill, McQueen shook shotgun shells by his ear and shaded his eyes with his Stetson. When he spied Petra and the village women washing clothes in the river, he tugged at his bandana suggestively. During the shootouts, he whistled through his teeth and rubbed his hands on his shirt before calming a spooked horse.

Sturges encouraged the ad-libs and, before long, everyone was vying for the camera. Vaughn skulked in the shadows like Iago; Coburn employed his strange, loping gait; Wallach, a past master at one-upmanship, sucked water from his fingers and played with his sombrero. McQueen's ad-libs—"Vin looks at Chris, grins, holds up five fingers"—were especially inspired, and the director made sure they were penciled into the script. Brynner was furious. He had an assistant report all unscripted moves. Finally, he confronted McQueen, who played dumb.

"Look, if I take my hat off, nobody will ever see you," said Brynner. (He flashes his famous pate only once, when Chris and the others are digging a fortification.)

"Oh, it was a big rivalry—they were at it day and night," said Sturges, savoring the memory. "Steve felt under pressure to assert himself. If he had been the Steve McQueen of *The Great Escape,* he would have squawked about the part and we'd have been in trouble. Instead, he just tried to build it up."

While he listened to Brynner's gripes and feigned concern, Sturges was excited about how each actor fought for his turf. He realized that McQueen, Coburn, and the others were gradually becoming indistinguishable from their characters, and that this would imbue the film with a fresh, anachronistic quality.

"In some cases, Yul was unfairly critical of Steve," the director said. "But you can't explain to these guys the way to make pictures. They're supposed to dream up things. You watch it and if you like it, that's the way it is. When Steve pushed his hat back on his head, it was his response to a thing. But Yul was convinced that Steve was scene-stealing, fussing around with his hat behind his close-up, and he had a guy watch McQueen's hat. Finally I said, 'Oh Christ, Yul, watch his hat.' You can't explain everything, but you do have to be the boss. I figured if something didn't work, I'd change the dialogue later or throw the scene out. If they didn't like it, fire me."

Deborah Sturges, a frequent guest at the Hotel Jacarandas, was hurt that her father tuned out even those closest to him when he was on a movie set. She had a term for his standoffishness: "reverse nepotism." It didn't help that her parents' marriage had pretty much run its course, and the director, taking his cue from McQueen and Bronson, was open to run-of-production "company." McQueen told Neile, "John cast Monteros because he's sleeping with her." Vaughn recalled seeing the director "sneaking up the backstairs" of the hotel with the actress, but he was quick to add, "It was our supposition that he had tried something and she had rejected him."

Deborah would only confirm that there were marital tensions and "a lot of angry wives. But that's true of every film set I've been on, particularly *The Great Escape* [where Jill Ireland left husband David McCallum for Charles Bronson]." Michael Sturges: "Let's be frank, Dad liked women. He was quite the ladies' man, but he was very careful to shield my sister and me from that stuff. I discovered it after the divorce, when I visited the set of *Ice Station Zebra* and crew members would wink and nod toward one of his many conquests."

In early April, Sturges returned to Churubusco Studio for the hotel and saloon interiors. Here, he shot Vin asking "How many you got?" and responding to Chris's single raised finger with a crooked smile and two fingers. (This sequence can be seen as a dry run for a similar exchange in

The Great Escape, when Richard Attenborough's squadron leader tricks McQueen into joining the mass breakout.)

On the last day at the studio, Sturges made a speedy getaway. The moment he yelled "Cut!" on the final take of the final scene, a studio hand, waiting for his cue, muscled open the soundstage door, and Sturges hopped into his conveniently parked Jaguar convertible. "I'd never seen anything like it," said Vaughn. "The car was sitting right there on the soundstage, its top down. He literally drove out of the building . . . and off into the afternoon sun."

Post-production, at this point, was well under way. Elmer Bernstein—intrigued by what he was reading about the Western— "lobbied" to write the score. Sturges, as he had with Tiomkin and Raksin, invited the young composer to his office for a conference. However, instead of handing him the script, he told him the story of the seven gunfighters and the bandit, and provided general pointers on the placement of "big music" and "character music." Bernstein, an Aaron Copland protégé who had worked his way up from session conductor to become one of Hollywood's most prolific composers (*The Ten Commandments, The Man with the Golden Arm*), preferred this way of working. He found Sturges "authoritative—but with a great charm to go with it." Sturges oversaw the scoring without imposing himself. In fact, he seldom visited the scoring stage.

"John didn't know a great deal about music and never spoke to you in musical terms," said Bernstein, who would score six Sturges films, including *The Great Escape* and *The Hallelujah Trail.* "But he was the most inspiring storyteller. If you spent the morning with John telling you the story and you left the room still not knowing what to do, you were in the wrong business. You could tell he loved music because his films left room for it. . . . We had relatively little contact on *Mag 7,* but we had terrific contact on every movie from then on; we would often talk about the music before he shot the film."

When Bernstein screened an early assemblage of *The Magnificent Seven,* he was shocked by how deliberate the pacing was. "If you look at it without music, you'd be surprised how slow-moving it is," he said. "I realized immediately there that the function of the music would be to get on top of the film, drive it along. It had to have tremendous life and vigor. *The Great Escape* didn't need that kind of help, this one did."

Bernstein delivered what is arguably, after John Williams's *Jaws* and *Star Wars* themes, the most recognizable overture in the history of the medium, one that would soon be appropriated by Madison Avenue (for the Marlboro Country campaign) and later imitated and parodied (by Bernstein himself for *Three Amigos!*). The composition begins with a lively fanfare à la Copland's "Billy the Kid" suite and Jerome Moross's *The Big Country* score and then, as the action shifts, incorporates darker refrains (with conga, clave, Indian log drum), indigenous folk music (marimba, mariachi horns), and, for the budding Chico-Petra romance, soft melodic interludes (violin, flute, solo guitar). Like Bernstein's other scores, this one allowed for tonal inflections—ominous and inexorable (for Calvera), tender and childlike (O'Reilly), tortured and discordant (Lee). In concert, they became an aural treatise on the ambiguous nature of heroism.

"Every once in a while—it doesn't happen often—you hit on something that really feels quite thrilling," Bernstein said. "I remember being very excited when I found that opening rhythm. It was like a surge of energy." In the liner notes for a compilation film-score CD, the composer added, "In this and another picture done much at the same time (*The Comancheros*), I said almost everything I had to say on the subject of Western Americana." Lawrence Kasdan—who traces his dream of directing to *The Magnificent Seven*, which he discovered as a wide-eyed twelve-year-old—considers Bernstein's music the "greatest Western score there ever was." For composer John Ottman (*The Usual Suspects, Superman Returns*), the theme is iconic—"so strong it has become a part of American culture." Mirisch called it "deathless," adding that Bernstein's contribution is "such an integral part, we can no longer separate the movie from the music."

In retirement, Sturges remembered the moment he walked into a rehearsal hall and heard Calvera's theme. "That was one of the best scores ever written—just brilliant!" he said. "Bernstein played the title first on the piano, and discussed the use of Indian drums. Oh, wow! Then we recorded the main theme. They usually do that, start with the biggest band and gradually drop musicians until they wind up with two or three instruments. . . . The guy who played the witango on a guitar was one of the best in the world. It was very modern music and very effective, but it's also very legitimate in terms of Mexico. . . . You know,

UA didn't even do a soundtrack album. The jerks said [the music] wasn't any good, said it didn't have a theme." (In 1966, UA attempted to redress this blunder with a *Return of the Seven* single and album. The original soundtrack album was released on CD in 1998.)

On his working relationship with Bernstein, Sturges added, "The thing is, I gave him a chance to play music. I learned that from [George] Stevens and from cutting pictures. When you're doing a picture like *The Magnificent Seven,* you have to pace the music. You can't just have it happening all the time. *Boom, boom, boom!* There have to be spaces where you start over. For example, when Calvera and the bandits return to the village and discover the seven, I went clear back [to a variation on the opening theme]. I dreamt up that little thing where the kid is waving to the bandits, but he's really signaling another kid on top of the hill, who waves to the kid at the bottom of the hill, who runs in to warn Chris and the others. Pure visual suspense, furthered when you have good music. And we did."

Wallach attributed much of his character's forcefulness to the thundering score. "I only wish I had heard that music when I was riding that goddamn horse," he said later. "I would have ridden better."

While still on location, Sturges shot the film's memorable trailer, which began *"They were seven . . . and they fought like seven hundred!"* The stars posed on a cloth number 7. There was no question of who stood where. Brynner, thumbs in his gun belt, was at the front, followed by McQueen, then Buchholz, Bronson, Vaughn, Dexter, and Coburn. It had all been worked out contractually in advance. (Wallach may have lost the clown samurai to Buchholz, but he was generously compensated with second billing after Brynner.)

Deciding who wrote the film would prove more difficult. Once he realized how much work Sturges's "typing job" entailed, Roberts lobbied the Writers Guild for a credit. Newman blew up. This had happened to him on three previous pictures. Before he shared credit with a "script doctor," he said, he would remove his name.

When the WGA supported Roberts's claim, Newman said, "OK, give it to Roberts." Roberts countered, "No, take my name off it." Finally, an Alan Smithee nom de plume was submitted. (This was a rarity at the time. Pseudonyms were usually reserved for films that had been severely re-edited or written by someone who was blacklisted.)

"Who the hell is this?" Sturges shouted when shown a poster with the fake credit. "In a pig's ass there won't be a screenwriter! I own this picture; it's a big investment. And whether you know it or not, it's a hit picture. I'm not about to have the press say, 'Who the hell is so-and-so?'"

Eventually, Roberts received sole credit—and raves from critics unfamiliar with the WGA arbitration. The *Los Angeles Times* praised Roberts for the very qualities that had distinguished Newman's work on *Ace in the Hole* and *Man with the Golden Arm:* "His characters are subtle, complex, rather understated individuals; they ring true. And his lean, mean dialogue is, by turns, virile, rowdily funny and then, abruptly, not always predictable." Sturges insisted to the end, "Pretty much all the good stuff in it was in the original script." (UA's publicity department, obviously out of the loop, credited Newman with "a script that crackles with action, atmosphere and dialogue.")

Had he sat on the arbitration panel, Mirisch said, he would not have awarded Roberts credit. "And I liked him. He did a lot of work on the film. He was very helpful. But the whole spin of the picture, the characterizations and all that were Newman's. Unfortunately, his stubbornness robbed him of an important credit." (Whether intentional or not, Newman would have his revenge: *Cat Ballou,* his Western spoof starring Jane Fonda and Lee Marvin, opened the same year as *The Hallelujah Trail* and, besides winning an Oscar for Marvin, easily out-performed the epic Sturges comedy.)

Because of its accrued cult status and ongoing popularity—for years it was the most aired film on TV—it is assumed that *The Magnificent Seven* was an immediate box-office success. The press handouts for *The Return of the Seven* furthered this impression by referring to the original as "an instantaneous and world-wide hit." This was not the case. Arriving the same year as *The Apartment, Psycho,* and other more adult attractions, the horse opera seemed hopelessly out of sync. Consequently, UA treated it as standard Western fare, with a mediocre promotional campaign and late-November slot. In urban markets, it was co-billed with a low-budget crime thriller or a children's pirate fantasy. Recalled Larry Cohen, who wrote *Return of the Seven:* "The first picture was not a hit in the U.S. It never played in a decent theater. I saw it at the Metropolitan in Brooklyn." Vaughn found it playing an empty theater in San Fernando Valley.

Variety adjudged the film "a rip-roaring, rootin' tootin' Western with lots of bite and tang and old-fashioned abandon." The trade paper applauded Sturges's "crackling good direction" and "superior craftsmanship" but found the third act maudlin, anti-climactic. Bronson, ironically, came off as the most sympathetic of the bunch; McQueen was seen as "an actor who's going places." The *Los Angeles Times* found Sturges's direction "superbly staccato; making a knife-sharp use of pauses and silences, it brings out both the humor and melancholy, the humanity as well as the evil inherit in the situation." Overall, the critic added, the film was "genuinely magnificent — a Western to rank along with *Shane, High Noon* and *Stagecoach.*" The New York critics, busy championing artier, more socially aware filmmakers such as Ingmar Bergman and Stanley Kramer, whose *Inherit the Wind* had just opened, were less impressed. They found the film draggy and irrelevant. Howard Thompson, the *New York Times* second-string critic, gave passing nods to McQueen and Wallach and praised the "dusty, slam-bang" action set pieces. He then provided a scene-by-scene comparison to subtitled Kurosawa and found the Western, overall, "a pallid, pretentious and overlong reflection on the Japanese original." Further, Brynner was miscast and Bernstein's score was loud and reminiscent of Tiomkin's music for *Giant.* The "gifted" Mr. Sturges's direction was described as "stately," a tip-off that the film is "going to take its own sweet time, moving at a thoughtful snail's pace." Not surprisingly, the Western did not join *Elmer Gantry, The Apartment,* and *Exodus* on Crowther's year-end Top 10 list.

"Of course that review hurt — it hurt me, hurt John," said Mirisch. "But you really didn't expect a *New York Times* rave. New York was never the prime market for Westerns."

When UA attempted to do the critics' bidding and shorten the film by twenty minutes, Sturges reminded the distributor that he and the Mirisches had invested $3 million in the picture and owned the negative. "I told them, 'I own this movie — you're not cutting a goddamn thing!'" he said later. "UA didn't think the picture was any good because the New York critics — who saw it at ten o'clock in the morning with phones ringing, people walking in and out — thought it was too slow. They said, 'Cut it down to as short as you can, lose the stuff with the

Old Man. Maybe we can get our cost back.' They didn't know what they had."

Two months later the film took up residence along the Champs-Élysées. Now called *The Seven Mercenaries,* it was immediately embraced by *Cahiers du Cinéma.* To reviewers-turned-filmmakers Jean-Luc Godard and François Truffaut, who had already championed the Westerns of Mann and Aldrich, the film represented the apotheosis of the Western as morality play. Later, John Carpenter would comment, "It was the beginning of the end of the Great American Western, a kind of last hurrah." Its unabashedly stylized approach laid the groundwork for the darker revisionist Westerns of Peckinpah and Aldrich and the spaghetti Westerns of Sergio Leone, who, following Sturges's lead, adapted *Yojimbo* as *A Fistful of Dollars,* starring Clint Eastwood as the Man with No Name. (The third in the Leone-Eastwood series, *The Good, the Bad and the Ugly,* was co-financed by UA and featured Wallach as a comic Calvera.) "I won't say Leone copied *The Magnificent Seven,*" said Sturges, "but he certainly profited by a lot of stuff in that picture, especially the multiple-character thing." Added Mirisch: "We stepped up the violence three, four, five notches in *The Magnificent Seven.* But those spaghetti Westerns went even further. They brought new levels to the violence that you didn't find in our picture."

When *The Magnificent Seven* opened in Tokyo in May 1961, it quickly became the top-grossing import of the year. "And why wouldn't it be popular?" asked the director. "It was a deliberate remake. We gave Kurosawa credit. I didn't copy what he directed, but I sure as hell copied what he wrote." According to Sturges, the Japanese master—already a John Ford fan—eventually phoned to say he was flattered by the change in idiom. He followed up with gifts—a kabuki doll and samurai sword. (Kurosawa was less amused by *A Fistful of Dollars:* Leone and his backers had failed to acquire the remake rights.)

At the Academy Awards in April, the Mirisch Company was well represented—by Billy Wilder's *The Apartment,* which took home five Oscars, including best picture and director. Unless a Western was cerebral and downbeat (*High Noon*) or screamed "epic" (*Giant, The Big Country*), it was shrugged off by the voting membership. That John Wayne's *The Alamo* earned seven nominations said more about the director-star's pushy, flag-waving campaign than any real affection for the film. In this climate Sturges and company were lucky to receive a nod. And that's what they got. Elmer Bernstein was nominated along with Tiomkin (*The Alamo*), André Previn (*Elmer Gantry*), and Alex North (*Spartacus*) and wound up losing to Ernest Gold (*Exodus*). Wallach, in retrospect an obvious choice for supporting actor, failed to make the cut. (Peter Ustinov won for *Spartacus*.) Brynner, sans Stetson, was the only one in the cast to appear onstage, presenting the best-actress award to Elizabeth Taylor for *Butterfield 8*.

By now consigned to second- and third-run theaters at home, *The Magnificent Seven*, like its eponymous heroes, refused to go away and in the coming months became what we now think of as a "sleeper hit" or word-of-mouth success. A mostly male demographic found it, raved about it, and—a rarity in the pre–James Bond/*Star Wars* era—returned for second and third viewings. And Sturges and the Mirisches felt, if not vindicated, at least assured that their initial hunches had been correct.

"Although it wasn't a huge domestic grosser in its initial release, it kept playing and playing and playing," said Mirisch. "Theaters kept booking it back, and the numerical number of engagements that it played was the highest we had on any of our pictures. It wasn't that, as many assume, it re-opened and something great happened; it just had its own audience that was very faithful to it."

Of all his films, Sturges was proudest of *The Magnificent Seven*. Yes, *Bad Day at Black Rock* was technically superior, the best job of "pure directing," he allowed. "But I would put *The Magnificent Seven* first because it's the best theater, the best job of staging and inventing characters. It's loaded with color and vitality. Not the kind of picture audiences had seen before."

Indeed, the very qualities that rankled some of the critics—the booming music, the ritualistic violence, the 1960s vernacular—made *The Magnificent Seven* the forerunner of today's high-concept escape, in other words, required viewing for adrenalin junkies. Like the Mirisches' *West Side Story*, released the following year, it worked as a participatory experience, to be mimicked in the dark of the theater or by choosing up sides in the backyard. Almost a half century later, as the Western genre lies all but dormant, the film seems, if anything, more modern than ever. This can be attributed to Sturges's near-seamless fusion of music, location photography, more liberal-than-usual language and bloodletting ("rape" and "damn" are used; the bandits are swarmed by villagers wielding machetes and farm implements, and one staggers from a hut with an axe in his back), and the cool, economical performances of McQueen and Coburn, who enabled the director to achieve a new kind of visual shorthand. The more intimate moments—O'Reilly lecturing the boys to respect their fathers, Lee cowering in the dark of his room— are skillfully interwoven into the story and provide unexpected texture.

Wallach's Calvera ranks with Lee J. Cobb's Dock Tobin in *Man of the West* and Burl Ives's Rufus Hannassey in *The Big Country* as one of the genre's more ambiguous villains. Instead of a one-note sadist, the bandit chief is an oddly sympathetic rogue, a seriocomic paterfamilias who craves the company of his peers. His undoing is in assuming Chris and the others are like him. He traps them and then returns their guns because to do otherwise would be to admit that some men who "deal in lead," to quote Vin, exist on a higher moral plain. Dying, Calvera asks, "You came back—for a place like this. Why? A man like you. Why?"

To this day, the debate continues over the film's tacit comment on U.S.-Mexican relations. Some have argued that the Western is insulting because it more than suggests that Latinos are an inferior race that must go, sombrero in hand, begging for protection and, by extension, validation. At a film festival, Mexican actress Katy Jurado demanded, "Why did they need those gringos? They couldn't fend for themselves?" Academics, meanwhile, read Chris and company's incursion south as a metaphor for imperialism and Cold War interventionism. "In *Rio Grande* the cavalry pursuit of Apaches provided an oblique commentary on the Korean War, and John Sturges' *The Magnificent Seven* was clearly a fantasy about Third World counterinsurgency," submit the authors of *The American West: A New Interpretive History.*

Playwright-filmmaker Luis Valdez (*Zoot Suit*) shrugged off much of this speculation. He recalled that as a young Chicano filmgoer he was amused by the *campesinos* in their "spotlessly clean" costumes, but he accepted them as a figment of "Hollywood reality." "It represented a silly level of censorship," he said. "The government was not disposed to let them show the poverty and filth of Mexico, though it obviously exists in some places. I think Sturges is to be congratulated for his eye for detail, particularly in the village sequences. He gave them a nitty-gritty quality." Also, like Peckinpah's *The Wild Bunch*, the Sturges film achieves a certain historical credence, said Valdez, adding, "The Mexican border was, and continues to be, a line of demarcation, a means of escape for American outlaws."

Based on the eventual success of *The Magnificent Seven*, Sturges was approached about doing the first of what would be three sequels (released in 1966, 1969, and 1972). The snag, of course, was that four of the seven were dead. Sturges's solution: The whole thing was a hoax. "There really was gold in the village, and they only pretended to be dead. The movie would open with Chris riding up to a house and inside are the other four. McQueen would be in on the finish. A theatrical gimmick, but it would have worked." Only Sturges saw the humor in this preposterous reversal, and it was quickly forgotten in favor of a *Magnificent Seven* TV series, which would be written and occasionally directed by Sam Peckinpah, whom Sturges admired for *Ride the High Country*. "We had a great setup. I was going to direct the first one and at least three others, and Sam was going to direct at least three and be head writer."

Peckinpah's take on the series was more subversive, to say the least. After the limited success of his now highly regarded series *The Westerner*, he saw *The Magnificent Seven* as another opportunity to deconstruct the form and, in the process, "rip up the soft underbelly of Hollywood." Peckinpah embraced Sturges as a fellow conspirator; Sturges, nonplussed, pegged Peckinpah as a drunk with a career death wish. "I wasn't interested in ripping up the soft underbelly of Hollywood, for Chrissake," Sturges said. "But that was Sam, you know; he needed conflict in his life."

Ultimately, the TV series, like Harry Luck, was done in by greed. "UA wanted a piece of it, the Mirisches wanted a piece of it—everybody wanted a piece of it. So everything fell apart," Sturges recalled. (After Walter Mirisch and Kathy Sturges gave their consent, a *Magnificent Seven* TV series aired on CBS in 1998. It ran for twenty-two episodes, with Vaughn in a recurring role as a judge.)

Buchholz, McQueen, and Brynner were all approached about doing the 1966 sequel, *Return of the Seven*, directed by Burt Kennedy from a script by Larry Cohen. McQueen, now a bona-fide movie star with *The Great Escape* and *The Cincinnati Kid* on his résumé, was committed to an auto-racing film in Europe (*Day of the Champion,* developed with Sturges, had just fallen through). Buchholz, who had returned to Germany after *One, Two, Three,* sent word back, "Without Sturges, I don't do it." Brynner, who went from the Sturges picture to a string of expensive flops (*Taras Bulba, Kings of the Sun*), was only too happy to reprise his man in black, even if he now led the "B" team (Robert Fuller, Warren Oates, Claude Akins, etc.) into action.

"I wouldn't touch those sequels," said Sturges, who was, in fact, announced for the second sequel, which was shot in Spain. "I made a lot of money on them because they couldn't make them without making the deal with me."

In 1991, Sturges put his share of earnings from residuals and VHS sales at $70,000. With regular DVD re-releases, the Western remains a lucrative annuity for the director's widow, Kathy Sturges. (Because the contracts were signed before January 31, 1960, the negotiated start date for TV residuals, the cast never participated in later earnings.) Over the years, a virtual cottage industry has grown up around variations and rip-offs, starting with *The Professionals* and *The Dirty Dozen* and including *Three Amigos!, Bad Girls, Silverado, Young Guns,* and Roger Corman's *Battle beyond the Stars,* with Vaughn as a futureworld Lee. Steven Spielberg said he thought about the Western when juggling his *Jaws* and *Close Encounters of the Third Kind* casts. "You know, I felt that I knew each one of the seven," Spielberg told Sturges. "It was more than seeing a movie."

To explain the film's hold on subsequent generations, Walter Mirisch quoted Chris's response to the Mexicans who timidly volunteer their village's meager resources. "I've been offered a lot for my work," the gunfighter says, lowering his eyes, "but never everything."

"That's a great theme of John's, isn't it? The stand of the decent people against tyrants," said Mirisch. "Periodically, there's talk of a remake. The problem, of course, is: How do you duplicate that incredible ensemble? It was a picture in which everything worked. I don't know why. Fate maybe. I do know it continues to resonate with audiences almost fifty years after it was made. The mission, the music, the title — they've become part of our language."

12

Grand Illusion

Following *The Magnificent Seven*, John Sturges wanted to do another ensemble piece, either *The Sons of Katie Elder* or that long-gestating project about an escape from a German prison camp. Since he had a non-exclusive contract with the Mirisches, he approached Hal Wallis about *Katie Elder*. Wallis liked the script but couldn't entice Paramount to back the picture. (It was made in 1965 by Wallis and director Henry Hathaway.) The Mirisches, meanwhile, worked overtime to keep Sturges happy and in the fold. Now in possession of the rights to the Brickhill bestseller, they assured Sturges they would co-finance the war film as soon as all parties could agree on a script. Little did anyone know that the adaptation would take the better part of two years, with successive drafts submitted by Walter Newman, W. R. Burnett, and James Clavell, who had been a POW in Singapore and was at work on a novel about the experience, to be published as *King Rat*.

In February 1961, the *New York Times* reported that McQueen would segue from MGM's "The Golden Fleecing" (filmed as *The Honeymoon Machine*) to *The Great Escape*. The columnist added, "Frank Sinatra and Dean Martin are being sought for the Mirisch Company–United Artists release," which at that point had an optimistic summer start date. Also announced (but soon abandoned) was a Sturges remake of George Stevens's *Vivacious Lady*, with McQueen and Lee Remick in the Jimmy Stewart–Ginger Rogers roles.

"I didn't want John to go elsewhere and get tied up in another film," said Walter Mirisch. "So I asked him if he wanted to stay with us and do *By Love Possessed,* which was ready to go. He wanted to work and indicated an interest in it. I was encouraged by his enthusiasm."

Written by Pulitzer Prize–winner James Gould Cozzens, *By Love Possessed* was optioned before its publication in 1957 by Ray Stark's Seven Arts Productions, which unaccountably paid $100,000, plus 10 percent of the profits, for a novel many found impenetrable. Billy Wilder and William Wyler were approached about directing; Ketti Frings (*Come Back, Little Sheba*) did the first screenplay. But when the project failed to gel, Stark struck a co-production deal with the Mirisches, who were looking for a post–*Peyton Place* vehicle for Lana Turner. She agreed to play an expanded version of Cozzens's tortured Marjorie Penrose. The movie—which interweaves adultery, suicide, embezzlement, and accusations of rape—also starred Jason Robards Jr. as Julius Penrose, Turner's partially paralyzed lawyer husband, and Efrem Zimbalist Jr. as Arthur Winner, Robards's law partner and Turner's straitlaced lover. Russell Metty, Douglas Sirk's cinematographer at Universal, shot the color-saturated, burnished-mahogany interiors; Elmer Bernstein contributed the rhapsodic score, and Charles Schnee (*The Bad and the Beautiful*) wrote the script, changing the setting from Pennsylvania to rural Massachusetts and, at Mirisch's insistence, dropping all flashbacks. Turner insisted on other changes, and Schnee, finally fed up with star's interference, had his name removed. (He is credited as "John Dennis.")

That Sturges was uncomfortable with the assignment was obvious from the outset. He rankled when asked about how faithful the movie would be to the book. "Eighty percent of the book was introspection," he said. "We are not going to try to cope with introspection. What we have done is sheer editing. If we told the book on the screen we would be making an eighteen-hour picture. . . . If you want that, read the book."

Though handsomely produced and more than capably performed, *By Love Possessed* left little doubt that Sturges was no Sirk—or, for that matter, Mark Robson (who had directed *Peyton Place*). Like Zimbalist's Arthur Winner, the film felt tentative and unfinished, afraid to indulge in the very carnality that is at the core of the character's salvation. The only marginally naughty moments were provided by Yvonne Craig as Veronica, who has a maddening habit of referring to herself in the third person ("Nobody treats Veronica like a tramp but Veronica"). Turner and Barbara Bel Geddes as Winner's bedridden wife turned in the most convincing performances.

"I would hypothesize that Lana Turner and Martha Hyer (in *A Girl Named Tamiko*) were women taking on male roles," said Michael Sturges. "In a weird sort of way Dad was ahead of his time. He was perfectly comfortable with women who were strong; but I don't think he was into having touchy-feely relationships with them. That made him very uncomfortable."

By Love Possessed opened in July, fanned by a promotional campaign that was as overwrought as it was misleading. "The story of a woman who was BY LOVE POSSESSED!" trumpeted a poster with Turner in clingy cocktail dress. "The Bold Best-Seller That Sent a Fever through America—Now Fires the Screen!" teased another ad. In a first for Sturges, UA prodded exhibitors to "Go All Out for the Women's Angle!" with perfume giveaways and women's previews. *Variety* turned up its nose at the "melodramatic clichés" while the *New York Times* found it "expertly made." To recoup its investment, UA struck a deal with TWA: *By Love Possessed* was among the first in-flight attractions. Mirisch chalked up the film's failure to timing. "It came at the end rather than at the beginning of a cycle of soapy, *Peyton Place*-type pictures."

Sturges's critics have speculated about his return to the melodramatic excesses of *Sign of the Ram*. Did something in the Cozzens novel bring to mind Grace's stories about Oak Park relatives? Perhaps it was the insular world of country-club attorneys, or the descriptions of languorous summers at the lake. It is more likely that he saw the film as a work-vacation, an opportunity to repair family ties and oversee rewrites on *The Great Escape*.

Sturges blamed it on ego and Mirisch's persistence. "You get to the point where you think you can handle anything. I knew I had no business making that picture. Sure it was well acted and staged, but it just didn't amount to anything. . . . I couldn't care less about those people. I didn't like 'em, didn't understand 'em. And if you don't understand people in a given situation and you don't like what's happening, you shouldn't try to make a movie out of it."

He added, sighing heavily, "But you do because you get talked into it and think you can get around it . . . or you need the money, or some goddamn thing."

In late 1961, Sturges reteamed with Hal Wallis on *A Girl Named Tamiko*, taken from Ronald Kirkbride's 1959 bestseller about changing mores in post-Occupation Japan. The director saw the movie — starring Laurence Harvey as Ivan Kalin, a Eurasian photographer desperate for a U.S. visa, and France Nuyen as Tami, a modern Japanese woman who falls in love with him — as an opportunity to again tackle the theme of postwar racism, this time as practiced by Americans in Tokyo.

Wallis — hailed as the producer who "takes pictures instead of trips" — decided only Sturges and a second unit would travel to Japan. (Harvey had accompanied Wallis on an earlier trip and cost the production a small fortune in bar tabs.) In a memo, Wallis explained, "We will plan on shooting in Japan as we did for *G.I. Blues* in Germany, using only doubles." During the week abroad, stand-ins for Harvey and Nuyen, always just turning from the camera, were photographed in front of shrines and Buddhist temples, walking hand-in-hand around Lake Biwa, site of Tami and Ivan's romantic getaway. The stars posed later before rear-screen transparencies.

While Sturges by this point was used to star tantrums, Harvey's antics clearly made the director uncomfortable. The British actor — known for his flamboyant manner and bisexual lifestyle — downed vast quantities of Pouilly Fuissé and kept the company waiting as he fielded calls from antique dealers. For laughs, he affected an effeminate swish and recited racy limericks. This "camping," as Nuyen called it, was meant to get the uptight director's goat. It worked. "Larry was so mischievous — he teased John mercilessly in front of everybody," recalled Nuyen. "And John, poor darling, was like a big cowboy lost in the middle of Saks Fifth Avenue lingerie. . . . He would stand there shaking his head, his ears red." (Colleagues and family members insisted that the director was not homophobic.)

Promoted as an interracial love story — "He was half Oriental . . . but he used the women of two continents WITHOUT SHAME OR GUILT!" — *A Girl Named Tamiko* opened in March amid fierce Oscar campaigning for *To Kill a Mockingbird* and *Lawrence of Arabia*. In a week's time, it went from first-run bookings to the bottom half of double bills. Though compulsively watchable and an improvement on *By Love Possessed,* it was dismissed by most critics. Ironically, the reviews made the film's point about pervasive anti-Japanese sentiment. *Variety* referred to costar Miyoshi Umeki as "a slant-eyed cutie." Crowther couldn't see beyond Harvey's boorish character and faulted Sturges and screenwriter Edward Anhalt for their anti-Americanism. "Odd," he noted, "is the fact that all the Americans we see are silly to downright vicious types, while most of the Japanese are forthright, courteous and charming."

Sturges in retirement shrugged off both melodramas as "clear misses." At gatherings, his family would gingerly sidestep any mention of them. "They were my dad as a fish out of water," observed Michael. "They never got said aloud," added Deborah. "We called them by their acronyms, like BLP."

The Mirisch Company, now a key industry player, celebrated its fifth anniversary in 1962 by announcing a slate of nineteen movies to be bankrolled for $60 million and released over the next two years. Among the titles was the World War II adventure *The Great Escape.* Walter Mirisch had finally acquired the book rights after Sturges assured Brickhill that the movie would stick to the facts and "do the thing justice"; that it would not be a typical "How We Won the War" bit of Yank braggadocio; and that the director would await clearance from the families of Roger Bushell, Harry "Wings" Day, and the other escapees who had been executed by the Gestapo. With Sturges's outline in hand, Brickhill returned to England. "When [the families] said OK and I gave him my word that I would employ (C. Wallace) Floody as a technical adviser . . . I just convinced him I was on the level," the director recalled.

In retirement, Sturges insisted that there never was much of a script for what would become his greatest triumph. The screenplay, finally credited to Clavell and Burnett, went through eleven drafts by at least half a dozen writers. It was, according to the director, "strictly cut-and-paste all the way." The sixty-four pages that landed on his desk were little more than character vignettes, a lot of talk and swagger in search of a cohesive storyline. William Roberts, Walter Newman, Burnett, and Nelson Gidding, another former POW, each took a crack at adapting the book but wound up "inventing things," according to the director, because they thought Brickhill's story was too farfetched. The book lacked a conventional three-act structure, and, in place of empathetic characters, contained sixty-some faceless prisoners who popped in and out of the action. Only RAF organizer Roger Bushell, known as "Big X," and a couple of others stood out.

Nor did it help from a promotional and marketing standpoint that, in reality, the Yanks had been moved to a different camp by March 1944 and played only a peripheral role in the breakout. If Hollywood were going to make the movie, Sturges would have to go back on his promise and manufacture American characters to be played by marquee names. United Artists also complained that there were no female characters, which could hurt ticket sales. The director who was becoming known for macho ensembles wasn't fazed by this. "We have nary a woman; they have no place in this story," he said at the time. "We figure we'll keep audiences happy without 'em." (Such declarations, however, did not keep UA's promotional department from conspiring behind the scenes to improve the demographic appeal.)

"There were great delays and frustrations," acknowledged Mirisch. "Newman and Roberts were our first writers, but what they turned in was very disappointing. Then we hired Burnett, and he didn't work out. We knew we had to go further. The book was our primary source for the escape, but we had to create characters. That's where Jim [Clavell] came in. We hung in and persisted and kept hiring writers until we found one who could deliver a first-class script."

Still, there was the problem of the ending.

As Sam Goldwyn had so famously groused when Sturges approached MGM with the project a decade earlier, "What the hell kind of escape is this? Nobody gets away!"

While an exaggeration—three of the seventy-six who went through the tunnel made it to freedom and fifteen were returned to the camp—Goldwyn had a point. This was a few years before *Cool Hand Luke* (1967) and *Easy Rider* (1969), and downbeat endings were not yet in vogue. Sturges, however, knew that the suspense and intrigue would be leavened by humor. He was a fan of Lean's *Bridge on the River Kwai*, and in that POW saga, he reminded UA, both William Holden and Alec Guinness died. His other models—Jean Renoir's *Grand Illusion* (1937) and Wilder's *Stalag 17* (1953)—also had more than their share of bleakly sardonic moments.

"When I said I wanted to make that picture everybody thought I was crazy," Sturges recalled. "I don't think anybody understood how an escape that doesn't come off could be a picture. I did. But I'll tell you, if I hadn't done *The Magnificent Seven*, which became a hit with an all-male cast, they never would have let me make *The Great Escape*. Never in a million years."

Brickhill's book, published in 1950, recounted in great detail the 1944 mass breakout from Stalag Luft III in Sagan, Germany (now Zagan, Poland). In about a year's time, Brickhill and six hundred other airmen (primarily British and Canadian, but also Polish, Norwegian, and Australian) worked secretly on three tunnels code-named Tom, Dick, and Harry. Tom was eventually discovered and Dick abandoned, but Harry, the longest of the three, was completed under the supervision of Squadron Leader Bushell and Canadian Floody, a.k.a. "the Tunnel King." The prisoners used what was available within the compound to dig a 25-foot-deep, 348-foot-long tunnel, complete with track and trolley, air pump and lights (spliced into the camp's electrical system). It was a remarkable bit of engineering, like the jungle bridge in Lean's picture, one that could only have been accomplished through full cooperation.

"It was about why our side won," Sturges said, punching his palm. "Here were these guys who had never seen each other in their lives, all different nationalities, who formed an organization to escape. They're a microcosm of the Allies, men who voluntarily formed the most professional army ever put together to wipe out the Nazis. I saw it as a movie about this uncontrolled, individualistic, do-it-your-way form of life — *our* way of life — which defeated those dictatorial sons-a-bitches."

More, it was a harebrained mission with our most precious gift, freedom, on the line. "That's the emotional content," Sturges continued. "An irresistible force meets an immovable object: Either these guys are going to get out or die trying. Something's got to blow. And it's real, it happened. That gives it dimension."

The Great Escape, originally to be shot in California with some German locations, was budgeted at $2.3 million, which after weather and script delays became $4 million, making it the most expensive gamble of Sturges's career. (In today's dollars, it would cost around $40 million and be considered medium budget.) The core production team included several Sturges and Mirisch regulars: Relyea, editor Webster, composer

Bernstein, assistant director Jack Reddish, cinematographer Daniel Fapp (*West Side Story*), and Wise protégé John Flynn, who worked as "second-second assistant" and doubled as a German soldier because Sturges liked his look.

"If you worked for the Mirisches or 'Miri,' as we called them, you would finish one movie and go right into the next—same grips, same gaffer, same prop and makeup people," recalled Flynn, who graduated to director on such films as *The Outfit* and *Rolling Thunder*. "It was a huge production that went way, way over budget, and it was obvious Sturges was under pressure. He was taciturn, but very much in control—the father figure."

Kirk Douglas and Burt Lancaster were sought for the principal POWs, now composites from the book; but their combined asking price of $1 million put them well beyond the budget. Martin and Sinatra, George Hamilton, John Mills, and Richard Harris were also mentioned for the leads. In late 1961, McQueen re-upped with Sturges, whom he lauded as "the best action director in the business." McQueen would play Captain Virgil Hilts, an American prisoner who favors sleeveless sweatshirts, but his participation was contingent on Sturges beefing up the role and utilizing his motorcycle skills in the climactic escape. A few months later, James Garner—a household name from TV's *Maverick* and a co-star in the Mirisches' *The Children's Hour*—came aboard as Hendley "The Scrounger." (Garner, an ex-GI who had scrounged for officers in Korea, acknowledged that there was "a little of me in the role.") Harris was set to play Roger "Big X" Bartlett (based on Bushell), until it was announced that he had been "detained" on *This Sporting Life* and would be replaced by Richard Attenborough. By the spring, Charles Bronson and James Coburn were signed as, respectively, Polish tunneler Danny and the Aussie Sedgwick, who insists on escaping with a large suitcase. Rounding out the British contingent: James Donald as Senior British Officer Ramsey, Gordon Jackson as Intelligence Officer MacDonald, "Wee" Angus Lennie as the "wire-happy" Ives, Donald Pleasence as the nearsighted forger Blythe, David McCallum as "dispersal" expert Ashley-Pitt, and British pop star John Leyton as Willie, Danny's best mate and protector. German actors Hannes Messemer and Robert Graf were cast as Colonel Von Luger, the camp's Kommandant, and Werner the sympathetic guard or "ferret." Jud Taylor was promised the third American character, Goff, Hilts's sidekick—provided he pay his own way to Germany. (In 1988, Taylor co-directed the made-for-TV *The Great Escape II: The Untold Story,* starring Christopher Reeve and inspired by Brickhill's final chapters, which dealt with the investigation into the murder of the captured escapees.)

"I had the cast of a lifetime, plus my pick of the best actors in Germany," said Sturges. "Three years later, there wasn't a studio in town that could afford McQueen, Garner, and Coburn."

As late as February 1962, Sturges intended to shoot in Idyllwild, California, where a small stand of pines in the San Jacinto Mountains would sub for Bavaria's Black Forest. "McQueen will join the director in the Alps in April for some motorbike sequences. The rest of the picture will be shot in California," reported the *Los Angeles Times*. In March, Reddish and Relyea flew to Munich to scout second-unit locations (train stations, meadowlands, towns along the Rhine). They rented an old Mercedes and, recalled Relyea, "hopped from town to town. We circled Germany twice looking for a place to put the camp." They telephoned Sturges: "Guess what? Germany looks like Germany, not California." Relyea and art director Fernando "Ferdie" Carrere next traveled to Zagan to tour what remained of the actual compound. Carrere, known for his meticulous research, returned with enough photos and sketches to duplicate Stalag Luft III, board for board.

Back in California, the Mirisch Company again faced labor problems. This time, however, it wasn't the actors or writers unions but the Screen Extras Guild (SEG). Sturges wanted to bus in half the background players from Los Angeles and supplement that number with college students from Palm Springs. For this, the production would need a waiver. SEG refused, citing a rule that said guild members must be employed "within a 300-mile radius of Hollywood." According to Sturges, this technicality—plus the cost of replicating German trains and ordnance—made shooting close to home prohibitive. The German film industry, virtually shut down since the war, took the opposite tack: instead of asking $30 to $40 a day for extras, they would charge $15. "They courted us," said Relyea, who made the arrangements. "They promised blanket work permits and said we could come and do whatever we liked." The University of Munich, with its English-speaking exchange students, was a handy source of extras.

In March, UA announced the picture would be shot in its entirety outside Munich at the Bavaria Film Studios in Geiselgasteig, where Wilder had just wrapped *One, Two, Three.* The intention was to start in early June, after construction of the compound, and shoot through the summer. Script revisions, unseasonable weather (it snowed on July 4), and McQueen, who eventually went AWOL, caused what was to be a sixty-day production schedule to more than double—at $30,000 a day.

"It is no longer true that you can shoot any part of the world in Hollywood," Sturges told the *L.A. Times,* justifying the location change. "You can't fake a literal representation—the vehicles, the trains, the Autobahn, the Swiss Alps—on the big screen."

Carrere, whose prison sets for *Birdman of Alcatraz* had caused Burt Lancaster to break out in a cold sweat, built a partial replica of the "escape-proof" prison camp in the forest directly behind the studio. "The idea was to be close to the studio, so we could duck into a soundstage when it rained and keep shooting," explained Relyea. Though Brickhill had nothing to do with the production and did not visit the set, his book provided a blueprint for the compound, right down to the dimensions of the bed slats (thirty by six inches) used to shore up the tunnels:

The compound was about 300 hundred yards square, and right round it ran two fences about nine feet high and five feet apart, each strung with about 20 close strands of rusting barbed wire. In between them, great coils of barbed wire had been laid, so thickly in parts that you could hardly see through it. Some 30 feet inside the main fence ran the warning wire. Just outside the northern wire lay the *vorlager,* containing the sick quarters and the long, grey concrete cooler with its barred windows. . . . The entrance to the compound was on the north side . . .

The huts were divided into 18 rooms about 15 feet square, each to be bedroom, dining-room and living-room for eight people, and three little rooms for two, reserved for those who could pull enough rank to deserve them. Furniture was elementary: double-decker bunks, a deal table, stools, lockers and a stove in one corner on a tiled base. The bunks consisted of four corner posts with planks screwed along the sides and across the ends at two levels. Short, flat boards rested across the side planks and on these one laid one's palliasse [mattress]: a bag of woven paper that looked like hessian and stuffed with wood shavings.

The guard towers or "goon boxes" were equipped with searchlights and machine guns. Sentries, Brickhill recalled, patrolled the fences with German shepherds "trained to go for a man's throat if necessary."

The actual camp was built in a cleared pine forest, which provided a sort of natural wall. So it was a stroke of good fortune that Bavaria Studios bordered the national forest. Or was it? Though the American company was granted a permit by the Interior Ministry to clear four hundred trees—the saplings to be replanted elsewhere, the mature trees to be replaced two-for-one—the deal did not endear the Americans to area conservationists. One proprietary forest ranger trained an eagle eye on the production.

"We took out ads, and hundreds of people showed up to take trees that had been dug up and bundled in burlap," recalled Sturges. "And we did replant after we built the set. But that one guy never forgave us because they had lost a year's growth. He spied on us throughout the shoot, cursing and shaking his fist from the tree line."

Like the Mexican village in *The Magnificent Seven,* the studio compound was what Sturges called a "360-degree set" that could be photographed from any angle. A reporter called it "the most depressingly realistic POW camp you ever set eyes on." It helped immeasurably, said the director, that some of the actual events in the story "took place not ten miles from this studio." The barracks interiors and a cross section of the tunnel, with fat lamps and operational trolley, were built inside the massive soundstages. During his visits, technical adviser Floody was in such demand, he was passed from department to department—"by appointment only."

"You must be getting something right," he told Sturges after squirming out of the studio tunnel, "because I'm having terrible nightmares."

Pleasence, a World War II veteran who sat out the war in a Baltic prison camp, also had flashbacks. "It was an exact reproduction of a prisoner-of-war camp, and just as frightening," he said.

No sooner than the barracks were framed, it began to rain. "It was so depressing—it rained forever," recalled Relyea. "We would go out and watch the painters trying to paint the buildings, and their ladders would keep sinking, so they would step up a rung to keep painting."

And then the rain turned to snow, which was unheard of in the spring, locals assured the crew. "Europe's worst weather in 38 years has been hurting our schedule," Sturges reported, adding presciently, "If only I could take 100 days instead of 60."

Later, he recalled, "It snowed and snowed . . . and then the snow began to melt. An absolute quagmire. You'd sink two feet in the mud. We brought in bulldozers and those things used to melt asphalt." Meanwhile, Sturges shot interiors. He did the scene in which Blythe secrets a pin across the room to trick Hendley and Bartlett into believing his eyes are fine. "After three weeks, we went back to the beginning—a very dangerous thing to do," said the director, who later would point to the moments between Pleasence and Garner as the heart of the film.

Like a good field general, Sturges seemed to be everywhere at once. (Most of Mirisch's involvement was over the phone from his Hollywood office.) On the weekends and evenings, he called upon his studio training and methodically broke down and reassembled the script. The new three-act structure: (1) introduction of the camp and fifteen principals; (2) Tom and its discovery by the Germans, Ives's death at the wire, Hilts's change of heart, and the decision by "X" to concentrate on Harry; (3) the escape and its tragic/defiant aftermath. Yet to be addressed was Hilts's role in the escape and how he wound up on a commandeered German motorcycle.

"[I] couldn't get it . . . the way I wanted it until almost a month after we started shooting, often working only a couple of days ahead," Sturges wrote Curtis Wong, who produced Criterion's 1991 laserdisc transfer. To keep track of character alliances (Danny-Willie, Hilts-Ives, Hendley-Blythe) and how the scenes dovetailed, the director plastered his office with maps, location photographs, and note cards. "I was the only one who knew what I was doing," he said, laughing.

By early June, the American cast members, followed by the Brits, began arriving. Instead of being shown the rehearsal hall, they were given a tour of the set and driven to their respective accommodations. Coburn and Bronson were in a Munich hotel. Steve and Neile McQueen had a house in Deining. Garner and Sturges had chalets in the "Bel-Air section of Munich." McCallum and his actress wife, Jill Ireland, rented a guesthouse on Lake Stamberg. Relyea, Flynn, and other crewmembers took apartments in Schwaba, the student quarter. McQueen, drawn to the Autobahn by its unlimited speed limit, was perpetually lost. The afternoon he was scheduled to check in, he missed the studio exit by 150 miles. Throughout the shoot, he would infuriate the local authorities by tearing to and from the studio in his Mercedes 300SL convertible. They rigged a speed trap especially in his honor.

"We have stopped a lot of your friends this morning, Herr McQueen," said a policeman who clocked the actor at more than 100 mph and confiscated his license. "But I must tell you, you have won the prize." Later, to keep from colliding with a tractor, he performed what he described to Pleasence as "a controlled crash" into a forest.

With more time on their hands than they knew what to do with, the British cast members read and socialized and generally behaved themselves. The Americans, not nearly as patient, gambled and complained. The Germans, used to imbibing on the set, consumed large quantities of beer—even at breakfast with their white sausage. The head electrician, according to Flynn, got so drunk he fell into the scenery on more than one occasion. Weekends were for play and travel. A map of the world hung in the main office. Color-coded pins showed "where everyone was because John was quite happy to let people go off and do things if they weren't working," said McCallum, unaccustomed to such extravagance.

"Because there was no script, we had to call everybody on a daily basis," recalled Flynn. "The English actors were completely fine with this. You'd call them and they'd get into make up and sit around in their little lawn chairs, listening to the radio or reading. They made it a picnic. They didn't care; they were being paid."

As he had on *The Magnificent Seven*, Bronson played the glowering narcissist. Flynn described him as "perpetually pissed off—he entered the room pissed off." Most afternoons he could be found shirtless, working a chaw of tobacco, scanning the horizon for his next romantic conquest. Deborah, the director's daughter, recalled him as "this very physical, very rough person" who, when he came to the house to discuss a role, "grossed my brother and me out" by spitting chewing tobacco into a coffee can.

"Charlie was a terrible misanthrope, a terrible sort of melancholy type, who had worked in a coal mine with his brother as a kid," said Sturges. "So he was a natural for Danny, the tunneler who's afraid to go back down into the tunnel."

Bronson being Bronson, he couldn't help raining on everyone's parade—or weekly card game, for that matter. Garner recalled that they almost came to blows during a Sunday night poker session. They didn't speak again during the shoot, but this didn't stop Bronson from sharing his days of deprivation and "weed soup" with the rest of the cast. Sturges finally took him aside.

"Charlie, I want you do something for me," the director said.

"Sure, boss."

"The days with the weeds and the soup?"

"Yup."

" . . . and the parents who gave you away because they couldn't feed you."

"Yup."

"They're all gone, Charlie. You're a highly successful actor on your way to being a star."

"You think so?"

"Stop talking about those days. Be happy."

Bronson's outlook did seem to improve, perhaps because he found unlikely allies in McCallum and his wife, Jill, pregnant with their third child. When McCallum was called away to London for post-production work on *Freud,* Ireland had a miscarriage and almost died. Bronson sat by her bedside and when she recovered, according to Flynn, "he was on her like an animal." Relyea may have naively facilitated the affair by loaning his apartment when Bronson asked, "Can I get a key to your flat? I have to get away from my hotel."

The public shows of affection became such a distraction that Sturges stepped in. "Look, I don't interfere in people's lives off the set," he told Bronson. "If they're professional, what they do elsewhere is none of my business. But I don't think you should be fooling around with Jill, even if it's innocent, when David's working."

Bronson agreed. "You're right, I won't do it." Later he told Sturges, "Just to show I'm on the level, I talked to David about it. I told him, 'David, I'm going to marry your wife.'" Sturges just shook his head in amazement.

"It's very difficult for me to speak of memories of Charlie Bronson," said McCallum. "Unbeknown to me, they became very good friends, and subsequently they got married. . . . There was an awkwardness about it, but at the same time one had to have a stiff upper lip and keep things as polite as possible for the sake of the children."

With production proceeding in fits and starts, rumors flew that the film was in trouble, possibly even in danger of being shut down. To squelch such talk, Sturges screened forty-five minutes of dailies from the first six weeks—mostly barracks dialogue and compound gags. Because the Hilts character was still evolving, there was little footage of McQueen. Jud Taylor recalled the funereal response: "There was a gray mood. Everybody thought, 'This film is awful. It doesn't seem real. It seems too light . . . kind of silly.'" Added Pleasence, who would later appear in *The Hallelujah Trail* and *The Eagle Has Landed,* "When I left, I was convinced the film was going to be a disastrous flop."

McQueen was furious. The dailies made him appear an afterthought. Worse, he complained to Neile, Garner "in that goddamn white turtleneck" was stealing the show.

"Steve hated dialogue, he always wanted to cut his own lines," said Flynn. "But here he was in the first weeks of rushes with these guys out of Masterpiece Theatre, and he's standing there like a tree."

"No, Steve didn't like it one bit," confirmed Garner. "Coburn and I got with him and went over the script, scene by scene. We figured it out: Steve wanted to be the hero—but he didn't want to do anything heroic."

Sturges chalked it up to basic insecurity. McQueen felt like a stuntman in the presence of Shakespeareans. He also was underpaid. Thanks to his three-picture contract with the Mirisches, even at $100,000, he wasn't making as much as Garner and Attenborough. On top of all this, *The Great Escape* followed three consecutive flops—*The Honeymoon Machine, Hell Is for Heroes,* and *The War Lover.* McQueen was scared.

"He was groping around, ad-libbing, trying to figure out how he could make the switch from loner to a member of the 'X' team," said Sturges. "I couldn't get Steve to realize that that was his part, the loner. He kept getting upset because he wasn't involved with the mechanism of the escape. Everybody was something: Jim was 'the scrounger,' Coburn 'the manufacturer' who could build an air pump, Attenborough was Big X. Steve needed something he could hang his character on."

McQueen called Stan Kamen, his Hollywood agent, who flew to Munich to calm his client. As soon as he left, McQueen disappeared. "Steve said, 'I'm not coming back unless that thing is fixed,'" recalled Neile. "He just drove around, letting off steam." Mirisch was less understanding. "On top of all the other aggravations," he fumed, "our star decided he wasn't satisfied with his role and stopped coming to work."

Sturges shot around McQueen. He told the Mirisches, "I want to jerk Steve out of the picture." He then phoned Garner. "Jim, you're the star of the picture because McQueen's out." That was on Friday. On Sunday, Kamen and several grim-faced associates were back in Munich. Midweek, McQueen, dressed in suit and tie, met with the director.

"Look, Steve, when I made *The Magnificent Seven,* you did what I told you to do and it came out fine," Sturges began. "But you believed in the scenes, and you believed that when I staged them they were good. Now all of a sudden you don't believe me. And if you don't believe the scenes, you're going to be lousy. I don't want you to be lousy."

Sturges's shoulders slumped. He had reached his limit.

"And frankly, Steve, I'm getting tired of arguing with you. If you don't like this part, to hell with it. We'll pay you off and I'll shift to Jim Garner."

Kamen and McQueen retired to the next room. Ten minutes later they emerged. "Steve wants to stay in the picture," said Kamen. "He'll do exactly as you say."

"Well, c'mon, fellows, let's not go to the opposite extreme," laughed Sturges. "I'm not asking him to check his talent or his brains. I'm just asking him to be a member of the team."

"So when can we get the script?" asked Kamen.

"When it's ready. Until then, you either trust me or you don't trust me."

"Oh, we trust you! We trust you!"

With the clock ticking and Mirisch on the phone daily complaining of cost overruns, Sturges scouted about for a nearby writer who could, in a few broad strokes, capture Hilts's hotshot personality. Ivan Moffat, a war buddy of George Stevens who had worked on *Shane* and *Giant* and now lived in England, answered the call. Moffat's contributions, during a two-week stay, were small but crucial. He wrote the scene in which Hilts tests a blind spot between guard towers by tossing a baseball at the fence and the exchange in which Bartlett and MacDonald con Hilts into becoming their advance scout.

While the baseball stunt, which earns the American his first stretch in solitary, neatly established the character's suicidal brashness, the meeting with Bartlett and MacDonald was more important. Here, Sturges answered McQueen's question: Why would someone like Hilts, an incorrigible loner, suddenly turn team player and risk everything for the greater good? In the scene, the RAF officers apply reverse psychology on the slow-thinking Yank, who plans to "blitz out" and keep going. They want him to reconnoiter the surrounding countryside and report back.

Hilts (finally reading between the lines): "*Wait a minute!* You aren't seriously suggesting that if I get through the wire and case everything out there and don't get picked up . . . to turn myself in and get thrown back in the cooler for a couple of months so you can get the information you need?"

Bartlett: "Yes. One has to ask some very strange things in the job I have.

MacDonald: "We'll give you a front place in the tunnel."

Hilts: "I wouldn't do that for my own mother."

MacDonald: "I don't blame you."

Hilts: "Well, OK then—"

Bartlett: "It's completely understandable."

Hilts: "Well, OK then."

Bartlett (exiting with MacDonald): "Yes. Well, thanks, Hilts."

To come were additional cave-ins and sight gags (the roof of one hut appears to undulate under the weight of hidden soil), and the humorous July 4th celebration by Hilts, Goff, and Hendley, who buy up the camp's potatoes for moonshine. Much of this sequence, including the Americans' comic "*Wow!*" when they taste the home brew, was improvised and has the feel of handheld cinema verité. "That was John's direction entirely," said Neile McQueen. "Steve couldn't get the timing right, and John stayed on him until he came up with that scorched-throat sound." The lighter moments, however, soon give way to tragedy as Werner discovers "Tom" and Ives steps over the warning wire and is machine-gunned scaling the fence.

Hilts now had a plausible explanation for his change of heart—"Sir, let me know the exact information you need; I'm going out tonight"— and McQueen got his wish. He was a member of the group and had earned a spot in the tunnel. His star billing assured that it would be the lead spot.

"Mechanically, it worked," said Sturges. "Because when he'd gone out and found out what was out there, it was logical that he would be the first man out of the hole, steering the others in the right direction."

The escape by train was done with a vintage steam engine and two passenger cars purchased from a junkyard. It was photographed live (no process shots) on the busy Munich-Stuttgart run. The most spectacular stunts—Hendley and Blythe's crash-landing in a German plane, Hilts's attempted escape by motorcycle—were, for obvious reasons, left until the end of production. Relyea, who described himself as a weekend pilot, doubled for Garner at the controls of the single-engine Bueker 181, a flimsy trainer purchased from a Belgium collector for $250. Repainted and decorated with a swastika, the hedge-hopping aircraft was an easy target for angry farmers. Recalling one implement that barely missed the prop, Relyea said, laughing, "Can you imagine telling your grandchildren that you were shot down by a rake?"

Relyea piloted the plane over Salzburg toward the Austrian Alps, and then, after it appeared to sputter and lose altitude, steered it into a stand of trees. (Sturges had already shot a mock-up of the plane, with Garner and Pleasence climbing out of the burning wreckage.) Today, such a crash-landing would be achieved with computer graphics, as it was in the 2004 remake of *Flight of the Phoenix*. In 1962, it was done by Reddish's second unit and six cameras, some undercranked to speed up the action. The aircraft was prepared by weakening the wings and punching out the cockpit glass. After a couple of practice runs between two flags, it was positioned about fifty yards from the trees, almost drained of fuel and held by a dead-man anchor. Once the engine caught, Relyea, seated beside a dummy, snapped the canopy shut and eased back on what was now, for safety reasons, half a joystick. The tether twanged taut and Reddish signaled the cameras were "at speed." Relyea thought, "The damn thing is flying!" Veering left and then right, he jabbed the rudder and passed between the trees, shearing wings and propeller. When he regained consciousness, all he could see were flailing arms and the dummy's head rolling about the cockpit like a marble.

Unlike the previously shot footage, which showed the burning mock-up in the road, the real fuselage came to rest in an embankment. Webster, gambling that the viewer's attention would be drawn by the smoke and fire, "fixed" the continuity glitch with a simple match cut.

The editor's contribution to the motorcycle jump was even more impressive. He made an entire generation think it was seeing an airborne McQueen when in fact it was his stunt double, Bud Ekins. The sequence was shot in a meadow outside Füssen on the Austrian border as a hundred extras in German uniforms looked on. McQueen gunned his converted Triumph 650 and rode parallel to the six-foot barricade. Then Ekins, his hair dyed yellow, executed the sixty-five-foot jump, followed by a controlled slide into fake barbed wire. "If you fall," Sturges instructed Ekins, "get up and run like hell toward the wire." According to Neile, McQueen had wanted to do the stunt and, in fact, rehearsed it with Ekins. But when his rear wheel grazed the rehearsal rope, Sturges decided it was too dangerous: "We couldn't take a chance with him bustin' a leg. Whether Steve could have done it, I don't know. He was pretty good."

McQueen did do the rest of his own motorcycle stunts, Sturges was quick to point out. "That's him in beer-bottle goggles playing a German soldier chasing himself." But to the actor's lasting frustration, it was the barricade leap that soon defined both the film and his career. Today, the moment rivals Gene Hackman's suicide run in *The French Connection* and McQueen's car chase in *Bullitt* as the iconic action sequence.

Sturges continued shooting *The Great Escape* until he ran out of money and had to start using crew members in bit parts (script supervisor John Franco played a Pyrenees guide). He had already cut numerous scenes from the script, including the "mole" breakout by Hilts and Ives, a cooler montage (Hilts eating, doing pushups, etc.), Blythe coping with his blindness, Danny and Willie in a rowboat narrowly avoiding capture by sentries. The final shot was supposed to be of Danny and Willie boarding a Swedish freighter. By this time Sturges and his "guerilla crew" were working out of the back of a Volkswagen van. He had hired a launch for the camera crew.

"We ran up to the freighter and asked the captain if we could make a shot of some guys climbing up the ladder," Sturges recalled. "The captain said no, he didn't want anything to do with Germans. We couldn't convince him this wasn't a German production. I kept yelling, 'I'm an American. We're not Germans!'"

This time the bad weather proved a blessing. The falling snow obscured the filmmakers. Sturges, seizing the opportunity, yelled to

Bronson and Leyton, "Get on the [ship's] ladder! Kick the rowboat away! Climb up the ladder!"

"That's all it took," he said. "With that, we folded."

The rough cut ran more than five hours; Webster and Sturges condensed it to just over three, their strategy being that the film would go out as a special "roadshow" with intermission and reserved seating. This didn't happen because, according to Sturges, prime theaters were "illegally block-booked" by competing studios, making it impossible to dislodge films. Ten minutes had to go, bringing the film to around two hours and fifty minutes. Lost were additional scenes between Hendley and Blythe, Hilts refueling his motorcycle and sampling Sedgwick's special escape rations, and Sedgwick trying the Americans' brew and finally opening his suitcase. "It was funny stuff," said the director. "Sedgwick, who's Joe Organization, stops by a stream, opens the thing and in it he has food, wine, change of clothes, a compass, and book. He starts nibbling the cheese, drinking the wine, reading the book. Got a big laugh. But it had to go. Length."

Sturges phoned Garner from the editing room. Over lunch the next day, he said, "Jim, the two best acting scenes in the picture are between you and Pleasence. The only thing wrong is they're on the cutting-room floor. I've got to stay with Steve on the bike." (McQueen's fear of getting lost in the large ensemble proved unfounded. He is onscreen more than anyone—forty-three minutes in total.)

"I thought it was very classy of John to call me and tell me before I got to the preview," said Garner, who would later star in *Hour of the Gun*. "I accepted it because of the way it was presented. He was a very classy guy."

For his stirring tuba-and-woodwinds score—reminiscent of the "Colonel Bogey March" in *Bridge on the River Kwai*—Elmer Bernstein recycled a martial theme he had written at age fourteen. It was "jaunty, nose-thumbing in character . . . adolescent rather than adult" and meant as a cheeky counterpoint to the foreground heroics. "Apart from that," he added, "it was simply a matter of getting behind the action and McQueen's character."

The catchy theme was whistled near and far, from the Friedrichstrasse to Times Square. Conductor Mitch Miller recorded "The Great Escape March," which became a hit 45 rpm record. "You know that tune has become the official song of the English national soccer team," said Bernstein. "Whenever I perform it in England, the audience will start to whistle along."

In April, *John Sturges' The Great Escape*—his name for the first time prominent above the title—was previewed in Santa Monica and Beverly Hills. These showings were "a huge success," according to the director. Still, UA wanted the film to come down further in length to increase daily showings. Sturges was livid.

"I knew it was too long, but we couldn't shorten the damn thing any more," he said. "We had multiple stories with ten different characters. It was constructed like a house of cards: Take one thing out and it all falls apart. Finally we dropped the scene where the tailor (Robert Desmond) shows 'X' his new line of civilian clothes made from blankets and uniforms."

Meanwhile, UA demanded hefty interest on the $1 million overage. Sturges and Harold Mirisch went to Pacific National Bank for a loan. The board agreed, provided it could see the film. "They loved it, but couldn't understand how the men got their civilian clothes. So back it went." (Not a fan of extended director's cuts, such as *Close Encounters of the Third Kind: Special Edition,* Sturges said that even if the earlier deletions could be found, he did not favor restoring them.)

By spring, strategic previews and benefit screenings had generated advance buzz. Columnists were calling Sturges's latest "the one to beat" at Oscar time. In May it was announced that the film had been selected for the Moscow International Film Festival in the Kremlin. Never one for hoopla, Sturges found a way to beg off; Clavell, Bernstein and the Mirisches tendered his regrets. In June, the world premiere was held in London at the Odeon Leicester Square Theatre. It was preceded by an RAF benefit screening and an afternoon screening attended by Floody and other surviving members of Stalag Luft III. This was the acid test. Would the men who lived the story accept the Hollywood embellishments, especially those in the second half, which even Sturges called "apocryphal"? A written prologue prepared them for liberties: "This is a true story. Although the characters are composites of real men, and time and place have been compressed, every detail of the escape is the way it really happened." The standing ovation quelled all fears.

"To a man, they said we had the spirit and feeling absolutely right," said Sturges, who was designated a "Friend of the Royal Air Force by the RAF at the London premier.

"They loved it, they were very moved," added Relyea. "They said it was very accurate. That doesn't necessarily sell tickets, but it does mean we made an honest picture." (In 2006, camp survivor B. A. James called the film "a load of rubbish," adding, "The first part of the film wasn't bad, but the second half was just Hollywood fantasy, an excuse for McQueen to ride his motorbike. There was no motorbike. Nobody pinched a plane either.")

UA's advertising campaign played up the epic scope of the Mirisch-Alpha release ("Great Adventure! Great Entertainment!"). The press book encouraged exhibitors to stage promotional gags that played on the film's theme. Most were in poor taste: hawkers dressed like RAF officers (their heads "swathed in bandages"), play tunnels in the lobby for children, shopping-center prison camps, complete with barbed wire, Doberman pinschers, and Nazi guards. "If local ordinance allows, a siren can go off from time to time . . . (and) live prisoners can sit behind the wire" with cutouts of the stars. During production, UA had suggested a "Miss Prison Camp" beauty contest. The lucky winner would appear onscreen, cradling the dying McCallum. "I thought better of discussing that with John," said Relyea.

Sturges's grand celebration of Allied cooperation premiered in Los Angeles on the July 4th weekend. It opened in New York a month later. As would become more evident as the decade progressed, the public and press were split over the director's work. Audiences allowed themselves to be caught up in the often over-the-top escapades; critics were in the mood for something earthier and more provocative, such as *Hud* and *The L-Shaped Room*, both released the same year. *Variety*, however, called the film a beautifully produced and directed cliffhanger in "the recent screen tradition of *River Kwai* and *Navarone*." While stressing that this was a film carried by story and strong production values, not marquee names, the trade paper singled out McQueen as a "throwback to the personalities of earlier screen eras." The *L.A. Times* (in a reprint of a review published in conjunction with the London premiere) raved, equivocally, "There have surely been literally hundreds of prison-break movies, civilian as well as military. *The Great Escape* digs, hammers and claws its way, if not to the top of the list, then awfully close to it." Crowther refused to give himself over to the swaggering heroics, justifying UA's decision to delay the New York premiere. Obviously looking for something grimmer, like Clavell's *King Rat,* he found Sturges's latest work superficial, overlong, and "Rover Boyish." McQueen's ball-and-mitt routine, hailed by others as a show of nose-thumbing bravado, was "a moronic running gag." Crowther continued: "It is callow and obvious play-acting, and the whole picture is that way, aimed to inveigle the viewer with blunt, chauvinistic showiness. . . . It's a strictly mechanical adventure with make-believe men."

Needless to say, *The Great Escape* was not among Crowther's "Top Films of 1963," which included *Cleopatra* and *It's a Mad, Mad, Mad, Mad World.* Sturges dismissed the slight as an ongoing vendetta — "Crowther panned every picture I ever made" — and contented himself with the box-office returns. The POW picture more than doubled its investment, earning over $16 million. Sturges said he and the Mirisches collected about 40 percent of the theatrical gross net. "It made a ton of money," he said, "and because I owned a third of it, I made a ton of money."

Popularity at the box office did not translate into support from his peers in the Academy. In February, when Oscar nominations were announced, *The Great Escape* had to make do with one, for Webster's editing. Paramount's *Hud* and UA's *Tom Jones,* which would bring Tony Richardson the best-director Oscar, dominated the field. Sturges's rightful place in the best-picture category was taken by 20th Century Fox's *Cleopatra,* a lavish flop. Attenborough, Bronson, and Pleasence, all deserving of supporting-actor nods, were overlooked. Richard Harris, who had passed on the Bartlett role, was among the best-actor nominees for *This Sporting Life.* McQueen, whose first and only nomination would come three years later (for *The Sand Pebbles*), contented himself with nascent superstardom — and a per-picture asking price that more than tripled.

Was the Academy slight political? Did Sturges's reluctance to campaign cost the picture nominations? "He was like me," observed Garner. "He wouldn't kiss-up to the big boys so they would push his films." Added Relyea, "John was not a Hollywood type. He didn't get votes by attending the right dinners and parties. I don't remember him going to a party, period. He was not that gregarious."

Robert Wise screened *The Great Escape* for friends shortly before his death in 2005. The former president of the Academy and two-time best director winner considered the movie, along with *Bad Day at Black Rock*, Sturges's finest achievement. He allowed that Sturges's low profile in Hollywood may have put him at a disadvantage with Academy members. "That could have been part of it, yes," said Wise.

Sturges shrugged off the apparent slight. "You don't think about those things," he said, adding, "There must have been some fairly good competition."

Since its release, *The Great Escape* has steadily gained in stature as a pop-culture touchstone. In 2001, it made AFI's list of 100 Most Thrilling Movies at number 19, ahead of *High Noon*, *Lawrence of Arabia*, and *Star Wars*. Among the movies that have either reworked the plot or referenced it: *Von Ryan's Express* (1965), *The Dirty Dozen* (1967), *Escape from Alcatraz* (1979), *Reservoir Dogs* (1992), Disney's *Parent Trap* (1998), *Hart's War* (2002), and *Chicken Run* (2000), with its trash-bin Cooler and tunnel trolley. James Cameron and the Wachowski brothers, the high-tech heirs of Sturges, have offered apocalyptic homages to the motorcycle chase. In 1986, *The Great Escape* and *The Magnificent Seven* finally cracked the Oscars, as part of Chuck Workman's compilation tribute, *Precious Images*. In 2006, Hummer aired a takeoff commercial. The film remains a cash cow for distributor UA/MGM, which released a collector's edition DVD to commemorate the sixtieth anniversary of D-Day.

The reason the film has aged so well may be that it was always an anachronism, the first hip how-the-war-should-have-been-fought fantasy, where the German guards seem to hang back to allow the stars their digs. Obviously influenced by time spent with Sinatra and McQueen, Sturges the aging beat imposed a 1960s vibe that presaged the anti-establishment escapades of *Kelly's Heroes* and *M*A*S*H*, both released in 1970. Crowther was right for the wrong reasons: it is an adolescent's view of war, as formalistic in its handling of POWs as *Gunfight at the O.K. Corral* was in its handling of Tombstone gunplay. But that was the point. By 1963, the small screen had become an integral part of America's daily routine. *The Great Escape* stood apart *because* it fused big music, big action, and larger-than-life characters. It felt like the last of a dying breed, at least until the cliffhanger escapes of Lucas and Spielberg.

Sturges, now at his peak creatively, knew instinctively when to dolly and when to anchor the camera to let a scene play out. He also knew the importance of pathos (Danny's attacks of self-doubt) and slapstick (prisoners falling through beds minus slats). The fluid tracking shots of the tunnelers, chest-down, riding the wooden trolley are as exhilarating today as when the film was first released, and the crane shots of McQueen on his final, foolhardy run up to the Swiss border still evoke Allied bravado. This is action filmmaking of a very high order, pared to the essentials and skillfully paced so that, as Hitchcock taught, the lighter moments make the explosions of violence, such as Ives's death on the wire, that much more disturbing.

Downbeat ending not withstanding, *The Great Escape* is, in many ways, an action-comedy, a lead-up, if you will, to Sturges's *The Hallelujah Trail.* Much of the humor comes from the clash of cultures within the compound. Sturges's Brits are officious optimists, not quite stereotypical in their stiff-upper-lip resolve; the Yanks are cagey, demonstrative. The breakout depends not only on teamwork but also on the ability of one culture to con and cajole another. The British exploit Hilts's recklessness while lecturing him on the commonweal. For Hilts to claim his place in the tunnel, he must fall into step with Macready, Chris, and the Wyatt of *Gunfight at the O.K. Corral,* and acknowledge, albeit begrudgingly, the need for allies. The Howard Hawks of *Rio Bravo* would probably disapprove. Sturges, however, grew up in the studio system and knew the importance of being a "team player." He knew that linking arms now could mean grandstanding later.

"*The Great Escape* holds up because there's nothing phony in it," said Ken Annakin, who co-directed *The Longest Day* (1962). "It has almost perfect direction in that you aren't conscious of the director, and yet his work is absolutely essential. He was the one who made McQueen appear to be behaving completely natural."

Sturges attributed the film's success to his experiences overseas in the Army Air Corps. He knew and liked the POWs of Stalag Luft III. "It was the film I put the most into," he said proudly. "That's why I used the possessory 'John Sturges' *The Great Escape.*' I found the story, over-saw the screenplay, cast the stars. On that one I did it all. . . . If I were the most skilled director in the world, I'm not going to make Spike Lee's *Do the Right Thing.* No way. I don't know that scene; I don't know those people. . . . You have to have the experience. When I made *The Great Escape,* I suddenly realized I had an ear. I was never a POW, but I was in the army for four years and knew the lingo.

"It's curious that nobody has ever made a good picture about the war who wasn't in the war. Very interesting."

While most fans recall McQueen's attempted escape by motorcycle and other action scenes, Sturges once again cherished the subdued gal-lantry of the men. "What makes it work are the scenes where Blythe realizes he can't see and plants a pin to try to convince Roger he can, and the quarrel between Hendley and Big X over playing God, who goes and who doesn't. That's what makes the picture work. It's the emotional involvement."

In the spring of 1963, Sturges formed Kappa Corp. The company an-nounced three pictures—*The Hallelujah Trail, The Law and Tombstone,* and *The Satan Bug*—as part of a four-picture deal with the Mirisches. Because the two Westerns were mired in rewrites and required signifi-cant pre-production, Sturges moved on to the relatively low-budget (at $6 million) contemporary piece, which would allow time between set-ups to hone the other projects.

A doomsday thriller based on a 1962 bestseller by Scotland's Alis-tair MacLean (writing as Ian Stuart), *The Satan Bug* appeared made to order: It combined Sturges's proven skills in police procedural and race-against-time cliffhanger. The novel—about a top-secret government laboratory in southern England—also had a scary, ripped-from-the-headlines topicality that had so far eluded the director. "I'm no 'message man,'" he said, "[but] this story is within the realm of possibility." It dealt with something new and horrifying in the Cold War arsenal: microbiological weapons.

In the novel, Dr. Giovanni Gregori, described as a "raving crack-pot," steals a supervirulent "bug" from a research center and threatens to unleash it on London unless the lab is razed. As a preview of the devas-tation to come, he exposes East Anglia to the botulinus. Pierre Cavell, an undercover agent with Scotland Yard's Special Branch, heads up the manhunt. Armageddon becomes personal when Cavell's wife is kidnapped by Gregori, who turns out to be an Auric Goldfinger-like megalomaniac bent on looting London's financial district.

Tired of living out of a suitcase and worried about his brother's failing health (Sturge would die during production), the producer-director decided to film close to home, in Palm Springs and environs. To Americanize what was essentially a pulp detective novel, he turned again to Clavell and Anhalt. They transposed the action from the gloomy marshes of Wiltshire to the blinding sunlight of desert highways and Joshua Tree National Park. They also contemporized the hero, now a Korean War veteran named Lee Barrett, and—per Sturges's instructions—moved the research facility underground.

"Biological warfare is a terror potential that exists in our times," the director told a visitor to the set. "[MacLean] placed the action on the English moors, but we feel we aren't losing any of the suspense quality by moving it to America. . . . For our climax, we'll try to depict what would happen if Los Angeles had to be evacuated in twelve hours. Wouldn't that be something?"

As re-imagined, Barrett became the prototypical Sturges hero: hip, unattached, and vaguely political, a rebel in windbreaker who lives on a boat and shows disdain for protocol. McQueen or Coburn would have been ideal casting, but both were now outside the director's price range. Therefore, Sturges went with his famous instinct for emerging talent and hired George Maharis, a McQueen manqué from CBS's *Route 66*. Richard Basehart, from another hit TV show, *Voyage to the Bottom of the Sea*, was cast as Dr. Gregor Hoffman, much expanded from the book's villain. Basehart sank his teeth into the role, especially savoring Hoffman's plea to seal E Lab. The speech, taken verbatim from MacLean and cued by Jerry Goldsmith's jittery electronic score, established the enormity of the threat lurking behind the massive, vault-like door.

In a week, all life—and I do mean all life—would cease in the United States. In two months, two months at the most, the trapper in Alaska, the peasant from the Yangtze, the aborigine in Australia—dead. All dead. Because I crushed the flask and exposed the green-colored liquid to the air. Nothing, nothing can stop the Satan Bug. What will be the last to go? Perhaps a great albatross winging its way around the bottom of the world. Perhaps an Eskimo in the Arctic. . . . But the seas travel the world over, and so do the winds. One day, one day soon, they too would die.

Hoffman's protestations go unheeded. Barrett—in one of the film's best sequences—dons oxygen suit and, with a caged hamster, enters the lab. Inside, Dr. Baxter, "father" of the Satan Bug, is dead from exposure to botulinus.

Veteran Dana Andrews drew the thankless role of the army general, who, mostly by phone, coordinates the dragnet and retrieval of the flasks, and Anne Francis replaced the previously cast Joan Hackett as the general's daughter, who may have once been involved with Barrett. Hoffman's henchmen were played by Ed Asner and Frank Sutton, both of whom would soon find success in TV sitcoms. By the time the film opened, Sutton was known as the sputtering drill sergeant in *Gomer Pyle, USMC*. Sturges wasn't amused. "These things hurt you," he said, shaking his head.

Sturges and art director Herman A. Blumenthal collaborated on the blueprints for the government research facility, now called Station 3. MacLean's lab was monolithic and foreboding, Victorian in style. The filmmakers kept the double-fence perimeter and Doberman guard dogs but opted for a minimalistic, more antiseptic look—amber guard station, heliport, concrete ramps, and air shafts. Below ground: a maze of glass offices, stainless-steel workstations, motion-sensor doors that whoosh open and shut. To complete the effect, Robert Surtees, shooting in widescreen Panavision, bathed Dr. Baxter's inner sanctum in an ominous red glow.

"We had to build the thing big enough to make it look right," Sturges explained. "But this was a budget picture. So what do you do? I said, 'It's underground! All you have to do is build a lot of [ventilation] stacks sticking up in the air and a cement thing with a door.' Jeez, what an idea! The set cost us nothing."

Sturges's excitement was short-lived. As would happen more frequently in the days ahead, he lacked the time and resources to pull off the appropriate ending. Following an extended two-way chase and a police sweep of the Los Angeles Coliseum (where a booby-trapped flask is found at the back of a concession cooler), the director took to the skies above Los Angeles. The script called for "interchanges and over-passes jammed bumper to bumper with motionless cars." Panic in the streets. Gridlock. City Hall said no.

"The sons-of-bitches wouldn't let me stop traffic. I went up and beat on the mayor's desk. I threatened the chief of police. 'You talk about hot taxpayers on the highway,' I said. '*We're* big taxpayers! *We're* the movie business!'"

To cover for the missing close-ups of the pandemonium, Sturges used "glass shot" composites backed by the faint sound of honking horns. It got the job done but, as he noted, "it looked phony and they [the critics] nailed me." Also missing, after the reasonably well-staged helicopter fight and Basehart's parting *"Oh, no—Los Angeles will be my epitaph,"* was the obligatory process shot of the villain falling to his death. Hitchcock, whom Sturges often cited in interviews, would have made more of the moment.

"Had the end been what I tried to do, it would have been a big hit," said Sturges, seated under a *Satan Bug* poster. "But all we had was the underground lab and the mad professor. For the clear liquid to be sinister, you have to show the care with which it's locked up; the scientists in [protective] spaceman suits. We did that. But we didn't get the panic in the streets, the motorists trapped on the freeways. What I wanted to do was shoot a picture showing what would happen if everybody tried to get the hell out of Los Angeles before something hit . . . show the nightmare of the evacuation."

While on location shooting *The Satan Bug*, Sturges conferred with John Gay about *The Hallelujah Trail*. "Come on out," he said. "Maybe we'll get a chance to work on the script." Gay thought this meant they would hash out a few ideas over the weekend. Instead, the story conferences took place during work hours, between setups. "There we were talking about the scenes and laughing away," said the screenwriter, still incredulous. "No wonder the actors threw us dark looks." Francis and Asner were particularly annoyed. For a director known for his tireless preparation, Sturges was surprisingly cavalier about continuity and retakes. In the released film, Maharis stumbles on a speech about the investigation, recovers, and continues. Asner's thug talks with a pronounced rasp late in the picture, but the karate chop to the jugular that caused the vocal abnormality was never shot.

"Every day while they were setting up shots for the next scene, he'd go walking off into the desert with Gay to talk about *Hallelujah Trail*," said Asner, still fuming over the slight. "He'd come back laughing his ass off, looking very, very different from his demeanor and communication with us. Obviously that's where his heart and mind were; he wanted to get through our film as quickly as possible."

"That was becoming increasingly John's pattern," confirmed Relyea. "The smaller films suffered because of that big thing to come."

To capitalize on Basehart's popularity abroad—and exploit the more immediate threat of arms proliferation in Europe—*The Satan Bug* premiered in West Germany in March 1965. Two weeks later, it opened in New York, ballyhooed by posters that warned: "Since time began man has hunted the ultimate evil. . . . Now the search is over." *The Satan Bug* was retitled "Station 3: Top Secret" in France and Italy, where, to Sturges's amazement, it became "a smash hit. . . . It ran forever." The reviews were mixed. *Variety* found it "a superior suspense melodrama" that "should keep audiences on the edge of their seats." Crowther liked the desert scenery and color photography but found the thriller short on thrills and long on talk, like your "average serial television show." The *L.A. Times* dubbed it "James Bond without the laughs . . . a cat-and-mouse game with spurts of violence."

By June, *The Satan Bug* was playing almost exclusively at drive-ins or on the bottom half of double bills. Beside *Goldfinger* and *Dr. Strange-love*, two wildly subversive takes on the Cold War mindset, Sturges's film seemed, in the parlance of the day, "out of it." The Fort Knox climax of *Goldfinger*, where soldiers are anesthetized by the villain's sexy air corps, said it all. For the new youth market, now well past the Cuban missile crisis, impending Armageddon was more hoot than horror.

Maharis came off as a glum Boy Scout next to Sean Connery's super-agent. "It suffered from the fact that we were not able to attract a frontline star," said Mirisch. "John pushed me on Maharis, and I finally agreed." Sturges refused to lay blame. "George was good, he had something," the director insisted. "But he just never clicked."

Despite glaring lapses in logic—why is security so lax at "the most secret chemical warfare establishment in the hemisphere," and why isn't Barrett contaminated by a broken flask that kills others instantly?—Sturges's first forays into science speculation now boasts a cult following and speaks to audiences familiar with SARS and anthrax. One cannot consider Wise's *The Andromeda Strain* (1971), George P. Cosmatos's *The Cassandra Crossing* (1976), Frankenheimer's *Black Sunday* (1977), or Wolfgang Petersen's *Outbreak* (1995) without acknowledging the earlier film. Among its strengths: the animated title sequence (with abstract virus multiplying and attacking a human form that dissolves into a desert highway); the endless wait in an abandoned gas station for the hurled botulinus; and Jerry Goldsmith's nerve-jangling score, which incorporates modular synthesizer.

Politically, *The Satan Bug* is, like the director, pro-action and anti-war—in other words, "Hollywood liberal." In the early scenes, Barrett shows signs of being a 1960s peacenik. But this quickly passes. And by the time he gets around to assessing the anonymous blackmailer's motives, he's speaking out of both sides of his mouth, ideologically. What kind of deranged messiah would hold the world at bay? Ann demands. "Take your pick," replies Barrett. "Extreme right, extreme left—from the 'I'd rather be red than dead' fanatics to 'bomb Moscow right now' fanatics."

The film's coda is delivered by Barrett to the tower at Los Angeles International Airport: "I'll put down safely, and I'll give you the flask—then we're right back where we started." This line, all but drowned out by the roar of helicopter rotors, is savagely sardonic, defeatist in tone—and illustrative of Sturges's new cynicism.

13

Roadshows

Basking in the success of *The Great Escape*—and now, according to *Show Magazine*, among the most powerful directors in Hollywood—John Sturges in the mid-1960s had his pick of projects. This freedom would prove a mixed blessing, and perhaps his undoing as an independent. He passed on *Patton, Earthquake,* and *Papillon* and chose *The Hallelujah Trail, The Law and Tombstone* (released as *Hour of the Gun*), and *Richard Sahib,* a David Lean–inspired battle of wills. The latter was an original story by Sturges and Clavell about an American rancher who, on a trip to Hindustan, teaches low-caste "untouchables" how to irrigate their land, thus earning the wrath of a powerful shah who exploits the drought conditions. Sturges wanted Spencer Tracy for the rancher and Alec Guinness for the shah. Part of the Mirisches' ambitious 1964 slate, the film was to be shot in Lone Pine until the Extras Guild demanded accommodations for five hundred Hollywood extras. "That was my favorite story of all time," Sturges lamented. "But the guild demands wiped it out." (In 1981, Michael Sturges attempted to resurrect the project with Sidney Poitier as the engineer, now visiting South Africa.)

The other promising Mirisch-Kappa projects announced but eventually abandoned: *The Yards of Essendorf,* a behind-enemy-lines adventure with runaway trains and either McQueen or Warren Beatty, and *The Artful Dodger,* a broadly played offshoot of *The Great Escape* that focused on Johnny Dodge, an American POW who in the closing hours of the war was wined and dined by Churchill and the German high command.

Sturges blamed his inability to launch projects on the growing bias against large-scale productions. He too was a fan of certain "daring" imports by Bergman and Truffaut, he said, but he didn't want them to replace Hollywood's mainstay, the big-budget spectacle.

Members of what he distastefully dismissed as "the club" think that "anything produced in CinemaScope or Cinerama, in color, with name stars and in Hollywood—is junk," he told the *Los Angeles Times*. "This is tantamount to asking us to go back to driving a horse-and-buggy, reading by kerosene and writing with quill pens. . . . When the most modern techniques for screening are available, we are cheating the public if we do not use them." Sounding more than a little parochial, he continued: "If only sex exposé is art and if only small-screen fare smacks of talent, then why do the world's respected critics, together with the industry, praise such films as *Bridge on the River Kwai, West Side Story* and *Lawrence of Arabia*?" (In a letter the following week, a member of "the club" rebutted, pointing out that Sturges had adapted Kurosawa, and that as filmgoers became better educated the director's "horse-and-buggy" notions would be exposed for what they were.)

Concerned that his brand of event movie would further suffer from inferior presentation, Sturges visited theaters showing his movies. Traveling with *The Great Escape,* he found lenses that hadn't been cleaned in years. "The screen is what the customer looks at," he reminded *Variety,* "but it's the last item to be considered in a redecoration job. And theaters wonder where the audiences have gone." At times, Sturges's company would pay to replace "dull, old screens," *Variety* reported.

As the battle raged over runaway budgets—*Cleopatra* had lost $18 million, the Marlon Brando remake of *Mutiny on the Bounty* $10 million; *Star!*, *Paint Your Wagon*, and *Hello, Dolly!* were in the wings— Sturges, like Robson and Wise, ignored the signs. His next film would be a showy $7-million "How the West Was Undone" lampoon starring, if available, Lee Marvin, Art Carney, and James Garner. Adapted from Bill Gulick's 1963 novel *Hallelujah Train,* it was pitched as a tall tale in the Paul Bunyon tradition, with square-jawed cavalry officers, drunken Indians, Bible-thumping suffragettes, and a wagon train loaded down with whiskey and champagne. *Sergeants 3* notwithstanding, Sturges still fancied himself a farceur, and moments of *The Great Escape* made his case. Now, his sendup of Hollywood's oldest genre would put him in the same league with the Mirisches' resident funnymen, Billy Wilder and Blake Edwards, who had just completed two Pink Panther comedies and was at work on his own epic spoof, *The Great Race*.

The Hallelujah Trail — which dropped Gulick's wraparound sessions between President Grant and a reporter but remained faithful to the book's boisterous tone — is a big, bawdy Western built on a single distasteful premise: men, especially Native American men, will do anything for alcohol. With the winter of 1867 weeks away, Denver miners realize they are about to be snowed in without a drop of "likker." On the advice of Oracle Jones, a grizzled scout-seer, they contract for eighty wagons of whiskey. Standing between the miners and their next drunk: Cora Temple Massingale and her women's temperance league, reservation-jumping Sioux, and Irish teamster drivers who are always threatening a strike. Colonel Thaddeus Gearhart escorts "the devil's cargo" and arbitrates the escalating disputes. The ruckus to follow, the viewer is told in deadpan *"O, Virgin West . . . O, Pioneer West"* narration, would henceforth be known as "The Battle of Whiskey Hills . . . and the subsequent Disaster at Quicksand Bottoms."

Working closely with John Gay, who had rewritten the Henry Hathaway segment of *How the West Was Won*, Sturges devised a number of elaborate sight gags — trees raining soldiers, Indians circling their wagons as the cavalry, whooping and hollering, lay siege — that would upend every Western cliché. "John and I acted out the parts — had such fun with it," said Gay. "We did everything in reverse — the heroic cavalry officer who's bumbling, the temperance woman who takes a drink. The idea was to do the opposite of the stereotype and exaggerate the stereotype at the same time. The whole thing had a comedic overtone that John liked very much."

Because of the preponderance of cowboy shows on television (*Bonanza*, et al.) and the diminishing box office of Westerns by Ford and Mann, the genre already had one foot in Boot Hill. Garner, after reading the script, instructed his agent to pass. "I just didn't think the story was very good," he said. "The premise was too outrageous. There wasn't enough truth in it to be funny." Garner, part Native American, was also offended by the script's firewater-swilling "Injuns."

Shot in Ultra Panavision 70 (a single-camera Cinerama process) on a Navajo reservation outside Gallup, New Mexico, *The Hallelujah Trail* was, from its inception, promoted as a roadshow attraction that would play the latest domed theaters and receive what Sturges called a "red-carpet presentation," with overture, intermission, reserved seating, and exit music. His stock company again included Ferris Webster, Elmer Bernstein, now-associate producer Robert Relyea, and Robert Surtees. Bruce Surtees, the cinematographer's son, was hired as assistant camera-man, or "focus-puller."

Failing to sign Garner, Marvin, and Carney, Sturges settled for a mix of marquee names, character types, and newcomers. Burt Lancaster re-united with the director as the stupefied, cigar-chomping Colonel Gear-hart; Lee Remick, much in demand after *The Days of Wine and Roses,* was signed for Cora Massingale; Brian Keith and Donald Pleasence were cast, respectively, as the apoplectic wagon master and prescient Oracle, whose every vision brings a celestial *"Hallelujah!"* In keeping with the custom of the day—*Little Big Man* was still five years away—Martin Landau and Robert J. Wilke were cast as Sioux chiefs. Their tribesmen were played by local Navajo, earning $10 to $15 a day, de-pending on whether they rode a horse.

"It's a spoof of all the Westerns you've ever seen," explained Lan-caster, doing what the studio billed as his "first foray into total comedy."

Sturges assured the skeptics, "No one's playing this to be self-consciously funny. No 'take-'ems.' This is a situation comedy in which they're all led step by step into worse predicaments. And it's all built up from an actual incident dug up by Bill Gulick for his novel."

The location shoot called for a three-hundred-member crew (two full units), several especially dangerous stunts (men catapulted from fall-ing horses and runaway wagons), a centerpiece sand storm (fifty tons of Fuller's earth scattered by six giant "ritter" fans), and a climactic stam-pede (photographed at ground level with horses and wagons thundering over buried cameras). Cost: $65,000 a day. The late summer weather held for two months and then, when thunderheads appeared, the com-pany retired to the Paramount backlot. Keith and Pleasence returned to Gallup in the fall for the Quicksand Bottoms finale.

"It was a hard shoot," recalled Bruce Surtees, who would graduate to cinematographer five years later on *Dirty Harry.* "We had dust storms and bad weather, and the location was a long distance from the hotel. And we were shooting in 70mm, which made life even more difficult."

The *Los Angeles Times*'s Art Seidenbaum was dispatched to Gallup for what was thought to be a promotional feature. Instead, he reported back on unemployment and poverty, Navajo protestors (who insisted the company was trespassing), and Sturges's shrimp-and-sake parties. "On a good Gallup day," Seidenbaum wrote, "the call goes out for more than 100 extra Indians to emote under the leadership of two blue-eyed chiefs imported from Hollywood. The signal is sent by radio (few Indians have telephones in their hogans but many own transistor sets). One of the local stations interrupts its Beatles music to issue casting bulletins. The Navajos report for work at the Gallup armory just after dawn, where they swap jeans and dark glasses for buckskin and braided wigs." Obviously not sold on the film's premise, Seidenbaum assured readers, "The Indians who go to Gallup on weekends to drink and go falling down drunk are the rare ones. While the script calls for laughing at both sides of the old American Indian arguments, the present condition of the Navajos is the most serious story in this part of the nation."

The wagon stampede—with its exploding champagne bottles and airborne Indians—was left until the end of the shoot. Sturges had returned to the studio. On November 12, stuntmen Buff Brady and Bill Williams approached Relyea about improving the gag by delaying their jump from a careening wagon. Relyea approved the change. The next day, the two men, in wigs and buckskins, climbed onto a covered wagon that was attached by cable to a pickup truck. The truck pulled the wagon into a ravine. Brady jumped clear, but Williams, whose costume may have become snagged, remained seated.

"The wagon catapulted into the air," recalled the still-devastated Relyea, "and Billy, his arms and legs flying like a rag doll, landed in front of me . . . and the wagon landed on him." Williams died instantly. His wife and two young children were watching from the other side of the ravine.

Sturges was "really shaken" by the accident and agreed with Relyea that it should be cut. The Mirisches, however, overruled them, and the fatal stunt remained in the movie and figured prominently in the trailer. That morbid reminder, juxtaposed with the wholesale mugging, left everyone feeling uneasy, said Gay; but at advanced screenings friends pumped the director's hand and congratulated him on a one-of-a-kind comedy. Simultaneous premieres were held at the Warner Cinerama Theatre in Hollywood and Loew's Capitol Theatre in New York. To make sure everyone knew it was OK to laugh, the invitation read: "All Hallelujah breaks loose . . . and spreads from coast-to-coast. *Hah! Hah! HAH! HAH! HAH!*" In attendance was the press corps, which then adjourned for what critic Judith Crist described as "the classiest and most lavish barbecue ever thrown in a parking lot on West 51st Street." (Crist included *Hallelujah Trail* on her list of the year's worst films.)

"At the premiere, those queasy feelings came back," Gay said. "The performances kept getting in the way. It should have been played more seriously, almost straight. But Keith and Pleasence were playing it for laughs. . . . I felt terrible for John."

Added Relyea, "On location we all felt that Lancaster doing an imitation of Lancaster—that huge, toothy smile—was hilarious, but nobody else did. There was a definite sense that you weren't watching *Ben-Hur* or *Gone with the Wind*."

John Sturges' The Hallelujah Trail opened in July 1965 and, not surprisingly, split the hometown and out-of-town papers. *Variety,* which screened a 152-minute cut, found it "freewheeling . . . beautifully packaged." The *L.A. Times* called it "one of the very few funny Westerns ever made, and possibly the funniest." The *New York Times* and *Washington Post,* which saw a 165-minute cut, found it belabored, overlong. The consensus: Surtees's color photography was topnotch; the animated map inserts were amusing; and a handful of sight gags were inspired. The score, described by Bernstein as "completely up for fun," almost qualified the film as a pre-*Paint Your Wagon* musical. It did not, however, mask Keith's sputtering Mr. Magoo performance, Landau's leering chief, or the deadly pacing. Indeed, Sturges's timing could not have been worse. This was the year of edgy adult fare, such as *Darling* and *The Spy Who Came in from the Cold,* and campy Westerns such as *Cat Ballou* and TV's *F Troop.*

When UA's "big, wide, adventure-packed" comedy failed to draw audiences in ritzy, reserved-seating theaters, which were limited to two performances daily, the distributor rethought its strategy and made a 145-minute cut available on a continuous performance, reduced-price basis. "I think we learned that Western fans don't like fables," said Walter Mirisch. Ticket sales barely reached $3 million.

Norman Jewison's *The Russians Are Coming! The Russians Are Coming!,* also produced by the Mirisch Company, opened the following year and, because it was more timely, easily out-performed the sagebrush send-up. Sturges was openly envious. "I was the kid on the lot with a little bungalow; John had fancier offices and a production company," recalled Jewison. "When he talked, you listened. He had that kind of presence. But when I made *Russians Are Coming,* he said hello. He loved the film, thought it was a great political satire. And after that, he was really kind to me, very supportive."

"*The Hallelujah Trail* is the only real disappointment I've had; I wish I hadn't made it," Sturges admitted later. "We all thought that was going to be a hit picture—until we hit an audience. I've never been so surprised in my life. I thought it was hilarious. Ten percent of the people who saw it thought it was hilarious; the other 90 percent asked if it was supposed to be a comedy. Jesus! That's disconcerting. But I can't blame anybody. I had full control."

Sturges acknowledged that "After that I couldn't sell the proverbial ice cubes to Eskimos. I had reached a point where if you were as successful as I was, a clunker will hurt you but it's not going to clobber you. But you better not make three in a row."

Determined to put the film behind him, Sturges now concentrated on three projects—a Mafia comedy developed with John Gay and seen as a possible vehicle for Jack Lemmon, a Grand Prix racing drama tailored for McQueen, and *Richard Sahib.* MGM announced that "by special arrangements" with the Mirisch Company Sturges would return to the studio to shoot *Ice Station Zebra* with Gregory Peck. That turned out to be premature: the Cold War thriller still needed a third act.

Only the McQueen project, called *Day of the Champion* and eventually set up at Warner Bros., showed any traction. In the summer of 1965, the director—already out-of-pocket $25,000 in pre-production expenses—flew to France and toured the Formula One circuit with McQueen and racing legend Stirling Moss, retained as technical consultant. They lined up Porsche and mounted Panavision cameras on the cars. The races at Reims, Monaco, and Nürburgring were shot by a second-unit crew as Edward Anhalt prepared the script. Sturges wanted to plumb the psyche of a driver who must win at any cost. As McQueen went on to *Nevada Smith* and then *The Sand Pebbles,* Warner Bros. announced a May 1966 start date. Alarmed that there still was no script, Sturges flew to Taiwan to confer with McQueen. A 7.8 magnitude earthquake cut his visit short.

"I'm fascinated by these drivers," the director said at the time. "I want to find and show what makes 'em tick. In a real way, they're like Hillary. They've got to climb mountains. They talk about ten-tenths driving, driving at your absolute limits all the time. Someone used to say that Stirling Moss was an eleven-tenths driver." Sturges added that at that point in his career he didn't mind being saddled with the appellation "action ace." "I'd challenge it if somebody meant that my films weren't thoughtful or believable."

Day of the Champion was canceled when *The Sand Pebbles* went four months over schedule and Robert Wise refused to let McQueen out of his contract. The delay allowed MGM's *Grand Prix,* directed by John Frankenheimer and starring James Garner, to reach theaters first. Jack Warner told Sturges, "We're going to be second. Close it down." Recalled Relyea, who was now working for McQueen's Solar Productions, "We did everything but make the movie. Somewhere in the Warner vaults there are millions of feet of film from three car races. We were in about $4 million."

Returning to his London hotel suite, Sturges told Dorothy, "Get packed, we're going home."

"I vividly remember him coming home early," said Michael Sturges, fourteen at the time. "He explained that the film was canceled. His oldest friend, Bobby Wise, had kept running over and over, and they'd passed the point of no return. They couldn't make the film any longer. . . . If Dad had made *Day of the Champion* lean and mean, the way he wanted to, his career might have gone in an entirely different direction. He might not have embarked on those big films."

In March 1970, Relyea and McQueen resurrected the project at CBS's Cinema Center Films. It was now known as *Le Mans* or *The 24 Hours at Le Mans.* The budget had climbed to $6 million-plus. Several names were floated, including Steven Spielberg and George Lucas, but in the end McQueen went with Sturges, "The greatest action director I know." From all reports, pre-production was a disaster because director and star were at cross purposes: McQueen saw the film as a quasi-documentary with actors wandering through the background; Sturges saw it as a human drama set against the colorful world of high-stakes racing. After filming the endurance race, Sturges shut down for two weeks to resolve script problems.

"The arguments over what the story was about never ceased," recalled Relyea, who was credited as executive producer. "Day after day, week after week, we shot No. 22 passing No. 23, No. 24 spinning out of control. Nobody spoke any words. John sat in his chair, stewing."

Neile McQueen described the deteriorating relationship as "volatile," adding, "Steve refused to listen to John. He decided *he* was the filmmaker and he would focus on the dangers to the drivers, everything mechanical—everything but the story."

Finally, when Cinema Center executives showed up at the London production office and announced they were taking over the project, McQueen announced he was going on vacation to Morocco. Sturges said, "Look, I'm too rich and too old for this shit. I'm going home."

"I assumed he meant back to his hotel," said Relyea. "He meant *home*—Studio City."

"I've never been able to take very much punishment, just haven't," said Sturges. "Steve went out of control on *Le Mans*. We never did get a script. So I just walked off the picture. If we had had a bad script, I could have fixed it. But the blank page was too much for Steve. You couldn't put anything down that he liked."

Le Mans was finally released in the summer of 1971, with Lee H. Katzin credited as director. "CBS paid him a $50,000 bonus if he'd bring any script in on schedule," said Relyea. "The disaster went from there. John was the only one with brains."

Sturges returned to *The Law and Tombstone*, the third picture in the Mirisch-Kappa deal and, it would turn out, a salve for his separation from Dorothy after twenty-one years of marriage. Michael described the divorce as "acrimonious" and financially costly for his father, who moved to a condo in Marina del Rey. Deborah characterized it as "painful, like all divorces," and the settlement as reasonable. (As a volunteer at the Motion Picture Country Hospital, Dorothy would meet Dr. John Messina. They married in 1973.)

For the more factual sequel to *Gunfight at the O.K. Corral,* Sturges, working from an original script by Anhalt, returned to Churubusco Studio in Mexico City. The Tombstone exteriors were shot in Torreón, where, near a train track, the crew erected a façade town, including Tombstone Epitaph, Fly's Photographic Gallery, courthouse, and three saloons. (Sturges planned to rent out the Western town to future productions.) The gunfight was shot over Christmas with fans assuring dust-blown authenticity; the climactic showdown with Ike Clanton was filmed in the courtyard of a hacienda near San Miguel de Allende.

Sturges, as usual, enjoyed playing tour guide. In an orientation letter to cast and crew, he provided pointers on travel arrangements and currency, adding:

> Shortly before Christmas, we will move to Mexico City for our interiors. [It] is one of the biggest and most sophisticated cities in the world, and you will find the restaurants, nightclubs, shops and hotels among the finest. If you want to be a *turista* on the side, the opportunities are almost endless. The beautiful resort town of Cuernavaca is only an hour and 10 minutes away by a four-lane express highway over the mountains, with Taxco (a national monument also world famous for its silver work) a short distance from there. I'm always afraid to add that Acapulco is only a half day by express highway and an hour by air. . . . Mexico City is very high—7,300 feet—and while there won't be any rain to speak of, it can be very chilly particularly at night, so warm clothes and a top coat are a good idea.
>
> I can't mention food without reference to possible intestinal trouble, delicately referred to as The Turistas, or whimsically as Montezuma's Revenge or the Aztec Two-Step. Don't worry about anything you eat or drink in the hotels or restaurants, or anything we will serve on location. But be sure about any water you drink, and I would certainly avoid completely any out-of-the-way places or roadside stands. If you do get a touch, our doctor has medicine that will knock it right on the head.

As a postscript, he noted that Mirisch-Kappa was not happy with the title *The Law and Tombstone.* "If you think of one you like, let us know."

The all-male cast included James Garner as the more callow Wyatt Earp, Robert Ryan as the now politically motivated Ike Clanton, and

Jason Robards as the consumptive Doc Holliday, who doubles in this retelling as Wyatt's conscience. An unknown named Jon Voight smirked from the shadows as gun-for-hire Curly Bill Brocius. The film was photographed by Lucien Ballard between stints on Peckinpah's *Ride the High Country* and *The Wild Bunch* and benefits from a stark look that mirrors Garner's performance. Webster, who by now could finish Sturges's sentences, turned in a near-perfect first cut, and Jerry Goldsmith composed the music, a simple but effective fusion of acoustic guitar and Latin percussion that only occasionally erupts into full symphonic score.

Garner reteamed with Sturges without hesitation. "I trusted John," he said. "So when my agent called and said he was doing a sequel to *O.K. Corral*, I said, 'Yeah, I'll do it.' I was happy to play the character because John always knew what he was doing. He could take five, six, seven factions in a story and bring them together. That takes an editing sense. . . . We didn't get into any great acting discussions. Wasn't needed."

Garner, no stranger to playing scoundrels (see *The Americanization of Emily*), welcomed the idea of Wyatt as murderous antihero in black hat, gloves, and vest. "I saw him as a vigilante out for revenge," said the actor. "He was a guy taken with his own power, who nobody could defy. He had no qualms about shooting those boys. . . . I think the movie's as accurate on that as any that's been done."

The location shoot was well organized and Sturges "all business," recalled Bill Fletcher, who played Sheriff Bryan. He described Torreón as "this quiet little agricultural-mining town with a single hotel and bar. On Saturday nights, the mariachis would play in the gazebo on the square, and the boys, in their Sunday best, would circle one way, the girls the other." In the evenings, Sturges invited the cast to the Hotel Río Nazas to screen dailies. "Not many directors do that," said Fletcher. "Henry Hathaway didn't. He was a real prick, Sturges a total gentleman."

This made his occasional reprimand all the more effective.

"They had to send assistant directors out to find Jason in the mornings," said Garner. "And they knew just the whore house and bars where he would end up."

One especially cold morning, Robards was scheduled for an 8 a.m. call. He turned up after lunch.

"Jason, that's the most unprofessional thing I have ever seen on a set," said Sturges in front of the crew. "You know what you've cost this company?"

Robards, now the repentant child: "I'll pay for it."

Sturges: "You can't pay for it. It's done. It's your lack of professionalism . . ."

"John read him off as politely as you could read him off," said Garner. "Jason was perfect from then on."

The retitled *Hour of the Gun* was released in 1967 to indifferent reviews and abysmal box office. It was not, as UA publicity promised, your "typical Sturges rouser." In a three-paragraph notice, Crowther dismissed the Earp-Holliday reunion as "totally conventional." *Variety*'s A. D. Murphy found it talky and sluggish, adding, "Reality often makes for poor drama." The ads and trailer traded on the Hal Wallis original — "Most legends of Wyatt Earp end with the gunfight at the O.K. Corral. Our story begins there" — and fed into the cynical mood of the day: "Wyatt Earp. Hero with a badge or cold-blooded killer? He lived through the gunfight at the O.K. Corral . . . that may have been a mistake." Barely netting $2 million in ticket sales — or $9 million less than *Gunfight at the O.K. Corral* — the venture cut short Sturges's career as producer-director: He would produce only one more film, *Chino*. (In 1992, MGM/UA accepted the rights to *Hour of the Gun* in lieu of $1.2 million still owed by Kappa Corp.)

At 101 minutes, *Hour of the Gun* was Sturges's shortest film in years. It was also a lean, soulfully elegiac coda to *Gunfight at the O.K. Corral* and *Last Train from Gun Hill*. Today, it is rightly hailed as a forerunner of *Will Penny* (1968), *The Wild Bunch* (1969), *Wild Rovers* (1970), and other revisionist Westerns fueled by the moral ambiguities of the Nixon-Vietnam years. For the Tombstone Marshal to obtain "justice" for his brother Morgan's murder, he must throw away his badge, much as Harry Callahan does four years later in *Dirty Harry*. His hands bloodied, Wyatt has become Doc's doppelgänger. He is no longer fit to uphold the law.

Sturges opens with a bald, matter-of-fact replay of the October 26, 1881, shootout between the Earps, Clantons, and McLowerys. Only this time, the director foregoes stockyard acrobatics and records the event as a dispassionate onlooker. From the first discharge of Holliday's scattergun to Ike Clanton's surrender, barely thirteen seconds elapse, making this the most compressed of all reenactments. From here, Sturges cuts to a funeral procession, the Boot Hill burial of William Clanton and the McLowerys, and Ike Clanton's speech about buying the law to forestall those factions—the railroad and homesteaders—that would "corner the range." This sets the scene for the ambush murders of Virgil and Morgan Earp, and Wyatt's methodical revenge. In a wry play on *The Magnificent Seven,* Doc goes in search of a posse and returns with a drunken gambler and a strike breaker.

Wyatt tracks Warshaw (Steve Ihnat), one of the killers, to Clanton's ranch. With Doc and his posse looking on, he masochistically demands the details surrounding his brothers' murders. What follows is the most savage moment in any Sturges film. "What'd he pay?" the marshal asks, sounding almost indifferent. "He paid $50." "Before or after?" "After." "A man's life . . . $50." Wyatt forces Warshaw to draw, and then empties his gun in him.

"Boy, you sure gave him a chance," says Doc, his voice dripping sarcasm. "I'd have just blown his head off as he lay in bed."

Thrusting a bottle at his friend, the gunslinger adds, "Those aren't warrants you got there, those are hunting licenses. . . . Go on, have one! If you're gonna kill like me, you might as well drink like me."

In reversing the Wyatt-Doc roles, *Hour of the Gun* subverts the mythic Western story, much as Arthur Penn and Sam Peckinpah, in turn, subverted the legend of Pat Garrett and Billy the Kid. The mortally ill Doc seeks redemption by saving his friend from himself.

"I don't care about the rules anymore," Wyatt tells Doc in Mexico.

"But they're the only rules there are," Doc replies. "And they're more important to you than you think. Play it that way, Wyatt . . . or you'll destroy yourself. I know you, you can't live like me."

Sturges's mise-en-scène telegraphs the moral confusion, as well as Ike Clanton's fate. The opening gunfight ends with Wyatt and Doc—one crouched, the other standing—covering one another. The collapsed depth of field, however, makes it appear that Wyatt is aiming at Doc and vice versa. The funeral-parlor viewing that follows is reminiscent of multilayered compositions in *Black Rock:* Clanton's window reflection is superimposed over his brother's and the McLowerys' publicly displayed corpses.

Hour of the Gun wanders during the second half—as Doc checks into a sanitarium, Wyatt contemplates his appointment as chief U.S. marshal, and the Americans join forces with the Federales. But the buildup to the final hacienda shootout could not be more eloquent or assured. Goldsmith's score and the languorous dissolves as two men ride down empty streets set the tone. The script called for an aqueduct battle and Wyatt shooting Clanton repeatedly, "like an executioner." Sturges, realizing the point had been made, opted for a single bullet and Wyatt's parting declaration, "I'm through with the law."

Sturges chalked up the film's failure to public sentiment. He was interested in reportage, the true story of O.K. Corral and its aftermath. (The equivocal "Within the limits of dramatic license, this is the story of what actually happened" became "This picture is based on fact; this is the way it happened.") He saw it as a political allegory with modern-day ramifications: the federal-minded Earps were the Democrats, the anti-government-interference Clantons were the Republicans. This, of course, was lost on Western fans, who proved John Ford's dictum in *The Man Who Shot Liberty Valance:* When the truth becomes legend, print the legend.

"My mistake was that I thought people would be fascinated by the real story about the quarrel between the Earps and the Clantons. You didn't just shoot people, there were trials, lawyers, citizens' committees. I thought the reality of the thing would catch people, who would say, 'Gee, that's the way it was? That's fascinating.' Not so. I got [preview] cards that said of all the stories told about Earp and Holliday, this was the dullest. They considered them fictional characters. They couldn't have cared less that that's the way it really was."

After the back-to-back box-office failures, the Mirisches cooled on their prime action director. For his part, Sturges said he had lost confidence in the producing team after Harold Mirisch's death in 1968. *The Yards of Essendorf,* the fourth picture in the Mirisch-Kappa deal, was put on hold. Walter Mirisch, who for the most part had enjoyed the six-picture collaboration—"quite extraordinary in this business"—later explained, "John was offered a big picture he wanted to do, and then started making pictures away from us . . . and we drifted."

Sturges, ever restless at fifty-seven, went back to being a gun for hire—albeit a handsomely compensated one. He was paid $500,000 and points to oversee MGM's *Ice Station Zebra* and, in 1968, a career high of $750,000 for Columbia's *Marooned,* making him the highest paid director in Hollywood. (By comparison, David Lean in 1969 was getting $500,000.) Unfortunately, the kinds of movies in which he now specialized—"grand-scale action films," according to his press bio—were out of fashion with Hollywood's new target audience: teenagers. The most popular films in 1967-70—the era of Vietnam, student protest, and love-ins—were *The Graduate, Easy Rider, Harold and Maude, Bonnie and Clyde,* and *M*A*S*H.* These were social satires that questioned, and rejected, the values of the older generation. They skewered what Sturges and establishment Hollywood held dear, the notion of valor through teamwork.

The director was oblivious to such arguments. He didn't have a satirical bone in his body and as a self-described "gadget guy" was now attracted to projects for their technical challenges. (Friends joked that if he mounted another depth finder on his boat, it would sink.) For Sturges, the Cold War was less about ideology than which side had the superior scientists and engineers. A decade earlier, when the Russians launched Sputnik 1, he and neighbor Mel Shavelson had tracked the satellite on a ham radio. They sat in the dark listening for the telltale beep that came every ninety minutes. "Nobody could believe that the Russians had done it before us," said Shavelson. "And that was a big point with John. He couldn't get over it." In the late sixties, the navy's "nukes" or nuclear submarines elicited the same awed reaction. "You practically need an MIT degree to swab the deck on one of those boats," Sturges said.

Ice Station Zebra, set aboard the U.S.S. *Tigerfish III* at the height of the Cold War, is so ramrod straight it could pass for a U.S. Navy recruiting commercial. It is also, at least when at sea, exhilarating entertainment on a grand scale, a hybrid of *Twenty-Thousand Leagues under the Sea* (1954) and *The Hunt for Red October* (1990). The title and central premise—an American sub races to the Arctic to investigate a disaster at a British weather station and retrieve a Russian space capsule containing film of American missile installations—were from Alistair MacLean's 1963 bestseller. The novel, full of musty Briticisms ("damn and blast it all"), was told from the perspective of an English secret agent being ferried to the North Pole. The U.S. commander was a secondary figure indebted to his passenger for the survival of his own boat. MacLean's not-so-veiled suggestion: When the chips are down, British diligence will always trump Yank impetuosity. The book was optioned in 1964 by producer Martin Ransohoff and set up at MGM, with Gregory Peck, David Niven, and George Segal the announced stars. Peck and Niven were naturals: they had co-starred in the popular 1961 adaptation of MacLean's *The Guns of Navarone*. It has always been assumed that Peck was in line to play the submarine commander. Not so, according to Sturges and press releases. Having played a sub captain (in *On the Beach*), Peck wanted the juicier role of the cynical American agent. Niven was announced as the British spy and Segal as the often-flummoxed commander.

Sturges read the script by Paddy Chayefsky and cringed. "Where the hell's the finish?" he asked the author of *Marty* and other working-class dramas. The book ended, after an interrogation aboard the sub, with the British hero unmasking the station's doctor as a Soviet spy-saboteur. It was talky and protracted, closer to Agatha Christie than Ian Fleming. Chayefsky's solution: Peck is a double agent working for the communists. "Talk about the butler did it!" Sturges said, bristling.

Peck's response: "I have no objection to playing a communist—I've played an anti-Semite, an alcoholic, and Captain Ahab. But this is preposterous, impossible. I won't do it."

W. R. Burnett and Harry Julian Fink worked on the script. But they only exacerbated the problems, said Sturges. "It was a bunch of clap-trap, patriotic bullshit," he continued. "I told Metro, not only will I not do this, I don't think you should. But Metro was under the gun from people who wanted to take over the company, and Ransohoff had spent something like $650,000 not getting the script and another $1.7 million on miniatures and underwater effects. They said, 'We'll give you anything you want, but you cannot turn this picture down.' So I threw the script in the trashcan and got a TV writer named Douglas Heyes. He came up with the confrontation angle between the American commander and the British agent. He did a helluva good job."

There were other novel-to-screen changes meant to clarify as well as boost box-office potential. The American commander, James Ferraday, was moved to center stage, and the British agent was rewritten as a glib James Bond type; a platoon of very green marines was placed onboard the sub; the saboteur-killer turned out to be a Russian double agent; and, most significantly, act 3, now played out on the ice pack, climaxed with a frantic search for the capsule and a standoff between Soviet paratroopers and the Marines.

With Peck no longer involved, Laurence Harvey was briefly mentioned for the Russian double agent. The role went to the much more expansive Ernest Borgnine. Rock Hudson—about to turn forty and experiencing a career trough—successfully lobbied Sturges for the role of Commander Ferraday, who pouts for much of the picture because he's kept in the dark about the mission. Jim Brown and Tony Bill came aboard as the grim marine captain and his second-in-command. Sturges was proud of casting Brown in his first non-race-specific role, telling the press, "It doesn't make any difference whether he's a Negro or not." Irish actor Patrick McGoohan, star of Britain's *Danger Man* TV series, was cast as the mysterious spy-hero, code-named David Jones. He has "the same excitement" as McQueen, said Sturges. With more than thirty featured parts, the adventure represented Sturges's largest all-male ensemble yet. Hudson joked that his leading lady was the submarine. (To appease investors about the lack of women, Sturges considered, and then rejected, a hallucinogenic dream sequence that included a discotheque and go-go dancers.)

Ice Station Zebra, budgeted at $8 million and intended for roadshow bookings, went before the cameras at MGM in June 1967. The shoot lasted three months and would have taken longer without the cooperation of the navy, whose non-nuclear U.S.S. *Ronquil* doubled for the *Tigerfish III.* Rather than brave subzero weather, Sturges made do with aerial shots of Greenland fjords and ice floes. These doubled for Siberia and were projected behind models of Soviet MiG-21s. (Sturges later admitted this was a mistake because, not only did the shots not match— four F4 Phantoms are seen from the ground, five MiGs streak toward the camera—the models looked fake. He likened MGM's obsolete special effects to "high-button shoes.") The sub's sixteen-foot superstructure, control center, and nuclear reactor took up most of Metro's massive soundstages. Construction was ballyhooed as "MGM's biggest shipbuilding job since *Mutiny on the Bounty.*" Hydraulic rockers pitched the mess hall, passageways, and torpedo room. Lot 3—coated in urethane-foam "ice" and ringed by a cyclorama skyline—contained the fire-ravaged station, including Quonset huts and radar dome. Michael Sturges, who visited the set, recalled Hudson and company in full arctic gear "traipsing through fake snow, baking in the middle of the summer, with wind machines blasting away." The eerie underwater shots were done in a tank with a ten-foot *Tigerfish* model, and the sub's-eye-view perspective was accomplished with cameras in watertight housings mounted on the *Ronquil's* deck and conning tower.

As he had on *The Great Escape,* Sturges worked from sketches, location photos, and note cards pinned to his office wall. The running joke was that only he knew where the ship was headed. "Do you understand the ending? Am I alive or am I dead?" Brown asked Bill between setups. "I don't know, I thought you knew," replied Bill.

The aerial inserts of the sub were filmed off the coast of Oahu. It was the closest Sturges came to being killed during a location shoot: "Camera operator John Stephens and I went thirty miles out in a helicopter. Big waves. Blowing forty-five knots. I got on the radio and tried to reach air-sea rescue. They were supposed to have gone out with us. A voice answered, 'You're out there in a goddamn helicopter!' It was too rough for *them.* Over two days we shot big, monumental seas. They were backlit to make them look cold and gray. Terrific stuff. When the pilot took the helicopter back to Kauai, where it was based, the rotors came off, and he was killed. It was about to happen. We got home just in time."

MGM fanned exhibitor interest with a "Lionpower" product reel. The twenty-five-minute short showcased, besides Sturges's December release, new projects by Frankenheimer, John Boorman, Robert Aldrich, and Stanley Kubrick, whose *2001: A Space Odyssey* opened in April and rendered the Cold War thriller instantly obsolete. One could detect a generational divide between the Sturges and Kubrick factions, a divide exacerbated by MGM's decision to pull *2001* early to make room for the submarine adventure. The premature closing, according to Jerome Agel "caused much trade speculation, some insisting that MGM sacrificed the engagement to open its long-completed *Ice Station Zebra* in time for Christmas business." Had studio bookers listened to preview audiences they might have released the movies in reverse order.

"Everybody at the San Jose preview loved the movie right up until the intermission, just as the sub breaks through the ice," said Michael

Sturges, who sat near the back of the domed theater with his father. "All the stuff in the sub was great. They really had 'em at the intermission. Then they come out on the ice and the whole thing, like a soufflé, goes *whoosh.* They came out going, 'It's too big. It's too long.' I was like seventeen, the perfect age, and I remember going, 'Too much.'"

The ironic denouement—Jones saves Vaslov by shooting Captain Anders (Brown), whom he mistakes for the killer—left viewers scratching their heads, and the final shot—a tableau of Ferraday and the Russian colonel (Alf Kjellen) staring at each other across the ice—proved as unsatisfying as it was heavy-handed. It was changed at the last minute to a teletype readout lauding the heroic rescue mission by the two great nuclear powers, "a further indication of international cooperation."

"We made it up as we went along, adding a whole bunch of gimmicks—the homing devices, the capsule in the ice, the blowtorch," Sturges admitted. "Then we threw a lot of yellow smoke around, killed Ernie (Borgnine), and went home. . . . They showed the film on a flight from London to New York and had to shut it off before the finish. The guy next to me was outraged. I felt like saying, 'You don't know how lucky you are.'"

Sturges waved off any talk of a pro-détente message. "Oh, I don't think it had any great political significance. It just dealt with an existing phenomenon in an interesting way. I tried not to make any point, other than conflict should be avoided if at all possible. I thought it important to make the Russian colonel something more than a shoe-pounding caricature. He had to seem rational."

The reviews ranged from mixed (Renata Adler, *New York Times:* "a fairly tight, exciting Saturday night adventure story that goes all muddy in its crises") to deferential (*Variety:* "Sturges' direction is professional and straightforward") to brutal (Pauline Kael: "the silliness . . . became almost satisfying, in a ritualistic, bad-movie way"). The initial roadshow bookings didn't help the box office. Nor did the more adult competition: *Bullitt, Candy, Barbarella, Rosemary's Baby, Petulia.* Said Sturges, "It's considered successful, but it won't break even until its second run on TV." Today, *Ice Station Zebra* holds the dubious distinction of being Howard Hughes's favorite sick-room diversion. "AP called me when he died," said Sturges. "They said he sat there in an oxygen tent, watching the picture over and over—forty-eight times!"

If anything, *Ice Station Zebra* has over the years gained in popularity. In a 2004 poll conducted by Warner Bros. and Turner Classic Movies, action buffs voted it one of the films they would most like to see on DVD. Mainly due to the miniature work and dive sequences (set to Michel Legrand's stirring theme), the adventure remains a classic example of late-studio-era craftsmanship, and an important influence on the high-concept movies of Spielberg, Cameron, and especially Bruckheimer.

Sturges said that he felt more empowered on *Ice Station Zebra* than at any point in his career. Ransohoff had deferred to his leadership and organizational skills. "I didn't start getting *real* power until I did that picture," he said. "I now had this all-father image. Everybody believed in me." Tony Bill, who would later produce *The Sting* and direct several pictures, admired the director's sangfroid. "I learned from watching how laid-back you can be," Bill said. "He was a no-frills, no-nonsense, get-the-job-done guy. Nothing precious about him or his manner. No yelling or screaming. He sat in his director's chair and very calmly and quietly said, 'Let's try that again.'"

Despite the weak ticket sales—*Ice Station Zebra* finally netted $4.6 million, slightly more than half its budget—the Sturges name still held cachet. In a business that prided itself on the well-turned action sequence, it was spoken in the same breath as Lean, Peckinpah, and Frankenheimer. More, Sturges was respected by the new crop of auteurist critics, such as Vincent Canby, who would follow Crowther at the *New York Times*.

It surprised no one, then, when Mike Frankovich, the ex-Columbia vice president who had just set up a production company at the studio, asked Sturges to direct *Marooned*. The science-speculation thriller would be based on Martin Caidin's highly technical novel about an astronaut stranded in orbit and the subsequent race by the United States and Russia to mount a rescue mission. The book was optioned before publication by Frank Capra, who was approaching seventy and had not directed a feature in four years. He hired Walter Newman to write the script and took the package to Frankovich, who loved it, but not with the semi-retired director attached. "I backed off from *Marooned* a beaten, discouraged man," wrote Capra in his autobiography. "Frankovich finally forced me into an impossible position: Make the film for under $3 million or give up the project. I gave up the project." (Capra would pass his option to son Frank Capra Jr., ultimately credited as associate producer.)

In the summer of 1968, Sturges was announced as director. However, he didn't report to Columbia immediately. He was busy researching another of his side ventures: a high-tech commercial tuna boat to be based out of Newport Harbor and Honolulu. (The eighty-five-foot *Lawaia* was launched in 1971, but, because of the resentment of local fishermen, never became a going concern.) Upon his return, Sturges threw out the Newman script and hired playwright-TV dramatist Mayo Simon, who was dispatched to NASA's Houston headquarters for research. Simon interviewed astronauts, astronauts' wives, and anyone he could find with a crew cut and pocket protector. Sturges envisioned the film as a nuts-and-bolts cliffhanger, the most accurate to date on NASA's day-to-day operations. It would be heavy on hardware and jargon ("kick the box," "we have negative retro-fire") but stress the importance of the human factor in the space race.

"John wanted me to spend a lot of time with the Apollo playbook," Simon said. "Everything had to be within the realm of possibility, completely accurate. Capra had turned it into a Capra-esque movie with a love story. I don't think he had a lot of feeling for the astronaut program. First thing John did was drop the romance. Then, because NASA had gone through the Mercury and Gemini programs and was now into the Apollo program, we expanded the story and made it about three astronauts stuck in orbit during a trip to a space lab, which, we were told, was on the drawing board."

Caidin, retained as technical adviser, approved the modifications, which, he said, kept "pace [with] the times." The Mercury capsule became the Apollo Ironman One, which is incapacitated by an electrical fire; the Russian craft was changed from a Voskhod to a Soyuz; and the American rescue vehicle was modified as a dart-shaped X-RV, forerunner of the space shuttle. On January 27, 1967, a real-life disaster almost caused the film to be scrubbed. Preparing for the first moon shot, Apollo I astronauts Gus Grissom, Edward White, and Roger Chaffee died when a flash fire engulfed their capsule. The events in the movie were too similar, said Columbia's front office. "Some people wanted to cancel the film because it would seem like we were taking gruesome advantage of this horrible tragedy," Simon recalled. "Frankovich said, 'No, no—let's change the premise.' So they sent me home to rewrite. I said, "OK, leaving the space laboratory, their retrorockets won't fire. And they don't know why.'"

Satisfied, Sturges proceeded with the casting, second-unit photography of NASA launches, and special effects, which would combine models, hydraulics, and, dangled from wires before a blue screen, a full-size mockup of Ironman One. Split-screen, popular after *Grand Prix,* was considered and rejected. Gregory Peck and David Janssen led the large ensemble as the tough-minded head of the U.S. Manned Space Program and senior astronaut Dougherty, respectively; Richard Crenna, James Franciscus, and Gene Hackman played the Ironman astronauts, whose response to the crisis range from decisive to analytical to panic-stricken; Lee Grant, Nancy Kovack, and Mariette Hartley appeared as the wives who stand by at Mission Control for updates. Frankovich, who was always looking over Sturges's shoulder, feared that the film was becoming too technical. "He was afraid it wasn't human enough," recalled Simon. "So I gave the women more to do, and I wrote in a scene [that was never used] between Peck and a college-age son—little personal things that kept intruding on the NASA drama." Some of these exchanges would anger feminists, who took exception to astronauts' wives depicted as cheerleaders who could best serve the space program, as Hartley's character says, by keeping "our feelings to ourselves, and let the men get on with their jobs."

With a more realistic budget of $8 to $10 million, production began in the winter on the Mission Control mock-up and continued through the spring at the Kennedy Space Center, where the race to launch the X-RV is further hampered by a hurricane. NASA, which had signed off on a judicious use of its logo, denied the filmmakers access to its Houston headquarters.

Sturges was at once excited about the project and nervous that, in the wake of *2001: A Space Odyssey,* it would look "phony." Much to the delight of image-conscious NASA, he favored gleaming surfaces over the period's equivalent to Mir space-station clutter. "I wanted to have the astronauts dirty and unshaven and their capsule grungy and cramped, like a phone booth," said Simon. "John didn't want that. He didn't like dirt. He liked Mexicans in clean white serapes and astronauts in clean spacesuits. I said, 'John, wouldn't it be great to get shots through their crotches and under their elbows—to get the sense of them all squeezed together?' He said, 'That's not how I work.' He had them design the capsule bigger."

The filmmaker's biggest challenge was to simulate conditions in deep space. Kubrick had solved that problem, but Kubrick wasn't sharing trade secrets. Columbia's effects department went low-tech: wires, hydraulics, rear-screen projection. Sturges was mortified but didn't let on to the press. "The biggest problem was making everyone look weightless," he told a reporter. "We used every trick in the book, which is all I'm willing to say. . . . After all, it is better to go to a film and be impressed rather than go and think, 'Oh, I know how he did that. It's not real.' The filmmaker should make his audience believe."

Adding to the mounting frustration: Everywhere Sturges looked there was Kubrick's embryonic star-child—staring back from billboards, posters, newspaper ads. Had the special effects bar been reset impossibly high?

"There really wasn't any competition," insisted Simon. "*Marooned* was scientific; it was about engineering. The Kubrick film was about evolution and the rebirth of humanity. One was nuts-and-bolts prose, the other poetry."

In post-production Sturges played down the chances of Americans being marooned in space. "The situation in this film is a possibility, not a probability," he said. "It is quite possible that men will someday be marooned in space, but because of the technical expertise we now have it is not really probable. However, should it actually happen, our film is a close approximation of the kind of rescue which will take place. . . . By the time the picture is released, the first orbiting laboratory will be about ready to go into space." On July 20, 1969, five months before the film's premiere, Neil Armstrong and Apollo 11's lunar module were on the moon.

Marooned was previewed for the National Association of Theatre Owners in Washington, D.C., where, at a pre-screening party attended by Sturges and Frankovich, "the top Washington brass [mixed] with the top Hollywood brass," reported *Washington Post* columnist Sally Quinn. The Hollywood premiere was held on December 12 at the Egyptian Theatre on Hollywood Boulevard. In attendance, besides the filmmakers and stars, were astronauts Walter Cunningham and Jack Swigert. The following day the space epic—rated G and running 134 minutes (minus suspense-snapping intermission)—began its exclusive reserved-seating run. The ads hailed "the epic adventure of three astronauts stranded in the hostile beauty of space while the whole world watched and waited." Drawing audiences across town were *Midnight Cowboy, Medium Cool, Alice's Restaurant, Butch Cassidy and the Sundance Kid,* and *Bob & Carol & Ted & Alice.* Again, the reviews varied wildly, from enthusiastic (*Variety:* "Superbly crafted, taut, a technological cliffhanger"; *L.A. Times:* "the ultimate movie statement to date about space exploration. . . . Sturges is one of the very best directors of masculine adventure, with a special gift for the dramas of technology") to noncommittal (*Life* magazine: "I ended up feeling nice and tense") to convoluted (*New York Times:* "This ambitious conscientious Columbia movie is admirably intelligent all the way") to grim (Pauline Kael: "Total, straight Dullsville"). Still, by scouring the secondary markets, Columbia could pull together enough positive press for a full-page ad. To the untrained eye, it seemed that the industry and media were more taken by Sturges's space epic than Kubrick's.

Trade paper predictions of strong box office did not pan out because for many the film—set to electronic beeps and high-pitched radio signals in lieu of a conventional score—proved too technical and impersonal. On April 13, as Columbia considered pulling *Marooned,* an eerily similar scenario played out. Trapped in orbit above the Earth, after their Apollo 13 command ship sprang an oxygen leak, astronauts Swigert, Fred Haise, and James Lovell radioed back, "Houston, we have a problem." For the next eighty-eight hours, as the world watched and the crew retreated to its lunar module, the movie's ads shrank from full page to discreet single-column box. When the crew returned safely, the larger ads returned, with such banners as "Well Done, Astronauts!" and "NOW *MAROONED* IS MORE than just a thrilling motion picture!"

The confluence of make-believe and breaking news did result in a box-office boost, but hardly of the magnitude experienced in 1979 by *The China Syndrome* after the accident at the Three Mile Island nuclear power plant. The space drama ultimately grossed $4.1 million, or less than *Ice Station Zebra.* It received Oscar nominations for cinematography, sound, and special effects—the most for any Sturges film since *Bad Day at Black Rock*. It won in the effects category.

Before *Marooned* was in theaters, Sturges was back at Goldwyn preparing *The Yards of Essendorf*. The World War II adventure—about an American who escapes from a prison camp and joins the French resistance in a plot to hijack a train—picked up "where *The Great Escape* left off," said screenwriter Stirling Silliphant. Sturges planned to film in France and western Canada, where he had already located an abandoned marshaling yard and three junked steam engines. He wanted Warren Beatty for the American behind enemy lines, Jean-Paul Belmondo for the lead resistance fighter, and Ursula Andress, Belmondo's girlfriend, for a Red Cross worker. Unhappy with Silliphant's script, Sturges turned to Mayo Simon, who, having little aptitude for he-man heroics, fared no better.

"I could have killed both writers," Sturges said, fuming over what would amount to a two-year gap in employment. "But the story was so good, Beatty agreed to do it with no script. His character, an American trying to get over the border into Switzerland, is cornered in a railroad yard and, like a hobo, gets under a train, which turns out to be carrying jewels, gold, priceless art. The resistance wants to capture the train, sabotage the place, and Beatty winds up helping them. . . . We had a runaway snowplow, big as a house—sixteen drivers, five hundred tons. It comes down this grade, out of control. Clobbers everything! We had two trains run together head-on at fifty miles per hour. . . . Nothing was explained or logically accounted for, but in a showman sense it worked. Everybody loved it, but UA wouldn't go for it because the writers couldn't lick the damn thing."

In March 1970, Sturges received the Golden Eddie Filmmaker of the Year award by the American Cinema Editors. In the fall of 1971, before turning to *Joe Kidd* (originally "Sinola"), he was announced for Universal's "Earthquake, 1980." He eventually backed away from the disaster film when it became obvious that the script by Mario Puzo was "more of a marquee gimmick than a story." He also passed on *Papillon* starring Steve McQueen and Dustin Hoffman.

Between 1972 and 1974, Sturges did two Westerns and a cop thriller—*Joe Kidd*, *Chino* (aka *The Valdez Horses*), and *McQ*. A telling departure: Instead of being carefully assembled ensemble pieces, the director's métier, they showcased three of the top box-office draws in the world: Clint Eastwood, Bronson, and John Wayne.

Elmore Leonard's script "Sinola" took its name from a New Mexico Territory border town and was inspired by Chicano activist Reies López Tijerina's 1967 raid on a federal courthouse. Leonard, whose Western stories included *3:10 to Yuma* and *Hombre,* backdated the episode to turn-of-the-century New Mexico and made Tijerina a would-be Zapata named Luis Chama. After breaking into Sinola's courthouse, burning land deeds, and briefly holding a judge hostage, Chama is tracked by a land baron and his "hunting party." Caught in between—but seemingly siding with the dispossessed—is former bounty hunter Joe Kidd. Producer Sidney Beckerman optioned the original script for $100,000 and took it to Eastwood's Malpaso Company, which set it up at Universal. Eastwood, who had just made *Dirty Harry* and was about to unseat Wayne as Box Office Star of the Year, had earlier attempted to interest Sturges in *Hang 'Em High.*

"We met, and he proceeded to butter me up," Sturges recalled. "'You're great, you've really got it,' he told me. I asked him if he was going to make a spaghetti Western. I told him, 'I don't make spaghetti Westerns.'"

Sturges saw Eastwood as a latter-day Tracy or McQueen, a reactive personality. "Like those guys, he's all business, knows exactly what he's doing. If you're a bullshitter, forget it." Eastwood, likewise, praised Sturges's all-business attitude: "It wasn't the greatest story in the world—and it never really had a good completion to it—but I had always admired John's work, especially *Bad Day at Black Rock,* and I wanted to work with him."

John Saxon, who had played a Mexican in *The Appaloosa,* was cast as the phony folk hero, Chama, and Robert Duvall returned to his villainous ways as Frank Harlan, the Chicago land speculator whose bodyguards use high-powered rifles and take Mexican villagers hostage. Gregory Walcott played Sinola's worthless sheriff. Sturges handpicked the locations, which included Lone Pine, Bishop, and Inyo National Forest. "You couldn't stand still for more than fifteen minutes in the high country where they built the Mexican village," recalled Bill Sparrow, who visited the set with his then-wife, Deborah Sturges. "It was freezing or below freezing every morning." Old Tucson stood in for Sinola, described as a "relatively new town . . . evidence of civilization's push into this remote area." The production crew—a combination of Eastwood and Sturges regulars—included Ferris Webster, cinematographer Bruce Surtees, and composer Lalo Schifrin, whose guitar-and-flute score owed more than a passing nod to Ennio Morricone's spaghetti Western themes.

Sturges said he went against his better judgment when he agreed to direct but not produce. This meant he did not have the final say on the script and often had to yield to Eastwood and Eastwood's omnipresent mouthpiece, executive producer Robert Daley. Sturges saw the protagonist as a bumptious charmer who, when cornered, would rise to the occasion; Eastwood saw him as the Hollywood version of his spaghetti Western persona, a loner with a big gun out for revenge. That there would be a difference of opinion over the character was evident from a story conference in Leonard's studio office.

"When I deliver this line to John Saxon, he's got several armed men behind him. Shouldn't I have my gun out?" Eastwood asked the writer.

"No, you don't have your gun out," Leonard replied.

Eastwood turned to Sturges. "Don't *you* think I should have my gun out? No? Well, why the hell not?"

"Because everybody in the audience has seen your pictures," the director said.

Sturges wanted the action to be playful and even included gags left over from *The Magnificent Seven*. In a bell-tower sequence, Kidd swings an olla like a pendulum, slowly lowering it until it crowns a guard. Eastwood, knowing his audience, insisted on more graphic violence. Their antithetical approaches resulted in a film that veers wildly in tone, from burlesque to cold-blooded retribution. In the final courthouse confrontation, Joe, seated in a judge's chair, swivels around and gets the drop on Harlan, who, appreciating the irony, almost smiles. Joe squints in close-up and squeezes the trigger.

The petty arguments drained Sturges, but he kept his emotions in check. Most nights after dailies he could be found in the hotel bar. And the combination of alcohol and altitude affected his stamina and gave him what Saxon called "this tired, glazed look." Schifrin described the director as "strangely detached." When he got excited, white spittle would form in the corners of his mouth, which some attributed to fatigue, others to his heavy smoking. "It only later occurred to [cast and crew] that the director was a boozer and in the downhill stages of his career," writes Patrick McGilligan in his biography *Clint*.

Surtees asked Saxon to "light a fire under John, he seems to be drifting." Observed Saxon later, "He was more interested in his commercial fishing boat with its sonic devices for trailing tuna—you could call it the next phase of his life—than he was in the film."

Added Duvall, who would later costar in *The Eagle Has Landed*, "Sturges was no spring chicken. He got tired after four or five weeks, and Eastwood, who's a control freak anyway, took over, like he did later from [Philip] Kaufman on *The Outlaw Josey Wales*."

At a loss for an action climax, Sturges drew inspiration from the abandoned *The Yards of Essendorf*. He had his crew lay an extra forty feet of railroad track over the weekend and, on Monday, improvised something out of a Buster Keaton film. Joe hopped aboard a conveniently parked train and crashed it through the railhead and into a saloon.

Sturges ended the picture with Walcott's sheriff asking, "Anything I can do for you, Joe?" Joe then rides out of town with the girl. In June, only a month from the film's release, Daley called Walcott in Rome and informed him, "We have to reshoot the tag of the film." Walcott raced back to the studio, and in forty-five minutes on the backlot, Eastwood reshot the ending. Now, after the sheriff delivers his line, Joe punches him in the face and growls, "Next time, I'll knock your damn head off."

Sturges felt betrayed by the changes because they had been made with Webster, *his* editor. "Throughout the shoot, Ferris, who was usually a pretty gruff fellow, catered to Clint, always called him Mr. Eastwood," said Walcott. "Clint kind of charmed him out of his boots." Midway through production the editor defected to the Eastwood camp, thus causing a rift in a friendship that had spanned fifty years and fifteen movies. (Webster would finish his career working on *The Outlaw Josey Wales* and other Eastwood films. Both he and Sturges retired to San Luis Obispo and lived only blocks from one another, but they never spoke, said Kathy Sturges.)

Joe Kidd opened in July, and though reviewers noted plot holes and character inconsistencies, it rode the Eastwood slipstream (created by *Dirty Harry, Play Misty for Me,* and a triple bill of the star's spaghetti

Westerns) and earned $6 million, making it the most successful Sturges film since *The Great Escape*. Sturges called it "an adequately successful picture. The script wasn't there, but all Eastwood pictures made money, including that one."

That summer Sturges and Bronson reteamed on a coming-of-age Western adapted from the Lee Hoffman novel *The Valdez Horses*. As part of a $1 million three-picture deal with Italian producer Dino De Laurentiis, Bronson had, and flaunted, script and director approval. For Sturges, who had weaned the actor from weed soup, this was an ignominious comedown.

To save on the budget, De Laurentiis announced that the Italian-Spanish-French co-production would be shot in southern Spain. Bronson, now an international star, played Chino Valdez, a half-Mexican, half-Indian who runs wild horses in Colorado, circa 1870. Fourteen-year-old Vincent Van Patten was cast as the runaway Jamie, who, by watching Chino, learns how to tame horses without breaking them. Bronson insisted that his wife, Jill Ireland, play a wealthy rancher's half sister, Catherine. The role was altered to accommodate the thirty-six-year-old actress's age, British accent, and marquee requirements. Marcel Bozzuffi (*The French Connection*) played Catherine's brother, who turns nasty when he finds her with the "half-breed." In the reworked canyon climax, Chino fights off the rancher and his men and then defiantly scatters the horses. The book's ending: Chino—"firing, fast as he could lever shells and take aim"—slaughters the ranch-born horses.

Cast and crew stayed in Almería and drove ninety minutes each morning to the desert set. Van Patten described the shoot as "tremendously long"—three months to a hundred days—and Sturges as "completely absorbed. You could tell he enjoyed what he was doing. . . . We'd rehearse and then he'd take me aside and show me exactly what he wanted—how to put on my coat or trade for moccasins with an Indian girl."

Sturges was less accommodating when it came to the crew's extended lunches and Bronson, who kept an RV on location for his wife and large extended family. "We'd break for lunch, which, because the wine was flowing, would stretch to two and a half hours," recalled Van Patten. "On a budget, Sturges wanted to move things along. But Bronson, at the time the top action star in the world, played prima donna.

He wouldn't emerge from his RV until he felt like it. Then he'd spend hours showing me and my brother how to throw a knife or find scorpions under rocks."

Still, Bronson was a good choice for the sullen Chino, the original horse-whisperer, Sturges insisted. The role required an animal physicality but also called on the actor's seldom-utilized tender side. Agreeing on Ireland, however, was a fatal mistake. When it was obvious her role wasn't working, Sturges flew back to the States and contacted Elmore Leonard. "We went out on his commercial fishing boat, made a big circle out, and talked about the script," recalled Leonard, who stayed at the director's Marina del Rey condo. "It wasn't a rewrite. He wanted a gunfight, a [saloon] fistfight, and a love scene. I watched what they had on a moviola, then wrote the scenes. My dialogue was full of explanations of why she's English and her brother, who speaks with a French accent, is Mexican. It's the only time I've worked like that."

Sturges finished *Chino* in late 1973. Six months later, De Laurentiis reassembled the actors and crew for a week of inserts and retakes. Because Sturges wasn't available, these were done by veteran Italian director Duilio Coletti. The film—called *The Valdez Horses* in Italy, *Wild Horses* in Spain, and *Valdez the Half-Breed* in Britain—was platformed out from Italy. It received a limited U.S. run in early 1976.

Little more than a frontier vignette, *Chino* pleased neither spaghetti Western fans nor the Bronson/*Death Wish* contingent. Sturges can be credited with the tracking shots of the stampeding horses and a more-respectful-than-usual depiction of Native Americans. The Western also contains the only nudity in a Sturges film and, compliments of Coletti, one of the most embarrassing sex scenes on record. Catherine and Chino become excited watching a wild stallion mount a mare. Sturges said he couldn't bring himself to watch whatever found its way into release.

"The only picture I made where I felt like apologizing," he winced. "I wanted to work in Spain so I shoveled everything under the rug. I never should have agreed to do the picture with Charlie's wife. She was hopelessly unsuited for the role. I should have spotted that and said, 'Let's call this thing off.' But you get egotistical; you think you can cope with anything."

The delay in release worked to Sturges's advantage. It kept him bankable and, in early 1973, the long-rumored pairing with John Wayne became a reality. In *McQ,* Wayne played a Seattle police detective who, during the investigation into his partner's murder, stumbles upon police corruption and a plot to recycle $2 million in confiscated drugs. Hobbled by internal politics, he eventually turns in his badge and operates as a private detective. Eddie Albert co-starred as the precinct captain whose knee-jerk reaction is to round up all "militants" and "freaks." Colleen Dewhurst appeared briefly but effectively as a lonely cocktail waitress who trades information for drugs.

Written and co-produced by Lawrence Roman and executive produced by Michael Wayne for his father's Batjac Productions, the Warner Bros. release was shot over the summer in Seattle and along the pristine beaches of Olympic Peninsula, backdrop for the car chase finale. Harry Stradling Jr. (*Little Big Man, The Way We Were*) photographed the film in widescreen Technicolor, and Elmer Bernstein reunited with Sturges for the sixth, and last, time to supply the ersatz *Shaft* theme. Instead of a six-shooter, Wayne cradled a submachine gun that was so lethal it rated its own "special weapon" credit. Instead of a horse, he saddled up a Pontiac Trans Am, referred to as the "Green Hornet." The sixty-six-year-old star did the picture, Sturges said, because his Westerns were no longer drawing large audiences, and he had made the mistake of turning down *Dirty Harry.* He would make up for it by playing Harry's Seattle cousin, "Dirty Duke." Another incentive: McQ, somewhat modeled on Sturges, lived on a boat in a marina. This meant that during production Wayne could bunk on his own boat, the *Wild Goose.* Wayne's mentor, John Ford, remained skeptical. "Duke's up in Seattle shooting some rubbish, playing a goddamn policeman," he said shortly before his death.

With its references to women's lib and extra-legal police methods — *"C'mon, pig, shoot me. Pull your piece and blow me up right here,"* a hippie taunts McQ — the thriller seemed an odd choice for Wayne, a staunch Nixon supporter. The story also contained implied references to Watergate — the hearings were in full swing and, when Wayne wasn't around, monopolized the production-office television. Sturges had gotten his star to agree to several career firsts, such as sauntering across a disco floor and dabbing white powder on his tongue, but Wayne drew the line at an exchange that smacked of liberal paranoia. The script ended with Captain Kosterman (Albert) offering McQ his badge back—in exchange for permission to continue his investigation, presumably to City Hall.

McQ: "Ed, in narco stuff, the threads run deep. I think Toms [Gulager] was too small to have laid it all out by himself. I think he took his orders from somebody sitting dirty someplace. That's where I want to go."

"Wayne was furious because his friend Nixon was in trouble and he thought Sturges was trying to put one over on him," said Roman. "I must have rewritten that scene twenty times, but I never could satisfy him. He saw it as political, anti-American. . . . I just thought by leaving it open-ended we might get a sequel out of the thing."

When it came time to shoot the scene, Wayne ignored McQ's "threads run deep" speech and cut to "Let's get a drink."

Sturges had his own ideas of how to streamline what he dismissed as a "mediocre, elaborately talky script." He issued the hero a supercharged Pontiac and an unregistered submachine gun. These accoutrements are showcased in the most accomplished sequences, including the climactic beach chase and shootout where a car, rigged with explosives, becomes airborne and corkscrews through the surf.

"God knows, we needed something in that picture," Sturges said. "So when I got up there on Olympic Peninsula, I looked at the beach and noticed a guy driving up it. 'Jeez,' I thought, 'that would be a terrific place to stage a chase, to get out there in a couple of feet of water with cars flying across sections of hard sand, the spray covering their windshields, practically destroying all visibility."

Sturges also had fun with the sequence in which the Trans Am is sandwiched between two semi-trucks in an alley and reduced to scrap. In retirement, however, he talked about the quieter moments shared by Wayne and Dewhurst, who played Myra, a melancholy addict-informant. Again belying the generalization that he couldn't direct actresses, Sturges coaxed an earthy, heartbreaking turn from the veteran stage actress. After Elsa Lanchester's landlady in *Mystery Street*, it's the finest performance by an actress in a Sturges film. "I'm always cast as a prostitute, the hardened woman," Dewhurst said, laughing. "When I did *McQ*, John Sturges saw that I came up a step—I'm a loose cocktail waitress."

The crime thriller wrapped in July, after the beach chase. Though bloodier than the norm for a Sturges picture—Myra's doorway murder was particularly shocking—the film received a PG rather than a threatened R rating by following MPAA recommendations to tone down the violence and profanity and "avoid showing exposed woman's breasts." In January, a studio publicist asked the director to participate in a pre-opening publicity stunt. Wayne was going to be roasted by Harvard's Hasty Pudding Theatrical Club. He would roll onto Harvard Square in an armored personnel carrier. Sturges, who avoided such gimmickry, called it "the worst idea there ever was. But Duke did it. He arrived on a tank, and they asked him about women's lib and LSD. And he won them over; he got a standing ovation."

McQ opened in early February. The New York ads carried the banner "Harvard's Man of the Year." The trailers worked the departure angle: "John Wayne is McQ . . . And this time, for the first time, HE'S A COP!" The critics—unable to see beyond Wayne's politics—found the film "stiff and perfunctory" (*Washington Post*) and "undistinguished" (*L.A. Times*) and pointed out the obvious, that Wayne, at sixty-six, was too old to be playing a maverick cop who guns his muscle car through intersections. Ticket sales stalled at just over $4 million (low for a Wayne movie). Not helping matters was the slew of more subversive cop thrillers, such as *The Seven Ups, Serpico,* and *Magnum Force,* the second Dirty Harry.

"It didn't fit Duke particularly well," Sturges conceded. "He liked things straight and clean—Disney-style. He said, 'Hell no!' to a longer bedroom scene with Dewhurst. Also, the story was extensively told with elaborate dialogue. Well, that's not Duke. I assumed we'd cut those things down. I wanted to tell the story visually, the producers wanted to tell it with words. I couldn't get these guys to understand that Duke was not the protagonist; he was, like McQueen and Spence, this reactive character. They wanted to keep giving him things to do, and Duke went along with them. And this meant in the end the movie didn't have a coherent style."

"McQ: John Wayne in Action," a behind-the-scenes featurette, shows Sturges puffing away furiously on a cigarette as he sets up shots. In the short, Wayne says of the director, he "knows what he wants and has a stick-to-it-ness to wait 'til he gets it." Not so, countered Roman and Bernstein. They recalled the filmmaker as "just going through the motions." Hollywood's premier escape artist, preoccupied with his other ventures, had begun his escape. "After shooting each day, he would disappear," said Roman. "What was he doing? He was in his room. He was designing a boat." Added Bernstein, "I hadn't seen John since *Hallelujah Trail.* I was shocked by how much he had changed. He was not the same man."

Sturges's seeming decline can be attributed to a number of factors, ego and age being the most salient. At sixty-four, he was feeling his years, and then some. His three-pack-a-day habit had taken its toll, and like Wayne, he was easily winded. (Four years later, he would be diagnosed with emphysema.) Also, out of frustration over his diminished powers of concentration, he was mixing his Cuba Libres earlier in the day. Everything was in flux, he complained. His brand of no-bull storytelling had fallen from favor. As proof, he pointed to his postwar peers — Wise, Brooks, Robson, and Dmytryk. They had been booted aside by a so-called new wave of film-school "auteurs" — among them, Scorsese, De Palma, and Coppola. And with nothing in the hopper, Sturges was too proud — and financially comfortable — to work just for the sake of working. So he focused more on the next stage. He leased property on Conception Bay in Baja, and anchored his fishing boat offshore.

Robert Aldrich, a longtime admirer, echoed others who lamented the director's disappearance. In *McQ,* Aldrich said, Dewhurst has "maybe the best moments of acting you've ever seen in a movie. There is a car chase on a beach at the end as good as anything in *The French Connection.* But nobody is going to remember that picture. If you get that kind of picture when you're trying to struggle back, it's going to put you down the tube. John Sturges hasn't been able to stay at the table."

The following summer, Sturges resurfaced in London attempting to raise money for "Three Who Went to War," a POW drama inspired by the 1915 "death march" of 12,500 British soldiers in Mesopotamia. The epic film, he told potential backers, could be done in Mexico. "A desert is a desert," he joked. "In Mexico you get hundreds of people who would make sensational Turks, with a little help from turbans." Between pitch meetings, he sat down with an *L.A. Times* reporter to discuss career strategy. The "burly old man in the aviator shades," as he was described, said he was looking at scripts and had, the previous summer, completed one about an escape through the Grand Canyon. Pointing to *The Godfather* and *The Poseidon Adventure,* he said that his kind of straightforward adventures—not those kitchen-sink dramas or "little quarrels between roommates"—were what filmgoers really craved. "Those contemporary life stories controlled the market for a long time, but now audiences are bored with pictures that don't take a strong approach."

Sturges's brand of storytelling, however, remained expensive. He needed $6 million to begin the POW drama, with its 285 speaking parts. "If you don't get the money, you don't do the picture. It's as simple as that. What good is a director without a picture to direct?"

Unable to secure financing for "Three Who Went to War," Sturges was recruited for a more traditional war movie, this one about a plot by Himmler to kidnap Churchill during the waning days of World War II. *The Eagle Has Landed,* from the 1975 bestseller by Jack Higgins, had been set up at Paramount by Jack Wiener and David Niven Jr. and the script assigned to Tom Mankiewicz, son of director Joe Mankiewicz and, with three James Bond movies to his credit, the hottest writer in town. "After I finished the screenplay," Mankiewicz recalled, "someone at Paramount said, 'You know who would be great for this? John Sturges.' I was so excited. I mean, *the* John Sturges . . . of *The Great Escape!*"

A meeting was arranged. Mankiewicz assumed it would be at the studio. Sturges, however, suggested a beach rendezvous in the Malibu Colony. He brought his boat up from Newport and rowed ashore. "It was very odd, sort of like the mountain coming to Muhammad," said Mankiewicz, who had a small beach house, with ratty furniture and no central heating. Sturges plopped down on the couch and asked about Joe Mankiewicz, whom he knew from the 1950 showdown with DeMille.

They then turned to the script, which Sturges said was terrific.

"Yeah, but the hero is a Nazi," Mankiewicz said, echoing Paramount's chief concern.

"No, no—that's not a problem at all," replied Sturges, polishing off his second gin and tonic. "That's what makes it interesting. These are honorable, disillusioned Germans, like the commandant in *The Great Escape.*"

"He was excited about the project, and very seductive," recalled Mankiewicz. "He seemed to understand everything that was right and wrong about the picture. I did notice he was drinking a lot, but I figured all the old-time directors did. I would have been disappointed if I'd had a chance to work with John Huston and he didn't have a cigarette dangling from his mouth and wasn't half in the bag."

Higgins's novel juggled numerous subplots, but its primary focus was Intelligence Officer Max Radl, who organizes the 1943 commando operation; Kurt Steiner, the war-weary colonel who leads his paratroopers on the mission; and Liam Devlin, a member of the Irish Republican Army now working for Berlin. An incorrigible boozer and romantic, Devlin is, by far, the most colorful character in the book. With the help of a smitten farm girl and a local Mata Hari, he prepares the way for Steiner and his men, who arrive in the Norfolk town of Studley Constable disguised as Free Polish on maneuvers. The kidnapping plot quickly unravels, and the Germans take the villagers hostage in a church. A battle with a nearby detachment of American Rangers leaves most of the Germans dead, but Steiner escapes and makes his way to the country manor where Churchill is staying. He is killed attempting to assassinate a man who turns out to be Churchill's double. Sturges dropped several subplots and added a twist: Steiner kills the decoy prime minister before he's killed.

Sturges wanted Michael Caine for Devlin. Caine sent back word that, because of recent bombings in London, he did not feel comfortable playing an IRA terrorist. "I like the script, but I have a new family. What if the IRA doesn't like my portrayal? How about me doing Steiner, the German commando, instead?"

Sturges had to laugh. "Isn't it amazing that thirty years after the war you'd have a British actor who would rather play a Nazi than an Irishman?" Richard Harris was announced as Devlin.

Paramount, not convinced that Americans would pay to see a movie with a Nazi hero, backed out of the project, and the producers, on the basis of Caine's name, took the picture to Lord Lew Grade's ITC Entertainment, which specialized in all-star melodramas, such as *Voyage of the Damned* and *The Cassandra Crossing*. *The Eagle Has Landed* was budgeted at a then-liberal $6 million. It was shot over an unusually hot summer in Cornwall, the Berkshire village of Mapledurham, and—for the opening train sequence that establishes Steiner's humanity (as he attempts to save a Jewish girl bound for a concentration camp)— Rovaniemi, Finland. Robert Duvall was signed to play Radl, who wears one black glove and an eye patch, and when Harris's IRA fundraising made him a liability, Donald Sutherland stepped into the Devlin role. Treat Williams, Sturges's latest discovery, was cast as an American captain who foils the plot. (Sturges took Williams under his wing and often invited the young stage-trained actor to dinner.) Other roles went to Jenny Agutter (Devlin's now older, less gullible admirer), Donald Pleasence (Himmler), Larry Hagman (a buffoonish would-be Patton), and Jean Marsh (a younger, less sympathetic version of Joanna Grey, Liam's contact in Studley Constable).

The blue-ribbon production crew, mostly British, included cinematographer Anthony Richmond (*Don't Look Now*), production designer Peter Murton (*Dr. Strangelove*), and Oscar-winning editor Anne Coates (*Lawrence of Arabia*). Lalo Schifrin provided the eclectic score, a fusion of martial anthem and Irish folk music. He said he was inspired by the theme of obsession and Sturges's aerial shots of the Bavarian Alps. "John didn't tell me what to write, but he did say it had to be big, for a full symphony," recalled the composer.

More intricate and logistically challenging than anything the director had undertaken in years, the location shoot dragged on for four months and was described by Caine as "one of the longest films I've been on." The production was based out of Twickenham Studios in London but traveled as far north as Lapland on the Arctic Circle. Sturges, who could not tolerate the bitter cold, confided, "I can't make another film like this or I'll kill myself." Mankiewicz checked in from Bermuda, where he was working on *The Deep*. The garrulous Wiener, new to producing and desperate to succeed, was noticeably agitated. He couldn't seem to get through to the director, whom he found uncommunicative. "He's behind schedule . . . and because he's under pressure, he's drinking a lot," Wiener told Mankiewicz. Sturges countered that the producers— "always hovering"—were so obsessed with staying under budget, they were sacrificing vital character detail. Initially, Caine sided with the director. "He's inclined to think 'Take One,' which I like," he said.

Duvall called Sturges an "Old School pro" who didn't encourage improvisation but was receptive to suggestions. "He was a big guy but he smoked a lot, so he tired at the end of the day and needed a boost," said Duvall, who spent a good portion of the Cornwell shoot horseback riding and dining on the local lobster. "At the end, I asked him if he would do a scene where Radl is put in front of a firing squad. It was my idea, but he filmed it. He wasn't neurotic like some of those old guys. Hathaway was a tyrant. He'd say, 'When I say, "Action!" tense up, goddamn it!' Sturges wasn't like that. He admired what actors could bring. I would have loved to have worked with him in his prime on *Black Rock* or *The Great Escape.*"

Mankiewicz said, yes, Sturges drank, but nothing like Robert Shaw or Richard Harris. Kathy Sturges, the director's second wife, added, "When I met him in Baja [in 1979], he was a social drinker. He knew when to quit. I never saw him drunk." Daughter Deborah, who spent two weeks on the set, said, "Dad totally ignored his health, and it was not outstanding on that movie. Of course, the disputes didn't help."

Sturges's method of appeasing the producers and getting back on schedule was to tear pages from the script. Because *The Eagle Has Landed* was so intricately structured, with one subplot feeding into another, this led to continuity problems and, Coates reported from the editing room, a lack of "coverage," including missing reaction shots and over-the-shoulder reversals.

"For me," said Mankiewicz, "that was so disappointing because the John Sturges of my fantasy didn't do stuff like that. He said, 'Fuck it, kid—let's go get the bastards.'"

Mankiewicz saw the film at a screening for foreign distributors. Sturges was not there. "He's on a boat somewhere in Mexico," Coates reported, adding that the director "hadn't been around much for the editing." Mankiewicz fidgeted through the screening. "There were great chunks taken out of the script," he said. "Some of it was unexplainable." For instance, when the Germans are trapped in the church and Steiner asks the American captain, "You thought we were going to break out of here, driving the women and children in front us?" now became the captain's accusatory response to Steiner's "I have hostages." Mankiewicz couldn't believe it. "My God," he blurted out, "he gave the whole moment to the wrong person!"

There were more problems with the sequence in which Radl discovers that he was duped, that Himmler was acting without Hitler's authorization. Mankiewicz called it "a crucial moment, where Duvall realizes that the last two hours have been a fraud." He asked Coates, "Can't we cut there to Duvall's close-up?" Embarrassed, Coates replied, "There isn't one. He didn't shoot it. . . . I'm using every foot of film that's in that scene."

Sturges's version of events is markedly different. He said he clashed with Wiener on the overall construction of the film and blamed the neophyte producer for his early departure. Contractually, he was once again painted into a corner: he had no control over post-production. "Same old story—producer interference," he said. "After I was off the picture, they hacked it up. Shot some tired newsreel opening. They didn't understand that you need to develop characters, let the audience understand their motivations, who they are. That way you pull for them in a crunch. I put in a bunch of stuff like that early on, things that indicated character. The editor cut all that down to nothing. So when you got to the big action sequences in the church and town square, nothing—they didn't play. The audience was not invested enough to care."

Caine took Wiener's word for what happened in post-production. Sturges in his eyes was now a "Hollywood old-timer" who talked incessantly about deep-sea fishing and retirement. "The moment the picture finished he took the money and went," Caine wrote in his autobiography. "Wiener later told me that he never came back for the editing nor for any of the other post-production sessions that are where a director does some of his most important work. The picture wasn't bad, but I still get angry when I think of what it could have been with the right director. We committed the old European sin of being impressed by someone just because he came from Hollywood."

Deborah Sturges was shocked by her father's appearance when they reunited stateside. "He was *really* unhappy, and because it had been truncated, threatened to take his name off the picture," she said. "I think the dispute with Wiener, the fact that the shoot was very hard on him physically, plus the kind of pictures he made didn't draw audiences any longer—that combination took its toll on Dad."

In contrast to the hoopla that attended *The Great Escape*, Sturges's latest received a half-hearted royal-command performance, which the director did not attend. The version that was screened for the trades ran 134 minutes and included a more leisurely *Great Escape*-like setup and spy Joanna Grey's backstory. It was trimmed by eleven minutes for the March opening and, reversing the usual critical response, received a rave in the *New York Times* ("a good old-fashioned adventure movie . . . stuffed with robust incidents") and a pan in the *L.A. Times* ("the same old maneuvers, the same old heroics, plus a large dose of truly terrible dialogue"). The news weeklies also split. Mankiewicz joked to director Richard Donner, "If you live in L.A. and get Newsweek, it stinks. If you live in New York and get Time, it's great."

Some reviewers made unfavorable comparisons to *Day of the Jackal* (1973), about a plot to assassinate Charles De Gaulle, and argued that, in the post-Vietnam era, a movie that glamorized war was not only passé it was in questionable taste. Released around the same time as Frankenheimer's much grimmer *Black Sunday,* the film fared poorly in the United States but was a modest success overseas.

The Eagle Has Landed—often confused with *Where Eagles Dare* (1968) with Richard Burton and Clint Eastwood—would turn out to be Sturges's last completed picture. Not a great film to go out on, but nothing to apologize for, either. As a swan song it was more accomplished than the final features of Wise, Robson, Fleischer, and Brooks. At its best, the Higgins adaptation is a lively, efficiently produced cliffhanger that benefits from postcard locations and sometimes jarring tableaux, such as the crucifixion death of a young German soldier on a mill water wheel. At its worst, it is disjointed and, in contrast to Zinnemann's rigorous *Day of the Jackal,* a morass of tones and acting styles. (Hagman's eager-beaver colonel is so broadly played he belongs in another movie.) For all its faults, Sturges saw the film as a vindication, proof that after the letdowns of *Chino* and *McQ,* he could still command a large-scale production.

Epilogue

The Best Escape

S turges said he never intended to retire. It was just that the interval between *The Eagle Has Landed* and that promising next project kept expanding. He woke up one morning to discover that the fishing trips to Kona and the Sea of Cortez, once a means of blotting out backlot politics, had become a new way of life. Further, he was not about to follow the lead of Richard Fleischer and others and make movies that were beneath him.

"It got to the point where the scripts that I liked couldn't seem to get financed, and the ones that got financed, where they came up with bags of money, I didn't like," he said. "And since I didn't need the money and I didn't have to keep stretching my career, I didn't see any point in making a picture that I felt was mediocre to begin with. God knows, it's hard enough to make them without starting off without any enthusiasm. . . . But then the spaces got longer and longer, until I realized I really wasn't doing anything. Then I said, 'To hell with it. I'm not going to do a picture just to do a picture.'"

Sturges didn't shut the door completely. His name still commanded respect, and there were additional offers. One was for a World War II submarine drama told from the viewpoint of the German crew—a natural after *The Eagle Has Landed* and *Ice Station Zebra;* another was an account of an unusual rescue mission during the Vietnam War. Relyea, now working as an independent producer, approached him about a detective thriller to be shot in New York. Relyea recalled, laughing, "John showed up in mismatched socks and, turning to the script, spent the next twenty minutes calmly explaining why he would be absolutely wrong for the picture."

In 1976, upon his return from England, Sturges was approached by Edward Pressman, a young producer who specialized in low-budget films by budding auteurs, such as Brian De Palma and Terrence Malick, but who now wanted to work with a major director on a more mainstream project. "I was a great fan of John's work," said Pressman. "He was a legend, one of those Old School Hollywood directors." After screening *The Eagle Has Landed,* which he found "a bit old-fashioned but a great film of its type," Pressman signed Sturges for *Das Boot,* an adaptation of Lothar Günther Buchheim's novel about life aboard a German U-boat in the North Atlantic. Set up as a U.S.-German coproduction, the movie would be shot entirely at Bavaria Film Studios. Robert Redford and Paul Newman were both mentioned for the U-boat captain, but Sturges wanted Gene Hackman and, as the war correspondent documenting life aboard the submarine, Richard Dreyfuss. He then flew to Munich with assistant Michele Rappaport to scout locations and oversee the construction of a soundstage submarine (modeled after a U-boat on display at a Chicago museum). Sturges, according to Rappaport, was "glad to be working again" and, even when things turned contentious, "not easily rattled." Pressman found the director gracious, vital—and expensive. Buchheim, however, was oddly evasive. "When I'd bring up the script," said Sturges, "he'd change the subject, talk about all the other pictures I'd made."

Buchheim and Bavaria Studios, it turned out, wanted Hollywood dollars but not Hollywood input. The author protested vehemently when his timeline was pushed forward, from 1941 to 1942, to accommodate American characters. Dreyfuss accused Buchheim of anti-Semitism and left the project. According to Wolfgang Petersen—who directed a six-hour television adaptation of *Das Boot* that was consolidated into a theatrical feature—the early scripts were "full of clichés, like a scene where the commander tells his first officer to turn machine guns on a group of poor American sailors swimming in the sea."

After two months of pre-production talks—and side trips to the Hamburg shipyard and Dachau concentration camp—it became clear that the screenplay was nowhere near ready, and it was Buchheim, not Pressman, who was calling the shots. Sturges, citing irreconcilable artistic differences, flew home. "Buchheim was thinking about filing a lawsuit—a 'T' had not been crossed on his contract," recalled Relyea. "Well, he didn't finish his sentence and John was gone." (Sturges was replaced by Don Siegel, who was even less accommodating and lasted only a few weeks. Buchheim would disassociate himself from the critically acclaimed Petersen film.)

Sturges's version of the story: "They hired me to do it. I went over there and to my amazement discovered the Germans hated the script and wanted to go back to the book. Well, I wasn't about to take a stand one way or another. I didn't think the script was all that great, but it had structure—first act, second act, third act. I didn't think you could make the book, take that purely atmospheric approach. So I said I wouldn't supervise a full rewrite and if they didn't like it, they had better call the whole thing off."

When *Das Boot* reached theaters in 1982, Sturges saw it with his daughter. He was envious: he could never have achieved such grueling realism (the result of a hand-held Arriflex on gyroscopic mount). "It's my kind of film," he told Deborah, "but this man did a better job than I would have." He later admitted, "I was wrong about the three-act structure. I thought it was excellent and the performances were marvelous. . . . It's another reminder that a director shouldn't try to do something he's not familiar with."

In 1980, Sturges read *Bat-21*, about Air Force Lieutenant Colonel Iceal "Gene" Hambleton, who was shot down over Vietnam's demilitarized zone. How Hambleton eluded the Vietcong and how the rescue team devised a radio code utilizing the colonel's photographic memory of golf courses had the makings of a first-rate adventure, the director decided. He announced plans to shoot in the Sacramento River Delta, until his declining health and the usual script problems caused the film to be shelved. (It was made four years later as *Bat*21*, starring Gene Hackman.) "I really liked that story, and we had the complete cooperation of the Air Force," said Sturges. "I liked the technique [of the rescue], how they used the concept of the golf game to get that guy out. It had a lot of humor, too. All you had to do is cut to the Vietcong listening in, trying to make sense out of the golf talk. Had to be funny."

Michael Sturges was skeptical about the project because his father had always been, if not pro-U.S. involvement in Vietnam, never outspoken on the subject. In retirement, the director was less anti-war than he was anti-South Vietnam. "The war, on the face of it, was a disaster because we went in on the wrong side," he insisted.

"If I had to criticize Dad, I think he beat World War II to death," said Michael. "Yes, *Bat*21* would have taken him into Vietnam, but I think his approach would have been: 'How can I turn it into a World War II movie?' as opposed to taking it on its own terms. A younger John Sturges, the guy who made *The Walking Hills* and *Mystery Street*, would have looked at Vietnam as the tremendous allegory that it was. In his later years, Dad was trying to tell war stories without waking up to the idea that the new war movies, like *M*A*S*H*, weren't about the glory of war; they were about the tragedy of war, the screw-up of war."

Unlike Robert Wise, who remained an industry fixture and would serve as president of the Academy of Motion Picture Arts and Sciences, Sturges had no desire to settle in Hollywood, where, as elder statesman, he could hold forth at guild functions and reminisce about "the good old days." He wanted out, far away from the four horsemen of the metropolis: traffic, smog, people, crime. (Besides being mugged in Marina del Rey, he had four Porsches stolen.)

And when the offers stopped, Sturges spent more time in Baja, where he leased property on a small bay the locals called Posada Concepcion. The endurance racer in him looked forward to the grueling, twelve-hour run from the border. Sometimes he drove a Dodge truck, more often his silver Porsche. "He would take a shot of tequila and drive like hell from the time he left Ensenada," said Bill Catching, who visited the director in Mexico. "I told him he was crazy to drive like that on a two-lane highway, chuck holes all over the place. He just shrugged." On one trip, between Guerrero Negro and San Ignacio, a crop-duster flew parallel to the road and challenged the Porsche. Sturges enjoyed recounting the incident, his speedometer inching upward with each retelling.

In Posada, he anchored the *Cochinito* seventy yards offshore. The conditions were to his taste: primitive. Nothing but scrub brush and sand to the water. He lived in a trailer. Later, he added a thatched-roof palapa and a system to pump diesel fuel from the beach to the boat. "John loved the notion of being self-sufficient in every way," said Bill Sparrow, who made several trips to Baja with his father-in-law.

It was in Mulegé, at weekly get-togethers with other Americans, that Sturges met Kathy Soules, who was almost half his age and married to a retired fireman.

"John was around seventy when we met, but I always thought he was younger," said Kathy. "He immediately fell in love with Conception Bay, where he fished for yellowtail and marlin. He built a workshop and a nice covered patio for the trailer. Then he built a brick house. After we got married, he sold that house and built another. These houses had to be self-contained because there was no well water or electricity. John solved this problem by buying a water truck in the states for our handyman, Rafael. They drove it down together and used it to fill our holding tank. There were two big diesel generators for power. John loved the machinery."

Kathy wasn't a film buff—indeed, she didn't know who John Sturges was when they were introduced—but she did share the director's love of boats and fishing, and after a lifetime of Hollywood phonies, he found her lack of pretense refreshing. When Kathy divorced, Sturges sold his Marina del Rey condo, and the couple shuttled between Baja and Kona. In 1984, they were married at the Santa Barbara Courthouse. In attendance were Deborah and her husband, Dr. Stephen Wyle, and Wyle's thirteen-year-old son, Noah, who would later star in the TV series *ER*.

"Talking about movies wasn't their thing," observed Michael. "It was hanging out together, companionship. I think there's something to be said for someone who's not forever raking over the coals of your past glory. That gets old fast. And that definitely was not his style. That may be why he didn't stay in touch with people—a fear that they were going to sit around and talk about the glory days."

Unable to find something suitable in Santa Barbara, John and Kathy moved to Morro Bay and then San Luis Obispo, a university town on California's Central Coast. Sturges designed the second place, a small ranch house of pine, flagstone, and black glass nestled in the Santa Lucia foothills. "I live a very quiet life," he said. "I don't have a big beach house like Bobby Wise. I don't get my jollies going to parties. Not my style." The couple wintered in Posada, driving the 960 miles in their Chevy Blazer, which was outfitted with auxiliary gas tanks and always loaded down with supplies and spare parts. The trips to Kona became less frequent, said Kathy, because "he felt it had gotten too built up—too many fast-food places and tour buses."

Sturges didn't let go easily. He talked about buying another Porsche (his ninth) and getting back behind the camera. "I want to do the return of Christ, but with a whole new concept," said the director, a fallen-away Episcopalian. "He'd show up in Texas—twenty-two, bearded, a hippie. He'd preach everything Christ preached. You know what would happen to him. The church would disown him; the cops would beat him up, kill him. Only I'd never say he was Christ. Deny that he was. Deny that the story was a parable. Just a guy who shows up in Texas. That would be one helluva movie."

Pausing, he took another pull on a Marlboro and suddenly felt every bit his eighty-one years. "Not sure I have the energy. Not sure I'm bankable. The bigger you are the more critical it is that you finish the picture yourself. David Lean at the end had to have a standby director."

Hollywood's premier escape artist had orchestrated his best escape. He was remembered by only a handful of friends and *cinéastes*. Wise's query was typical. "What became of Johnny? Is he still alive?" When Stanford University called to invite him for a retrospective, the director registered shock. "I'm out of the business, and *now* they recognize me." In October 1989, he wrote Jack NyBlom, owner of a repertory theater in San Jose: "Thanks for your letter. I'm really flattered by your plan [for a retrospective] and, of course, would be glad to be part of it. Only problem would be my health, since I've gotten very old while I wasn't looking."

As it became increasingly difficult to draw a breath, Sturges, like Huston and Peckinpah near the end, was tethered to an oxygen tank. Because of acute anemia, he received regular blood transfusions. He read and played gin rummy and Monopoly. He worked with Curtis Wong on supplementary materials for the laserdisc of *The Great Escape*. His audio-track commentary was gruff, unsentimental. Inevitably, the trips to Hawaii and Baja stopped altogether. The *Cochinito* was brought back to Santa Barbara to be refitted.

"The boat needs an able-bodied seaman, and I'm no longer that able-bodied," he said over the phone. "I'm selling the *Cochinito*. It's all part of backing off from the active life." He inhaled. "But, hey, my health isn't anybody's business. Just tell 'em I'm old."

On August 17, 1992, the director was admitted to a San Luis Obispo hospital. He died at four o'clock the next morning. Cause of death was given as cardiopulmonary arrest due to emphysema. Following a small gathering, his ashes were flown three miles out from Avila Beach and scattered.

Because Sturges had been out of the limelight for so long, the news of his death was slow in getting out. *Variety* and the *Los Angeles Times* carried stories four days later. Sturges, "who combined action with philosophical reflection," was celebrated for his "visceral, unflinching, deglamorized direction of gunfights and other violent scenes, but most of the violence in *Bad Day at Black Rock* was psychological," Joseph McBride pointed out in the *Variety* obituary. "One of the last of Holly-wood's old-time action directors, whose triumphs at the box office con-founded critics who tried to dismiss him as a 'technician,' died Tuesday," reported the *L.A. Times*. The *New York Times*, in a short piece riddled with errors, said Sturges's movies were "often mean and muscular and celebrated situations involving tough men in desperate situations." Two weeks later, *People* magazine acknowledged the action director's passing, noting "the careers of many tough-guy actors zoomed after starring in Sturges films."

Not surprisingly, given the dismissive treatment he received from Crowther and others, Sturges's death went all but unnoticed by the critical establishment. This writer's "Slow Fade to Credits: The Life and Films of Director John Sturges" was intended as a Sunday career retrospective, but because events rendered it immediately dated, it was repackaged as a tribute/obit. "When John left the scene, he really left the scene," observed Kathy. "I was surprised there wasn't more coverage. But people forget you fast if you haven't done anything recently." (When I wrote a piece on Sturges for the *Los Angeles Times* in 1996, an executive at Amblin Entertainment contacted me about getting in touch with the director to discuss his two shelved projects, *Richard Sahib* and *The Yards of Essendorf*.)

As the pendulum swung back toward formalistic action movies in the 1990s—due in large part to the high-concept blockbusters of Jerry Bruckheimer and the hyper-kinetic crime thrillers of Quentin

Tarantino—Sturges's style of moviemaking came back in vogue. Name an action director and chances are good that he will have been influenced by Sturges. Steven Spielberg, Clint Eastwood, Robert Redford, Andrew Davis (*The Fugitive*), John Landis (*Three Amigos!*), Edward Zwick (*Glory*), Lawrence Kasdan (*Silverado*), Peter Weir (*Witness*), William Friedkin, John Carpenter (*The Thing*), Kevin Costner (*Open Range*), Christopher Cain (*Young Guns*), Robert Zemeckis (*Back to the Future I–III*), Paul Thomas Anderson, and John Frankenheimer have all acknowledged a debt to the director.

Many remember exactly where they were when they discovered *The Magnificent Seven*. Andrew Davis was in the balcony of a theater in Madison, Wisconsin. He was fourteen. Writer Tom Mankiewicz was a freshman at Yale. "I must have seen it four or five times that first week," he said. "It was the absolute bravura of those guys, that larger-than-life-with-no-apologies quality." Carpenter saw it in Bowling Green, Kentucky. He was twelve. "It had everything; it encapsulated the entire genre for me," he said. "When I got to film school, I began to see all of his work and study the visual compositions. He has a diagonal composition that he uses a lot. It's distinctive, the way he frames master shots and close-ups. . . . He has to be the most underrated filmmaker of the postwar era, probably because he was unfavorably compared to Kurosawa and he mainly did action pictures." Lamenting the dearth of pure action movies, producer Harvey Weinstein said, "When I was a kid, we had *The Dirty Dozen* and *The Great Escape*. What do they have now? Fifty bad ones for every good one."

Ron Howard and Tony Bill have, independently, considered remaking *Bad Day at Black Rock*. "You could put it out today, and it would be so timely," said Howard. "It's riveting, a tough guy movie that rings true. There's never any posturing; those guys don't strut the way villains do today." England's Mike Newell (*Four Weddings and a Funeral*) recalled seeing *Black Rock* on his twelfth birthday. "After the film had finished, we all played the movie again in the field outside our house," he said. "We all wanted to play Tracy. If that's in you from early on, you don't want to only make films, you want to make [Hollywood] films."

Author Khaled Hosseini, a Western buff, paid tribute to Sturges in his best-selling *The Kite Runner*. Amir, his young protagonist, recalls, "We saw *Rio Bravo* three times, but we saw our favorite Western, *The*

Magnificent Seven, thirteen times. With each viewing, we cried at the end when the Mexican kids buried Charles Bronson." The lines were in fact autobiographical, said Hosseini, who first saw the Western in Iran in 1970. "There was something about the seven guys ganging up, defending these innocents against this band of brutes. My favorite was the James Coburn character who said so little. I remember crying when he was shot and died at the end."

When asked about his legacy, Sturges became noticeably uneasy. He refused to think in such high-flown terms. "I got into the film business in order to make a living, and I proved fairly good at telling a story," he said. "I guess you could say I was a pretty good action director, that I had a flair for staging. . . . If I'm remembered, I'd like it to be as a movie director, in the fullest sense."

Acknowledgments

This book would not exist without the cooperation and encouragement of the Sturges family. John Sturges and his wife Kathy invited a journalist to dinner and then urged on a budding biographer. They could not have been more generous. I am equally indebted to the director's children: Michael Sturges, who read portions of the manuscript and suggested other avenues of research, and Deborah Wyle, who arrived pulling a suitcase loaded with family correspondence and photo albums dating to her father's Oak Park infancy. Jon Stufflebeem, interviewed on his boat in Sausalito, provided a different, but no less important, perspective, and Bill Sparrow vividly recalled the director's Baja days. Millard Kaufman, Robert E. Relyea, Joel Freeman, Walter Mirisch, Armand Deutsch, Elmer Bernstein, Norman Jewison, and Robert Wise were also instrumental in telling Sturges's story. Each patiently submitted to "just one more question." Already a legend among film scholars, Ned Comstock at USC's Cinema-Television Library located production files, copied articles I may have overlooked, and, in general, made the project his own. Archivist Barbara Hall fulfilled much the same function at the Academy of Motion Pictures Arts and Sciences' Margaret Herrick Library/Special Collections. Mark Quigley of the UCLA Film and Television Archive arranged screenings of 35mm prints; Lauren Buisson and Julie Graham at UCLA's Charles E. Young Research Library pulled the RKO files; and the delightful Stephanie Zeman and Catherine Dodson at Davee Library on the University of Wisconsin-River Falls campus made the daunting task of digging through mountains of boxes seem, well, less daunting.

Because this is the first Sturges biography, much of the research was by necessity primary-source interviews. These were supplemented by family anecdotes, photos, and letters, including one from the six-year-old Johnny to Santa. Unfortunately, the adult Sturges was no sentimentalist who squirreled away memorabilia. That task has fallen to his daughter, Deborah. Forty-one of the director's annotated scripts, retrieved from a storage unit in San Luis Obispo and donated by Kathy Sturges, are kept at the Margaret Herrick

Library's Special Collections. The collected papers of Dore Schary, Paul Osborn, and Walter Mirisch can be found at the Wisconsin Historical Society Archives in Madison; MGM, Universal, and Warner Bros. production files, including in some cases executive meeting notes, are stored at USC's Cinema-Television Library; the scripts and production notes for *Underwater!* are in UCLA Arts Library's Special Collections. The UCLA Film and Television Archive has some prints of the Columbia films, including *Alias Mr. Twilight* and *The Sign of the Ram*. The Motion Picture Division of the Library of Congress has unpreserved copies of *Alias Mr. Twilight* and *Keeper of the Bees*. Neither film, at this time, is available for viewing or copying. The George Eastman House in Rochester, New York, has Sturges's personal 35mm print of *Thunderbolt*, which it is presently evaluating for restoration.

For sharing their memories, I thank Lee Aaker, Jack Ackerman, Aki Aleong, Richard Anderson, James Arness, Edward Asner, Polly Bergen, Walter Bernstein, Tony Bill, Ernest Borgnine, Richard Brooks, Myriam Bru, Chris Buchholz, Martin Caidin, William Campbell, John Carpenter, Bill Catching, Larry Cohen, Jerome Courtland, Andrew Davis, Colleen Dewhurst, Ted Donaldson, Robert Duvall, Clint Eastwood, Richard Egan, Hillard Elkins, John Ericson, Richard Fleischer, Rhonda Fleming, William Fletcher, John Flynn, Anne Francis, William Friedkin, James Garner, John Gay, Gary Gray, Kelo Henderson, Gloria Henry, Lee Hoffman, Earl Holliman, James Hong, Khaled Hosseini, Jimmy Hunt, Eugene Iglesias, Teddy Infuhr, John Ireland, Hawk Koch, Fred Koenekamp, Chris Langley, Ruta Lee, Elmore Leonard, James Lydon, A. C. Lyles, Don Mankiewicz, Tom Mankiewicz, David McCallum, Chad McQueen, Neile McQueen-Adams, Ricardo Montalban, Terry Moore, Lori Nelson, France Nuyen, John Ottman, Michael Pate, Alexander Payne, Edward Pressman, David Raksin, Robert Redford, Lawrence Roman, Jane Russell, John Saxon, William Schallert, Lalo Schifrin, Marshall Schlom, Melville Shavelson, Henry Silva, Mayo Simon, Bruce Surtees, George Takei, Vincent Van Patten, Robert Vaughn, Jon Voight, Eli Wallach, Wally Young, and Gregory Walcott.

For their research assistance, comments, and moral support, I also am indebted to Ken Annakin, Stephen B. Armstrong, Tony Beres, Stephen G. Bloom, Henry Breitrose, Jerry Condit, James Curtis, Brian De Palma, C. J. Eschelbach, Scott Eyman, Harry Flynn, Alexa Foreman, John Frankenheimer, Karen Gilette, Tom Goldrup, Carl Gottlieb, Shirley Graves, Alan Hess, Heather Holmes, Ron Howard, Laurie Jacobson, Eric Johnson, Eirik Knutzen, Chris Langley, Roger Letson, Boyd Magers, Ana Martinez-Holler, Charlie Matthau, Joseph McBride, Ron Miller, G. E. Nordell, James and Serena Murray, Jack NyBlom, Marvin Page, Karen Pedersen, Deborah Peters,

Charles Pignone, Dennis Piotrowski, Michele Rappaport, Van T. Roberts, Frank Robinson, Candice Russell, Paul Schrader, Ron Smith, Sandy Spanier, Sandra Stelts, Edward E. Stratmann, Sandy Sturges, Susan Tavernetti, Bob Thomas, Mike Thomas, Luis Valdez, Jeremy Walker, Josie Walters-Johnston, Kathleen Broome Williams, Curtis Wong, Valerie Yaros, Peter Yates, Steven Yvaska, and the late Bill Kelley, whose affection for Sturges rivaled my own.

Once again, University of Wisconsin Press spotted an omission in film scholarship and sallied forth heroically. Senior acquisitions editor Raphael Kadushin and Wisconsin Film Studies series editor Patrick McGilligan led the charge. Patrick believed in this project before anyone and shepherded it through the proposal and revision stages. His suggestions on how to makes Sturges the man come "more to the fore" were invaluable. My principal editor in San Jose, California, was Donna Lovell, who kept me focused and on track. She made judicious cuts to "move the narrative along." Donna passed the manuscript to James Murray, my style-book guru, who passed it to the University of Wisconsin Press's freelance copy editor, Jane M. Curran. Tony Lioce worked his special magic on the opening chapters. The Press's unflappable Adam Mehring oversaw the editorial process and folded in last-minute tweaks, and Carla Aspelmeier commissioned the wonderful cover by Bruce Gore.

A very special thanks to my wife, Donna, and our sons, Andrew Lovell and Dan Goldberg, who helped in ways they'll never know; to my mother, Audrey, who as always showed uncommon patience; and to Roman and Rose Yanish and the rest of my Minnesota family, who provided a haven and wheels to continue the research in Wisconsin. Thank you, all!

Filmography

RKO, 1932–1939: As Assistant Technicolor Consultant, Assistant
Sound Editor, or Assistant Editor

Of Human Bondage, 1934
The Gay Divorcee, 1934
The Last Days of Pompeii, 1935
Becky Sharp, 1935
Alice Adams, 1935
The Dancing Pirate, 1936
The Garden of Allah, 1936
Shall We Dance, 1937
Gunga Din, 1939

RKO, 1940–1941: As Editor

They Knew What They Wanted, 1940
Tom, Dick and Harry, 1941
Scattergood Meets Broadway, 1941
Syncopation, 1942

Army Signal Corps and Air Corps, 1942–1945: As Director of Training
and Orientation Shorts

The Operation and Maintenance of the B-51
IFF (Identify Friend or Foe)
Thunderbolt (editor, co-director with William Wyler), 1945 but delayed until
    1947, when Monogram Pictures released it with James Stewart introduction

Columbia Pictures, 1945–1949: As Director

The Man Who Dared, 1946
Shadowed, 1946
Alias Mr. Twilight, 1947

For the Love of Rusty, 1947
Keeper of the Bees, 1947
Best Man Wins, 1948
The Sign of the Ram, 1948
The Walking Hills, 1949

MGM, 1950–1955: As Director

Mystery Street, 1950
Right Cross, 1950
The Magnificent Yankee, 1950
It's a Big Country (segment director), 1951 but released in 1952
Kind Lady, 1951
The People against O'Hara, 1951
The Girl in White, 1952
Jeopardy, 1953
Fast Company, 1953
Escape from Fort Bravo, 1953
Bad Day at Black Rock, 1954
The Scarlet Coat, 1955

Freelance and on Loan Out from MGM

The Capture (RKO), 1950
Underwater! (RKO), 1955
Backlash (Universal), 1956
Gunfight at the O.K. Corral (Paramount), 1957
The Spirit of St. Louis (Warner Bros., three days of retakes), 1957
The Old Man and the Sea (Warner Bros., replaced Fred Zinnemann), 1958
The Law and Jake Wade (MGM), 1958
Saddle the Wind (Universal, two days of retakes), 1958
Last Train from Gun Hill (Paramount), 1959
Never So Few (MGM), 1959 but released in 1960
Sergeants 3 (Warner Bros.), 1962
A Girl Named Tamiko (Paramount), 1962

United Artists–Mirisch Company, 1959–1967: As Producer-Director
(unless otherwise noted)

The Magnificent Seven, 1960
By Love Possessed (director only), 1961
The Great Escape, 1963
The Satan Bug, 1965

The Hallelujah Trail, 1965
Hour of the Gun, 1967

Independent, 1967–1976

Ice Station Zebra (MGM), 1968
Marooned (Columbia), 1969
Joe Kidd (Universal), 1972
Chino (Dino de Laurentiis, a.k.a. *The Valdez Horses;* producer-director), 1973
McQ (Batjac and Levy-Gardner; distributed by Warner Bros.), 1974
The Eagle Has Landed (ITC, distributed in U.S. by Columbia Pictures), 1976

Projects Announced but Abandoned or Directed by Others

The Sons of Kati Elder (Hal Wallis; pre-production, casting), 1955–59
633 Squadron (Mirisch; pre-production, preliminary casting), 1958
The Wreck of the Mary Deare (MGM; pre-production talks), 1958
Vivacious Lady (Mirisch; casting, Paris locations), 1962
Richard Sahib (Mirisch; story by Sturges and James Clavell, preliminary casting
    and locations), 1964–65
Day of the Champion (Warner Bros.; pre-production, background races in
    Europe), 1965–66
The Artful Dodger (Mirisch; script conferences), 1966
Guns of the Magnificent Seven (Mirisch; pre-production, casting), 1968
The Yards of Essendorf (United Artists-Mirisch; story by Sturges; script by
    Stirling Silliphant-Mayo Simon), 1968–70
Le Mans (Solar Productions; pre-production, background races in France),
    1970
Earthquake, 1980 (Universal, pre-production), 1971
Das Boot (Bavaria Studios; casting, script conferences, location scouting in
    Germany), 1976
Bat*21 (TriStar; script conferences, locations), 1980

Notes

Prologue: The Case for "The Other Sturges"

Author interviews with John Carpenter, Ricardo Montalban, Robert E. Relyea, John Sturges, Michael Sturges, Deborah Wyle.

Arnold, William. "Who Is This Jerry Bruckheimer Guy, Anyway?" *Seattle Post-Intelligencer,* Jan. 13, 2006.

Jones, DuPre. "The Merit of Flying Lead." *Films and Filming,* Jan. 1974.

———. "The Power of the Gun." *Films and Filming,* Feb. 1974.

Sarris, Andrew. *The American Cinema: Directors and Directions.* New York: Dutton, 1968.

Chapter 1. Sturges with a Blast of Rum

Author interviews with Bill Sparrow, John Sturges, Kathy Sturges, Michael Sturges, Robert Wise, Curtis Wong, Deborah Wyle.

Chapter 2. Youth

Author interviews with C. J. Eschelbach, Jon Stufflebeem, John Sturges, Kathy Sturges, Michael Sturges, Sandy Sturges, Deborah Wyle.

Anonymous. "Marin Varsity Wins Oregon Game." *Mariner.* Marin Junior College, Oct. 30, 1929.

———. *Mariners' Log, Vol. 1.* Marin Junior College, 1930-31.

Barringer, Emily Dunning. *Bowery to Bellevue: The Story of New York's First Woman Ambulance Surgeon.* New York: W. W. Norton, 1950.

Cherry, Richard. *Action,* Nov.–Dec., 1969.

Staff. "'Sky Train' Scheduled to Arrive at Tamalpais Theater Tomorrow." *Marin Journal,* April 9, 1931.

Sturges, John. *Bad Day at Black Rock,* laserdisc. MGM.

Thomas, Kevin. "He-Man Movies for Feminine Tastes." *Los Angeles Times,* Sept. 6, 1967.

Wakeman, John, ed. *World Film Directors.* Vol. 1. New York: H. W. Wilson, 1987.

Chapter 3. RKO

Author interviews with Richard Fleischer, Robert E. Relyea, John Sturges, Robert Wise.

Jewell, Richard B., with Vernon Harbin. *The RKO Story*. New York: Arlington House, 1982.

Kanin, Garson. *Hollywood*. New York: Viking Press, 1967.

Lasky, Betty. *RKO: The Biggest Little Major of Them All*. Englewood Cliffs, NJ: Prentice-Hall, 1984.

Parrish, Robert. *Growing Up in Hollywood*. New York: Harcourt Brace Jovanovich, 1976.

Scheuer, Philip K. "Jean Arthur Will Star in Garson Kanin's Play." *Los Angeles Times*, Nov. 20, 1945.

Selznick, David O. "RKO 1931–1933." In *Memo from David O. Selznick*, ed. Rudy Behlmer. New York: Modern Library, 2000.

Staff. "Color Pictures Keep Hollywood Film Hub." *Los Angeles Times*, May 10, 1936.

Thompson, Frank. *Robert Wise: A Bio-Bibliography*. Westport, CT: Greenwood Press, 1995.

Chapter 4. War & Wyler

Author interviews with Joel Freeman, G. E. Nordell, Dennis Piotrowski, Jon Stufflebeem, John Sturges, Kathy Sturges, Deborah Wyle.

Agee, James. *Agee on Film*. New York: Modern Library, 2000.

Capra, Frank. *The Name above the Title*. New York: Macmillan, 1971.

Crowther, Bosley. "Thunderbolt Shows Air Power over Italy." *New York Times*, Oct. 27, 1945.

Dunne, Philip. "The Documentary and Hollywood." In *Nonfiction Film Theory and Criticism*, ed. Richard Meram Barsam. New York: E. P. Dutton, 1976.

Madsen, Axel. *William Wyler*. New York: Crowell, 1973.

Maslowski, Peter. *Armed with Camera*. New York: Macmillan, 1993.

Orriss, Bruce W. *When Hollywood Ruled the Skies*. Hawthorne, CA: Aero Associates, 1985.

Chapter 5. Columbia Years

Author interviews with Jerome Courtland, Ted Donaldson, Rhonda Fleming, Gary Gray, Gloria Henry, Teddy Infuhr, John Ireland, Terry Moore, Jon Stufflebeem, John Sturges, Michael Sturges, Deborah Wyle.

Agee, James. *Agee on Film*. New York: Modern Library, 2000.

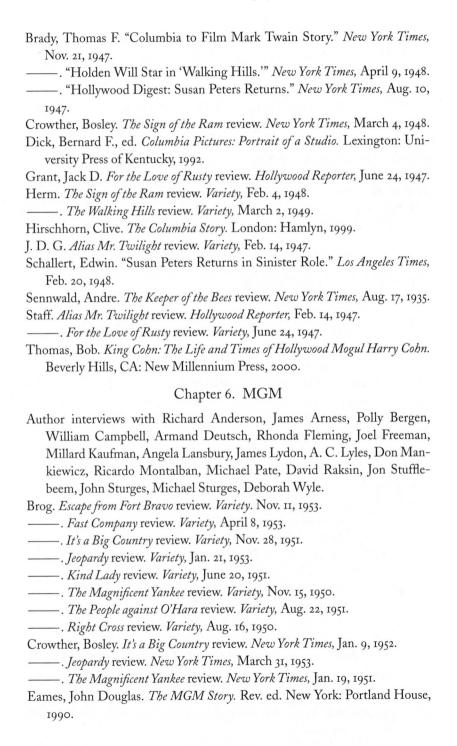

Brady, Thomas F. "Columbia to Film Mark Twain Story." *New York Times,* Nov. 21, 1947.

———. "Holden Will Star in 'Walking Hills.'" *New York Times,* April 9, 1948.

———. "Hollywood Digest: Susan Peters Returns." *New York Times,* Aug. 10, 1947.

Crowther, Bosley. *The Sign of the Ram* review. *New York Times,* March 4, 1948.

Dick, Bernard F., ed. *Columbia Pictures: Portrait of a Studio.* Lexington: University Press of Kentucky, 1992.

Grant, Jack D. *For the Love of Rusty* review. *Hollywood Reporter,* June 24, 1947.

Herm. *The Sign of the Ram* review. *Variety,* Feb. 4, 1948.

———. *The Walking Hills* review. *Variety,* March 2, 1949.

Hirschhorn, Clive. *The Columbia Story.* London: Hamlyn, 1999.

J. D. G. *Alias Mr. Twilight* review. *Variety,* Feb. 14, 1947.

Schallert, Edwin. "Susan Peters Returns in Sinister Role." *Los Angeles Times,* Feb. 20, 1948.

Sennwald, Andre. *The Keeper of the Bees* review. *New York Times,* Aug. 17, 1935.

Staff. *Alias Mr. Twilight* review. *Hollywood Reporter,* Feb. 14, 1947.

———. *For the Love of Rusty* review. *Variety,* June 24, 1947.

Thomas, Bob. *King Cohn: The Life and Times of Hollywood Mogul Harry Cohn.* Beverly Hills, CA: New Millennium Press, 2000.

Chapter 6. MGM

Author interviews with Richard Anderson, James Arness, Polly Bergen, William Campbell, Armand Deutsch, Rhonda Fleming, Joel Freeman, Millard Kaufman, Angela Lansbury, James Lydon, A. C. Lyles, Don Mankiewicz, Ricardo Montalban, Michael Pate, David Raksin, Jon Stufflebeem, John Sturges, Michael Sturges, Deborah Wyle.

Brog. *Escape from Fort Bravo* review. *Variety.* Nov. 11, 1953.

———. *Fast Company* review. *Variety,* April 8, 1953.

———. *It's a Big Country* review. *Variety,* Nov. 28, 1951.

———. *Jeopardy* review. *Variety,* Jan. 21, 1953.

———. *Kind Lady* review. *Variety,* June 20, 1951.

———. *The Magnificent Yankee* review. *Variety,* Nov. 15, 1950.

———. *The People against O'Hara* review. *Variety,* Aug. 22, 1951.

———. *Right Cross* review. *Variety,* Aug. 16, 1950.

Crowther, Bosley. *It's a Big Country* review. *New York Times,* Jan. 9, 1952.

———. *Jeopardy* review. *New York Times,* March 31, 1953.

———. *The Magnificent Yankee* review. *New York Times,* Jan. 19, 1951.

Eames, John Douglas. *The MGM Story.* Rev. ed. New York: Portland House, 1990.

Eyman, Scott. *Lion of Hollywood: The Life and Legend of Louis B. Mayer.* New York: Simon and Schuster, 2005.

Markfield, Wallace. "Remembrances of 'B' Movies Past." *New York Times,* Aug. 3, 1975.

McNulty, John. "Overlooked Lady." *New Yorker,* Dec. 10, 1949.

Montalban, Ricardo. *Reflections: A Life in Two Worlds.* New York: Doubleday, 1980

Parrish, Robert. *Growing Up in Hollywood.* New York: Harcourt Brace Jovanovich, 1976.

Pate, Michael. "Along the Big Trail." *Western Clippings,* nos. 60 & 61, Sept.–Oct., 2004

Pryor, T. M. *Right Cross* review. *New York Times,* Nov. 16, 1950.

Schary, Dore. *Heyday.* New York: Little, Brown, 1979.

Scheuer, Philip K. "Yankees, Rebels, Indians in 'Bravo' Tug of War." *Los Angeles Times,* Dec. 10, 1953.

Staff. "Film Directors Guild Split by Recall Move." *Los Angeles Times,* Oct. 15, 1950.

———. "Intriguing Premise Lost in Hazy Story." *Fast Company* review. *Hollywood Reporter,* April 8, 1953.

———. *Mystery Street* review. *Time,* Aug. 7, 1950.

———. "$100 Million Worth of Films Planned at MGM by Mid '50s." *Hollywood Reporter,* Feb. 9, 1949.

———. "Rough on the Redskins." *Time,* Dec. 14, 1953.

Thompson, Howard. *The Capture* review. *New York Times,* May 20, 1950.

———. *Escape from Fort Bravo* review. *New York Times,* Jan. 23, 1954.

———. *The Girl in White* review. *New York Times,* May 31, 1952.

———. *The People against O'Hara* review. *New York Times,* Sept. 6, 1951.

———. *The Scarlet Coat* review. *New York Times,* July 30, 1955.

Vinc. *Mystery Street* review. *Variety,* May 17, 1950.

Watt. *The Girl in White* review. *Variety,* March 19, 1952.

Weiler, A. H. *Kind Lady* review. *New York Times,* Aug. 8, 1951.

———. *Mystery Street* review. *New York Times,* July 28, 1950.

Zagoria, Sam. "Movie Director Finds Actor Had Real-Life Experience." *Washington Post,* June 22, 1950.

Zimm, Maurice. *A Question of Time,* radio script. Aired Sept. 18, 1950.

Chapter 7. A Walk in the Sun

Author interviews with Ernest Borgnine, Richard Brooks, Jerry Condit, John Ericson, Anne Francis, Joel Freeman, William Friedkin, Millard Kaufman, Chris Langley, John Sturges, Michael Sturges, Deborah Wyle.

Baldwin, Bill. "Good Day at Black Rock." *Cinemeditor,* Winter 2000.

Brog. *Bad Day at Black Rock* review. *Variety,* Dec. 15, 1954.

Crowther, Bosley. *Bad Day at Black Rock* review. *New York Times,* Feb. 2, 1955.

———. "Best Films of 1955." *New York Times,* Dec. 25, 1955.

Kael, Pauline. *I Lost It at the Movies: Film Writings, 1954–1961.* Boston: Little, Brown, 1965.

Kaufman, Millard. *Bad Day at Black Rock,* shooting script. May 14, 1954.

Lovell, Glenn. "Significance of 'Black Rock' More Evident as Years Pass." *San Jose Mercury News,* Oct. 14, 2000.

Schary, Dore. *Heyday.* New York: Little, Brown, 1979.

"Schary Plans New Story of 'Black Rock.'" *Los Angeles Times,* Dec. 30, 1954.

Strickling, Howard. Reports on *Bad Day at Black Rock* preview polls. Los Angles, Hollywood and Encino theaters, October–December.

Staff. "Frontier Town Host to Movie—Its 460th." *New York Herald Tribune,* Aug. 15, 1954.

Sturges, John. Commentary. *Bad Day at Black Rock,* laserdisc. MGM.

Chapter 8. At Sea

Author interviews with Jack Ackerman, Ernest Borgnine, Richard Egan, Carl Gottlieb, A. E. Hotchner, Eugene Iglesias, Fred J. Koenekamp, Terry Moore, Lori Nelson, Robert E. Relyea, Jane Russell, Franklin J. Schaffner, Jon Stufflebeem, John Sturges, Luis Valdez, Deborah Wyle, Wally Young.

Brog. *Underwater!* review. *Variety,* Jan. 12, 1955.

Crowther, Bosley. *The Old Man and the Sea* review. *New York Times,* Oct. 8, 1958.

———. *Underwater!* review. *New York Times,* Feb. 10, 1955.

Hemingway, Ernest. Letter to Leland Hayward re *The Old Man and the Sea.* July 17, 1955. Warner Bros. Collection, USC Cinema-Television Library.

———. Letter to Madelaine Hemingway re *The Old Man and the Sea.* Feb. 14, 1953. Rare Books and Manuscripts, Special Collections Library, Pennsylvania State University Libraries.

Higham, Charles. *Kate: The Life of Katharine Hepburn.* New York: W. W. Norton, 1975.

Hill, Michael E. "TV's 'Old Man' Taking on the Giants." *Washington Post,* March 25, 1990.

Hopper, Hedda. "'Big Rainbow' Will Star Jane Russell." *Los Angeles Times,* Sept. 26, 1953.

Hotchner, A. E. *Papa Hemingway.* New York: Carroll and Graf, 1999.

Johnson, Erskine. "Reticent Hemingway." *Los Angeles Mirror-News,* April, 21, 1960.

Pryor, Thomas M. "New Filming Set for Flight Story." *Los Angeles Times*, Dec. 28, 1956.

Russell, Jane. *Jane Russell: My Path and My Detours: An Autobiography*. New York: Franklin Watts, 1985.

Scheuer, Philip K. "*Underwater!* Effective Subsea Adventure Film." *Los Angeles Times*, March 4, 1955

Scott, John L. "Stars, Press Go Overboard for 'Underwater!' Preview." *Los Angeles Times*, Jan. 11, 1955.

Swindell, Larry. *Spencer Tracy: A Biography*. Cleveland: World, 1969.

Young, Wallace. Letter to author re: *Underwater!* Dec. 6, 2004.

Zinnemann, Fred. *A Life in the Movies: An Autobiography*. New York: Charles Scribner's Sons, 1992.

Chapter 9. Gun for Hire

Author interviews with William Campbell, Rhonda Fleming, Earl Holliman, John Ireland, Elmore Leonard, Robert Parrish, Henry Silva, Ron Smith, Jon Stufflebeem, John Sturges.

Cook, Bruce. "The War between the Writers and Directors, Part II." *American Film*, June 1979.

Crist, Judith. *Take 22: Moviemakers on Moviemaking*. New York: Viking, 1984.

Crowther, Bosley. *Gunfight at the O.K. Corral* review. *New York Times*, May 30, 1957.

———. *Last Train from Gun Hill* review. *New York Times*, July 30, 1959.

———. *The Law and Jake Wade* review. *New York Times*, June 7, 1958.

Douglas, Kirk. *The Ragman's Son*. New York: Simon and Schuster, 1988.

Hopper, Hedda. "Paramount Picture Scheduled for Ladd." *Los Angeles Times*, Nov. 9, 1955.

Schallert, Edwin. "'Katie Elder' Feature Gets Spurring." *Los Angeles Times*, Aug. 25, 1955.

Scullin, George. "The Killer." *Holiday*, Aug., 1954.

Shurlock, Geoffrey M. Letters on *Backlash*. Motion Picture Association of America, April and May, 1955. Universal Collection, USC Cinema-Television Library.

Staff. "Race between Older, Newer Directors Seen." *Los Angeles Times*, Jan. 5, 1958.

Wallis, Hal, and Charles Higham. *Starmaker: The Autobiography of Hal Wallis*. New York: Macmillan, 1980.

Whit. *Gunfight at the O.K. Corral* review. *Variety*, May 15, 1957.

Chapter 10. The Rat Trap

Author interviews with Aki Aleong, Bill Catching, Hillard Elkins, James Hong, Millard Kaufman, Hawk Koch, Ruta Lee, Boyd Magers, Neile McQueen, Walter Mirisch, Michael Pate, Charles Pignone, Robert E. Relyea, Marshall Schlom, Henry Silva, John Sturges, Michael Sturges.

Buchwald, Art. "Lollobrigida vs. Howard Hughes." *Los Angeles Times,* March 27, 1959.

Crowther, Bosley. *Never So Few* review. *New York Times,* Jan. 22, 1960.

Lovell, Glenn. "Significance of 'Black Rock' More Evident as Years Pass." *San Jose Mercury News,* Oct. 14, 2000.

Murrow, Edward R. *Person to Person* interview with Sammy Davis Jr. CBS, Nov. 4, 1955.

Pate, Michael. "Along the Big Trail." *Western Clippings,* no. 33, Jan.-Feb., 2000.

Powe. *Never So Few* review. *Variety,* Dec. 9, 1959.

Scheuer, Philip. "Clan Won't Quiet Down to a Bedlam." *Los Angeles Times,* July 11, 1961.

Scott, John L. "Sinatra Thrives on Killing Pace." *Los Angeles Times,* Jan. 25, 1959.

Tube. *Sergeants 3* review. *Variety,* Jan. 24, 1962.

Weiler, A. H. "Screen: *Sergeants 3* Opens at Capitol." *New York Times,* Feb. 12, 1962.

Chapter 11. Seven the Hard Way

Author interviews with Elmer Bernstein, Walter Bernstein, Myriam Bru, Christopher Buchholz, John Carpenter, James Coburn, Larry Cohen, Norman Jewison, Neile McQueen, Walter Mirisch, John Ottman, Robert E. Relyea, John Sturges, Michael Sturges, Luis Valdez, Robert Vaughn, Eli Wallach, Deborah Wyle.

Burr, Ty. "Coburn, Baby, Burn." *Entertainment Weekly,* May 11, 2001.

Capua, Michelangelo. *Yul Brynner: A Biography.* Jefferson, NC: McFarland, 2006.

Crowther, Bosley. *The Magnificent Seven* review. *New York Times,* Nov. 20, 1956.

Hine, Robert V., and John Mack Faragher. *The American West: A New Interpretive History.* New Haven, CT: Yale University Press, 2000.

Hopper, Hedda. "Dean Jones Stars in Sturges Film." *Los Angeles Times,* Dec. 17, 1959.

Kennedy, Paul P. "Shooting a 'Magnificent Seven' in Mexico." *New York Times*, April 10, 1960.

Lovell, Glenn. "Eli Wallach Remembers the Good, Bad and Ugly." *San Jose Mercury News*, April 20, 1992.

———. "The King and Yul Brynner." *San Jose Mercury News*, Nov. 28, 1982.

———. "'Seven' Sequel Is Crushing Bore." *Hollywood Reporter*, July 25, 1972.

Preminger, Otto. *Preminger: An Autobiography*. New York: Doubleday, 1977.

Scheuer, Philip K. "Mirisches' Budget Set at $20 Million." *Los Angeles Times*, Apr. 15, 1959.

———. "Strikes Expected to Halve Shooting." *Los Angeles Times*, March 7, 1960.

Schumach, Murray. "Producer Scores Mexican Censor." *New York Times*, May 20, 1960.

Staff. "Anthony Quinn Files 3 Suits." *New York Times*, Feb. 4, 1960.

Stinson, Charles. "'Magnificent Seven' Magnificent Western." *Los Angeles Times*, Nov. 25, 1960.

Thompson, Howard. *The Magnificent Seven* review. *New York Times*, Nov. 24, 1960.

Tube. *The Magnificent Seven* review. *Variety*, Oct. 5, 1960.

Chapter 12.   Grand Illusion

Author interviews with Dana Andrews, Ken Annakin, Edward Asner, Elmer Bernstein, James Coburn, John Flynn, Anne Francis, James Garner, John Gay, James Hong, David McCallum, Neile McQueen, Walter Mirisch, France Nuyen, Robert E. Relyea, John Sturges, Michael Sturges, Deborah Wyle.

Anby. *By Love Possessed* review. *Variety*, June 14, 1961.

Archer, Eugene. "Gene Kelly Plans to Direct '*Gigot*.'" *New York Times*, Feb. 23, 1961.

Coe, Richard L. "Off-B'way Has a Joyous Gem." *Washington Post*, May 21, 1963.

Crowther, Bosley. *A Girl Named Tamiko* review. *New York Times*, March, 15, 1963.

———. *The Great Escape* review. *New York Times*, Aug. 8, 1963.

———. *The Satan Bug* review. *New York Times*, April 15, 1965.

———. "Top Films of 1963." *New York Times*, Dec. 31, 1963.

Hopper, Hedda. "McQueen Will Star in 'I Love Louisa.'" *Los Angeles Times*, April 15, 1963.

Jares, Joseph. "Hit Movie Director Seeks Track 'Oscar.'" *Los Angeles Times*, Nov. 11, 1963.

Klein, Doris. "Fast-Rising Star Has Speed Thing." *Washington Post*, Feb. 6, 1966.

Lovell, Glenn. "Director Sturges Panned the Scan." *Los Angeles Times*, Aug. 4, 1996.

———. "France Nuyen Laments Ageism in Hollywood." *San Jose Mercury News*, Nov. 23, 2002.

Mirisch, Walter. *I Thought We Were Making Movies, Not History*. Madison: University of Wisconsin Press, 2008.

Scheuer, Philip K. "A Film to Bug You—Some of Our War Germs Are Missing." *Los Angeles Times*, March 21, 1965.

———. "Garner, McQueen in 'Great Escape.'" *Los Angeles Times*, Feb. 21, 1962.

———. "*The Great Escape* Is Top Suspense Thriller." *Los Angeles Times*, July 2, 1963.

———. "How to Make $100 Million in the Motion Picture Business." *Los Angeles Times*, Sept. 23, 1962.

———. "Man's Struggle for Freedom Is Substance of Three Movies Now Being Made in Europe." *Los Angeles Times*, Aug. 5, 1962.

———. "Men Tunnel Their Way into Sunlight." *Los Angeles Times*, Aug. 1, 1962.

———. "'Mutiny' Director, Find Make Deals." *Los Angeles Times*, March 12, 1962.

———. "Paramount Sets 12 for 2-Year Release." *Los Angeles Times*, Feb. 5, 1964.

———. "Stay-Home Record Topped by Wallis." *Los Angeles Times*, Jan. 24, 1962.

Schumach, Murray. "By Hollywood 'Possessed.'" *New York Times*, Jan. 15, 1961.

Sturges, John. Letters to Curtis Wong re: *The Great Escape*, March 19 and June 1, 1991. Private collection.

Sturges, John, and Elmer Bernstein, Robert Relyea, and Bud Ekins. Commentary. *The Great Escape*, laserdisc. Criterion, 1991.

Sturges, John, and Cast and Crew. Commentary. *The Great Escape*, DVD. MGM.

Tube. *The Great Escape* review. *Variety*, April 17, 1963.

Weiler, A. H. *By Love Possessed* review. *New York Times*, July 20, 1961.

Whit. *The Satan Bug* review. *Variety*, March 12, 1965.

Chapter 13. Roadshows

Author interviews with Tony Bill, Dino De Laurentiis, Colleen Dewhurst, Robert Duvall, Clint Eastwood, William Fletcher, James Garner, John Gay, Elmore Leonard, Tom Mankiewicz, Walter Mirisch, Robert E. Relyea, Lawrence Roman, John Saxon, Lalo Schifrin, Melville Shavelson,

Mayo Simon, Bill Sparrow, John Sturges, Kathy Sturges, Michael Sturges, Bruce Surtees, Vincent Van Patten, Jon Voight, Gregory Walcott, Deborah Wyle, Peter Yates.

Adler, Renata. *Ice Station Zebra* review. *New York Times,* Dec. 21, 1968.

Aldrich, Robert. *Robert Aldrich Interviews.* Edited by Eugene L. Miller and Edwin T. Arnold. Jackson: University Press of Mississippi, 2004.

Caine, Michael. *What's It All About?* New York: Turtle Bay Books, 1992.

Canby, Vincent. "*Eagle Has Landed* on Screens with Lively Splash of Adventure." *New York Times,* March 26, 1977.

———. "To be Au Courant at the Laundromat." *New York Times,* Dec. 14, 1969.

Capra, Frank. *The Name above the Title.* New York: Macmillan, 1971.

Champlin, Charles. "Car Films Going on All Cylinders." *Los Angeles Times,* Sept. 29, 1965.

———. "*Marooned*—A Cliff-Hanger in Space." *Los Angeles Times,* Dec. 7, 1969.

Crowther, Bosley. *The Hallelujah Trail* review. *New York Times,* July 2, 1965.

———. *Hour of the Gun* review. *New York Times,* Nov. 2, 1967.

Friedman, Tom. Sturges interview in "*McQ:* John Wayne in Action." Kaleidoscope Films, Aug. 30, 1973.

Greenspun, Roger. "Film: Eastwood Western." *New York Times,* July 20, 1972.

Haber, Joyce. "Sci-Fi Films Put Hollywood in Orbit." *Los Angeles Times,* July 1, 1968.

Jewison, Norman. *This Terrible Business Has Been Good to Me.* New York: Thomas Dunne Books, 2004.

Kael, Pauline. *McQ* review. *New Yorker,* Feb. 11, 1974.

Kifner, John. "John Wayne Plays a New Role: The Invader of Harvard Square." *New York Times,* Jan. 16, 1974.

Lovell, Glenn. "Colleen Laughs at Life." *Fort Lauderdale Sun-Sentinel,* Feb. 4, 1977.

McGilligan, Patrick. *Clint: The Life and Legend.* London: HarperCollins Entertainment, 2000.

Mills, Bart. "Making a Mint by Keeping It Simple." *Los Angeles Times,* Aug. 24, 1975.

Murphy, A. D. *Hour of the Gun* review. *Variety,* Oct. 4, 1967.

———. *Ice Station Zebra* review. *Variety,* Oct. 23, 1968.

———. *McQ* review. *Variety,* Jan. 23, 1974.

Quinn, Sally. "Administration Turns Out." *Washington Post,* Nov. 10, 1969.

Rick. *Marooned* review. *Variety,* Nov. 19, 1969.

Scheuer, Philip K. "Films' Future Seen Lying with Director." *Los Angeles Times,* April 2, 1964.

———. "Kim Novak to Pair with Mastroianni." *Los Angeles Times,* May 4, 1964.

———. "Satire on Italy Filmmakers Readied by Shavelson, Moll." *Los Angeles Times,* Dec. 3, 1963.

———. "Silliphant: He'd Rather Be a Writer." *Los Angeles Times,* Mar. 24, 1968.

———. "'Snobs' Only Seek Diamond-in-Rough." *Los Angeles Times,* Dec. 11, 1963.

———. "William Holden Up for Greatest Job." *Los Angeles Times,* Dec. 3, 1963

Seidenbaum, Art. "Indian Spoof Makes the Scalp Tingle." *Los Angeles Times,* Nov. 1, 1964.

Staff. "Murky Lenses, Screens, Color Prints: Angry Spots before John Sturges' Eyes." *Variety,* Dec. 24, 1969.

Staff. "Universal Starts on 'Earthquake, 1980.'" *Los Angeles Times,* Sept. 6, 1971.

Stan. *The Eagle Has Landed* review. *Variety,* Dec. 22, 1976.

Thomas, Kevin. "A Change of Pace for Rock Hudson." *Los Angeles Times,* Sept. 21, 1967.

———. "He-Man Movies for Feminine Tastes." *Los Angeles Times,* Sept. 6, 1967.

———. "North Pole Finds a Place in the Sun for 'Ice Station.'" *Los Angeles Times,* July 17, 1967.

———. "Policeman Becomes Private Eye in 'McQ.'" *Los Angeles Times,* Feb. 1, 1974.

Thompson, Howard. *Marooned* review. *New York Times,* Dec. 19, 1969.

Warga, Wayne. "Author, Director All Out for Space-Age Authenticity." *Los Angeles Times,* April 27, 1969.

Whit. *The Hallelujah Trail* review. *Variety,* June 16, 1965.

———. *Joe Kidd* review. *Variety,* July 12, 1972.

Epilogue: The Best Escape

Author interviews with Tony Bill, John Carpenter, Bill Catching, Andrew Davis, Clint Eastwood, John Frankenheimer, William Friedkin, Khaled Hosseini, Ron Howard, Tom Mankiewicz, Jack NyBlom, Alexander Payne, Edward Pressman, Michele Rappaport, Robert Redford, Robert E. Relyea, Bill Sparrow, John Sturges, Kathy Sturges, Michael Sturges, Robert Wise, Curtis Wong, Deborah Wyle, Peter Yates.

Chase, Chris. "At the Movies." *New York Times,* Feb. 19, 1982.

Folkart, Burt A. "John Sturges: Director of Classic Actions Films." *Los Angeles Times,* Aug. 21, 1992.

Lovell, Glenn. "Director Sturges Panned the Scan." *Los Angeles Times,* Aug. 4, 1996.

———. "The Full-Color, Wide-Screen World of the Late, Great John Sturges." *San Jose Mercury News,* Aug. 21, 1993.

———. "Helmer Sturges Leaves Rich Legacy." *Variety,* April 6, 1998.

———. "Slow Fade to Credits: The Life and Films of Director John Sturges." *San Jose Mercury News,* Aug. 23, 1992.

Lyman, Rick. *Watching Movies: The Biggest Names in Cinema Talk about the Films That Matter Most.* New York: Times Books, 2003.

McBride, Joseph. "Filmmaker Sturges Dies of Heart Attack." *Variety,* Aug. 21, 1992.

Saroyan, Strawberry. "Newell 'Smiles' on Feminism in the '50s." *Variety,* Dec. 19, 2003.

Siegel, Don. *A Siegel Film.* London: Faber and Faber, 1993.

Sturges, John. Letter to Jack NyBlom, Oct. 28, 1989. Private collection.

Thomas, Kevin. "The Men Who Launched the Movie." *Los Angeles Times,* May 2, 1982.

Bibliography

Agee, James. *Agee on Film*. New York: Modern Library, 2000.

Aldrich, Robert. *Robert Aldrich Interviews*. Edited by Eugene L. Miller and Edwin T. Arnold. Jackson: University Press of Mississippi, 2004.

Alton, John. *Painting with Light*. Berkeley: University of California Press, 1995.

Anderson, Lindsay. *About John Ford*. London: Plexus, 1999.

Barringer, Emily Dunning. *Bowery to Bellevue: The Story of New York's First Woman Ambulance Surgeon*. New York: W. W. Norton, 1950.

Bergan, Ronald. *The United Artists Story*. New York: Crown, 1986.

Biskind, Peter. *Easy Riders, Raging Bulls*. New York: Simon and Schuster, 1999.

Blair, Betsy. *The Memory of All That*. New York: Alfred A. Knopf, 2003.

Breslin, Howard. "Bad Time at Honda." In *No, But I Saw the Movie: The Best Short Stories Ever Made into Film*, ed. David Wheeler. New York: Viking Penguin, 1989.

Brickhill, Paul. *The Great Escape*. New York: W. W. Norton, 1951.

Buford, Kate. *Burt Lancaster: An American Life*. New York: Alfred A. Knopf, 2000.

Caine, Michael. *What's It All About?* New York: Turtle Bay Books, 1992.

Capra, Frank. *The Name above the Title*. New York: Macmillan, 1971.

Capua, Michelangelo. *Yul Brynner: A Biography*. Jefferson, NC: McFarland, 2006.

Chamales, Tom T. *Never So Few*. New York: Charles Scribner's Sons, 1957.

Chodorov, Edward. *Kind Lady*. New York: Samuel French, 1963.

Coursodon, Jean-Pierre, with Pierre Sauvage. *American Directors*. Vol. 2. New York: McGraw-Hill, 1983.

Cozzens, James Gould. *By Love Possessed*. New York: Carroll and Graf, 1998.

Crist, Judith. *Take 22: Moviemakers on Moviemaking*. New York: Viking, 1984.

———. *The Private Eye, the Cowboy and the Very Naked Girl*. New York: Holt, Rinehart and Winston, 1968.

Deutsch, Armand. *Me and Bogie*. New York: G. P. Putnam's Sons, 1991.

Dick, Bernard F., ed. *Columbia Pictures: Portrait of a Studio.* Lexington: University Press of Kentucky, 1992.

Dickey, James. "Charles Bronson: Silence under the Fist." In *Close-Ups: The Movie Star Book,* ed. Danny Peary. New York: Workman, 1978.

Douglas, Kirk. *The Ragman's Son.* New York: Simon and Schuster, 1988.

Dunne, Philip. "The Documentary and Hollywood." In *Nonfiction Film Theory and Criticism,* ed. Richard Meram Barsam. New York: E. P. Dutton, 1976.

Eames, John Douglas. *The MGM Story.* Rev. ed. New York: Portland House, 1990.

Eyman, Scott. *Lion of Hollywood: The Life and Legend of Louis B. Mayer.* New York: Simon and Schuster, 2005.

Ferguson, Margaret. *The Sign of the Ram.* Philadelphia: Blakiston, 1945.

Finn, Ed. *The Legend of the O.K. Corral.* Tucson: Rio Nuevo, 2005.

Gill, Anton. *The Great Escape: The Full Dramatic Story with Contributions from Survivors and Their Families.* London: Headline, 2002.

Gottlieb, Carl. *The Jaws Log.* New York: Dell, 1975.

Gulick, Bill. *The Hallelujah Trail.* New York: Berkley, 1994.

Hemingway, Ernest. *The Old Man and the Sea.* New York: Charles Scribner's Sons, 1952.

Higgins, Jack. *The Eagle Has Landed.* New York: Pocket Books, 1975.

Higham, Charles. *Kate: The Life of Katharine Hepburn.* New York: W. W. Norton, 1975.

Hill, William. *Sir Michael Caine: The Biography.* London: John Blake, 2006.

Hine, Robert V., and John Mack Faragher. *The American West: A New Interpretive History.* New Haven, CT: Yale University Press, 2000.

Hirschhorn, Clive. *The Columbia Story.* London: Hamlyn, 1999.

Hoffman, Lee. *The Valdez Horses.* New York: Berkley, 1973.

Hosseini, Khaled. *The Kite Runner.* New York: Riverhead Books, 2003.

Hotchner, A. E. *Papa Hemingway.* New York: Carroll and Graf, 1999.

Huston, John. *An Open Book.* New York: Alfred A. Knopf, 1980.

Jewell, Richard B., with Vernon Harbin. *The RKO Story.* New York: Arlington House, 1982.

Jewison, Norman. *This Terrible Business Has Been Good to Me.* New York: Thomas Dunne Books, 2004.

Kael, Pauline. *5001 Nights at the Movies.* New York: Henry Holt, 1991.

———. *I Lost It at the Movies: Film Writings, 1954–1961.* Boston: Little, Brown, 1965.

———. *Going Steady.* New York: Atlantic Monthly Press, 1970.

Kanin, Garson. *Hollywood.* New York: Viking Press, 1967.

Kauffmann, Stanley. *A World on Film.* New York: Dell, 1966.

Kaufman, Millard. *Plots and Characters: A Screenwriter on Screenwriting.* Los Angeles: Really Great Books, 1999.

Kirkbride, Ronald. *A Girl Named Tamiko.* New York: Frederick Fell, 1959.

Kubrick, Stanley. "Letter to MGM re exhibition of *Ice Station Zebra.*" In *The Making of Kubrick's 2001,* ed. Jerome Agel. New York: Signet, 1970.

Laskin, Emily, ed. *Getting Started in Film.* New York: Prentice Hall, 1992.

Lasky, Betty. *RKO: The Biggest Little Major of Them All.* Englewood Cliffs, NJ: Prentice-Hall, 1984.

Lavery, Emmet. *The Magnificent Yankee.* New York: Samuel French, 1946.

Law, John. *Reel Horror: True Horrors behind Hollywood's Scary Movies.* San Francisco: Aplomb, 2004.

Lipsky, Eleazar. *The People against O'Hara.* New York: Doubleday, 1950.

Lyman, Rick. *Watching Movies: The Biggest Names in Cinema Talk about the Films That Matter Most.* New York: Times Books, 2003.

MacLean, Alistair. *Ice Station Zebra.* Glasgow: Fontana Books, 1982.

———. *The Satan Bug.* Glasgow: Fontana Books, 1971.

Madsen, Axel. *William Wyler.* New York: Crowell, 1973.

Maslowski, Peter. *Armed with Camera.* New York: Macmillan, 1993.

McGilligan, Patrick. *Clint: The Life and Legend.* London: HarperCollins Entertainment, 2000.

Mirisch, Walter. *I Thought We Were Making Movies, Not History.* Madison: University of Wisconsin Press, 2008.

Montalban, Ricardo. *Reflections: A Life in Two Worlds.* New York: Doubleday, 1980.

Munn, Michael. *John Wayne: The Man behind the Myth.* New York: New American Library, 2003.

Nolan, William F. *McQueen.* New York: Congdon and Weed, 1984.

Orriss, Bruce W. *When Hollywood Ruled the Skies.* Hawthorne, CA: Aero Associates, 1985.

Parrish, Robert. *Growing Up in Hollywood.* New York: Harcourt Brace Jovanovich, 1976.

———. *Hollywood Doesn't Live Here Anymore.* Boston: Little, Brown, 1988.

Parish, Robert, and Ronald L. Bowers. *The MGM Stock Company: The Golden Era.* New Rochelle, NY: Arlington House, 1973.

Porfirio, Robert. "Dore Schary (1905-1980)." In *Film Noir Reader 3: Interviews with Filmmakers of the Classic Noir Period,* ed. Robert Porfirio, Alain Silver, and James Ursini. New York: Limelight Editions, 2002.

Preminger, Otto. *Preminger: An Autobiography.* New York: Doubleday, 1977.

Previn, André. *No Minor Chords: My Days in Hollywood.* New York: Double-day, 1991.

Quinn, Anthony, with Daniel Paisner. *One Man Tango.* New York: Harper-Collins, 1995.

Quirk, Lawrence J., and William Schoell. *The Rat Pack: Neon Nights with the Kings of Cool.* New York: HarperCollins, 2003.

Rainsberger, Todd. *James Wong Howe: Cinematographer.* La Jolla, CA: A. S. Barnes, 1981.

Raksin, David. *Hollywood Composers.* Los Altos, CA: Stanford Theatre Foundation, 1995.

Ringgold, Gene, and Clifford McCarty. *The Films of Frank Sinatra.* New York: Citadel Press, 1971.

Rioux, Terry Lee. *From Sawdust to Stardust: The Biography of DeForest Kelley.* New York: Pocket Books, 2005.

Russell, Jane. *Jane Russell: My Path and My Detours: An Autobiography.* New York: Franklin Watts, 1985.

Sarris, Andrew. *The American Cinema: Directors and Directions.* New York: Dutton, 1968.

Schary, Dore. *Heyday.* New York: Little, Brown, 1979.

Selznick, David O. "RKO 1931–1933." In *Memo from David O. Selznick,* ed. Rudy Behlmer. New York: Modern Library, 2000.

Siegel, Don. *A Siegel Film.* London: Faber and Faber, 1996.

Sinai, Anne. *Reach for the Top: The Turbulent Life of Laurence Harvey.* Lanham, MD: Scarecrow Press, 2003.

Stratton-Porter, Gene. *The Keeper of the Bees.* Bloomington: Indiana University Press, 1991.

Swindell, Larry. *Spencer Tracy: A Biography.* Cleveland: World, 1969.

Terrill, Marshall. *Steve McQueen: Portrait of an American Rebel.* New York: Donald I. Fine, 1994.

Thomas, Bob. *King Cohn: The Life and Times of Hollywood Mogul Harry Cohn.* Beverly Hills, CA: New Millennium Press, 2000.

Thompson, Frank. *Robert Wise: A Bio-Bibliography.* Westport, CT: Greenwood Press, 1995.

Thomson, David. *A Biographical Dictionary of Film.* New York: William Morrow, 1981.

Twain, Mark. "The Jumping Frog." In *Great Short Works of Mark Twain,* ed. Justin Kaplan. New York: Harper and Row, 1967.

Wakeman, John, ed. *World Film Directors.* Vol. 1. New York: H. W. Wilson, 1987.

Walcott, Gregory. *Hollywood Adventures: The Gregory Walcott Story.* Wilson, NC: Wilson Daily Times, 2003.

Wallach, Eli. *The Good, the Bad, and Me: In My Anecdotage.* Orlando, FL: Harcourt, 2005.

Wallis, Hal, and Charles Higham. *Starmaker: The Autobiography of Hal Wallis.* New York: Macmillan, 1980.

Windeler, Robert. *Burt Lancaster.* New York: Berkley, 1985.

Zinnemann, Fred. *A Life in the Movies: An Autobiography.* New York: Charles Scribner's Sons, 1992.

Index

Note: Page references in italics refer to illustrations. JS refers to John Sturges.